Please Note!   Some of the addresses in the
original printing of this issue are no longer valid.
Please use the corrected addresses below:

Orgone Biophysical Research Lab
Greensprings Center, PO Box 1148
Ashland, Oregon 97520 USA
Tel/Fax: 541-552-0118
Email: info@orgonelab.org
Internet site: www.orgonelab.org

Natural Energy Works
Distribution for this issue of Pulse of the Planet
Greensprings, PO Box 1148
Ashland, Oregon 97520 USA
Tel/Fax: 541-552-0118

Pulse of the Planet #4, 1993

On Wilhelm Reich and Orgonomy

Research Report and Journal of the
Orgone Biophysical Research Laboratory, Inc.
ISSN: 1041-6773

Cover: Wilhelm
Reich in Tyrifjord,
Norway in 1939.
See page 64 for
the full picture
and article by
Ellen Siersted.

Editor: James DeMeo, Ph.D.
Production Assistant: Theirrie Cook, B.A.

Contents: Page No.

Pulse of the Planet
Back Issues

USA Orders: Price as given below, postpaid.
Foreign Orders: Add $2 per issue for surface mail, or $5 per issue for airmail. Payment only in US funds by International Money Order, or a check from a bank with US Branches.
Send Funds To: Orgone Biophysical Research Lab, PO Box 1395, El Cerrito, CA 94530 USA.

Issue #1, 1989: (bound xerox-54 pages) $10
- "Cloudbusting, A New Approach to Drought" by J. DeMeo; "Recent Abnormal Phenomena on Earth and Atomic Power Tests", by Y. Kato; "Postscript on the FDA's Scientific Evidence Against Wilhelm Reich", by J. DeMeo; "Response to Martin Gardner's Attack on Reich and Orgone Research", by J. DeMeo.

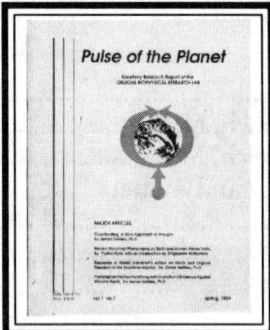

Issue #2, 1990: (softcover-96 pages) $15
- "The Orgone Energy Continuum: Some Old and New Evidence", by J. DeMeo; "Nuclear Bomb Tests & Earthquakes: Dangerous Patterns & Trends", G. Whiteford; "Psycho-Physiological Effects of the Orgone Accumulator", Muschenich & Gebauer; "Wilhelm Reich, Discoverer of Acupuncture Energy", by B. Senf

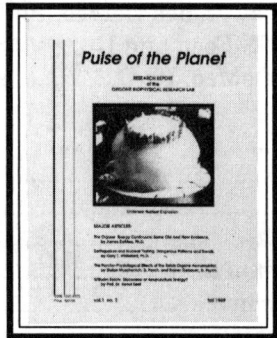

Issue #3, 1991: (softcover-144 pages) $20
- "Origins & Diffusion of Patrism in Saharasia", J. DeMeo; "Body Pleasure & the Origins of Violence", J. Prescott; "Orgone Accumulator Therapy of Severely Diseased People", H. Lassek; "Treatment of Infectious Diseases with Orgonotic Devices", M. Brenner; "OROP Arizona 1989", J. DeMeo.

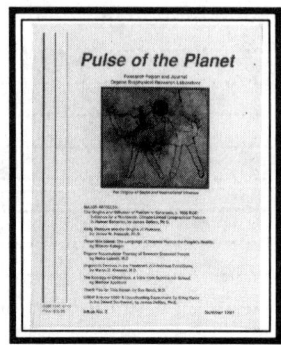

Pulse of the Planet #4, 1993.
ISSN: 1041-6773

Copyright © 1993

DISTRIBUTION TO BOOKSELLERS
Natural Energy Works,
PO Box 864, El Cerrito, CA 94530 USA
(510) 526-5978

SUBMISSION GUIDELINES: Manuscripts should be sent in duplicate to the Editor, in care of the Orgone Biophysical Research Laboratory. They should be typed, double-spaced, on 8-1/2 x 11 inch paper, with 1 inch margins. Citations should be gathered as endnotes, and include author(s), title of book or article, name of journal, volume, number, page numbers, publisher, publisher's location, and year. Authors are responsible for the accuracy of references. Drawings and charts should be made with black ink on white paper, and be clearly labeled and identified with a concise legend or key. Author(s) occupations, affiliations and academic degrees should also be given. Photographs may also be submitted. Letters to the Editor should be kept as short as possible, and contain any necessary citations. Manuscripts accepted for publication will be copyrighted by the Orgone Biophysical Research Laboratory, Inc., but will remain the permanent property of the author(s). Questions regarding permission to reprint should be directed to the author(s). RESPONSIBILITY for the contents of original articles and letters rests with the authors, and not the Editor. Inclusion of an article or communication does not imply agreement of the Editor with its contents or conclusions. ART AND LINE DRAWINGS are also required for each issue; submissions will be much appreciated and gratefully acknowledged.

Editor's Page

We are pleased to present in this issue of *Pulse*, the translated articles of Wilhelm Reich on bioelectricity and the basic antithesis of vegetative life functions. Our thanks to Barbara Koopman for undertaking the original translations, and for making the materials available. These are milestone research papers, rich with detail and information routinely ignored or even censored from textbooks — including textbooks on sexuality! Today, biologists and physiologists are focused upon the "mind-body" connection. And yet, as pointed out in the article by R.D. Laing, Reich's important work on this subject is almost never mentioned.

Reich undertook this important research in the 1930s, in Scandinavia, while literally "on the run" from Nazi terror. The included article by Ellen Siersted gives some historical background to the period when the experiments were undertaken. With minimal help and resources, Reich established a small laboratory, and empirically solved the riddle of the *unity between psyche and soma*, providing important experimental evidence — all within a few years. This is testimony to Reich's personal energy and contactfulness, and to the accuracy of his basic starting assumption: *the sex-economic basis of human behavior*. These papers are the foundation-stones for his later biophysical work, on the cancer biopathy, bions, and orgone energy.

The world of science is gradually verifying these and other findings of Reich. This issue of *Pulse* provides a summary article and other smaller reports and letters addressing Reich's biophysical discoveries, including amazing electron microscope photos of bions by an Australian researcher. Articles, by Katagiri and others, touch upon the issue of *atmospheric oranur* from nuclear bomb tests and reactor accidents. Included are summary reports on recent cloudbusting projects in Israel and Namibia, Africa — projects which provided powerful corroboration of Reich's original findings on desert greening through use of orgonomic principles. Whether acknowledged and accepted by institutionalized science or not, Reich's findings are increasingly the subject of very concrete and practical life-positive applications.

Not all of the articles contained in this issue are pleasant to read — such as the documentation on horrific medical experiments and the FDA's war against the natural health movement — but they all constitute essential information not widely known. Also included is a controversial article with a strong challenge to the conventional "wisdom" on the HIV theory of AIDS. The reader should find all the articles, both new and old, illuminating and of current interest.

The works of Wilhelm Reich have always provided essential insights and unavoidable steps toward the solution to major social, health and environmental problems. Science and society continue to stumble over the same old problems, decade after decade, through a calculated evasion of Reich's pioneering research findings. As he stated, the way out of the trap is clearly marked, though few appear willing or able to take the necessary steps toward and through the open door. This issue of *Pulse* is but another marker along the trail.

James DeMeo, Ph.D.
Director of Research
Orgone Biophysical Research Lab
El Cerrito, California, USA

Translator's Preface*
by Barbara G. Koopman, M.D., Ph.D.**

Now that the concepts of vaginal orgasm and genital primacy are under fire from many quarters, [1974] including such researchers as Masters and Johnson, it is especially timely that Reich's experiments in sexuality should appear in English translation. Though they predate the above investigations by decades, they offer a far deeper understanding of the mysteries of orgastic functioning. Here Reich signals the cardinal importance of genital orgasm as a regulator of the total energy economy. His view represents a far broader concept than that of local climaxes fired off from various erogenous zones. To Masters and Johnson, if I understand them rightly, an orgasm is an orgasm no matter what triggers it, and therefore, vaginal orgasm is of no special importance for sexual health. They fail to distinguish between a local climax (partial discharge) and the total bodily convulsions of genital orgasm as described by Reich. It is only the latter that can fully discharge the sexual tension accumulated in the living organism. (Partial discharge of tension only begets more tension. The differential between energy buildup and energy discharge provides the somatic core of the neuroses.) Not even multiple consecutive climaxes can accomplish this libidinal-economic task.

The thinking that culminated in the monumental *Function of the Orgasm* of 1942 (1) is already present in the early biological papers translated here. According to Reich, the orgasm is, physiologically speaking, far more than a mechanical filling and emptying of fluids. It also entails a process of bioelectrical charge and discharge and is therefore a paradigm of all life functions, such as the beating of the heart, wherein mechanical filling and emptying in systole and diastole is accompanied by a buildup and ebbing of bioelectrical energy (as manifested in the electrocardiogram).

Reich reasoned that mechanical tumescence and detumescence do not adequately explain orgastic phenomena, since erection, ejaculation, and detumescence can occur without any trace of satisfaction or may even evoke displeasure and disgust. For satisfaction to ensue, he postulated, there must be a bioenergetic charging and discharging of the sexual apparatus and of the total organism, in addition to the mechanical accumulation and ebbing of body fluids.

In a long series of carefully controlled experiments (published herewith) he was able to corroborate this hypothesis. He first established that both erogenous and nonerogenous skin sites served as loci for the buildup of bioelectrical potential, with the erogenous zones showing a much wider range in both buildup capacity and loss of charge. Subjects connected to an oscillograph regularly

showed a sharp upward deflection when an erogenous zone was stimulated, but *only* if subjective feelings of pleasure were experienced. If an identical stimulus on the same subject evoked displeasure or annoyance, there was a sharp *downward* deflection of the graph, corresponding to a sharp decrease in bioelectrical charge (withdrawal of charge from the skin surface). For example, an erect penis produced no upward deflection of the graph unless pleasurable excitation was felt by the subject. The oscillograph reading always reflected accurately the *amount* of pleasure experienced. Thus a *subjective* experience of pleasure was *objectively* quantified by the instrument and coincided with a demonstrable buildup in bioelectrical potential. This bioelectric energy behaved differently from electromagnetism and was considered by Reich to be functionally identical to Freud's "libidinal energy" — now no longer a Freudian metaphor but an empirically demonstrable energy, which he later termed *orgone*.

The same biophysical energy was reflected as *pleasure* if it flowed *outward* to the skin surface, with resultant buildup of charge at the skin site; as *anxiety* if it flowed *away* from the skin surface, causing a lowering of charge at the skin site and increased central (visceral) tension. In higher organisms, the autonomic nervous system mediates this expansion and contraction; in lower life forms, organic and inorganic chemical substances subserve this vital pulsatory function.

These experiments show conclusively the basic antithesis of sexuality and anxiety. Energy flowing from center to periphery is functionally identical to pleasure; energy flowing from periphery to center is functionally identical to anxiety. It is the *direction of flow* of this energy that determines the one or the other.

The capacity to experience genital orgasm with full bioenergetic (orgonotic) charge and discharge entails plasmatic motility of the organism — that is, an absence of armoring, which is the somatic counterpart of psychic conflicts. (Reich likened the armored body to an undulating serpent that had been tied down in many places with consequent compromise to its motility.) Reich's view is functional rather than dualistic: psyche and soma are two sides of the same coin and share as their common functioning principle orgone energy functions. Therefore, orgonomic psychiatry concomitantly treats both character structure (psychic aspect) and physical armoring (somatic aspect). Success or failure depends largely upon the patient's capacity to overcome energy stasis and tolerate the higher excitation of his organism consequent to the unblocking of the energy flow...

As for the technical details of the translation, I have tried to offer a faithful rendering of the original. It is an enlightening experience to trace Reich's thinking in German, step by step, from his origins in psychoanalysis to his breakthrough into psychobiology and the ultimate discovery of life energy functions.

The footnotes, with rare exceptions, are Reich's, as they appear in the original text. I have chosen to leave his bibliographical references in German. Occasional words or phrases, not in the original text, have been added in brackets for greater clarity of translation. ∎

---

1. Reich, W.: *Discovery of the Orgone, Vol.1, Function of the Orgasm*, Orgone Institute Press, Rangeley, ME, 1942; Reprinted by Farrar, Straus, & Giroux, NY, 1971.

* First published in *The Impulsive Character and Other Writings* by Wilhelm Reich, (translated by Barbara G. Koopman) Meridian Books, 1974, pp.xvii-xxii.
** Barbara Koopman, M.D., Ph.D., was former editor of the *Journal of Orgonomy* (1985-1991) and is a practicing orgone therapist in New York City.

The Basic Antithesis of Vegetative Life Functions*

by Wilhelm Reich, M.D.
translated by Barbara G. Koopman, M.D., Ph.D.**

1. Point of Departure and Basic Hypothesis

As disturbances in genitality became more crucial in the economic view of mental illness, I was still a long way from appreciating the far-reaching consequences which an understanding of the orgastic function would have in various fields.

Whereas before, genital disturbance was seen as a symptom that might or might not occur in a neurosis, I had definitely established that, in general, such disturbance was pathognomonic of, and essential to, the development of neurosis. I now had to pursue — within the clinical framework of research in neurosis — the relationship between mental illness and disturbances of natural sexual functioning. The years following publication of *Die Funktion des Orgasmus* (1927) were devoted to a study of character problems. The psychic apparatus, in particular the ego, must deal with blocked sexual excitation; the means of dealing with this blockage is the basic problem of character formation. Further research on the sex-economic aspects of mental illness forced me back to the original starting point, the better to deal with the difficult problem of anxiety.

On the one hand, my revision of the orgasm theory (1) showed that it, first and foremost, was the logical continuation of Freud's original libido theory, and that it in no way contradicted the psychoanalytic theory of the neuroses. On the other hand, my work on the relationship between anxiety and sexuality was incompatible with the classical formulation of eros and death instinct, and definitely contradicted it, since (if correct) it did away with the basic assumptions of that theory.

In my opinion, sexual excitation and anxiety are antithetical functions of all living substance in general, and of the psychic apparatus in particular. It is this basic antithesis that gives rise, secondarily, to the other well-known antagonistic functions of the instinctual apparatus. Thus I equate every primary motor excitation, that is, every reaching out to the external world of objects, with the psychoanalytic concept of

"libidinal drive." I doubt Freud's correctness in giving "libido" such a broad connotation, but would rather construe it simply as, life energy (though not in the old-fashioned Jungian sense of psychic monism). While Freud sees a hypothetical death instinct as antithetical to sexual (libidinal) excitation, I see *anxiety* as a *primary* irreducible tendency of the living organism. I base this on a *dialectic dualism* of living substance, in general, and of the psychic apparatus, in particular.

In addition to my revised theory of the instincts based on dialectic principles, I also see an identity of so-called functional and somatic processes. This view differs from the following three older views about the relationship of psyche and soma:

1. The soul (psyche) builds the body for itself; it is eternal, absolute, "primary" (metaphysical idealism).

2. The soul (psyche) is a secretion of the brain (vulgar mechanistic materialism).

3. Psyche and soma are two independent causal entities, mutually interrelated (psychophysical parallelism).

I see the dynamic interplay of psyche and soma as a *functional psychophysical identity*. It seems meaningless to speak of two separate autonomous processes which obey their own laws, or of a one-sided dependence of one upon the other. Rather, we will try to prove that the known, primary psychic and somatic functions are absolutely identical with regard to basic life processes, and that under certain circumstances they split into antithetical functions — so that we may speak of a functional antagonistic duality.

At this point, one may wonder about the usefulness of another formulation of the body-mind relationship when there are already so many around. I myself would have taken this attitude and refrained from pure speculation. However, in the course of studying basic sexual functions, I realized that the lack of clarity in this regard had led to typical errors in formulating its role in sexuality — including those of the psychoanalysts, who had hitherto given us our most complete insight into sexual matters. However, some basic clinical observations, described below, enabled us to break ground toward an understanding of that borderline territory between the psychic and the physical. †

It may not be amiss to say a few words here about the way in which we dared approach this most sensitive of all fields. We start from the structure of the individual, as laid bare by

---

1.   Cf. my paper on "The Orgasm as an Electrophysiological Discharge", *Zeitschrift für Politische Psychologie und Sexualökonomie* Vol. 1., 1934. [article follows in this issue of *Pulse of the Planet*]

*   Translated from "Der Urgegensatz des Vegetativen Lebens." *Zeitschrift für Politische Psychologie und Sexualökonomie,* Vol.1, 1934. Reprinted with the kind permission of Barbara Koopman and Orgonomic Publications, Inc. This English translation first appeared in *The Journal of Orgonomy* 1(1-2):4-22, 1967 and 2(1): 5-23, 1968.
**   Barbara Koopman, M.D., Ph.D., was former editor of *The Journal of Orgonomy*, 1985-1991, and is a practicing orgone therapist in New York City.

---

†   Reich later revised this manuscript to reflect his character-analytic contributions to psychoanalysis, as well as his sex-economic discoveries of muscular armor and technique of vegetotherapy. These later findings of Reich were a radical simplification and clarification of Freud's ideas on id, ego and superego. See Reich, W.: *The Bioelectrical Investigation of Sexuality and Anxiety*, Farrar, Straus & Giroux, NY, 1982 - JD.

> "...since the psychic apparatus is also part of the biophysical apparatus, certain laws pertaining to the former must also govern the latter...Only with the aid of laws *in common*, first discovered in the psychic realm, can we make progress in physiological problems as well."

psychoanalytic theory. According to the latter, the psychic apparatus is composed of three structures — interconnected, mutually interacting, and even partly overlapping in their origin. They are *id, ego,* and *superego.(2)* The superego is the representation of the external social reality (that is, of the existing social order whatever it may be) *within* the individual; the id is the sum total of all the given biological needs which, so to speak, "are rooted in somatic processes." The biological and social aspects of the individual are in conflict with regard to need gratification or denial: the basic conflict is that between need and external world. It is only within this context, according to psychoanalysis, that the psychic structures begin to emerge. The originally undifferentiated id "separates off a part of itself," namely, the ego, which takes over the function of perception and transforms the id impulses into orderly, coordinated activity. The ego, insofar as it serves these functions, is wholly on the side of the id. It is a "pleasure ego," which responds to the stimuli streaming in by differentiating the individual from the chaos of perceptions, both internal and external, and, on the basis of the pleasure and unpleasure it experiences, separates itself from the external world. Everything that is pleasurable becomes part of the enlarged pleasure ego. Everything that is unpleasurable is assigned to the external world. The phenomena of introjection and projection, of incorporation and dissociation (particularly in psychoses), can be traced to this phase of differentiation between id and external world, primarily to the nursing period where, according to unequivocal clinical findings, the mother's breast is incorporated into the pleasure ego. Probably, it is the final withdrawal of the breast that for the first time leaves behind strivings — out of the "narcissistic reservoir" — for pleasure objects of the external world (object libido).(3) Later the ego must mediate between the urgent needs of the id and the prohibitions of the outside world, as well as heed the latter; therefore, the ego, up to now only a part of the id, comes in conflict with the id, as the defender of outside interests. To begin with, however, this process is at the service of the ego, which wants to maintain itself. Thus, even very early in life, two tendencies arising from a common source come into conflict with each other: self-preservation, fear of "punishment," prevents the gratification of other needs of the id. At first, this occurs out of fear of punishment, failure, loss of love, and the like. Later the forbidding figures of the external world, or rather, certain of their qualities, are taken into the ego, "introjected," and from then on the ego limits its needs in response to an "inner morality." What was formerly anxiety or perceived as such, now becomes an inner conscience, equipped with the full force of an anxiety drive. From now on the ego remains as the mediator between biological needs and social demands.

With this brief summary of the psychic apparatus, it is easy to sort out the scientific areas of research in sex economy. Studying psychic structures and their relationship to one another is really the domain of clinical psychoanalysis. Ques-

tions pertaining to the superego lead to sociology as a theory of laws regulating social existence. If, however, we delve deeply into id and ego functions, especially id functions, and into instinctual sources, we arrive at physiological and biological questions. Here the psychological boundaries become blurred. Here we come upon clearer and more inevitable issues at the scientific core of psychology, which, in the last analysis, still elude understanding: for example, the *quantity* of excitations, whose interplay is the basic problem of psychodynamics; or the problem of how affect becomes linked to conceptionalization and perception; the transformation of sexual feeling into anxiety or hate, etc. Obviously, to understand the borderland between psyche and soma, we must begin with the nature of the drives and affects themselves. While biology and physiology go from physical phenomena to the more complex, "higher" psychic functions, psychoanalysis, by a process of reduction to the simplest laws, goes from complicated psychic phenomena to their sources, the drives. Sex economy continues this study into the field of physiology, since, as a science of sexual functioning, it cannot stop at the boundaries of the psychic realm, as psychoanalysis, because of its method, is forced to do. It seems obvious that physiological and psychological research *must* meet in certain problem fields if they proceed correctly. The meeting ground is that of the *vegetative nervous system* with its relationship, on the one hand, to the basic biological functions, and, on the other, to psychic mechanisms.

We need to say a few words more about how sex economy assumes the right to step from sexual psychology into the physiological realm. Such attempts by psychoanalysts like Ferenczi, F. Deutsch, and Groddeck, among others, suffer from the fact that the psychoanalytic *method of interpretation of meaning and association* was carried over to the physiological field. Thus, they tried to find a "psychic meaning" in the sex act, that is, to make the sex act an expression of some third entity, analogous to a psychic phenomenon — for example, a regression to the mother's womb (Ferenczi, Groddeck). A number of years ago, I had already tried to show that basic physiological functions could not be interpreted psychologically. Only the *disturbances* of such functions could be psychogenic.

There is, however, another way of going from psychology to physiology without carrying over into the physiological realm laws which are valid only psychologically. Dialectic observation teaches us that the psychic apparatus has a biophysical origin and that, therefore, two kinds of laws must be invoked. The first set of laws should deal with the psychic apparatus in terms of what it shares in common with this biophysical origin — such as tension and discharge, stimulus response, etc.; the second set of laws should deal with those features which differentiate the psychic from the physiological, which are solely its own and, therefore, antithetical to the physiological. In this category, for example, are repression of instinctual drives, introjection, projection, identification, etc. Without this clear distinction between psychophysical identity and antithesis — and if one applies psychological laws to physiological phenomena, as did Groddeck — errors result. But since the psychic apparatus is also a part of the biophysi-

2. Freud, "Das Ich und das Es," Intern. Pychoanalyt. Press, Vienna.
3. Cf. Reich: *Der triebhafte Charakter*, Intern. Psychoanalyt. Press, 1925. [English translation in Reich, W.: *The Impulsive Character and Other Writings*, New American Library, NY, 1974].

cal apparatus, certain laws pertaining to the former must also govern the latter. This applies especially to the law of tension and discharge. Only with the aid of laws *in common*, first discovered in the psychic realm, can we make progress in physiological problems as well.

The following will show to what extent this is useful.

2. Sexual Excitation and Anxiety

The Problem of Anxiety

In 1895, Freud noted that patients with functional heart symptoms or acute anxiety states also showed characteristic disturbances in their sexual life; "free-floating anxiety" appeared whenever sexual excitation did not culminate in satisfaction, and especially often when intercourse was interrupted. From these facts, Freud correctly concluded that sexual excitation which is denied motility and the chance to become conscious must necessarily change into anxiety, since the latter appears in place of, and does away with, the sexual excitation. On the basis of these findings, he differentiated between "anxiety neurosis" and "anxiety hysteria"; in the latter, the anxiety is no longer "free-floating" but is bound to certain ideas. In such a case, it is assumed that the anxiety stemming from dammed-up sexual excitation becomes symptomatically "bound" (as, for example, in a compulsive symptom). In analyzing such a symptom, we break it up into its components by uncovering its latent psychic content or by preventing its expression (as, for example, when we stop a compulsive ritual). Anxiety then appears in place of the symptom, a process which may be regarded as the binding up of otherwise free anxiety into a symptom.

The original concept — that blocked sexual excitation turns into anxiety — was later set aside by Freud as unimportant, and anxiety was conceived mainly as a "signal" of the ego at the threat of danger. Yet the question remained as to how the ego "can give a signal," and it seemed important to find out the nature of the excitation in this process.(4)

Let us start by orienting ourselves in the complex realm of psychic anxiety. Our point of departure is the basic formula worked out by psychoanalysis. When one is threatened by a real external danger, such as a traffic collision or an attack by a dog, a state of anxiety ensues; the same thing occurs when certain patients, that is, anxiety hysterics and phobics, fantasize compulsively, without basis in fact, that a beloved person might meet with an accident. The first kind of anxiety, rationally based, we call *reality anxiety*; the second, irrational in nature, we call *neurotic anxiety*. Analytic delving into the latter shows that it is a reaction of the ego to an unconsciously felt, pressing, and at the same time forbidden, impulse (as, for example, when a mother feels a murderous impulse toward a beloved child). Thus, we speak of "instinctual danger," and maintain that there is also some reality in this kind of internal danger — namely, that behind it is a drive which the ego perceives as dangerous and, therefore, must overcome. The difference then, between reality anxiety and neurotic anxiety is that in the former the danger lies in the external world, while in the latter it lies within the self. What is common to them is that both partake of *reality danger*, since the fulfillment of a forbidden impulse is also dangerous insofar as it threatens the ego's integrity. Thus neurotic anxiety, too, is, in the last analysis, reality anxiety.

There are, however, certain kinds of patients, *actual neurotics* (I prefer to call them *stasis neurotics),* who suffer from anxiety but do not attach their anxiety to any sort of idea, conscious or unconscious. Actual anxiety, or stasis anxiety, is the pure expression of an undischarged need tension, which is converted to anxiety whenever the inner perception of the need or its motor release is unacceptable. The absence of real danger, then, makes the difference between stasis anxiety and neurotic anxiety; what they do have in common, however, is need tension. We might add that stasis anxiety is without content, while neurotic anxiety is already connected to certain ideas.

A further difficulty in the problem of anxiety is that sometimes anxiety appears as a *result* of instinctual inhibition (stasis anxiety), while at other times it is the very *cause* of the instinctual inhibition. Thus, for example, a little boy's fear of losing his penis is the cause of his repressing the impulse to masturbate. On the other hand, we see that the boy develops anxiety *after* he has repressed his masturbation and may perhaps have developed a fear of the dark as well. How can anxiety as the cause, and anxiety as the result, of instinctual inhibition be reduced to a common denominator? Freud, in "Inhibition, Symptom and Anxiety" (1926), abandoned his original view of anxiety as the result of instinct inhibition and took the position that anxiety is actually the cause of the inhibition.(5) We, on the contrary, do not subscribe to an "either-or" alternative, but see instead a process uniting both views at once. In order to understand this, we must clear up the semantic inaccuracies that arise when we speak of the various kinds of anxiety. The anxiety arising in the masturbating boy because he fears some damage to his penis is not the same as the anxiety affect he develops *after* he has repressed the instinctual drive. The former could very well be a simple fear or expectation of danger, to avoid which he represses his drive. In other words, in the first case, the affect of anxiety does not develop fully but only partially, while in the second case it comes *to full* fruition. In the former case, the emphasis is on *signal anxiety* [apprehension]; in the second, it is on the *affect of anxiety*. Signal anxiety, which leads to repression of the instinctual drive, can only become the affect of anxiety when a need tension (that is, sexual stasis) is already present. This holds true for every sort of anxiety, including reality anxiety.

In homosexuals, for example, we see a "castration anxiety" that keeps them from embracing a woman; but this anxiety becomes an affective experience only if they have been abstinent for a long time. On the other hand, erythrophobes lose their anxiety as soon as they let themselves masturbate — long before the fear of genital injury is resolved.

Thus neurotic anxiety arises from the confluence of objective signal anxiety *and* blocked sexual energy. The defense against the drive (inhibition) leads to stasis and hence the affect of anxiety; on the other hand, the experiencing of anxiety results in the fixation of the instinctual repression.(6)

Just what is the relationship of reality anxiety to stasis anxiety? Is it possible to see these two conditions, so different in their origin, as having a common source? Freud denies this and again differentiates stasis anxiety from other kinds. (7) In

---

4. "...the question as to what the anxiety consists of, has become of less interest." (Freud, *Neue Folge der Vorlesungen,* p. 115).

5. " It is not the inhibition that creates the anxiety, but the anxiety is there first, the anxiety is what causes the inhibition." (Freud, *loc cit.,* p. 119).

6. Cf. My detailed remarks in *Die Funktion des Orgasmus,* 1927.

7. "Anxiety as the signal of the ego may (also) serve the development of anxiety in the anxiety neurosis through physical damage. That is the libido itself which is thereby changed into anxiety, we shall no longer maintain." (Freud, *loc cit.,* p. 130).

a real, acute danger situation, one reacts with anxiety; recalling the episode in fantasy may evoke the original experience of anxiety in proportion to the vividness of the memory. What is so crucial about this? The only answer is — the affect. When vividly recalling a real danger once experienced, the individual reacts as if this danger were once more real. This affect must correspond to a specific bodily innervation which had occurred in the original experience. Stasis anxiety corresponds to a *specific physical innervation*. Is there a common denominator here, or a fundamental difference? The main difference is that, in stasis anxiety, an impulse or instinctual demand, pressing from within toward the outside is not given an opportunity for movement. To cite a comparison: it is as if a compressed gas were kept under pressure and now exerted a counterpressure, which we can equate with the stasis. In the case of reality anxiety, however, especially in panic states, there is a sudden withdrawal of all cathexis [energy] to the inside. The end result is the same: an internal blocking of energy. In terms of our analogy, it is as if a gas were first in an uncompressed state and an external force were suddenly to compress it. In both cases, an increase in gas pressure would result; only, in one case, the cause would be a prevention of expansion, while, in the other, it would be compression. Thus reality anxiety and stasis anxiety share a common source, namely dammed-up excitation. Normally, reality anxiety disappears; it does not become fixated. It can, however, continue as neurotic anxiety. This occurs when a realistically experienced danger and its resulting blocked excitation are caught up in an already existing need tension. This is seen most clearly in the traumatic neuroses.

Although we have found that the blocking of excitation is the *common denominator* of every affective anxiety experience (fright, reality anxiety, neurotic anxiety, stasis anxiety), there are still many problems to be solved. How is the excitation of neurotic anxiety related to that of reality anxiety, and how are both related to pure stasis anxiety? Simple consideration leads to the borderland between psyche and soma. The blocking of the excitation is a physiological problem that can be understood from two angles: its subjective psychic and objective somatic expressions.

Sexuality and Anxiety as Antithetical Excitations of the Autonomic Nervous System

In further pursuing the manifestations of anxiety, I was able — as a result of painstaking resistance analysis — to observe directly the change from genital to cardiac excitation, from sexual feeling in the genitals to anxiety sensations in the heart regions.(8)

As long as patients do not allow themselves to become conscious of a sensual sexual excitation, they experience anxiety which is felt as physically localized in the heart and diaphragm regions. If, however, they allow the sexual feelings to become conscious, the anxiety sensation of tension or oppression disappears and the genitals become turgid (erec-

tion, vaginal lubrication, etc.) Furthermore, in anxiety, physical symptoms appear that are the exact opposite of those in sexual excitation. Anxiety is characterized by cold shivers (from contraction of the skin blood vessels), pallor, urge to urinate or defecate, sudden sweats, increased heart action, with occasional systolic skipping, and dryness of the mouth; in men, shrinking of the penis; in women, complete dryness of the sex organs (vaginismus). By contrast, sexual excitation shows the following features: feelings of warmth (in women, particularly in the genitals, neck, and breast), turgidity and active secretion by the genital organs, the heart quiet or in diastolic excitation ("cardiac expansion"). In the heart and diaphragm regions there are sensations akin to those of the anxiety state, yet markedly different from them: patients mention "tightness" or "oppression" when they feel anxiety; "expansion" when they feel sexual pleasure. Such expressions are very meaningful to us, for they are the direct language of an inner state of being, as will be shown below.

The antithesis of sexuality and anxiety can easily be shown in other examples. The genitals "shrink" in anxiety (as a result of vasoconstriction) and expand, stretch and fill up in sexual excitation. In fright, there is a sudden energetic emptying of the peripheral blood vessels, especially from the musculature of the extremities, which we experience clearly as a "paralyzed" feeling. If a reflex defense action occurs, the anxiety feeling comes "later" that is, the sensation of paralysis follows the action; or, after a single strong systole, the heartbeat stops for a few seconds.

Thus, the excitation of the two contrasting states runs its course in the vegetative nervous system, but, in the case of sexual excitation, the *vagal* [parasympathetic] reaction predominates, while in anxiety the *sympathetic* reaction is uppermost. Here we should note that the vagal and sympathetic, as systems, constitute a functional unity, while possessing at the same time innervations which are antithetical to each other. We also know that, under certain circumstances, both branches of the autonomic nervous system react synchronously — for example, in fright, one may get both peripheral vasoconstriction (sympathetic), as well as a sudden diarrhea-like loss of feces and urine; or both branches can simultaneously block each other — for example, blocking of the sympathetic fibers of the celiac ganglion gives rise to hemorrhages of the intestinal mucosa. Furthermore, the feelings of anticipation that occur in both sexual arousal and anxiety states are different and antithetical to each other, yet still related, for in both experiences qualitatively similar sensations occur in the heart and diaphragm regions, the seat of the celiac ganglion. These sensory phenomena must bear a close relationship to the epileptic aura. Careful examination of epileptics reveals that the aura-like sensation preceding the attack has the character of pleasure anxiety, sometimes mainly of pure anxiety, sometimes mainly of pure pleasure; if the latter, it is felt in the genital region.

The above facts justify our modifying the original Freudian assumption that libidinal excitation which is denied motor

---

8.   Many analysts claim that they are unable to confirm my findings that every correct analysis finally reaches a stasis neurosis; yet this fact is undeniable. For many years, I could not understand these objections, until it finally became clear that they involved differences in technique and depended upon whether or not stasis anxiety developed during the course of the analysis. Since most of the affect is bound up in character reactions, one does not get energy in the unbound state if the character analysis remains incomplete.

A follower of my character-analytic technique has compared it to the smashing of the atom; indeed, we get sufficient affect only if we

take the character apart via this technique. As a result of differences in technique, large theoretical differences were bound to occur over the years, for the simple reason that the patients' reactions differed according to the approach. For this reason, my formulation of the basic antithesis of sexuality and anxiety, and my reduction of the various secondary drives to anxiety, and of stasis anxiety to free genital streaming, were not duly understood; likewise, the statements of this paper will scarcely be confirmable unless the technique of character analysis is used.

> **" We thereby formulated for the first time the sex-economic view of the emotions, the concept of a functional antithesis of body center and body periphery... the system, Sexuality-Vegetative Apparatus-Anxiety, is functionally identical to the system of fluid movement of the organism."**

discharge can "change over" into anxiety. Rather, what is involved is a different kind of innervation and excitation of the vegetative nervous system itself. Thus excitation of the body *periphery* gives rise to sexual sensations, whereas excitation of the body center (heart and diaphragm regions) leads to feelings of anxiety. We thereby formulated for the first time the sex-economic view of the emotions, the concept of a functional antithesis of *body center* and *body periphery* — a concept that has fundamental significance.

Our view that pleasure (sexual excitation) and anxiety are antithetical phenomena within the same nervous apparatus, that is, the vegetative apparatus, ties in with the view well known in the physiology of anxiety — namely, that there is a functional relationship between anxiety and vegetative excitation. The *new* factor we introduce is that, first of all, the vegetative system also has a relationship to the sexual function (as the antithesis of the anxiety function) and that here, too, an *antithetical* innervation of the vegetative apparatus is involved. On the basis of the above, let us now proceed to present evidence that the system, Sexuality-Vegetative Apparatus-Anxiety, is functionally identical to the system of fluid movement (blood and cellular fluid) of the organism.

The Misch Choline Experiment

The physiological problem of anxiety has been approached from many angles. The tie-in with carbon dioxide regulation in tachycardia, the anxiety attacks accompanying angina pectoris, the spasms of bronchial asthma, and similar illnesses pointed constantly to a definite physiological factor in anxiety. Painstaking research into the function of the orgasm had started with the problem of anxiety as a complex psychic phenomenon and had probed it to the boundary of the physiological realm. It remained for the latter to provide the rest of the solution, like the apposition of two sides of a tunnel. However, this did not occur, partly because nerve physiology was stuck in mechanistic neuromuscular experimentation that allowed of no theoretical meeting ground; also, because the connection between anxiety and sexuality, the key to the problem, was frowned upon in physiology, and the door was blocked by traditional attitudes toward sexuality, long since proven wrong. It was all the more significant, then, that two analytically trained psychiatrists, Doctors Walter and Kathe Misch, attempted to approach the physiology of anxiety by means of pharmacological experiments, and they did this by taking the problem of anxiety neurosis as their starting point.

They were very skillful in combining the therapeutic with the theoretical. Their article on "The Vegetative Origin of Neurotic Anxiety and Its Medical Treatment" (*Der Nervenzarzt*, Vol. 5, No. 8, 1932), notes that in their lengthy reports at the 1910 Congress, Oppenheim and Hoche had pointed out the futility of all medical efforts of a pharmacological or hydrotherapeutic nature.

The Misch experiments started out with the pure syndrome of anxiety neurosis (peripheral vasoconstriction, tachycardia, arterial hypotonia, mydriasis, decreased salivary secretion, cold sweats, debility of the musculature, with tremor and diarrhea), symptoms which point to a high degree of autonomic excitation, predominantly sympathetic. It was

easy to assume that there must be a drug that would remove the anxiety syndrome, dilate the peripheral blood vessels, slow down the heart, lower the blood pressure, promote salivary secretion, and restore the striated musculature — in other words, an agent that would affect the parasympathetic system. The whole group of choline preparations turned out to be just such agents, which, in the authors' words, "fit into the somatic anxiety syndrome like a key into its lock"; these can "not only do away with the somatic anxiety syndrome, but can also put an end to the psychic experience of anxiety in a flash." Intramuscular administration of 0.1 percent acetylcholine produced within a few minutes marked erythema, a subsidence of the tachycardia almost to normal, and the disappearance of subjective physical symptoms. At the same time, the anxiety state, usually so intractable, vanished, giving way to a feeling of complete well-being. When choline preparations were given orally (Pacyl, four to six tablets daily; Hypotan, three tablets daily) there was no recurrence of severe anxiety states.

It was further shown that the effect of choline is greater the more free-floating and unanchored the anxiety. (In cases of compulsion neuroses, for example, not much could be accomplished.) They attributed the results mainly to the counteracting effect of the choline on the sympathetic nervous system. Table 1 depicts the two syndromes, according to Misch.

	Table 1	
	Anxiety Syndrome	**Choline Effect**
Peripheral blood vessels of the skin	contract	dilate
Heart action	speeds up	slows down
Blood pressure	rises	falls
Pupils	dilate	constrict
Salivary secretion	diminishes	increases
Musculature	loses normal tone	regains normal tone

In contrast to the authors of this excellent experiment, I prefer to emphasize the theoretical rather than the practical, therapeutic aspects, since prevention of anxiety seems more important to me than its treatment, though I do not in any way minimize the latter. But the far-reaching question of preventing neurosis demands, first of all, the most complete theoretical application of this experiment. I had already postulated, from my psychoanalytic treatment of the neuroses, that the problem of the "somatic core of the neurosis" is a pathological state of excitation of the vegetative nervous system. This experiment does so much to confirm this view that it seems worthwhile to pursue it further.

> **"...sex economy denies the primary character of destructive drives and sees them, rather, as deriving phylogenetically from the function of dammed-up libido on the one hand, and from avoidance of anxiety on the other. "**

The Two Primordial Forms of Psychic Tendencies: "Toward the World" — "Away from the World"

If we now pursue the antithesis of sexual excitation and anxiety in its psychic ramifications — if we look for its expressions in so-called "higher" psychic functions — we strike, first of all, a mass of seemingly unrelated mechanisms and functions. To begin with, if we classify them genetically and theoretically, the assumption of a basic antithesis in autonomic life functions is unavoidable for an understanding of the higher psychic antitheses. Psychoanalysis differentiates a whole series of psychic pairs of antithetical strivings, beginning with the *individual* versus the *external world*. The libidinal interest directed toward the self is called *narcissistic libido;* that which is directed toward the external world, *object libido*. The latter arises from the "narcissistic reservoir" of libidinal energy. The cathexis of objects of the external world is likened to the amoeba's sending out pseudopods, which can then be retracted. This "pulling-in of the libido," the withdrawal of interest, is considered a return to the "narcissistic" state, as, for example, in falling asleep; yet, at any time, the interest can be directed outward from the ego toward objects (as in waking up, falling in love, etc.). Object libido can again become narcissistic libido, since its origin is in the narcissistic libido. The opposition between the individual and the external world is accordingly represented as a conflict between narcissistic libido and object libido. While both kinds of libido constitute a single entity, they can also come into opposition with one another. This occurs when object gratification comes into conflict with the narcissistic need for self-preservation. The incestuous love of a little boy for his mother regularly conflicts with his narcissistic self-interest, especially in terms of his concern for his penis. Thus renunciation of a drive and repression of an object-directed impulse regularly stem from narcissistic interests and result, first, in a withdrawal of object cathexis. [object interest - JD]

Let us examine another antithetical pair — namely, an aggressive impulse and the anxiety aroused at the prospect of discharging the aggression. We would immediately see this anxiety as arising *solely* from the blocked impulse since every aggressive impulse that is blocked results in anxiety. The only question is whether the aggression is a primary drive (as psychoanalytic theory maintains) or a secondary drive, which I believe it must be. The psychoanalysis of ambivalence teaches us that aggression is a reaction to the denial of libidinal gratification. Aggression and libidinal striving [sexuality - JD] have in common that both reach out *toward the world* or toward objects in the world; they are differentiated only by their aim. The libidinal drive seeks to achieve pleasure; the destructive drive seeks to abolish a source of unpleasure in the external world, either by destroying the object of unpleasure or by incorporating it. Libido and aggression thus have the same tendency — toward the world; however, in their goals, they show a decided antithesis. If, simultaneously, one loves and hates the *same* object, the love impulse tends to put a brake on the hate impulse and to transform it into a guilt feeling, as a compromise between love and hate directed toward the *same* object. On the other hand, frustrated love can turn into hate or can enormously increase existing hate. From the mixture of sexuality and destructiveness, sadism arises. Perhaps the best way to express this phenomenon is to say: if the individual cannot get to the world by way of love, then he will try to destroy it. Put in another way, the individual will replace the unattained libidinal gratification with an act of aggression. The common antithesis to both types of object striving is anxiety, which I see essentially as a *flight away from the world* into the self. This is what we mean by narcissistic regression — that is, the withdrawal of cathexis into the self. It may come about through an external blocking of drive gratification or by an internal prohibition against approaching the outside world. In both cases anxiety, or incipient anxiety, ensues. The tendency *"toward the world"* (libidinal or aggressive) is thus basically opposed to the tendency *"away from the world"*. The latter, in its most primitive biological state, is seen as a withdrawal into the self. On a higher biological plane, this reaction is never lost; it is only supplemented by a secondary muscular one, [namely], spatial separation from the primary source of the unpleasure. In the further development of coping with the external world, there appears the aggressive removal of the source of the unpleasure or danger (destruction) and, finally, intellectual foresight and mastery of external difficulties.

From these functional relationships, we can deduce that destructive aggression, which plays such a major role in social as well as individual life, represents a phylogenetically and an ontogenetically *later function* than the two primary drives, sexuality and anxiety. It will be shown that this slight difference from Freud's view that libido and aggression are drives stemming from the same biological level, has far-reaching clinical and theoretical as well as sociological differences. Thus, sex economy denies the primary character of destructive drives and sees them, rather, as deriving phylogenetically from the function of dammed-up libido on the one hand, and from avoidance of anxiety on the other. The fact that the muscular system, the apparatus of destruction, has its origin in the mesoderm, that is, a secondary embryonic structure, while the apparatus of the sexual and anxiety functions is already present in the protozoon, may strengthen this view from the standpoint of historical development.

The following considerations are crucial to an understanding of the psychic apparatus: the blocking of either an aggressive or libidinal drive produces anxiety, but anxiety is avoided whenever the aggression is blocked or turned against the self — in other words, when it has become a self-destructive trend. Elsewhere I attempted to explain in detail why *I have to reject the assumption of a primary drive toward self-destruction,* and why I see all phenomena pertaining to it in a different light. In any event, the development of anxiety stands in an antithetical relationship to masochistic, self-destructive tendencies — which contradicts the view of many analysts that anxiety is the expression of an inner perception of self-destructive tendencies. The latter holds true only if we differentiate blocked aggression from aggression against the self. Let us summarize our genetic view of the pairs of contrasting drives:

Genetic-Dialectic Antithesis of Drives †

External World	Ego
Object libido	Narcissistic libido
Object cathexis	Anxiety
Libidinal object cathexis	Aggression (combination results in sadism)
Aggression	Anxiety
Aggression	Self-destruction through turning against the self (masochism)
Drive	Morality

Steps in the Development of the Anxiety Reaction

Narcissistic regression	withdrawal into the self; protozoic reaction
Flight	spatial removal from the object; metazoic reaction
Destruction	abolition of the source of the danger; metazoic reaction
Civilized coping with existence	(intellectual planning; human-social reaction

Object Relation *Toward the World*	Narcissistic Relation *Away from the World*
Object love	(Sexual) anxiety
Hatred	(Aggressive) anxiety
Destructiveness	Guilt feeling or self-destruction
Coping with tasks (work accomplishment)	Schizophrenic autism

So much for the psychological postulates derived from the reduction of complex phenomena to simple ones. They support our main point concerning anxiety neurosis, namely the antithesis of sexual excitation and anxiety. Neither hate (destruction or aggression) nor drives toward self-destruction, neither muscular flight nor intellectual mastery of dangers, are met with in pure anxiety neurosis. The latter seems to us particularly suitable for discussing the problem of the border line between the psyche and soma.

The psychoanalytic theory of drives understood the antithetical nature of the drives, but differed from the dialectic

---

† Reich's use of the word "genetic" in 1934 held the meaning of "causal-historical," - JD.

approach in its lack of genetic derivation of this antithesis and in the assumption of an *absolute* basic dualism of the drives (Eros-death instinct). It made its major contribution when it tried to understand the organic in terms of drive dynamics, but was forced to land in the metaphysics of the death instinct, because it provided the inorganic with a soul [psyche], without directly deriving the source of the psyche itself from the inorganic. And it lost the chance of finding a way out of the metaphysical blind alley, when its proponents viewed our attempts at a dialectical-materialistic solution as a hostile act against the very heart of the theory. In doing so, the psychoanalytic theory of drives had become subservient to its religious and social milieu and had thereby sacrificed its scientific future.

Tendency to Assume Spherical Shape

Approaching the problem from a different angle, it is easy to show that many living organisms in a state of flight from the world, that is, in *narcissistic* regression, have a tendency to assume a spherical shape; or, when there is a fully developed skeleton, approximate that shape. A few examples will suffice.

If one touches the horns of a snail with a blade of grass, the snail retracts its horns but otherwise remains motionless. After a while, it will slowly extend its horns. When touched again, it retracts its horns more quickly than it did before and also starts withdrawing into its shell.

An earthworm at rest or in motion is elongated, "loose." If touched on the head, it will pull back, becoming shorter and fatter, or else it will curl up. Where the capacity to withdraw into itself has been lost, we no longer see a change from elongated to spherical shape, but, rather, a *curling up of the body* — in other words, a sort of illusory spherical form. That is what happens when a hedgehog is threatened. The extremities are drawn up close to the body, the back is rounded, and the head is drawn close to the legs. One thinks of the position of the embryo, which, of course, is not an "anxiety position" but represents an adaptation to the smallest space.

In the protozoon, one can best observe this drawing back into the self. The pseudopodia, which earlier had given the cell a multiform appearance, disappear; surface irregularities are smoothed out; the cell assumes an increasingly ball-like shape. Similarly, before cell division and after copulation, the spherical form predominates.

The "shaking with fright" of the metazoan is doubtless similar in principle. The teleological explanation — that a smaller area offers less surface to be attacked — does not suffice. This superficial, rationalistic interpretation only brings us closer to theology, but not a step further. We can explain this phenomenon differently.

If a cat feels threatened, its first movement is to hunch its back, that is, its vertebral column. The contraction of the piloerector muscles likewise belongs here; this appears as "hair standing on end." The spherical shape, either in the form of withdrawal of protruding organs (pseudopods, snail's horns, etc.) or of curving of the back and retraction of head and extremities, thus appears as a result of the tendency "away from the world." In contrast, we see bodily elongation, extension of the extremities and head, in short, a "spreading outward from the body's center" as a result of the function "toward the world." Later we will recognize the logical extension of this function in the fusion of two organisms.

But first, we must examine a few facts which reveal the above-mentioned functions in their basic vegetative form.

3. The Antithesis of Sexuality and Anxiety: The Basic Autonomic Model

Fluid Flow and Psychic "Trend" in the Organism

To understand what follows, let us summarize matters up to this point:

1. In anxiety states, the body fluids, blood and other liquids, flow away from the periphery. In sexual excitation we find the opposite: heightened turgor of peripheral blood vessels; erythema of skin and mucous membranes; increased secretion of salivary and genital glands.

2. Sudden chemotaxic dilation of the peripheral vessels relieves anxiety (choline effect). Blocking of sexual motility, that is, of peripheral turgor, produces anxiety (adrenalin effect).

3. On a phenomenological basis — quite apart from these physiological findings — we are compelled to postulate in the psychic apparatus two directions of psychic interest: "toward the world" and its opposite, "away from the world."

4. In the biological world, quite generally we find two antithetical directions or functions, resulting in the spherical form or its opposite, elongation and expansion.

We note that everywhere the direction of fluid flow is the same as the psychic direction, or, better, the biological direction. The tendency "toward the world," expansion, corresponds to the centrifugal flow; the tendency "away from the world," assumption of the spherical form, and anxiety formation corresponds to the centripetal flow. We especially want to know whether we are dealing with a coincidental similarity, or an important, hitherto overlooked *fundamental* law of living things. It would be of the utmost significance for our concept of the functional identity of psychic and somatic functions. Let us, then, bring together a few elementary facts, the sum total of which will enable us to understand clearly a series of otherwise totally incomprehensible relationships between psychic and somatic functions.

In unicellular organisms, as well as in multicellular life forms that have not yet evolved a circulatory system, we note a plasma movement that bears a certain orderly relationship to primitive life functions. In plant cells, the plasma shows rotating and circulatory movements. These movements respond promptly to electrical stimulation. Thus weak electrical stimuli slow down the plasma movements, while strong stimuli stop them completely.

The nature of plasma movement, whether spontaneous or altered by electrical stimuli, is seen most clearly in the amoeba. Its protoplasm contains corpuscular elements that turn out to be round, water-filled vesicles. The so-called contractile vacuole is such a spherical vesicle, which, from time to time, breaks down and discharges its fluid content. According to Max Hartmann, the movement of the amoeba is directly related to the plasma flow. When the amoeba moves forward, plasma flows from the center to the periphery, and thus the plasma pseudopod first comes into being. It is then retracted into the amoeba's body. If the amoeba is touched, the plasma flow is reversed — that is, the plasma flows from the periphery of the pseudopod back into the center. The withdrawal of the pseudopod corresponds to this. If the amoeba has put out several pseudopods and by chance touches something solid, the plasma flows in the direction of the pseudopod contacting the solid, while the other pseudopods are withdrawn by the emptying of the plasma.

When the amoeba is ingesting food, the plasma always flows toward the periphery. The amoeba reacts negatively to chemical, thermal, electric, and photic stimuli — that is, the plasma flow is deflected from the latter. According to Rhumbler, Engelmann, Harrington, Davenport, and others, if light is suddenly thrown on food being ingested by an amoeba, the creature stops feeding, even disgorges the devoured shreds, and draws into itself. An amoeba flows freely in red light, is stopped by blue light, but always moves in the direction of continuous beams of light. In the amoeba there is nothing but the vegetative plasma flow to sustain the system of life processes.

Let us summarize the most important biological discoveries regarding plasma flow and the structuring of forms that accompanies it. First, according to Rhumbler, during centrifugal plasma flow, the cell body's thin, fluid plasma mass (endoplasm) is changed into the thick, fluid plasma of the periphery (ectoplasm). During centripetal flow (also called spherogenic flow), when the flow is in the opposite direction, the thick, fluid ectoplasm is changed into thin, fluid endoplasm. This observation may well confirm Kraus's idea that what we are seeing here, in the basic living phenomenon of movement, is hydration or dehydration of a colloidal substance — in other words, a change in the density of the substance through *change in the water content*.

According to Max Hartmann, most phenomena pertaining to the movement of pseudopods show that the physical state of the protoplasm is primarily fluid. The movement itself according to available studies, is a result of the continuous change from expansion to contraction, in the plasma of one-celled organisms no less than in the muscles of multicellular ones. Here, too, there is a change from *contraction* (tendency: spherical form) to *expansion* (tendency: elongated form). In another connection, we shall return to fluid movement as the common denominator of plasma movement and muscle movement. Significantly, according to Hofer and Gruber, protoplasmic bodies that have lost their nuclei will go on forming pseudopods for days on end.

Everyone agrees with the well-known view of Butschli, Berthold, and Quincke, that the flowing movement of pseudopods can be explained by hydromechanical laws of surface tension. At the boundary between two immiscible fluids (as, for example, oil and water, or salt electrolyte and colloid electrolyte), surface tension and surface energies come into play, as they do in plasma also. There are two aspects to these energies: first, the internal pressure exerted from the center outward, which seeks to enlarge the surface; second, the surface tension exerted from the periphery to the center (and, beyond this, tangentially toward the surface curvature). The internal pressure is in direct proportion to the surface tension and in inverse proportion to the radius. If the surface tension of the surrounding medium is lower than that of a drop of plasma, the plasma surface tension wins out and a spherical form perforce results (state of equilibrium). It is thought that a pseudopod is formed when, for any reason, the surface tension falls at any spot on the surface. This idea misses the essence of the process, for, in that case, there would be only *passive* movement. Actually, the plasma flow arising from within points to an *active* process from the inside. This might perhaps lead to too hasty vitalistic assumptions, which we have every reason to avoid. Certainly, the effect of the internal pressure alone does not suffice to explain the endogenous tendency toward expansion, for then we would have to know why the nonliving drop is *not* in motion though it, too, has a pressure from within. In the living organism, however, there must be something other than mechanical tension to produce active motion.

Of importance in this connection are Butschli's experimental models set up to demonstrate the plasma flow in living organisms. When water drops are left standing with a mixture of oil drops and calcium carbonate over a period of time, oil foam drops result which, after a rinse with water, usually begin to flow without much change in shape. If the water is replaced by thinned-out glycerine and the oil drops pressed down by a glass slide, they not only float about but form variously shaped continua. In addition, one can observe the same *centrifugal* axial streams and counterstreams at the edges that are seen in the amoeba in a state of pseudopod formation. And, in amoeba and oil drop alike, a temperature elevation greatly speeds up the formation of artificial pseudopods.

Hartmann considers surface energy to be the prime mover in pseudopod formation but thinks that, despite the many hypotheses, no one has explained what causes a rise or fall in surface tension. According to Jensen anabolism is supposed to cause decreased surface tension, while catabolism results in an increase — accordingly, in the former, there is an expansion; in the latter, a contraction. The essence of this process is supposed to be an increase in the number of molecules in catabolism or a corresponding decrease in anabolism.

Be that as it may, we still have no reason to doubt that in the two opposing directions of the amoeba's plasma flow, the archetype is laid down for the two psychic directions postulated above: the "sexual" toward the world and the "anxious" away from the world. Here some corollary problems arise, which, with one exception, we shall merely touch upon but not pursue further in this paper.

First, it is clear that the leap from passive motion, caused by mechanical change in the oil drop's surface tension, to the active, *endogenously* conditioned plasma flow of the amoeba, holds within itself the riddle of the origin of the living from the nonliving. †

In addition, the problem of surface tension leads us to the question of cell division, which we will discuss elsewhere. Finally, the question arises as to how we go from the two directions of plasma flow to the complicated libido-anxiety phenomenon. For only by demonstrating continuity of function can we establish our basic hypothesis that sexuality and anxiety are antithetical primary functions of living matter.

Kraus's "Fluid Theory of Life"

After I rejected the primary dualism of sexuality and death instinct postulated [by psychoanalysis], (9) the logical continuation of psychoanalytic libido theory led toward a basic concept — that is, in addition to the frequently described relationship between fluid flow and anxiety or sexual excitation, there is a functional antithesis between the *center of the organism* and the *periphery*. We begin to understand anxiety, fundamentally, as a *central* stasis of fluid (psychologically expressed as a central "excitation"); and pleasure, in general, as well as sexual pleasure in particular, as a peripheral expansion of the bodily fluid (psychologically, a peripheral excitation). In the former case [anxiety], there is simultaneously a peripheral discharge of fluid and a *central* excitation. In the latter [pleasure], a central discharge and *peripheral* excitation. In the anxiety state, tension is felt centrally

---

9.   See "The Masochistic Character" in *Charakteranalyse*, 1933.
†   Later confirmed in Reich's work *Die Bione*, Sex-Pol Verlag 1938; *The Bion Experiments*, Farrar, Straus & Giroux, 1979 - J.D.

(congestion); in sexual tension it is felt peripherally (as in erection). The question remains whether these tension states have any connection with decrease in surface tension in peripheral discharge or the increase in surface tension in peripheral hyperemia. To clarify this, let us recall the actions of two drugs, adrenalin and alcohol, which have opposite effects on the circulatory system. The physiologic effect of adrenalin is the direct production of anxiety. Alcohol reduces tension and anxiety, as does choline, through dilatation of the peripheral vessels. We then must know more thoroughly the relationship of the vegetative apparatus to the vascular apparatus, since it stands in concrete, functional relationship to the affect of anxiety as well as to sexual excitation.

Let us turn now to Kraus's "fluid theory of life" [*Nasse Theorie des Lebens*] . In my estimation, it seems to do the job expected of a nerve physiology text, that is, to summarize the phenomena and functions of living substance in a basic, unified view. I would minimize the objection that it would be dangerous to build on this theory because it is, itself, controversial, since there are certain criteria for the usefulness and correctness of a theory that make a judgment possible. From psychoanalysis, we know how seldom new discoveries can count on the favorable response of colleagues in particular and scientists in general. There is not too much to be said for the oft-extolled objectivity of scientific criticism. Living in the midst of the scientific hustle and bustle shows us how greatly criticism is beclouded by personal likes and dislikes, traditional thinking, and friendships within the specialty field. It is almost impossible to make an objective judgment on new theories in a specialty with which one is unfamiliar. To rely only on the plausibility of a new viewpoint seems dangerous, because the plausible need not always be right and, also, because there is too much risk of lapsing into preconceived notions and biases. When, however, several disciplines, *independently* and without any inkling of their respective results, or any preconceived idea of agreeing with one another, always seem to converge toward one certain conclusion and toward similar or identical views; when, finally, certain problems can be solved only by such two or three independently arrived-at theories and not by any others — then we have no doubt that *these* theories, and not heuristically valueless, isolated ones, have the greater probability of being right.

By the same token, when it is shown that certain discoveries of the biologist Hartmann, the internist Kraus, and the psychologist Freud, arrived at independently, all converge in a certain direction; when, finally, my own sex-economic research into the function of the orgasm and its relationship to the vegetative nervous system leads me in the same direction; when the above cited findings partly confirm my theories and partly serve to form a unified picture of the psyche-soma relationship — then we cannot allow doubts about a strange new theory to deter us from using it, so long as the critics do not have a better, more plausible one to take its place.

I will limit my presentation of Kraus's theory to the basic points essential to an understanding of our problem. For the reader who wishes to delve more deeply, I recommend a careful study of Kraus's work "Allegemeine und spezielle Pathologie der Person" (*Klinische Syzygiologie*, Leipzig: Theime, 1926).

First, let us recall that in the plasma movement of the amoeba we determined in principle the same two antithetical directions seen in the tendency "toward the world" and "away from the world"; and that, further, the psychic tendencies and the physiological direction of the fluids are in the closest conceivable relationship to each other.

Some of Kraus's basic ideas concretely approximate my own views derived from character analysis.

Kraus starts from the premise that living substance is essentially composed of colloids. Colloids are solutions of substances in water that do not show molecular dissolution, but rather flocculation into quite large particles. From colloid solution to salt solution there are many gradations. Thus, the distinct boundary between the organic and inorganic, so long controversial, becomes blurred. The colloid, like the salt solution, is an electrolyte: it is differentiated from the salt solution by its inability to permeate a membrane. Kraus sees in the biosystem an arousal system, a "relay-like" release mechanism, an apparatus for charging (that is, storing) and discharging energy — located throughout on the energetically charged boundary surfaces. The most important boundary surfaces are those located between salt electrolyte and colloid electrolyte. The life process is characterized by the ability to remove oxygen, the production of carbon dioxide, and the generation of electrical energy at the boundary surfaces. Salt solution is an essential factor for life, appearing long before the development of blood. To Kraus, the transport and distribution of substances appear to be far more important for the reproduction of life processes than metabolism, that is, than the purely chemical transformation of the ingested substances themselves.

The life process may be defined as *a self-activating* vegetative flow, essentially as *fluid convection*. We must differentiate the following: the mechanical convection of fluid, such as blood and lymph circulation; the directed convection of digestive juices; and, finally, most important of all, the microscopic movement of protoplasm. The overall movement of fluids in the organism has far more significance than merely that of supplying various regions with nutritive substances; rather, functioning occurs only because border surfaces of varying potential are formed, in endless number, between fluids of different densities and composition. To these charged boundary surfaces, the purely mechanical surface tensions are added as a vectoral factor. *The biosystem functions through equalization of boundary surface tensions* — that is, the surfaces of unequal charge behave exactly like electrodes in an electrolytic system. The organic membranes and interfaces between the salt electrolyte and colloid electrolyte function mainly as boundary surfaces. In order for an electric current to flow, there must be not only a charging of the membranes (electrodes), but also a connection between the two; the body fluids, being electrolytes, serve as this connection, but not only as that. The biosystem itself not only generates electrical energy, but also equalizes these charges and generates currents between and within the inner membranes through the conducting substance of the organism itself. Thus a conductor experimentally placed from without would only result in a short circuit. The electricity arises from the movement of fluids; in the capillaries, for example, according to Kraus, unbound electrical charges wander about freely. The potential gradients mentioned originate in the boundary surface between fluid in motion and fluid at rest. In their equalization, electrical energy is converted into mechanical energy.

However, this "fluid theory of life" is validated only when what occurs in the protoplasm can be brought into some sort of relationship with the laws of colloidal solutions.

Let us consider briefly this theory of Kraus. He is undoubtedly describing, without labeling it, the same process I regard as the basis of the orgasm — that is, transformation of mechanical tension into electrical charge (*tension-charge process*); then, transformation of electrical discharge back into mechanical discharge (*discharge-release process*). Accordingly, the orgasm would be the most potent special case of general vegetative movement.

If, in the mimosa plant, one touches the lower half of the pulvinus, or perhaps applies a heat stimulus, the leaf falls — there is negative galvanization. At the same time, one observes a discharge of water from the leaf joint and a corresponding decrease in turgor. If, on the other hand, one stimulates the upper side, the leaf elongates. If the mechanical reaction is blocked, the electrical one still occurs. If, when the twig is immersed in water, the pulvinus becomes overly turgid, that is, erect, the leaf does not drop, because it is difficult to expel the water. All plants and plant organs react electrically.

Thus we maintain that water absorption goes hand in hand with an increase in turgor and expansion ("erection"); water expulsion, with the leafs falling and a decrease in turgor. The significance of this experiment for an understanding of penile tumescence and detumescence will be shown elsewhere. In principle, the processes are functionally identical.

In the tiny cells of Cucurbita pepo, which has a circular plasma movement, Velten found a plasma combination consisting of a darker, more colloidal substance and a lighter, more watery, hyaline substance. Both together, according to Kraus, form the so-called critical fluid mixture, which is a basic characteristic of all living substances. On observing microscopically the behavior of such "critical fluid mixtures" in living substances, we see that the granules are initially at rest. If granules from the denser layer reach the thinner, less viscous layer, those with a greater water content show lively Brownian movement. If a weak induction current is now sent through the cell, a great number of granules begin to show molecular movement; the flow slows down. When the electrical effect gets stronger, swellings appear at various points. Then the plasma cord either shows spherical excrescences or sends out fine plasma threads. If the stimulus is interrupted, the excrescences are again withdrawn, and the regular plasma flow continues. The swellings are accounted for by absorption of water from the layer of plasma with the greater water content. This can continue until the swelling site is completely severed from the plasma cord and swims about freely in the cellular fluid.

Every organic body shows a stable hydrodynamic system, the most essential functions of which are metabolism for tissue growth and for eliminating solids, metabolic wastes, and salts; water evaporation from the heart and lungs; water replenishment through ingestion of food and drink and from metabolism, etc. The water content of bodies remains the same, on the average. According to Kraus, in adults it is approximately 70 percent; blood is 80 percent, skin 70 percent, the brain 75 percent, and so on. We have already indicated that the plasma movement is most important. Stern (10) was able to determine that the plasma movement is slowed down by weak electrical stimuli and stopped by stronger ones. Essentially, the following changes occur in plasma when stimuli are applied: intermittent acceleration and deceleration, tumescence and detumescence, expansion and contraction, mixing and separating, precipitation and dissolving of substances appearance and disappearance of granules; also,

---

10. *Elektrophysiologie der Pflänze*, Springer, 1924.

> **" The investigation of the function of the orgasm, in which we see a fundamental process of living matter, taught us that tension and charge, discharge and relaxation, stand in a certain functional relationship to each other. "**

changes in viscosity (Kraus).

The effects of stimuli (electrical as well as others) consist of rearrangements of ions and changes in ion concentration in medium, cell fluid, and plasma.

A. W. Greeley was the first to test the general idea that the effects of an electrical current on ions are due to changes in ion concentration and their effect on the colloidal system. He found that acids and salts with cations of higher valence make the plasma more viscous, while alkalis and salts with anions of higher valence make it more fluid. From this, Kraus reached a basic conclusion: if every stimulus applied to a protoplasmic substance threatens the stability of the colloidal substance, it is because the complexes of colloid-inorganic electrolytes become rearranged; this generates changes in the energy potentials at the membrane surfaces, which in turn promotes electrical discharge. Now, since organisms are constantly exposed to external and internal stimuli, it follows that the basic characteristic of living matter is the change in energy potential and the equalization of potential gradients that occur as an alternation between charge and discharge, tension and relaxation.

At this point, we may raise a basic question. Charge and discharge, tension and relaxation, are physical processes which govern inorganic nature as well. To begin with, that which is living is differentiated from the inorganic by a *self-activating* alternation of these functions. What produces this self-activation? The investigation of the function of the orgasm, in which we see a fundamental process of living matter, taught us that tension and charge, discharge and relaxation, stand in a certain functional relationship to each other. Mechanical tension leads to an electrical charge, and the electrical discharge leads to a mechanical relaxation, which, in turn, is transformed into mechanical tension, and so on. Is it, perhaps, just this specific relationship of mechanics and electricity that constitutes the essential characteristic of living matter? We will return frequently to this question.

It is important for our study to consider, first, that analytic psychology sees the basic mechanism of the psychic apparatus as a system of alternating "libidinal" tensions and relaxations so to speak. Our concept of drives stands or falls on the idea that we are dealing with psychic events, tension and relaxation, charge and discharge of energy. That would have less meaning if it were merely an analogy. But there is more to it than that: there are homologies; there are identities.

We cannot give here, in full, the comprehensive and enlightening arguments that Kraus has provided to clarify his thought processes for the reader. Neither is it important in this connection to submit his arguments to criticism. We would not be in any position to furnish such criticism. Assuming the correctness of his basic concept, that the living system (consisting of the organic boundary surfaces, the colloid electrolyte/salt electrolyte system, the biosystem as the electrolytic relay apparatus, etc.) is activated by the vegetative fluid flow, then Kraus's experiments on living preparations take on an extraordinary importance for us. We shall briefly summarize them. Their point of departure is a view which Kraus has summarized as follows: "There is no individual life process which cannot in some way, directly or indirectly, completely or partially, be explained by ion activity. Like oxygen, electrolytes cannot be replaced by anything else. Most illnesses, too, functional as well as so-called organic ones, have their ultimate basis in the vegetative flow."

Potassium and Calcium as Vegetatively Functioning Ions

The animal organism coordinates a voluntary muscle innervation with an involuntary innervation (independent of consciousness) of smooth muscles, glands, and circulatory system, for the performance of vegetative functions (of heart, intestines, and sexual organs). However, vegetative function is contained in the voluntary muscles, perhaps in the form of muscle tone, as the result of continuous vegetative innervation. In the celebrate [organisms with brains], the vegetative system is represented by a particular type of nervous organization, that is, the joining together of sympathetic and parasympathetic ganglia. We may ask if living organisms without a developed vegetative apparatus have something which performs those tasks later evolved as vegetative system functions: peristalsis, circulation, muscle tone, and turgor. In metazoa lacking a skeletal system, we already find nerve ganglia developed. In unicellular and multicellular organisms, up to a certain stage of development, there is no regularly structured nervous system. What, then, takes the place of that function in such creatures? This raises a question as to the morphological forerunner of the vegetative nervous apparatus. Such completely unspeculative questions are necessary when we start from unconscious psychic processes and arrive at problems of living function in general.

For a long time, physiology has studied the specific effect of ions upon the colloidal system, the basic substance of all living matter. If there are chemical substances:

first, that can *strengthen* or *weaken* the effects of vegetative innervation;

second, that can *replace* these effects;

third, that can *potentiate* or *neutralize* each other in their effect; and, finally,

fourth, that are a specific component of protoplasm, as, for example, lecithin-cholesterol —

then one is justified in assuming that these inorganic substances, prior to the development of the vegetative apparatus, fulfill its later functions. It is even possible that this apparatus is an organized, later development of simple chemical substances.

Here the experimental attempts of Kraus, Zondek, and Dressel, among others, when basically in accord, are of pioneer significance .

Kraus concludes from his experiments that, in the biological system, the effect of nerves, drugs, and electrolytes are mutually interchangeable with respect to tissue hydration or dehydration (which, as we learned, is the basic function of living matter). Organic tissues are a combination of membranes and fluids. The membranes are complexes of protein, phosphates, and sterols; they also contain colloids, especially lecithin and cholesterol. Salt electrolytes are found in the most diverse forms and combinations. Only those salts in dissolved, ionized form are chemically active as stimulants — especially the cations (sodium, potassium, calcium, magnesium, and iron), and the anions (chloride, phosphate, sulfate, iodide, and carbon dioxide). These salt electrolytes either slow down or speed up the water flow, especially tissue hydration and dehydration. Since tumescence and detumescence are directly related to variations in surface tension, they are basic to the biophysical problem of tension and discharge. "In the interaction between colloid electrolytes and certain antagonistic salt electrolytes for the hydration of colloid membranes and particles lies all functioning and all functional adaptation."

Zondek began by pointing out that potassium (as well as sodium) has a diastolic, that is, relaxing effect, which leads to peripheral expansion; while calcium, on the contrary, has a systolic or constricting effect, giving rise to central tension. What we are concerned with, essentially, is the movement of fluids: one ion brings water to the heart, another removes water. Kraus and Zondek directly observed the water flow in a frog preparation and were also able to divert it away from the curve of the main flow. In other experiments, it was found that *the vagus* [parasympathetic] *acts like an addition of potassium* to the nutrient fluid of a muscle preparation, *the sympathetic like an addition of calcium.*

Kraus comes to the perfectly logical conclusion that nerves and muscles are not independent structures, but, rather, that the nervous and muscular systems together form a "syzygy" or functional unity. In particular "the vegetative nervous system, in its role as a protoplasm connector, sets up relationships between the membranes of different organs." As a connective plasma mass, the nervous system is subject to the laws of colloid electrolytes. Thus the potassium and calcium groups, with their antithetical effects, are always present. The vegetative nervous system is merely continuing, in an organized way, a function which, in principle, already exists in animals lacking a nervous system, namely: the function of plasma flow, hydration and dehydration, contraction and expansion, tension and discharge, by means of the ions of the salt electrolyte. We must now establish that cholesterol and lecithin, components never missing from organic colloids, behave in the same way as calcium and the sympathetic system, or potassium and the parasympathetic. The antithesis between lecithin and cholesterol is first expressed by the fact that lecithin is a hydrophilic, that is, water-absorbing, colloid, while cholesterol is a hydrophobic, or water-repelling, colloid. Dressel set up a lecithin-cholesterol mixture as a physiological model in order to test the effects of salt electrolyte on colloidal substances. Under certain conditions, (approaching a physiological concentration similar to the electrolyte's molecular structure), the following occurs: when a lecithin-cholesterol mixture is added to potassium or calcium chloride, the antagonism between the ions becomes evident. Thus potassium chloride causes an increase in surface tension of the lecithin-cholesterol mixture, while calcium chloride causes a decrease. Alkali behaves like potassium, acid like calcium. This is highly important to our understanding of certain organ-neurotic phenomena.

A lecithin-Ringer solution applied to a frog's heart stops the heart in *diastole*, that is, it has a *vagal* [parasympathetic] effect, while the cholesterol-Ringer solution does the same in *systole*, producing a *sympathetic* effect. *However, this effect on the heart muscle is antithetical to the effect on the peripheral muscle.* Potassium causes a tonic contraction of the peripheral

muscle, or potentiates the effect of an electrical stimulus. Calcium, on the other hand, diminishes the effect of an electrical stimulus and causes the muscle to relax. This antithetical effect of the electrolytes on heart and peripheral muscle, which Kraus does not further explain, is of great significance to our investigation. It clearly indicates the antithesis of effects between central heart function and peripheral muscular organ function. In this antithesis, also, calcium and potassium behave exactly like the sympathetic and the vagus [parasympathetic]. Vagal innervation enhances the tone of the peripheral smooth and striated muscles; sympathetic innervation decreases it, like potassium and calcium respectively in the frog experiment. On the other hand, the vagus (depressor nerve) slows down the heart to *diastolic* standstill; the sympathetic (accelerator nerve) acts on the heart muscle in a manner opposite to its effect on peripheral muscle. That is, it heightens its activity and tone, and, when hyperstimulated, brings the heart to *systolic* standstill. Furthermore, the vagal effect can be decreased or even stopped by the addition of calcium, and enhanced by the addition of potassium. The sympathetic effect on the muscle can be neutralized by the addition of potassium — further proofs of the functional identity of the vegetative nervous system and certain antagonistic ion groups. The tonic effect of digitalis can be blocked by potassium and enhanced by calcium, as the former paralyzes the heart, while the latter stimulates it. A surplus of calcium in the tissues produces H-ion dissociation; a potassium surplus produces OH-ion dissociation. An H-ion surplus means death of the tissue. Of potentially great importance to our understanding of vegetative functions are the following findings of Kraus: potassium (that is, the hydro-*philic* ion) predominates in the epithelium; calcium (the hydro*phobic*, water-repelling ion) predominates in connective tissues — as does potassium in growth and calcium in age. In cancer tissue, potassium as well as calcium are reported to occur abundantly, which might, perhaps, explain the tissue's tendency to proliferation (abundance of potassium !). Findings of this sort allow us to postulate life-affirmative effects in the potassium-ion group and life-destructive ones in the calcium-ion groups.(11) According to Kraus, muscle tone basically is not the expression of any mysterious nerve fluid, but rather a

11. In the available physiological explanation of anxiety, is there any confirmation of the death instinct hypothesis which currently holds sway in psychoanalytic theory? A supporter of the latter might say the following: if the cumulative effect of the potassium-ion group represents the sexual function, then the calcium effect would represent the death function, the dying off of the tissue. I would then counter with the same observations I made in my investigation of character, plus one further argument: the potassium-ion concentration makes itself felt as an instinctual drive. The calcium-ion concentration, on the other hand, is not experienced as a drive, which would correspond to *wanting* to die, but rather is felt as *anxiety*. The death drive is by no means silent or mute, but what is referred to as the death drive, namely the retrogressive movement of life energy, makes itself clearly noticeable as *anxiety*. This idea takes us even a step further. It is true that the calcium group produces phenomena like those seen in a dying person: contraction of the peripheral vessels, pallor, anxiety, trembling, and so on. But these phenomena are only objectively presented, not subjectively willed, like the potassium-ion effects. It is also true that the calcium-ion group shows the effect of promoting and speeding the process of aging and dying. But we would be mistaken not to see that this is a result of blocking sexual function, and that the organism defends itself against the increase of inner tension in the form of anxiety. If, finally, chronic anxiety processes were to hasten dying, this would not prove the existence of the death instinct but only the life hostile effect of sexual repression, inasmuch as vagus inhibition promotes sympathetic function, that is, the desiccation, the enervation, the crawling back into oneself — in short, the rejection of all life functions. Thus, we cannot find here arguments in support of the death instinct theory, which represents an apology for the life-negative effect of society and illness.

plasmatic *electrolyte turgor*, an expression of saturated muscle charge. Thus growth and increase in strength must rest on conditions whereby more is gained than used up in the process.

On peripheral blood vessels, the vagus has a dilating effect, which increases surface tension, while the sympathetic constricts the vessels, decreasing surface tension. In glands, too, like the submaxillary, there is antagonistic innervation. Thus, according to Claude Bernard, the sympathetic produces sparse, tenacious secretion (calcium is hydrophobic!), while the vagus [parasympathetic], by contrast, stimulates ample fluid secretion. Secretion experiments have shown that the increased pressure of the gland parenchyma is due to vagal innervation, specifically to tissue expansion and increased turgor. The latter, according to Kraus, speeds up the blood flow and not (or not *only*) the other way around. Bernard notes that cutting the sympathetic nerve of the neck heightens tissue tonus; this is explained by the ablation of the sympathetic-suppressing effect of the vagus [i.e., the sympathetic unopposed by the vagus].

The Antithesis between Center and Periphery

Table 2 summarizes the functions of sympathetic and parasympathetic nervous systems, which together are called the "vegetative" [or autonomic] nervous system. The summary

---

Table 2
Functioning of the Autonomic Nervous System

Organ	Sympathetic System (Anxiety)	Parasympathetic [Vagus] System (Pleasure-sexuality)
Smooth muscle of iris	(−) Relaxation of pupil constrictors; dilation of pupils	(+) Pupil constriction; narrowing of the pupils
Tear glands	(−) Inhibition; "dry eyes"	(+) Stimulation; "glowing eyes"
Salivary Gland	(−) Inhibition; "parched mouth"	(+) Stimulation; "mouth watering"
Facial sweat glands	(+) Stimulation; skin moist	(−) Inhibition; dry skin
Sweat glands of buttocks	(+) Stimulates gland secretion	(−) Inhibits gland secretion
Blood vessels	(+) Constriction; pallor	(−) Dilation (erythema); flushing of the skin without perspiration
Piloerector muscles	(+) Piloerection; hair bristles, "goose flesh"	(−) Relaxation of pilorectors; smooth skin
Scalp muscles	(+) Excites muscles; hair "stands on end"	(−) Inhibits, relaxes muscles
Bronchial muscles	(−) Dilation, relaxation	(+) Constriction, tension
Heart muscle	(+) Excitation, accelerated heartbeat	(−) Inhibition, slows pulse
Esophagus	(−) Inhibition	(+) Stimulation, contraction
Stomach, pancreatic gland, small intestines, kidney, large intestine, rectum	(−) Inhibition of digestion, peristalsis	(+) Stimulation of peristalsis and digestion
Adrenal	(+) Stimulation of adrenalin secretion	(−) Inhibition of adrenalin secretion
Urinary bladder	(−) Inhibits expulsion muscle	(+) Contraction, urine expulsion
Sphincter muscle of bladder	(+) Excites and closes sphincter; inhibits urination	(−) Inhibits, relaxes the sphincter; stimulates urination
Male genital: penis	(−) Flaccidity (vasoconstriction)	(+) Enlargement, erection
Male genital: scrotum	(+) Excites, tightens smooth muscles	(−) Inhibits, relaxes smooth muscle
Female genitals	(−) Inhibition of female sex glands; "dry vagina", decrease of blood supply	(+) Excitation, vasodilation; moist vagina, increased blood flow

---

Table 3.

Autonomic-Vegetative Group	General Effect on Tissue	Center / Periphery Effects
Sympathetic		
Calcium (group)	Lowering of surface tension	Systolic / Vasoconstriction
Adrenalin	Water expulsion (hydrophobic)	Heart muscle stimulated
Cholesterol	Striated muscle: relaxed	Intestinal inhibition
H-ions †	Decreased susceptibility to electrical stimulation	
	Increase O₂ consumption	
	Increased blood pressure	
Parasympathetic - Vagus		
Potassium (group)	Increased surface tension	Diastolic / dilation
Choline	Water absorption (swelling of tissues)	Heart muscle relaxation
Lecithin	Tetanic contraction of muscle	Intestinal stimulation
OH-ions	Increased susceptibility to electrical stimulation	
	Decreased O₂ consumption	
	Decreased blood pressure	

is from Muller's *Lebensnerven und Lebenstriebe* (Berlin: Springer, 1931, 3rd ed.).

The table illustrates the great diversity of innervation in the various organs. Sometimes it is the parasympathetic that stimulates muscles, sometimes the sympathetic. Thus the bowel and stomach musculature is stimulated by the parasympathetic and inhibited by the sympathetic, while in the heart the opposite prevails. Though, in general, the sympathetic relaxes the smooth musculature, it contracts the muscles of the peripheral vessels and causes vasoconstriction. Note that the sympathetic inhibits the salivary glands, but stimulates the adrenals, while the vagus acts in exactly the opposite way. It is of particular interest that, in one and the same organ, for example the bladder, the sympathetic stimulates the muscle that prevents urine passage, but relaxes the muscle that expels the urine by a squeezing action; and the parasympathetic does the opposite. The retractor muscle of a dog's penis is stimulated, not relaxed, by the sympathetic; the same applies to the smooth musculature of the human testes. On the other hand, the smooth muscle of the iris dilates [the pupil] under [sympathetic] stimulation, and contracts it when the [sympathetic] is inhibited. The parasympathetic does the opposite.

It would seem as though the laws of innervation are completely arbitrary. Up to now, physiology has formed no opinion on the matter, at least as far as I can judge from the available literature. And yet we may postulate that the "irregularity" of the innervation is only an apparent one, and that it has, nonetheless, a certain lawfulness. Along with the sympathetic and parasympathetic innervation, there is a *functional unity* of the two systems which we can understand only on the basis of the organism's *function as a whole*. Table 3 is based on this functional unity.

In the sympathetic group's effects, we again come upon anxiety; in the vagus group's effects, sexual excitation. The vagus (sexual) effect is, essentially, the function of organ expansion and peripheral tension; the sympathetic (anxiety) effect is, essentially, the function of peripheral contraction and central tension — if we consider not the individual organs, but the organism's total functioning. The periphery and the center are in an antagonistic functional relationship to each other; expansion and contraction, as basic functions, govern the innervation-as-a-whole of the organism.

The following facts are summarized in Table 3:

1. The antithesis of potassium (parasympathetic) and calcium (sympathetic) groups: expansion and contraction.

2. The antithesis of periphery and center, with respect to excitation.

3. The functional identity of the sympathetic or parasympathetic functions with their chemical stimulus substances.

4. The dependence of organ innervation on the functional unity and antithesis of the organism as a whole.

To begin with, a whole series of hitherto unexplained physiological phenomena are made clear by the functional antithesis of center and periphery. For example, the vagus inhibits the heart but stimulates the voluntary muscles, while the sympathetic, by contrast, stimulates and contracts the heart but inhibits the muscles: the functional connection is shown only if one considers the musculature as part of the periphery of an organism and the heart as part of the center. Every fright reaction shows this antithesis: paralysis of the muscles of the extremities and stimulation of the heart. Here we already see the functions of the organism not bound to separate organs, but to a common lawfulness governing the organism as a whole, an arrangement in which the organs are merely a means to the end. *It is not the excitation of a nerve that causes movement; rather, an impulse of the organism as a whole, concretely represented in its functional unity (plasma syncytium), brings its message to the nerve, in accordance with its direction and function.* This does not in any way lead us into teleology or the assumption of a hyper-individual entelechy. For, we now see also that the functional unity of the multi-

† The original version of this paper inadvertently reversed the H-OH identity, but was corrected by Reich as of 1942 - J.D.

celled organism derives from the functional unity of the unicelled organism. Both show the same two basic lawful characteristics of expansion and contraction, not only in their functional relationships, but also in the means and organs involved in performing the functions. In both cases, there is the genetic-functional identity of plasma and blood, plasma and nerves, plasma and muscles. It remains to be seen whether the developmental theory can confirm this functional identity. In any event, it seems physiologically demonstrated that, in plasma, the same inorganic substances (potassium and calcium) and the same organic substances (lecithin and cholesterol) perform the functions of expansion and contraction later fulfilled by the collective morphology of the vegetative (vagus-sympathetic) nervous system. The antithesis of the two basic functions is continued in the antithesis of the parasympathetic-sympathetic innervation. The parasympathetic is, essentially, the system of peripheral excitation and central discharge, that is, of libidinal *expansion* — psychologically, the direction "toward the world." The sympathetic is essentially the system of peripheral discharge and central excitation, that is, of anxious *drawing into oneself* — psychologically, the direction "away from the world — back into the self."

At this point, the antithesis between sexuality and anxiety can also be placed in the overall view of organic natural phenomena. Anxiety, as a psychic affect, is neither an "expression" nor a "result" nor an "accompaniment" of the sympathetic crawling-back-into-the-self, but *a direct inner perception of the process*, functionally identical with it. Likewise, sexual pleasure, in its entire gamut, from the simplest state of relaxed well-being to the height of sexual excitement, is the inner perception of the parasympathetic function of reaching out or expansion, which goes hand in hand with the increase in surface tension, mechanically and electrophysiologically. It is the inner perception of fusion and merging with the world, of fully stepping out of oneself, it is functionally identical with

what happens physiologically. In this sense, and in this sense only, does it seem possible to understand the body-mind problem; and the separation, in principle, of the so-called functional from the so-called organic nature of illness becomes untenable. The differences are only in the mode of approach of pathogenic stimuli or in the vulnerable points of a person's biosystem. Illnesses begin sometimes as toxic, traumatic, or physiochemical irritations; at other times, as a social inhibition of the individual's psychic motility. They achieve the same effect: a disturbance of the individual's energy equilibrium. In this light, for example, we see schizophrenia neither as "psychogenic" nor "somatogenic," but solely as a disturbance, somehow induced, of basic vegetative functions that are essential for life.

Antithetical in their *direction* of flow and, concomitantly, antithetical in psychic experience, sexuality and anxiety have, so to speak, sprung from a *single* source; moreover, the specific excitations of anxiety and sexuality can change into one another, or even fully supplant one another. They are, therefore, not absolute opposites, but relative ones, identical even in their antithesis. During anxiety and sexual pleasure, the sensations in the region of the celiac ganglion (diaphragm and heart) are, initially, scarcely distinguishable from one another. Only the further course of the excitation determines whether the development is to be toward anxiety or sexual pleasure.

A new view of phenomena and processes deserves careful consideration only when it makes possible the discovery of a common denominator for a series of facts, hitherto unexplained, or explained only with the help of multiple hypotheses. This principle of natural scientific research must also be demonstrated in our hypothesis. As for its consequences, I am fully aware of their extent, though they cannot be adequately surveyed at this time. ■

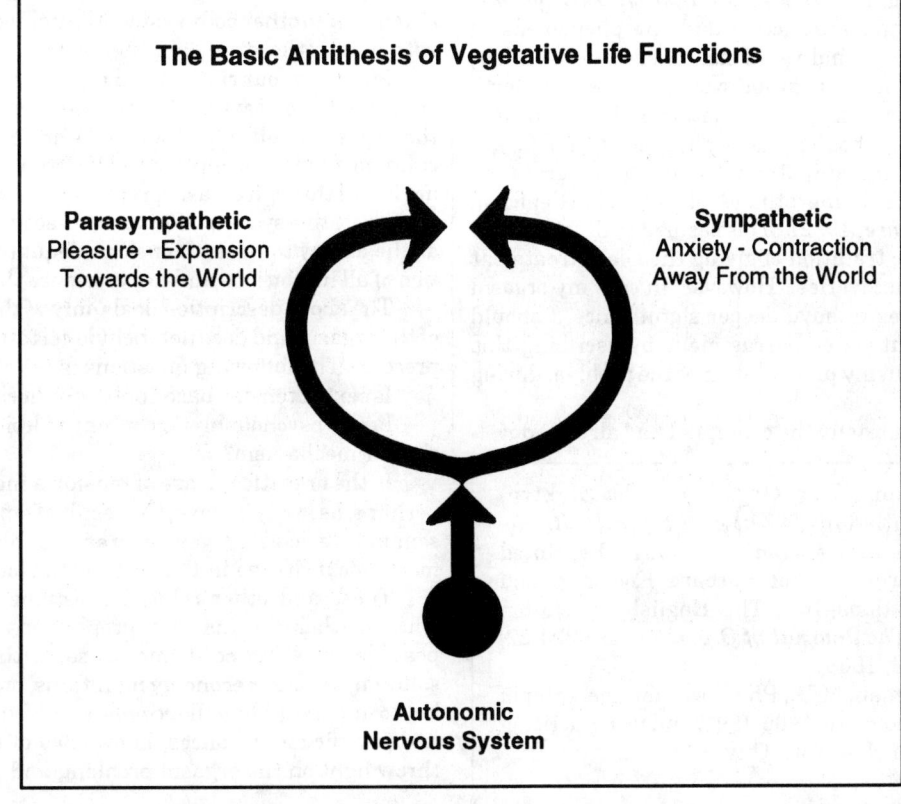

The Basic Antithesis of Vegetative Life Functions

Parasympathetic
Pleasure - Expansion
Towards the World

Sympathetic
Anxiety - Contraction
Away From the World

**Autonomic
Nervous System**

The Orgasm as an Electrophysiological Discharge*

by Wilhelm Reich, M.D.
translated by Barbara Koopman, M.D., Ph.D.**

1. A Review of Present-Day Knowledge [1934]

It is only in recent years that physiologists, for the first time, have begun to focus attention on the orgasm phenomena — the key factor in sex-economic theory. But, since the psychic aspects of the orgastic process are either wholly neglected or physiologically oversimplified, any purely phenomenological description completely misses the mark. Muller, in his collected writings, *Die Lebensnerven* (Springer, 1930, 3rd ed.), certainly refers to the relationship between orgasm and smooth muscle contraction but makes no mention at all of disturbances in orgastic function or the process of physiological excitation. I know of no existing animal or human experiments dealing with this problem, though they are easy to implement — easier than many. In the literature of sexology, many disturbances are described, but their relationship to unconscious psychic processes, sexual physiology, and sociological determinants of sex life is not entirely understood. In psychoanalytic writing, the function of the orgasm was not dealt with until 1925. Therefore, from 1923 to 1927, I undertook to integrate the clinical data on orgasm obtained from psychoanalysis and what was already known about sexual functioning in general. In my book *Die Funktion des Orgasmus* (1927), I brought orgastic function and the phenomena of anxiety into close functional relationship, each to the other, and both to the autonomic nervous system. After I set forth these fundamental hypotheses, no mention of them appeared in the literature of psychoanalysis or physiology, and only in very narrow circles was any attempt made to integrate my orgasm theory into existing studies of neurosis (Fenichel, *Spezielle Neurosenlehre*, 1932). This seemed to illustrate the well-known scientific tradition of giving the silent treatment to certain kinds of discoveries. However, in case my orgasm theory one day proves to have deeper significance, I should prefer to forestall future embarrassment by ascribing this neglect to some lack in my presentation of the problem during the past eight years.

I will summarize briefly the concepts I had already developed at that time as to how the orgastic process works. The orgasm corresponds to a change in concentration of the vegetative excitation; this excitation is transferred from the autonomic nervous system to the sensorimotor system. During the course of the excitation, we may distinguish the following phases: 1) a tension-free accumulation of sexual energy in the vegetative system; 2) a spontaneous or voluntary concentration of this sexual excitation in the genital system (with developing sexual tension and vasomotor activity); 3) advancing involvement of the sensory system (excitation of the erogenous zones; forepleasure and preorgastic phase of coitus); 4) transfer of excitation to the motor system (muscle tension at the climax and involuntary muscular contractions); and 5) ebbing of excitation in the vegetative system (quiescence: genital and sensorimotor systems relaxed).

The completeness of the orgasm and the orgastic release itself depend directly upon the amount of sexual excitation concentrated at the genitals and the thoroughness of its ebbing away from the vegetative system.

I had already distinguished a *centrifugal* and *centripetal* direction of flow from the beginning to the end of the orgastic excitation. The question as to what kind of excitation could undergo such a change of direction and transfer from the autonomic to other body systems remained unanswered, along with many others.

Moreover, our clinical and psychoanalytical observations on neurosis and sexual disturbances pointed to the following: the orgasm itself appeared to be an excitation phenomena culminating in a complete reduction of psychic activity and mediated through a basic process of tension and relaxation of the vegetative system. We came to recognize *orgastic potency* as the ability to release tension adequately through elimination of all inhibitions and to experience this release in the ego.

The above description deals only with the phenomenology of the orgasm and does not include certain basic aspects of the process. The following questions must still be clarified:

Is sexual tension based only on a mechanical phenomena?

Is the psychoanalytic concept of libido stasis based on a similar mechanism?

Is the orgastic release of tension a mechanical discharge, perhaps, as many believe, the result of emptying the engorged seminal vesicles or vas deferens, or is it based on some mechanical change in the surface tension of the sex organs?

These and other related questions must be answered, since neither therapy nor prophylaxis of the neuroses is possible, in a sex-economic sense, without their adequate solution. If, as sex economy maintains, orgastic potency is the key to understanding the *economy* and dynamics of psychic life and psychic disturbances, knowledge of the neuroses should throw light on the orgasm problem, and vice versa.

* Translated from "Der Orgasmus als Elektrophysiologische Entladung," *Zeitschrift für Politische Psychologie und Sexualökonomie*, I, 1934. Reprinted with the kind permission of Barbara Koopman and Orgonomic Publications, Inc. This English translation first appeared in *The Journal of Orgonomy* 1(1-2):4-22, 1967 and 2(1): 5-23, 1968.
** Barbara Koopman, M.D., Ph.D., was former editor of *The Journal of Orgonomy*, 1985-1991, and is a practicing orgone therapist in New York City.

2. Some Unusual Features of Sexuality

Assuming that the process of sexual tension and relaxation has a simple mechanical basis leaves many observations unexplained; these, however, easily fit together, if, in addition to a mechanical process of tension release, we postulate the occurrence of *an electrophysiological discharge during orgasm*. This should be experimentally demonstrable.

First, the concept of *mechanical tension* is only fully applicable to the male, since it *fails to account for what happens in the female*. From a mechanical concept such as this, one could easily conclude, as most sexologists do, that lack of orgasm is natural in the female. The sociological origin of this concept has been amply described elsewhere.(1) The unmistakable appearance of orgastic phenomena in the healthy female — completely equivalent to that of the male — therefore requires explanation. She shows the same kind of movements as the male: rhythmic, clonic contractions of the involuntary musculature; also the same preacme peripheral concentration of excitation and postacme centripetal ebbing of excitation, exactly like the male's.

In coitus interruptus, the mechanical discharge may be complete, and the excitement during acme even greater than usual. Nevertheless, the experience remains unsatisfying, and the feeling of relief from tension is either lacking or incomplete.

In coitus condomatus, the male has full mechanical discharge, but the feeling of satisfaction is greatly reduced. The decrease in tactile sensation *cannot* account for this, since the simple sense of touch is still present; what is missing or diminished is the feeling of pleasure. It is precisely this fact that needs explanation. The role of the tactile pleasure receptors on the nerve ends does not explain much, and is itself questionable and in need of much further clarification. In addition, the unmistakable signs of stasis, such as irritability, nervousness, and lack of pleasure in one's work — so often associated with coital use of a condom — attest to the absence of an adequate discharge of tension.

Analytic interviews reveal that in both monogamous and polygamous intercourse, *two basically different sensations arise from tactile excitation*, depending on the type of vaginal secretion produced. Patients describe one type of secretion as "watery," "slippery," or "runny"; the other as "oily," "thick," and "abundant." The former produces a weaker, qualitatively different sensation than the latter. Apparently they correspond, respectively, to the more serous or more colloidal secretions of the female genital glands.

The most striking fact is the relationship between *genital friction and contraction of the genital musculature*, the tonicity of which is greatly increased during erection. But, in addition, every friction movement brings on an involuntary contraction if one does not consciously tighten against it. As friction increases, the involuntary muscle contractions increase in intensity until, as the climax approaches, these are transformed into rapid series of spontaneous and uncontrollable *clonic spasm*s, which pursue their course even though the friction movement has ceased.

If friction brings the contractions to the clonic stage, it may — even before this stage — produce contractions of otherwise voluntarily innervated muscles, such as abdomen, face, and upper and lower extremities. This most essential

aspect of "the diffusion of excitation through the entire body" has been referred to previously in the purely phenomenological description of the orgasm.

We must still account for the fact that orgastically impotent, compulsive characters feel no sexual gratification, despite the capacity for mechanical release. We must also explain why, in patients suffering from ejaculatory impotence, genital friction appears to produce no corresponding muscle contractions in vas deferens and pelvic floor.

Very striking and hitherto unexplained (except by recourse to mysticism) is the fact that *a special kind of sexual resonance* can occur between a man and a woman — that is, an attraction later confirmed by a harmony of sexual rhythm. It may happen at the very first glance, though neither are yet aware of it.

Let us remove this "resonance" from the realm of genitality, which cannot account for it — nor can any single qualities of mind or appearance of the partners. We are then left with a certain something, which in popular parlance is called "radiating sex appeal" or having "sexual magnetism." Such a spontaneous, mostly unconscious object choice usually turns out to be harmonious — barring complicating difficulties. The question still remains, however, as to what constitutes this "harmony."

When the erect male organ touches the moist mucous membrane of the vagina, there arises an almost irresistible *urge to complete contact* between the two organ surfaces. The man feels this as an urge to penetrate fully; the woman, to receive completely. In contrast to this "genital magnetism," so to speak, we find this urge greatly diminished or completely absent in orgastically impotent men and frigid women, despite the presence of vaginal lubrication. There may even be a deliberate wish, fully conscious, to avoid penetration and pull out. Another striking feature is that the penis has to overcome a certain resistance in order to withdraw. This can result in a sensation of unpleasure or actual pain. The same thing happens in patients who consciously or unconsciously tighten their pelvic musculature during coitus and are then overwhelmed by the excitation. Such people tend to develop great anxiety prior to intercourse or sexual excitation.

If the vagina is dry, intercourse gives no pleasure at all, or a mild tactile pleasure at best, even when the friction movements lead to a mechanical release in the male.

Masturbation is less satisfying when done with a dry hand than with a saliva-moistened hand; the therapist might bear this in mind when treating patients with disturbed potency. Likewise, if the inside of a condom is moistened before use, a greater sensation is felt.

There is no simple way to explain why slow and gentle friction produces much stronger sensation than harsh and rapid movements. Purely tactile-mechanical explanations do not suffice. Carefully recorded sex histories from analytic subjects reveal that there are two types of genital friction movements: one is a deliberate straining and pushing of the entire torso; the other, a more spontaneous, undulating movement arising from the pelvis itself. We find the first type in people with heightened muscle tonus, or in affect-blocked types, who have to exert conscious effort to overcome their vegetative inhibitions, etc. The second kind occurs only in people who are muscularly relaxed and psychically unblocked. The first type we know is a substitute for *spontaneous* movement. But the meaning of the second type requires further explanation. In a similar vein is the question of why individu-

---

1. Reich, "Kritik der burgerlichen Sexualreform," *Geschlechtsreife, Enthaltsamkeit, Ehemoral*, Vienna, Munster press, 1930, p.15.

> **"... genital friction movements result in involuntary contractions of both the smooth and striated musculatures...*every friction movement, i.e., every change in surface contact between the vaginal mucosa and the penile surface, leads to a muscular contraction in healthy individuals.*"**

als with strongly erotic natures but lacking free-flowing sexuality may feel themselves as unattractive.

Finally, we have to point out one additional hiatus in our understanding of the complex orgasm phenomenon: after orgastic release, the genitals suddenly become refractory to any further excitation, and it becomes impossible to invoke a mental image of the sex act, or at best such images are completely drained of emotion. It is untenable to attribute this to a mechanical release of tension based on vascular engorgement of the genital organs, since the hyperemia abates only very gradually. It appears to be a direct *result* of the sudden drop in genital excitability rather than its cause. In order to explain this phenomenon in neurological terms, one would have to clarify how the end-organ receptors suddenly lose their receptivity right after climax.

All of the above considerations irresistibly point to the assumption that the orgasm represents *a form of electrical discharge*. To my knowledge, this is a concept new to the field of science, though it may have occurred here and there as a popular notion. We must now consider to what extent genital function can support this hypothesis. If this holds up, we must then explore and consolidate the relationship between mechanical relaxation and electrical discharge.

3. Mechanical Tension — Electrical Charge — Electrical Discharge — Mechanical Relaxation

The orgastic function must be an integral part — and a very elementary one at that — of the world of nature. It contains in clear form the basic functions of all living substance: tension, relaxation, charge and discharge, as well as the two fundamental directions of flow of vegetative excitation, which will require further careful elaboration. The orgastic discharge brings a feeling of pleasure and merging with the love object, its blockage leads to anxiety and a feeling of isolation. It holds the key to an understanding of the life-mind problem .

The prime feature in orgastic function is the vegetative excitation of the genital tract. Erection is basically a hyperemia of the genital blood vessels, particularly of the genital arteries (vagal [parasympathetic] innervation). The genital musculature (ischiocavernosus and bulbocavernosus muscles) is also under vagal stimulation and responds with increased tonus. This causes compression of the penile venous system, which is more superficially located than the penile arteries. The resultant backup of blood produces the erection. (Anxiety is the opposite process: sympathetico-tonic innervation contracts the arteries, relaxes the genital musculature, and results in a loss of erection.) The more completely vagal [parasympathetic] excitation takes over, the more strongly it compresses the urethra and bladder; in other words, the stronger the tone of the peripheral genital muscles, the stronger the ensuing contractions that force the semen past the muscle and vascular barriers.

In the female, the erectile process follows the same principle as in the male: arterial hyperemia and secondary venous engorgement of the corpora cavernosa clitoidis and bulbo

vestibuli (the vascular spaces around the clitoris and anterior vaginal wall).

We must therefore distinguish the following components in the process of *mechanical tension*: in the male, *tension in the seminal vesicles and the vas deferens*; in both sexes, a *heightened tension of the tissues themselves* (secondary to increased turgor of the genital glands and tissues), tension resulting from the *engorgement* of the corpora cavernosa, and surface tension in the *skin* and *mucous membranes*.

The well-known feeling of genital tension during sexual excitement has a direct mechanical basis, the increasing vegetative tension of the tissues themselves. Clinical studies of sexual disturbances, particularly in women, reveal that every *voluntary* tensing of the striated genital musculature either blocks or hinders sexual satisfaction. We know from the above formulation that the release of mechanical tension is quantitatively proportional to the intensity of the excitation. Therefore, the more relaxed the organism is (apart from purely vegetative tension), the greater is the pleasure experienced from this release.

The next question is — how does mechanical relaxation come about after vagal [parasympathetic] excitation has led to mechanical tension? Let us recall our earlier observation that genital friction movements result in *involuntary* contractions of both the smooth and striated musculatures.

Every friction movement, i.e., every change in surface contact between the vaginal mucosa and the penile surface, leads to a muscular contraction in healthy individuals. During resting contact, or in the absence of movement, no contractions develop (except at the end stage); the tonus may even drop slightly.

We know that galvanic stimuli, both "make" and "break" currents, produce contractions in muscle tissue. Striated muscle gives a rapid contractile response and relaxes just as quickly when the stimulus ceases; on the other hand, smooth muscle reacts with long, drawn-out undulations. It appears unmistakable that muscle contractions occurring with genital friction movements have the same characteristics as those due to electrical stimulation.

As the friction movements mount in frequency and intensity, the waves of contraction increase; as the climax is reached, tetany occurs — exactly as if induced by a rapid series of electrical stimuli — that is, a prolonged spasm at the peak of contraction. This tetany is then released with or without further friction movement by a series of *clonic contractions*, that is, by involuntary, automatic contractions of the entire genital musculature. It is not the tetanic contraction, but rather the ensuing clonus which brings about orgasm and the release of tension; the convulsive movements diminish and give way to a feeling of complete relaxation and subsequent drowsiness. It is now clear what ejaculation and release of tension entail. Under the stimulus of friction movements, a generalized excitation or tension is built up; during orgasm, this is released by a series of spontaneous muscular contractions which are independent of stimulation. The energy charge is dissipated and quiescence follows.

It is left to the physiologists to check these facts, make any necessary revisions, and determine exactly *what kind* of electrical activity is actually involved. At present, we are satisfied with the insight that an electrical discharge is present. The strong clonic contractions resulting from this discharge empty the seminal vesicles against the resistance of the tonically narrowed penile musculature and bring about a secondary, mechanical discharge. *Just as, before, mechanical tension was needed for an electrical charging of the genitals, now an electrical discharge is necessary for mechanical relaxation.* Since this reciprocal interplay between electrical and mechanical activity is an essential feature of the orgastic process, let us distinguish the *"tension-charge"* and *"discharge-relaxation" reactions* that, taken together, constitute the orgasm.

In order for there to be a complete feeling of release and satisfaction, it is not the mechanical but the electrical discharge that is essential, as the following discussion will make clear. Even minimal electric charges are sufficient to cause an evacuation of the seminal vesicle. However, the *feeling of gratification* does not depend upon seminal evacuation, but rather is proportional in intensity *to the prior mechanical tension, to the ensuing electrical charge, and to the amount of resistance that has to be overcome during the transition to clonus.* Accordingly, when ejaculation occurs during sleep, or during partial erection, there is little or no feeling of pleasure and relaxation; the completeness of release depends directly on the strength of the preceding erective tension. It also follows that one of the essential features of orgastic potency is the rhythm and force of the ejaculation, and not merely its occurrence.

We can now understand why coitus condomatus is wholly or partially unsatisfactory, even though a mechanical release of tension takes place. Clearly, the build-up of electrical charge is deficient, since the friction movements in this case are less pleasurable; but, above all, the preacme muscular contractions fail to occur and culminate in tetany. The clonic spasms are less intense, fewer in number, and weaker than normal. Thus, coital use of the condom raises a very important question as to how the electrical excitation is discharged, where it is localized, and what direction it takes in the two sexual partners.

We must therefore postulate the setting-up of an electrical system in each partner respectively, and we must ask how each of these systems is related to the other; since excitation and gratification depend precisely on this reciprocal relationship, which involves tactile as well as other factors.

For a clearer understanding, let us recall the set-up and functioning of a simple electrolytic system.

If we fill a glass container with dilute hydrochloric acid and introduce two platinum electrodes connected to [opposite poles of] an electric power source (but not to each other), an electric current will flow through the solution. If we connect the electrodes together with a good conductor, such as an iron wire, this produces a short circuit and the current bypasses the solution. However, if the current is passed into the solution, electric charges accumulate at each electrode. Soon we note that chlorine (anion) collects at the anode (positive pole) and hydrogen (cation) at the cathode (negative pole). According to Arrhenius's theory, the hydrochloric acid molecule does not decompose, but rather, each component atom is oppositely charged (chlorine negatively, hydrogen positively) and bound to a positive and negative ion, respectively. The electrodes constitute two *surface boundaries* that carry a strong charge when the current is connected. Then, according to the theory,

the negative chloride ions and positive hydrogen ions lose their originally random distribution in solution and become attracted to the oppositely charged electrode. The hydrogen (positive) ions go to the negative terminal (cathode) while the chloride (negative) ions go to the positive terminal (anode); at these electrodes, their ionic charge becomes neutralized and they are transformed into uncharged atoms. Thus, in the foregoing process of electrolysis, the charges of the cathode and anode do not directly neutralize each other, but do so through the intermediary of the positively and negatively charged ions present in the electrolytic solution.

We know, furthermore, that when two fluids are separated by a membrane or by a boundary surface (as the interface between two immiscible liquids is called), an electric surface potential is generated. If two such surface potentials are separated by a conducting fluid medium, ionic currents arise. This results in an equalization of the potential difference and a cancellation of the charge.

Pure water, a nonconductor, is not an electrolyte. Saliva, on the other hand, is a conductor. Thus, not by chance, clinical material reveals that erotic sensations are greatly reduced if the vaginal mucosa is moistened with water; with saliva, sensation is more intense, though not nearly so great as with the vaginal secretion, which is a colloidal acid solution .

As we know, the intensity of the pleasure sensation depends upon the proportion of watery to colloidal secretion. "Watery" secretion produces less pleasure than a "thicker", "oilier" one. How does this fit into our overall scheme?

First, the arrangement of membranes, boundary surfaces, and fluids during coitus points to the presence of a complete electrolyte system.

(a) male circulation
(b) male boundary layer (penile epidermis)
(c) female secretions (conducting medium)
(d) female boundary layer (vaginal mucosa)
(e) female circulation

We may consider the penile and vaginal surfaces as the two boundary surfaces or electrodes of the system. The acid vaginal secretion (which is an electrolyte) represents the contact medium (or conductor) between the two surfaces. The male and female circulations and the mutually stimulating plasmatic excitations in the autonomic nervous system represent the inherent sources of electrical charge on the organs of sexual contact. The equalization of the potential gradient occurs *between the two surface potentials: penile epidermis and vaginal mucosa.* In this scheme, we must distinguish three separate electrical phases: 1) the electric current generated by the male circulation; 2) the corresponding current in the female; 3) the electrolytic equalization of their respective charges through genital contact. The latter process must occur by means of ionic convection through the vaginal secretions, with the genital surfaces acting as electrodes. To support these assumptions, the following would be required:

1. Demonstration of the electrolytic properties of the vaginal secretions (electrical resistance, ionic composition, etc.).

2. Demonstration that the genital surfaces really are the locus of buildup of potential. (In this connection, the following should also be shown: the potential difference between the erect and flaccid organ; the relationship between amount of engorgement and degree of electrical charge; the reaction of the erect organ to an artificial electrode; and the ability of an intact skin or mucosal surface to discharge electrically.)

3. Demonstration of the polarity of charge, negative or positive, of the male and female surface potentials, respectively.

4. An experimental study of the electrolytic potential of various subjects according to their character structure, with special reference to the sexually disturbed female.

If we regard the sex act as basically an electrical process, we are able to understand the phenomena of genital magnetism, as well as the muscular contractions produced by friction movement. According to physical laws, the extent to which a potential gradient between two charged surfaces can be equalized depends directly on the completeness of their mutual contact. By the same token, neutralization will be less extensive if the contact is less complete. The impulse toward *complete* contact of the genital surfaces, that is, toward complete penetration followed by complete separation, we can explain by the following events: the partial release of tension occurring during genital contact and the rebirth of tension occurring when the organs are separated. We may thus distinguish two different kinds of *pleasure sensation*: the first stems from the *partial* release of tension occurring during friction-free contact; this is a precursor of the final orgastic pleasure in which the total charge is spent and the tension fully released; the second type occurs during friction contact, as a result of stimulation and the associated muscle contractions. Likewise, this motoric pleasure, surely the archetype of all motor-derived muscular pleasure, is an anticipation of the process that culminates in orgastic clonus. Let us call the first kind *"relaxation pleasure"* and the second *"tension pleasure."* Essentially, the former comes from a *decrease* and the latter from an *increase* in the surface potential gradient. The process is unequivocally clear with regard to the motionless phases of coitus, where there is anticipatory release of tension, as well as to the postorgastic phase when such release has been totally accomplished.

We are less clear in regard to the basis of "tension pleasure." According to our theories, tension should be experienced as unpleasure, not pleasure, which usually is the expression of a reduction in tension. The tension mounts somewhat after a friction movement, but abates considerably when the genitals rest together motionless; this permits a further rise in tension during the next friction movement, which is once again experienced as pleasurable. How can this ongoing increase of tension be reconciled with the accompanying feeling of pleasure ("tension pleasure")? Certainly each new friction movement increases the electric surface potential; but at the same time, the ensuing spasmodic muscle contractions discharge this accumulated energy, and *it is these contractions which render the experience of increasing tension as pleasurable rather than unpleasurable.*

There are two observations to support this hypothesis. First, Kraus concluded experimentally (without relating it to our problem) that a nerve under excitation *builds up* tension while a muscle under excitation *discharges* it through contraction.

During friction movement, both the contacting surfaces and the autonomic nervous system are becoming charged with energy, while at the same time, genital muscle contractions are releasing energy.

According to this, forepleasure consists of a simultaneous charge plus *partial* discharge. It was on this very concept that, in 1923, I based the phenomenological description of the sex act in my article "Zur Triebenergetik."(2) According to this, forepleasure is seen as a *dialectic* process, by which we may explain how a rise in tension can be pleasurable. Secondly, we find that, during genital friction, masochistic perverts experience the build-up of pleasure as unpleasure, and are compelled to avoid the *heightening* of pleasure sensations. At the same time, we find that a basic characteristic of sexual masochists is the *voluntary* contraction of the genital musculature in order to avoid the involuntary muscular contractions. This shows that if the latter are suppressed, the friction movement itself becomes merely an unpleasurable process of charge (like a continuous tickling stimulus) and will therefore be avoided.

In contrast to forepleasure, the final orgastic pleasure is a pure pleasure process and comes entirely from the muscular discharge; the muscular contractions discharge the nervous excitation by a process not entirely clear at the present time. The latter assumption is inescapable, since after orgasm the nervous system is refractory to further excitation and no further charging of the autonomic system is possible for a certain amount of time, whether by friction or fantasy; the surface of the genitals is not excitable either. However, the potential for a new buildup of charge is directly dependent on this discharge. This is seen in the greater orgastic potency resulting from regular, satisfying sexual activity, and its disturbance when satisfaction is seldom forthcoming.

In the frigid woman, deliberate tensing of the entire musculature suppresses involuntary muscle contractions, while dryness of the vaginal mucosa prevents the buildup of charge from friction movement.

How much of this dysfunction is psychogenic and how much is autonomic in origin will be discussed elsewhere.

In patients suffering from premature ejaculation, the genital musculature may reach too quickly the point of involuntary spasms (jerky ejaculations) or may simply fall into a state of tonic involuntary contraction (seminal emission only). In such cases, the excitation is transferred too soon from the autonomic nervous system to the musculature; physiologically, the actual process is still a mystery.

Furthermore, in both sexes one can discern differences in sexual behavior based on differences in orgastic potency. I should like to summarize them briefly here and try to consider their implication carefully with regard to sexual mores.

It is apparent that individuals who can experience friction-induced orgastic convulsions are much more likely to be monogamous than those whose sensations come only from mechanical discharge. The former have no need to inhibit polygamous impulses or follow moralistic codes; rather, their monogamy stems from the wish to repeat a vital, satisfying experience, in accordance with sex-economic principles. Naturally, this presupposes complete sexual harmony between the partners. There is no difference in this regard between men and women. On the other hand, if a suitable partner is not available, as so often happens under present sexual circum-

2. *Zeitschrift fur Sexualwissenschaft*, 1923, p.552.

> "... as the orgasm is based upon *elementary* natural principles, we would be extremely interested in determining if the process of tension-charge governs the orgastic function alone, or whether, as a universal phenomenon in nature, it represents a basic law of all living functions."

stances, the capacity for monogamy shows its opposite side in a tireless search for the right sex object. Polygamous behavior thus motivated cannot be considered neurotic, though prolonged sexual stasis can lead to neurosis. This questing activity does not arise from sexual repression but, on the contrary, is the expression of natural sexual impulses. After the appropriate partner is found, monogamous behavior is automatically resumed and lasts as long as the relationship is harmonious and mutually satisfying. In accordance with sex-economic principles, desires and fantasies concerning other mates are either greatly attenuated or not translated into action. This remains the case as long as no new partner presents an equal or greater appeal than the original mate. However, if the new relationship promises to afford greater pleasure, the earlier one is irrevocably broken off.

These facts run irreconcilably counter to the entire setup of sexual mores in present-day society, where material ties and responsibility toward children are in conflict with principles of sex economy. For this reason, it is precisely the healthiest individuals who suffer the most from sex-negative societal restrictions.

In contrast to this is the behavior of the orgastically disturbed, those who are incapable of electrical charge and discharge. Since they get less pleasure from intercourse, they are in a better position to tolerate the lack of a sex partner for a shorter or longer period, or they are less selective, since the sex act does not mean very much to them. If they are polygamous, it is the result of a sexually disturbed personality structure.

They regularly show more or less deep-seated disturbances in their work capacity, which is not the case among those achieving full orgastic release. They are more able to submit to the restraints of marriage; however, their fidelity is based not on sexual contentment, but on moralistic inhibitions; in other words, not on sex-economic principles but on socially imposed sexual morality. They very easily undergo neurotic regression to infantile conflicts. Their polygamous relationships are scarcely satisfying, and their long-term addiction to this form of activity makes them less and less likely to find an adequate sex partner. They are often in a better position to submit to the demands of bourgeois society but pay for it with various neurotic complaints that take their toll on the entire family group, especially the children. We see clearly right here how the illusion of "hereditary factors" can operate. If such individuals undergo successful analysis and achieve orgastic potency, they modify their behavior and begin to develop all the attributes of the genital character. (3) For sex economy, orgastic impotence holds the key to an economic and dynamic understanding of every kind of neurotic disturbance, symptomatic or characterological. Accordingly, it indicates dysfunction — not in the mechanical tension process (which would correspond to erective impotence) — but in the electrophysiological process of contact, charge and discharge.

The orgastic disturbance is relatively independent of the mechanical processes of hyperemia and surface tension, even though these are essential prerequisites to orgasm.

From all of the foregoing, a host of further questions arises, the most important of which is the following: inasmuch as the orgasm is based upon *elementary* natural principles, we would be extremely interested in determining if the process of tension-charge governs the orgastic function alone, or whether, as a universal phenomenon in nature, it represents a basic law of all living functions. ∎

---

3. See my study of the genital character in *Charakteranalyse*, Berlin Sexpol Press, 1933, p.16. [Also: *Character Analysis*, Farrar, Straus, & Giroux, NY 1972.]

Works by Wilhelm Reich
Published by Farrar, Straus & Giroux, NY
The Bioelectrical Investigation of Sexuality and Anxiety
The Bion Experiments
The Cancer Biopathy
Character Analysis
Children of the Future
Early Writings, Volume One
Ether, God and Devil / Cosmic Superimposition
The Function of the Orgasm
Genitality in the Theory and Therapy of Neuroses
The Invasion of Compulsory Sex-Morality
Listen, Little Man!
The Mass Psychology of Fascism
The Murder of Christ
Passion of Youth
People in Trouble
Record of a Friendship: The Correspondence of Wilhelm Reich and A.S. Neill
Reich Speaks of Freud
Selected Writings: An Introduction to Orgonomy
The Sexual Revolution

These and other titles available from:
Natural Energy Works
    PO Box 864, El Cerrito, CA 94530
Wilhelm Reich Museum Bookstore
    PO Box 687, Rangeley, ME 04970
American College of Orgonomy
    PO Box 490, Princeton, NJ 08542

Experimental Investigation of the Electrical Function of Sexuality and Anxiety*

by Wilhelm Reich, M.D.
translated by Barbara G. Koopman, M.D., Ph.D.**

Foreword

The following experimental paper is another in a series of reports dealing with the function of the orgasm and the autonomic life processes. Earlier, as I had anticipated, I was able to demonstrate experimentally this breakthrough into the realm of the autonomic life processes. To understand this report, biologists and physiologists must have some knowledge of my two recent papers: "The Orgasm as an Electrophysiological Discharge" (1934) and "The Basic Antithesis of Vegetative Life Functions" (1934). This paper, as well as its predecessors, should be regarded as a preliminary communication only. I should like to confine myself primarily to a presentation of the purely empirical findings and postpone tying this all up theoretically until I have adequately clarified a whole series of important but unclear findings in the broad and increasingly complex field of sex-economic research.

1. Basic Summary of Clinical Aspects

In my paper "The Orgasm as an Electrophysiological Discharge," I tried to tie together all the clinical data on sexual functioning which would remain incomprehensible unless based on an electrical theory of sexuality. According to this view, the process of sexual excitation is an electrical charging of the erogenous zones on the surface of the organism; the orgasm itself is a discharge of the potential built up as a result of preorgastic friction. Furthermore, noting the autonomic excitation that occurs after release of character armor and muscular tension, I came to view sexuality and anxiety as two distinct processes of excitation ("streamings") of the biological organism, which stemmed from the same autonomic source yet moved in diametrically opposite directions. Accordingly, sexuality would encompass everything related to peripherally directed excitation, streaming, energetic charging, and expansion. In essence, it is perceived subjectively as the feeling of pleasure. By contrast, anxiety includes everything related to excitation and flow centrally directed—away from the world. This would correspond to centrally innervated vegetative tension, felt and expressed as "tightening", "oppression", "inner tension", etc. (cf. my paper, "The Basic Antithesis of Vegetative Life Functions").

*   Translated from the monograph *Experimentelle Ergebnisse uber die elektrische Funktion von Sexualitat und Angst*, Sexpol Press, Copenhagen, 1937. Reprinted with the kind permission of Barbara Koopman and Orgonomic Publications, Inc.
**   Barbara Koopman, M.D., Ph.D. was former editor of *The Journal of Orgonomy* (1985-1991), and is a practicing orgone therapist in New York City.

This hypothesis is based on character-analytic observations and sex-economic principles. It has been confirmed and established in the Psychoanalytic Polyclinic [Vienna] after years of thorough testing. I knew from the start that its full significance would unfold in the field of neurosis and character pathology if one could find experimental support for the clinical phenomena on which it is based.

In the course of putting my theory to the test experimentally, it seemed as though I had stumbled across the core problem of the basic life process itself—as an inevitable outgrowth of my purely clinical observations. For if sexuality and anxiety represent two basic antithetical functions of living matter, we must prove and reproduce this fact experimentally.

From clinical observations on sexuality, I derived the following formula for the function of orgastic excitation: the first stage of sexual excitation is heightened turgor of the tissues, that is, an increase in mechanical tension secondary to blood engorgement; the second stage is an increase in surface electrical charge (rise to acme); the third is the discharge of potential built up during the involuntary muscle contractions; the fourth is the mechanical relaxation following the decrease in hyperemia. The "tension—charge—discharge—relaxation" formula of the orgasm requires the most careful experimental verification. This is especially so because it contains in essence the fundamental manifestation of life. The orgasm is a basic manifestation of living matter, and the tension-charge formula can in no way be applied to non-living phenomena. A survey of the literature—albeit incomplete—plus exhaustive inquiries to physicists and physiologists yielded the following information: in nonliving nature, there exists no process whereby mechanical tension leads to electrical charge and mechanical relaxation follows electrical discharge. On first reviewing the clinical data, I questioned whether this specific dialectic relationship between mechanical and electrical processes demonstrated some basic principle of biological functioning. The significance of this question is very clear. The tension-charge formula is, however, only a hypothesis derived from clinical observations and facts; if it is to lead to more useful theory and practice, it must be supported experimentally.

Review of Literature

In the available physiological literature, I could find no data to support the tension-charge formula and the basic autonomic antithesis of sexuality and anxiety. On the other hand, there were reports of experiments on the electrical functions of the skin.

The first report on the skin as a source of an electromotive force is found in correspondence between C. Ludwig and DuBois Reymond (*Akad. Verl. Ges.*, 1927). They described two different types of experiments: those dealing with the skin as a *conductor* of electricity (variations in resistance) and those dealing with the skin as a *generator* of electricity (source of the e.m.f.). H. Rein demonstrated the existence of an electric potential between closely adjacent skin areas. The skin's ability to act as an [electrical] membrane was shown by the fact that whenever the skin under both electrodes is injured, the potential difference disappears (*Z.f. Biol.* 85, 195, 1926). Philip Keller demonstrated that the skin potentials undergo continuous change (*Klinische Wochenschrift* 2, 1081, 1929). C.P. Richter studied the influence of diurnal and seasonal variations on skin resistance and found that in normal subjects skin resistance was lower in the morning than at other times of the day. From the above experiments, one concludes that fixed "normal" values for the direct current resistance of human skin cannot be established, since the results are extremely variable, fluctuating according to age, sex, experimental setup, diurnal and seasonal factors, etc. (Rein, *Handbuch*). However, Philip Keller was able to demonstrate that under rigorously controlled experimental conditions there were no significant differences among persons of different ages and sex. Interestingly enough, there was a marked negativity of the palm of the hand as compared with other regions of the body (56 mV versus 20-30 mV). Keller further demonstrated that even the most delicate touching of the human skin leads to a completely reversible increase in positive potential of the affected region. In addition, he showed a relationship between skin reaction and that of the sweat glands.

These experiments on the electrical function of the skin neglected to consider its erogenous function—that is, they failed to relate skin reactivity to skin erogenicity and to the affects of sexuality and anxiety. They also failed to investigate how the specifically erogenous zones differ from the rest of the skin. Theoretically, one would expect some attempt to explain the appearance of *local* variations in the skin zones studied. For example, perhaps some process in the sweat glands might be responsible for the increase in positive potential. But this kind of explanation errs by confusing the means of fulfilling a function with the function itself. This would isolate a function which is limited to a certain skin zone and set it apart from the functional unity of the organism as a whole. For example, as was shown, the surface of the hand responds to a shock by becoming negatively charged. One then might try to relate this reaction to a change in the functioning of the sweat glands on the hand. While this is not incorrect, it still obscures the more *basic* fact that when an *organism* is frightened it is the *total organism* which reacts, and, in this case, the surface of the hand represents only a detail of this total functioning.

In considering the results detailed below, it is important to realize the following:

1. The electromotive function of the skin has been established beyond doubt.

2. The skin has the ability to act as a membrane.

3. Normal values for skin potential cannot be fixed.

The theoretical explanation of my experimental results is based on the following concept: the electrical function of the skin is not a purely localized, isolated reaction, but, rather, the expression of a unitary function related to the bioelectric totality of the organism.(1) The skin may be regarded as only a special kind of membrane, since *the total biological organism is composed of a complicated salt electrolyte, colloidal electrolyte, and membrane system*. The relevant literature, especially the fundamental experiments of Kraus, Zondek, and others, I have already cited in my work "The Basic Antithesis of Vegetative Life Functions."

Tarchanoff and Veraguth found that the skin potential varies according to psychic stimulation. I will return to this fact later. Tarchanoff grouped these observations under the term "psychogalvanic response". Clinically, the following facts are significant in the field of psychopathology: the skin reacts electrically under the stimulus of affect: and even more important, there is a functional relationship between the *kind* of affect and the *direction* of electrical charge. The literature on the relationship between autonomic excitation and the emotions is so extensive that it is not possible to give a critical summary here. This will be done elsewhere in a more comprehensive theoretical review of the entire field.

For the present, we need only note that the literature offers no concept of the simultaneous functional identity and antithesis of the emotions and the autonomic apparatus. Rather, the physiological phenomenon is considered an "epiphenomenon" of the affect, or the affect is considered the "result" of an autonomic excitation. Thus the former view regards affect as lacking any objective biophysiological basis, since physiological phenomena are considered only epiphenomena. The latter view is a mechanistic concept which considers affect the "product" of an autonomic excitation. This idea is similar to the neurologists' myth that thinking results from secretions in the brain. Our present hypothesis—namely, that affect and autonomic excitation represent an indivisible and inseparable functional identity, and that the one is inconceivable without the other—opens up a significant perspective for exploring the borderland between psychology and physiology.

Lastly, we must emphasize that our present study brings genital pleasure into the realm of experimental research.

---

1. [An energy field around all living organisms—from slime molds to man—was demonstrated experimentally by Dr. H. S. Burr, a Yale neurophysiologist. Such demonstrations had only become possible in the early 1930s with the advent of the vacuum tube triode. Both Reich and Burr (the latter over a period of many years) used an amplifier of this type with high input impedance for the measurement of bioelectric potentials in the living organism. Dr. Leonard J. Ravitz, employing similar techniques, was able to show in human subjects a high degree of statistical correlation between polarity and intensity of these energy fields and various emotional states. For an excellent bibliography on the electrodynamic field, the reader is referred to Ravitz's article "History, Measurement and Applicability of the Electromagnetic Field in Health and Disease," *Annals of the New York Academy of Sciences*, 98, 1962.—*Trans.*]

2. Observations with the Oscillograph

In performing the following experiments, we used as our general frame of reference "The Basic Antithesis of Vegetative Life Functions" plus a specific hypothesis that we evolved step by step. These were supported consistently by well-known clinical facts. To avoid error, we set up experimental controls so that our working hypothesis would not bias the results. In the course of the work, there were many occasions where clinical theories seemed inadequate. In essence, it all boiled down to testing the correctness of the postulated "tension-charge" formula, or so-called orgasm formula.

The Biological Resting Potential

The first demonstrable aspect of the electrical function of sexuality is the electrical resting (or ground) potential shown by the *uninjured* skin or mucous membrane surfaces. The literature of the past few years contains an abundance of experimental evidence for this fact. Despite this, knowledge of the electrical surface charge is not well-known even in physiological circles. [The following procedure illustrates the phenomenon.]

Scratch the skin surface of an experimental subject who is hooked up to an oscillograph. Place the ground electrode on the injury site and apply the grid electrode, without pressure, to various intact skin areas. The light tracing on the oscillograph will show a deviation from the previously steady absolute zero line, and will register as a sudden jump to another region of the graph. The electrical surface charge of the uninjured skin has affected the grid potential (read as zero on the tracing), by increasing or decreasing its value. That it is, in fact, the uninjured portion of the skin which is involved in this reaction can easily be demonstrated by the following: if leads from two injury sites are simultaneously connected to the apparatus, there is *no* deviation from the zero line and the light tracing remains absolutely steady.

Physical Basis of the Experiments

To understand the experimental results, we need an explanation, albeit simplified, of the physical principle of the apparatus employed. It is based on the fact that a balanced electrical circuit will be affected by the introduction of a human body into the hookup. The effect of this will be manifested by a deviation of the otherwise steady tracing on the oscillographic film record. This tracing is produced by the reflection of a beam of light from a small mirror attached to a thin coil of the oscillograph; the latter is rotated by variations in strengths of the electromagnetic field (see the above diagram).

It is most important to understand the relationship between the electrical potential of the body and that of the apparatus. For this, a quick review of the principle of the vacuum tube amplifier is necessary.

We must first of all understand why an increase in charge of the body surface results in a positive deflection, and a decrease, in a negative deflection. This is related to the working principle of the amplifier tube, whose current is influenced by these changes in charge. The amplifying tube is a vacuum tube inside which a glowing cathode filament is placed opposite a "cold" anode. Between the two is the "grid," a kind of metal screen. The anode and cathode are attached, respectively, to the positive and negative poles of a battery (the "anode battery"). The so-called anode current is defined as a flow of "positive current" from the anode to the cathode. From the heated cathode (or filament), electrons, negatively charged, are emitted and generate a negative current flowing to the grid and then to the anode. The anode has a positive charge, and, since opposite charges attract, it attracts the negatively charged particles emanating from the cathode. Between the anode and cathode there exists a potential difference, the so-called anode potential.

There is also a potential difference between the grid and the cathode, which are connected together by a shunt, to form a secondary circuit. The grid, which is constantly bombarded by the electrons, tends to take on a negative charge. As this occurs, the electron flow is partially repelled by the grid, while the anode, with its positive charge, still continues to attract the remaining electrons. As a result, *the more the grid increases in negative charge (or decreases in positive charge), the more it repels electrons back to the cathode, and the fewer the electrons that reach the anode; therefore, the weaker the current from cathode to anode and the lower the potential difference, or grid potential between the grid and the cathode. Likewise, the less negatively charged (or more positively charged) the grid becomes, the more electrons reach the anode, and the stronger the current becomes.* To recapitulate, the first case (increasing the negative charge of the grid) results in a decreased (anode) current; the second case (increasing the positive charge) results in an increased (anode) current.

If we now connect any two regions of the human body, A and B, to the cathode and grid respectively, thereby completing the circuit, the light tracing either remains steady or is deflected to the left or right. If it remains steady, it means the resting current of the apparatus, that is, the grid potential, has not been affected. This may occur for two reasons: first, the two regions of the body may have the same charge. If there is no difference in charge between them, there is no potential gradient to generate a current. This also occurs when two separate injury sites are connected to the apparatus. If, however, one injury site and one intact site are connected, an electrical gradient will exist between the two. This potential gradient affects the previously constant grid potential, which registers as a steady zero line before the body is hooked up to the circuit. The apparatus is so constructed that the zero line remains at a steady level when the subject is not connected to the apparatus; that is, the current in the apparatus, and therefore the grid potential, remains steady. The zero line is arbitrarily chosen according to the setup of the equipment; therefore, use of another apparatus might result in another set of absolute values if a different zero line were chosen.

If two skin zones have markedly different charges or if one of them is injured, the light beam is deflected from the zero point. If the deflection is to the left (for a given hookup of the oscillograph), the skin zone connected to the grid has a greater charge than that of the grid potential. This results in a potential gradient between the skin and the grid and an increase in the positive charge of the grid. As noted before, this in turn causes an increase in the flow of electrons from cathode to anode, an *increased* current in the apparatus, and an increase in the grid potential: the oscillograph tracing is deflected to the left. On the other hand, when the grid is connected to a skin zone having a lower charge than that of the grid, the grid potential *decreases*. In this case, the grid takes on an increased negative charge, the electrons are repelled, and the current decreases, since fewer electrons can pass through the (relatively more negative) grid to the anode.

In summary: when the grid becomes negative, it indicates a decrease in electrical charge; when positive, an increase in charge.

The choice of the terms "up," "down", "left", or "right" is also an arbitrary one, but must be retained consistently for the entire series of experiments. If the oscillograph connections are reversed or the skin leads connected to the cathode instead of the grid, obviously many of the observed relationships would be reversed. For example, if we wish to indicate "positive" by an upward (or left) deflection, and "negative" by a downward deflection, the positive terminal of the apparatus must be connected to the body zones having a positive charge.

There is also the very important problem of polarization phenomena arising from the use of metal electrodes. We resolved this by installing a two-million-ohm resistance in the circuit between the subject and the vacuum tube, so that for practical purposes there is no actual flow of current, and only the potential differences are measured. Since there is no current flow, there is no polarization. According to the information supplied by the manufacturer, the actual flow of current from the body to the apparatus is of the order of 10^{-6} mA.

Using the experimental setup described, we measured the potential of the skin test sites in proportion to the grid potential. Through a series of trials with the same experimental hookups, we determined that all skin sites, with the exception of the easily excitable "ticklish" or "erogenous" zones, had a resting potential in the neighborhood of 10-40 mV. Repeated trials on the same subject gave the same results consistently—that is, variations of 1-5 mV. With certain exceptions, to be noted later, the potential of most of the skin surface was symmetrically equal on corresponding right and left sides of the body.

Figure 1. Average skin potential

Electrophoto 1 shows the resting potential (RP) of a female subject suffering from hysteria. The potential of the axilla appears the same on the left and the right, about –18 mV., and this is confirmed by a control test. As with all nonerogenous skin zones, a horizontal line results. The electrocardiographic tracing is also present and can be recognized on all of the photographs by its regularity. The direction of the cardiac deflection depends on whether the left or right arm is used as the site of the ground electrode. The reason for this is still unclear. The zero line of the apparatus remains constant.

A uniformly horizontal tracing is characteristic of the *biological resting potential* of the uninjured skin surface of an organism. It shows that a *constant electrical charge is being generated, with only rare fluctuations while at rest, from the interior of the organism to its surface.*

The Resting Potential of the Erogenous Zones

A few skin sites stand out as having a much higher potential than the nonerogenous zones of the body—namely, those which play a leading role in sexual sensitivity and excitability: penis, vaginal mucosa, tongue, inner surface of the lips, anal mucosa, nipple, palm of the hand, earlobe, and, interestingly enough, in some subjects with apparently marked intellectual abilities, the forehead. *These areas are different in their electrical functioning from the rest of the skin surface.* In particular, they have the capacity to register a resting potential much higher—or much lower—than that of other regions. On the latter, I found a resting potential of 0 to about –40 mV. By contrast, the sexual zones repeatedly showed deflections of up to 200 mV or one fifth of a volt; and there are several indications that their uppermost limit of potential has not been fully delineated.

Here we reach a problem which is central to the entire question [of electrical functions].

From clinical experience with psychiatric patients, we know that the sexual zones show a sensitivity and capacity for arousal far surpassing those of the rest of the body. When these functions are intact, one feels them subjectively as sensations of streaming, itching, tingling, pleasurable flushing, etc. The nonerogenous skin surfaces show these qualities to a far lesser degree or not at all. *Now is it possible that the intensity of excitation of a sexual zone corresponds exactly to its electrical charge?* To determine this, a further series of observations is necessary.

The erogenous zones may: 1) have a charging capacity that lies within the limits of variation of the rest of the skin; or 2) far surpass the upper limit of charge of the general skin surface.

A second basic phenomenon shown by the oscillograph may clarify in part these special properties, namely, *the wandering of the light tracing*, that is, the steady, gradual rise or fall of the potential.

The "Wandering" of the Potential

Electrophoto 2 shows the state of electrical charge of a semierect penis during the course of half an hour. The scale of the apparatus is adjusted so that a vertical deflection of one centimeter corresponds to 10 mV. The first deflection is about +35 mV, and the second deflection is about double that of the grid potential arising from an injury site. Control reference to the zero-potential level gives only minor deflections of about 3-4 mV, which are negligible. A third measurement results in a +40 mV deflection: a control test of the nipple gives about +20

" My results would seem to confirm exactly a mechanical-plus-electrical hypothesis:
...an increased surface charge must be added to the mechanical congestions before a feeling of
sexual tension, experienced as pleasurable, can arise. "

Figure 2. Potential of semierect penis

mV, and the final measurement of the penis, about +70 mV.
The EKG tracing is clear; the zero line remains constant.

The points marked by two crosses and forming a loop
down below register a negative potential: this represents the
control done by pressing the electrode on the penis. I will
return to this point later. We must now grasp two basic facts
which are absolutely essential for a correct understanding of
the entire problem:

1. *There is no rise in potential unless erotic, streaming
sensations accompany the tumescence. The organ can even be
fully erect without any rise in potential. The increased potential
is always associated with the subjective feeling of pleasure and
vice versa*, as will be shown later by other experiments. The
original assumption that erection is always associated with
increased charge proves to be false. My results would seem to
confirm exactly a mechanical-plus-electrical hypothesis: for,
evidently, an increased surface charge must be added to the
mechanical congestion before a feeling of sexual tension,
experienced as pleasurable, can arise.

2. In general, variations in potential height are gradual,
not sudden: figuratively speaking, the potential "wanders"
quickly or slowly up and down. Repeated control experiments
with inorganic materials show that this slow organic wandering has a special quality, a certain steadiness, easily recogniz-
able with experience. The fact that these changes in potential
are reflected in consciousness by changes in
the feeling of excitation, of *streaming*, demonstrates an amazing parallelism between
the objective, quantifiable events and their
subjectively felt intensity. (Control experiments with inorganic substances will be
discussed later.)

Electrophoto 3 shows a weak wandering
potential of the left palmar surface of a
female hysteric subject. With the electrode
resting in place, the potential rises from +15
mV to about +30mV; the electrocardiogram
is visible; the tracing shows only half of the
total run; 2.3 mm. of filmstrip equals about
a one-second interval. The tracing therefore represents changes
in potential for a period of about twenty-five seconds. (For a
precise gauging of the results, the beginning of the tracing
should be disregarded.)

Electrophoto 4 shows the wandering potential of the
same palmar surface one day later. The potential reads about
+35 mV at the beginning, then rises more steeply than on the
previous day; that is, the rise in excitation per unit of time is
greater than on the first tracing. This corresponded perfectly
to the way the patient felt:
she was in a much better
mood during the second experiment than on the day
before.

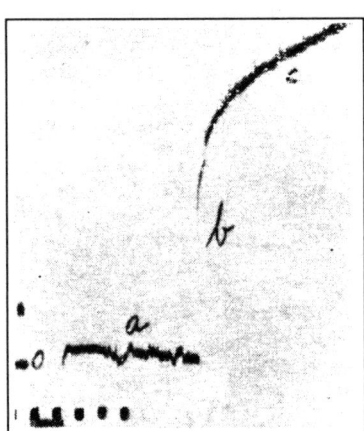

Figure 4 . Steep rise in
potential of the palm

3. *The rise in potential
must be regarded as the response of the organ to the
stimulus of gentle touching
with the electrode.* However,
the intensity of the excitation, as we can show, is related not to the intensity of
the stimulus, but rather to
the organ's state of excitability, or, better, its readiness to be excited.

Photos 5 and 6
show the excitation of
the anal mucosa of a
female subject upon
contact with the KCl
electrode, on two differ-
ent days:

Photo 5: here we
have wandering poten-
tials of about +25 mV.
The subject was in a
happy mood, and was
particularly interested
in knowing what the
tracing showed.

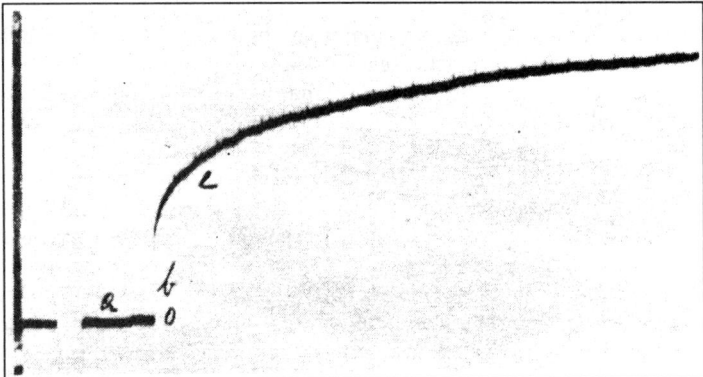

Figure 3. "Wandering" of the potential of a palm

Figure 5. Anal mucosa
of a woman in a state of
sexual excitation

Figure 6. The same mucous membrane in a state of depression (menstruation)

Photo 6: here we have a slight lowering of the potential, which starts out as –15 mV and remains "horizontal."(2)

On the day of the experiment, the subject was in a state of premenstrual depression. Here, too, the type and position of the potential recorded indicates the subject's emotional state. How does this relationship come about?

4. *The wandering potential represents a preorgastic, streaming excitation or discharge.* For a given person, it varies according to his changing emotional states.

5. *The preorgastic potential (POP) of the same erogenous zones varies from person to person.* On the other hand, the resting potential of nonerogenous zones is more or less the same regardless of the subject.

Thus the preorgastic potential sits on the resting potential like a mountain slope on a pain. It bespeaks a heightened biological activity on the periphery of the organism. In order to determine how the *intensity of subjective feeling* is related to the *quantity* of electrical charge, we need a further series of experiments and controls.

Tickling and Pressure Phenomena

Thus far we have examined phenomena that demonstrate the existence of an electrical charge on the periphery of the organism at various sites and various times without the mediation of an external stimulus. That such an electrical charge exists is the fundamental hypothesis on which the electrical function of sexuality is based; however, what sexuality really is, is not yet understood.

In general, the basic biological manifestation of sexuality is motor activity accompanied by the rhythmic friction of two excited body surfaces rubbing against each other. We know also, through direct experience, that this is associated with a subjective feeling of pleasure. But, until now, the objective component of this friction-induced sensuality has not been known. To confirm the electrical theory of sexuality, we must readily demonstrate that both phenomena (objective and subjective) have as their common denominator changes in electrical potential occurring at the pleasure site. The simplest form in which sexual pleasure is felt is the sensation of itching or tickling. These cause an automatic release of the impulse to scratch or to rub, and these actions seem to have a basic similarity to sexual friction. These phenomena seem to be generally present among metazoal organisms.

From clinical data, we know that a feeling of pleasure cannot be "commanded" into existence; the harder the mind tries to induce it, the less likely it is to appear. This is especially true when one tries to observe it in an experimental situation. Electrophoto 7 shows the stimulation of a male tongue—first by a resting electrode; then by gentle friction with the electrode; and, finally, by thrice-repeated pressure with the electrode.

The experimental setup is as follows: the ground electrode is placed on the left foot, while the grid electrode is placed without pressure on the tongue. We note that when the circuit is closed a ground potential of about +20 mV appears, which in

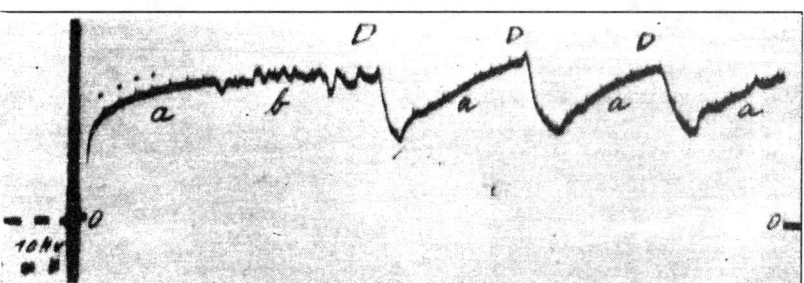

Figure 7. Mucous membrane of the tongue:
a = wandering; b = tickling; D = pressure

the course of about twelve second rises another 10-12 mV. As the tongue is gently stroked with the electrode, there is a further slow rise in the ground potential. We then see fluctuations of potential on either side of the ground-potential line, sometimes symmetrical, sometimes in a more or less positive or negative direction.(3)

This "tickling effect" can be demonstrated on any area of the body surface. However, repeated control experiments have failed to elicit it when the electrode is rubbed against inorganic substances (see below). We will return later to the significance of this "tickling effect." On the tracing, one may observe that the positive (rising) arm of the oscillating deflection is generally steep, while the negative (downward) deflection is shorter and more gradual. This will be shown to be of some significance later. The EKG follows exactly all the fluctuations in potential. At "D", the electrode is pressed gently but firmly into the tissues of the tongue. The result is an immediate drop in potential of about 15-20 mV which returns slowly up to the previous level when the pressure is released. We also note that

---

2. One may object that the wandering potential could be the result of local conditions in the electrode. However, any phenomenon which might arise from the electrode *alone* would appear *in every case*. (Cf. also "Results of control experiments," below).

3. The results observed here are in agreement with phenomena already known in the field of experimental physics. When two objects of different materials are brought together, an electrical field is generated between their two surfaces just within the boundary layers. For example, we may connect two different objects such as hair and a hand, respectively, to opposite poles of a current meter; if we approximate them carefully so that they are just touching, they will act upon each other at molecular distances, i.e., 10^{-8} cm. Thus, explain the physicists, the electrons are attracted from one body to the other and become "absorbed" on the surface of the latter. This gives rise to an electrical field with extremely short lines of force within the boundary layers of the two objects. This is called the "double-layer effect," and the voltage so produced is termed the "contact potential." The latter may be anywhere from .001 V to 1 V, as in our results. If the hand is rubbed over the hair, the two objects together constitute a "condenser": the lines of force become more concentrated, and the contact potential increases as the condenser becomes increasingly charged. This is registered on the current meter as a sudden deflection of the needle (i.e., sudden increase in current). Both objects may be insulating materials, or one of them may be a metal; however, both may not be conductors. (From R.W. Pohl, *Elektrizitätslehre*, 1935, p.196.) These explanations of physics say nothing about how the increased charge on an erogenous skin surface arises.

as the potential returns to its former level, it directly continues to follow the original "wandering" despite the interruption. This was regularly shown when the pressure was repeated on three additional trials. The pressure reaction also occurs on nonsexual areas, but without the wandering effect.

Electrophoto 8 shows the tickle elicited by the KCl electrode on the inner surface of a girl's lower lip. The negative deflection during tickling comes from an unintentionally heavy pressure on the electrode; the sudden rise at "K" coincides with the beginning of a strong itching sensation. When the tickling stimulus is withdrawn, the potential drops somewhat, and the wandering in a positive direction gradually resumes.

Figure 8. *Mucous membrane of the lips:*
*K to * = tickle phenomenon*

The degree of rise in potential of the tickling effect is related (1) inversely to the intensity of the pressure: the gentler the tickling, the steeper the rise; (2) directly to the excitability of the site; and (3) directly to the state of psychic readiness.

However, we cannot quantify this relationship until we can measure the *intensity* of the sensation. Yet everything seems to indicate that the rate of change in potential gives us the very yardstick we are seeking. As far as we can determine, the potential variations generated at or near ground level are not related to organ excitability or subjective mood and can be elicited at any time. However, we have never seen a steep rise in ground potential that was not accompanied by a simultaneous sensation of itching. Electrophoto 9 shows just how great the sudden jump in potential can be when the subject is in a suitably receptive mood.

The charge on the palmar surface yields a resting potential of about +20 mV. At the first tickling stimulus, it suddenly rises to about +55 mV. It then falls, apparently as a result of heavy pressure, to +10 mV, and climbs to +70 MV when the stimulus is repeated a second time. One may clearly see how the ground potential (along with the EKG complex) quickly builds up with each successive stimulation. We must, therefore, draw a careful distinction between: (1) the rise in the ground potential; and (2) the frictional fluctuations at or near ground potential level.

Electrophoto 10 shows the electrical charge on the same palmar surface after a two-minute rest. The ground potential starts off here at a level of +60 mV, compared to +20 mV obtained previously; it slowly begins to "wander"; then jumps to +85 mV when the tickling stimulus is applied; it then continues wandering up to +95 mV, while showing significant deflections due to the friction effect. When the tickling stimulus is removed, the tracing sinks slowly for 5mV over a period of about twelve seconds; thrice-repeated pressure with the electrode increases the negative drop by about 25 mV. A line drawn to join the points where the ground potential reappears after letup of pressure will represent the direct continuation of the ground potential's gradual fall.

From observations and control experiments, we maintain that inorganic substances show no such regularity and lawfulness in the process of acquiring electrical charge, and that these are properties specific to the organic world. We will return later to the implications of these facts in connection with other experiments.

Figure 9. *Strong tickle reaction of the palm:*
a = resting potential; k = tickling reaction

Figure 10. *Same palm one minute later:*
D = pressure

We have now established the following facts:

1. *Tickling stimuli which elicit a pleasure or itching sensation increase the electrical surface charge.*

2. *Pressure stimuli regularly decrease the surface charge.*
Does this lawfulness have a universal significance?

The same female subject, retested in a neutral frame of mind, shows about the same amount of charge on the left and right palms, that is, a symmetry of charge. In both cases and in the controls, the ground potential is almost still. Wandering is minimal (Photos 11 and 12). Careful evaluation of the control data amassed leads to the following conclusion: *in a given sexual organ, the capacity for excitation and the quantity of electrical charge can vary greatly from one time to another.*

Figures 11 and 12. *Symmetrical resting potentials of right and left palms*

Tickling near the Electrode

In evaluating the tickling effect, we had to consider the following objection: were the results simply an expression of the potential gradient between the friction material and the skin? We therefore produced the tickle phenomenon in the following way: the electrode rested motionless on the skin site to be tested, while the skin area *adjacent* to the electrode was gently stroked with a dry cotton pledget or feather (both nonconductors). Again, the tickling effect appeared, just as it did when the electrode itself was used as a stimulus (Electrophoto 13).

Figure 14. *Pleasure response (* to *) of an excited nipple*

Electrophoto 14 gives the results of such an experiment. We observe the nipple potential of a female breast during the course of one minute. The grid electrode rests on the nipple while the subject tickles the nearby aureole with a pledget of dry cotton. The asterisk indicates the start of the tickling. Up to this point, we see a horizontal resting potential of about +20 mV. As soon as the tickling begins, it suddenly jumps higher and then slowly increases until just before the end, when it again rises rapidly to about +45 mV. Then, as the tickling stops, it falls again. The subject reported that she twice felt a strong sensation of pleasure "right at the beginning and toward the end." At the latter time, she even reported the fantasy of a child sucking her breast. She was, of course, unaware of what the tracing registered, and when shown a photograph of it exclaimed, "That's the God's truth all right!"

Since the quantity of the potential (objective parameter) corresponds to the intensity of the pleasure [subjective parameter], we may draw the following conclusion: *the vegetative pleasure currents are photographically reproduced by the variations in electrical charge on the erogenous skin surface.* The details of this will be discussed later.

(The thickness of the light-streak tracing is due to interference transmitted by the house current, which was not filtered out in this experiment.)

In this type of experiment, we must emphasize that the testing and reporting of sensations by the subject has a distracting influence on the subject's attention, and, therefore, tends to inhibit the development of vegetative streaming. Because of this, we would expect that in a spontaneous and undisturbed situation the intensity of sexual streaming would be significantly greater.

ing his feelings, and the gentler the tickling (that is, the less contact there is between the tickling instrument and the skin), the more exact the results. We observed that quantitatively the objectively visible potential deflections reproduced—with photographic accuracy—the *intensity* of the [subjectively] felt pleasure experience. This was even more accurately reproduced when the intensity of the pleasure *currents* (*streaming*) was considered.

The experiment can also be performed in reverse by having one person indicate the reading of the tracing while the subject compares it to his own pleasure feeling. Naturally, this is not so satisfactory a method as the first.

Figure 13. *Tickle reaction of palm: tickling adjacent to resting electrode*

In order to verify the functional identity of *objective* variations in potential and *subjective* sensations of tickling, the following experiment was performed.

A control subject observes the apparatus [in one room]; the experimental subject is placed in an adjoining room and connected to the recorder by a long cord. The subject, who must be capable of observing his feelings, is then told to indicate whether the tracing wanders or stays steady; whether the potential is rising or falling, etc. He is to do this, not on the basis of tactile sensation—but *according to the amount of tickling he feels.* The greater the subject's accuracy in observ-

Figure 15. Reaction of penis to regular friction

The same experiment was conducted with the electrode placed on the penis; the results were the same. A regular friction stimulus applied near the electrode produces regular waves on the tracing (Photo 15). In this run, the apparatus was set at its lowest range of sensitivity (1/10). The deflections are in the 15-20 mV range.

In no case was a rise in potential observed where there was no feeling of pleasure associated with the stimulus. An indispensable requirement for conducting this experiment is the subject's ability to distinguish between a streaming sensation of pleasure and simple tactile or thermal sensation.

Anxiety and Unpleasure

In reviewing the literature on psychogalvanic skin reaction, I could find no statement as to any distinction between pleasure and unpleasure or anxiety phenomena. Physiologists who were consulted stated that no distinction could be made and that an increased negative charge would always result. But my concept of the antithesis of pleasure and anxiety, based on clinical observations, threw doubt on this. If psychic excitation is functionally identical to fluctuations in autonomic excitation, and the latter are observable as waves of electrical potential, then their view is untenable. Since the sensations of pleasure and anxiety are antithetical to each other (though identical *in origin*), this opposition should also apply to the direction of their electrical flow. The difficulty is that up to now, so far as I know, no one in the field of nerve and skin physiology has distinguished the *direction* of electrical flow resulting from excitation of an organ. Therefore this had to be worked out in the course of the present experiments.

Thus far we have quantified the various skin potentials as per their relationship to the grid potential, which is arbitrarily set at zero. We have also compared the potentials of various skin zones to each other. These differences are relative, since both sets of potentials are variable. We must now delineate more accurately a third aspect of electrical functioning.

The Direction of Change in Potential

So far we have called a potential positive or negative in relation to its value above or below the arbitrarily chosen zero level of the grid potential (e.g., +15 mV or –40 mV means 15 mV over or 40 mV under the zero potential, respectively). One may further distinguish the *direction* of change in potential, and speak of a "rising" or "falling" potential; these may be read directly from the milliammeter of the apparatus.

We must keep clearly in mind that any rise in potential indicates an increase in positive potential, regardless of whether this occurs above or below the arbitrary zero line; the same applies to a fall or increase in negative potential. Let us stop considering the absolute or relative difference of the changes in potential, but observe only their direction of change. For example, a change from –40 to –20 mV would still be considered a positive change; likewise, a change from +5 to +30, or from –10 to +10 mV. Similarly, any change on the milliammeter from a higher to a lower figure is considered a negative change, and will show on the tracing as a movement from left to right, or on the photo of the tracing, as a movement from above to below.

Lowering of the Surface Potential During Anxiety and Unpleasure

At the risk of repetition, we recall so far that stimuli that result in a streaming sensation of pleasure *increase* the electrical charge on the body surface. This is expressed as a rise in potential, that is, as a positive change in a grid potential. The light tracing is deflected to the left, the milliammeter registers an increased current flow, and the photo of the tracing shows an upward deflection.

Figure 16. X = reaction of vaginal mucous membrane to a stimulus of annoyance

Electrophoto 16 shows the change in potential accompanying a feeling of *annoyance*. The charge is measured at the vaginal introitus of a female hysteric (the same subject whose anal potential was measured previously). The vaginal measurement was done the same day as that of the premenstrual anal mucosa (cf. Photo 6).

The ground potential starts off at about –15 mV and quickly sinks to –25 mV. We will recall that the subject felt depressed and found the procedure quite disagreeable. She was isolated in a nearby room and was attached to the apparatus by a long cord. The ground electrode was attached to the leg and, like the grid electrode, was of KCl. The subject was asked simply to place the electrode on the labia majora. We noted a gradual decrease in potential, and then, suddenly, a steep negative deflection; at the same moment we heard a loud cry of annoyance from the adjoining room: a drop of KCl had fallen on the sensitive mucosal surface and irritated it. This point is marked by an "X" on the photo.

At the point indicated by the second "X", the subject became irritated once again and the potential dropped sharply about 20 mV.

A feeling of annoyance is accompanied by a decrease in electrical charge of the erogenous zones. Why does sexual excitability so quickly disappear in a state of irritation? When one is irritated, bioelectric excitation runs in a direction opposite to that of the sexual excitation: *therefore a decrease in surface charge occurs instead of an increase.*

Photo 17 shows a similar occurrence on the tongue of a male subject. The ground potential starts quietly at about +2 mV; at K, tickling with the electrode begins; the ground potential rises gradually; at E, a sudden loud cry is made to frighten the subject; the potential drops about 20 mV; a repeated shout results in another potential drop, much less than before (not shown in this photograph). A third cry has no further effect. We note that the tickling effect, as well as the electrocardiogram, conforms to the drop in potential.

> **" It is as if the living organism reaches out toward the world by charging its surface electrically. The charging of the periphery during pleasure excitation would seem to have the same functions as pseudopod extension in an ameba or feeler extension in a snail."**

Figure 17.
Tongue:
K = tickle
E = fright

Before seeing the actual tracing, the subject, a psychology student, drew us a graph depicting his tongue sensations. His diagram bears an amazing likeness to the curve of the ground potential. Only the effects of the tickling stimulus are missing.

From clinical work in sex economy, we are familiar with an interesting subjective phenomenon: patients occasionally report that when frightened they feel something like an electric shock on the tongue. A patient reported a similar sensation when he suddenly discovered that his wife had been unfaithful.

In a state of anxiety or fright, there is a concomitant drop in electrical charge of the body surface. This is more pronounced at sexual zones than on the rest of the skin. A flaccid penis, which typically accompanies anger or anxiety, regularly shows a lowering of potential.

It is easier to obtain an anxiety reaction than a feeling of pleasure. We use an exploding paper bag or a sudden loud striking of a gong. On one occasion, the electrical response did not occur. The subject reported that the stimulus had caused an instantaneous feeling of *rage*. This raises the problem: what is the relationship between rage and the negative potential change produced by annoyance and anxiety?

In the above, we have some experimental support for the sex- economic concept of the biological *antithesis of pleasure and anxiety*: they are oppositely directed electrical currents. *During pleasure, the surface of the organism becomes more positively charged with respect to the interior; during displeasure, irritation, or anxiety, it becomes more negatively charged.*

Now that we have demonstrated the functional identity of pleasure, with a peripherally directed current flow, and of anxiety, with a centrally directed current flow, we still have an important objection to consider—namely, the appearance of the so-called cold erection or pleasureless erection of the penis. Experiments show that mechanical hyperemia is not sufficient to cause a feeling of pleasure: compression of the penile root and consequent blood congestion does *not* cause a change in potential. In addition to blood flow, something else must occur for excitation to result. The "streaming" quality felt during pleasurable erection is due to *mechanical hyperemia plus the electrical charging of the surface*: pleasure currents are felt only when there is a rise in the electrical potential. We draw a further conclusion from this: namely, that the biopsychic tendency "toward the world" and its opposite "away from the world", "withdrawal into the self", have an objective functional basis in the antithetical direction of streaming of the bodily electrical charges. *It is as if the living organism reaches out toward the world by charging its surface electrically. The charging of the periphery during pleasure excitation would seem to have the same functions as pseudopod extension in an ameba or feeler extrusion in a snail.* Similarly, *the discharge of*

the periphery, and concomitant decrease in potential, would be the direct expression of a creeping back into the self. This problem should certainly be explored further in animal experimentation.

The Basic Antithesis of Vegetative Life Functions

The Sugar-Salt Experiment. In the tickling experiment we were able to elicit streaming sensations of pleasure; however, we are not entirely clear about them since we cannot specify their range of intensity, that is, quantify the capacity to accept electrical charge. Clinical experience has shown that the surface of an organism is not charged artificially from without but biologically from within, from the "vegetative center," so to speak. This reaction requires the elimination of all inhibitions and external disturbances. In all previous experiments, we allowed pleasure feelings to be artificially "pumped up", so that they did not stream spontaneously. As a result, the excitation always acted like a cautious snail afraid to venture out of its shell. In order to achieve a spontaneous reaction, we conducted the following experiment with several subjects.

The cathode is placed in a vessel filled with normal saline. The grid electrode is wrapped in a saline-soaked cotton pad. One end of this long pad is placed in a dish containing concentrated sugar solution. The other end of the pad is thoroughly moistened with a solution of either sugar or salt. The subject then sucks on this end of the pad while placing a finger in the vessel containing the cathode, in order to complete the circuit. The technical correctness of this arrangement will be considered later.

Figure 19. Reaction of
same tongue to salt

Figure 18. Reaction of
tongue to sugar

We begin by giving sugar, without her knowledge, to a female subject known from her therapy to have a strong oral-erotic tendency. The first part of Electrophoto 18 shows no curve since the tracing is too far to the left, that is, so far in a positive direction that it is out of the field. In the second part, a certain amount of adaptation has obviously occurred. In the third part, we see a curve rising in a positive direction, which clearly reproduces the sucking movements; it is analogous to the tracing produced by friction, with a steep rise followed by a more gradual falling off, and an increase in ground potential. In the second part, the zero line is displaced to the right, that is toward the negative, for the sake of accuracy. The curve begins at a minimum of +70 mV and rises approximately another 20 mV. In a second subject (male), with no particular oral-erotic tendency, there was an initial rise of +mV (4) followed by an increase of 30 mV.

When we repeat the same experiment, using a concentrated salt solution, we obtain a diametrically opposite result, even to the form of the tracing itself: the ground potential starts at about −55 mV, does not vary up and down as in the sugar experiment, but plunges downward in an almost constant drop (Electrophoto 19).

If we apply salt to the mouth unexpectedly, we see a large negative deflection toward the right margin, in the opposite direction to that occurring when sugar was used.

The oral excitation quickly leaps out toward a pleasurable stimulus and pulls back from an unpleasant one. Thus, the opposition between pleasure and unpleasure can be experimentally demonstrated and photographed. It is an objective fact, independent of any preconceived notions. The basic antithesis of vegetative life functions is manifested by pleasure, the peripherally directed flow of electricity, and by anxiety or unpleasure, the centrally directed flow.

Figure 20. Reaction of tongue to sugar

The Form of the Excitation. So far we have considered only the height and direction of the excitation curve. But in comparing the sugar and salt reactions, one is stuck by still another difference. The excitation curve of sugar is very "lively". In Electrophoto 20, we can clearly see the following: an increase in the positive deflections, that is, the most outwardly directed, toward-the-world strivings; but, in addition, we see strong negative deflections, which in turn give way to even stronger positive ones—deep clefts followed by steeply rising peaks. A very similar picture results when honey is sucked: each increase of excitation precedes a retreat. The reaction to salt, on the other hand, lacks this effect. Here (Electrophoto 21) we find a more or less regular "quiet" drawing back, once the first steep plunge of the ground potential has occurred. With different subjects, even the minor 2-3 mV fluctuations seen here are lacking: the excitation drops off uniformly.

---

4. [The original manuscript fails to give a figure for the initial rise. —*Trans.*]

Figure 21. Reaction of same tongue to salt

The "Disappointment" Reaction. When one administers sugar first and then salt, the reactions follow the pattern described above, though in varying degrees. We may also note an habituation effect with repeated administrations of a sugar-salt sequence. With each successive run, the reaction to sugar shows a progressively lower potential. Likewise, the reaction to salt is not so intense as in the first trial, when the stimulus is unexpected.

On the other hand, if the salt is applied before the sugar, the reaction is completely negative, and the subsequent administration of sugar does not induce a rise in potential; the sugar actually results in a steep drop in potential.

This finding clearly indicates the biological nature of these reactions. Once the salt has been applied, the tongue behaves as if it had become cautious and refuses to be tempted; it reacts with anxiety even when sugar is given. On repeated trials, we find that [after "disappointment"], the tongue does not respond to sugar with an increase in charge until one-half to one hour later. Even so, we do not get the steep jump in charge seen on the first application of sugar, nor do we see the "lively" behavior shown in Electrophoto 21. The friction potential, normally seen with sucking, shows only small deflections and appears rather "sluggish".

In dealing with phenomena of electrical excitation, one may discern not only *quantity* and *direction* of flow, but varying degrees of *liveliness*, as well. The same organ may respond to a given stimulus in a quick and lively fashion at one time, and in a slow or sluggish manner at another, depending on its "mood." From this, we may draw the following conclusions:

1. The electrical response of a sexual organ depends not so much on the stimulus as on the state of readiness of the organism as a whole.

2. A "disappointed" organ reacts slowly and "cautiously."

3. When *habituation* to a given stimulus occurs, there is a reduction in the range of potential change, both positively and negatively; that is, upward or downward deflections occur closer to the zero line.

We thus have experimental confirmation of some well-known aspects of sexual activity.

The response to a sexual partner is not always—indeed

only rarely—contingent upon the amount of stimulation offered. Rather, it depends almost entirely on the individual's state of sexual readiness

Also, during sexual activity, the genitals may experience a disappointment reaction, such as described above. A state of sexual arousal may be difficult or impossible to obtain. Instead of erection or vaginal secretions, flaccidity, dryness, even vaginismus may ensue in a wake of severe genital anxiety, unpleasant circumstances, or painful associations. The genital is totally dominated by the impulse to withdraw; the opposite reaction, of erection, of "reaching out to the world", cannot occur. Thus, in cases of impotence or frigidity, the important consideration is not so much whether there has been a sexual threat at one time, but rather whether at that particular time the organ responded with a negative biological anxiety reaction which subsequently became fixed. For the subjective experience of genital anxiety to have a lasting effect, it must be structurally anchored in the form of a [conditioned] negative electrical response. In contrast to this is pleasure anxiety, which I shall discuss later.

Hypotheses Concerning the Pleasure Response. Control experiments on the above are feasible only if one becomes familiar with the peculiarly "cautious" quality of the peripheral electrical charge. The charge will not "venture out" in the presence of a third party, in the face of possible disturbance, or if the attention is not completely directed away from the outside world. We, therefore, need a series of complex setups to ensure valid results.

In charging the periphery to capacity, the decisive factor seems to be not the rise in potential itself, but the amount and extent of the deflections involved. The tracings of the sugar reaction show a rise in potential broken by deep clefts, corresponding to strong withdrawals of charge. From clinical data, we know that the greater the waves of excitation produced by coital friction movement, the greater the pleasure obtained. If the excitation mounts in a steady rise [rather than in peaks and clefts], the sex act will not be as pleasurable, even if the same potential heights is eventually reached. It seems to depend upon the alternation of quiescence and activity, on the step-wise buildup of charge to the maximum charging capacity.

The tracings of the tickling response show alternate up and down movements corresponding to an increase and decrease of charge, respectively; we cannot properly call this decrease a "discharge". In the sugar response, the excitation on the tongue behaves like a suckling calf, which pulls away from the udder only to press forward again with increasing eagerness. It seems probable that each new movement leads to a fresh wave of pleasure. One thinks instinctively of a tiger or cat crouching before a leap—*contraction before maximum extension.* In this case, the state of contraction is not associated with any relaxation, but expresses a state of extreme inner tension. Since the charging of the periphery also reflects a directly observable state of tension, we must conclude that there are two different kinds of tension involved. Just before springing, there is a state of *central* tension in the organism; the greater this tension, the greater the motor impulse at the periphery. The withdrawal of charge from the periphery must necessarily

lead to an increase of tension centrally. *Thus the electrical excitation springs, so to speak, from the center to the periphery.* This state of central tension can be directly perceived if during coitus one happens to stop a particularly pleasurable friction movement and lies perfectly still: one immediately feels a strong inner urge to resume the friction movement, that is, to build up the peripheral charge. We will consider this to-and-fro movement of the excitation in more detail later.

Therefore, we must carefully distinguish *four different types of negative electrical response at the periphery*:

1. Central tension stemming from charging of the periphery.
2. Peripheral orgastic discharge.
3. Anxiety reaction
4. Extinction of the source of charge: death.

In all four cases, there is a reduction of the surface charge: the first is in order to recharge to a higher level—pleasure; in the second, all excitation above the resting potential is discharged to the outside—orgastic discharge; in the third, the tension remains fixed centrally—anxiety; the fourth corresponds to death. According to previous experimental results, dying tissues become increasingly negative as the central source of charge is extinguished.

By sorting out the various functions having the same direction of electrical excitation, we can better organize our wealth of data.

Electrical Excitation During Kissing

The Inadequacy of Direct Leads. From the very beginning of our investigations, we felt that a photographic tracing of electrical excitation in coitus would be an experimental goal of prime importance. However, our initial experimental setup, using direct leads from the test sites, made attainment of this goal seem unlikely. It is impossible to use direct leads for measuring the charge at the genitals during coitus. The manipulation alone would inhibit any excitation. Also, a direct lead is not entirely free from mechanical instability, which can give rise to unsteadiness and irregular, even broken contacts. Finally, there is another difficulty to be overcome: namely, to rule out possible mechanical artifacts of the electrode itself. This is necessary even though the controls showed no deflections resulted from rubbing the electrode (or its rubber-sheathed tips) against glass or a cloth soaked in electrolytes. At first, there seemed no way out, as I labored under the misconception that the excitation could be tested only by direct leads. It was at this stage of the experiment that we took the following tracing of an ejaculatory excitation curve (Electrophoto 22).

The subject was orgastically disturbed. The act of masturbation was interrupted just before the ejaculation. The electrode (KCl) rested on the glans penis throughout the ejaculation. At the beginning of the climax, we see a positive rise in

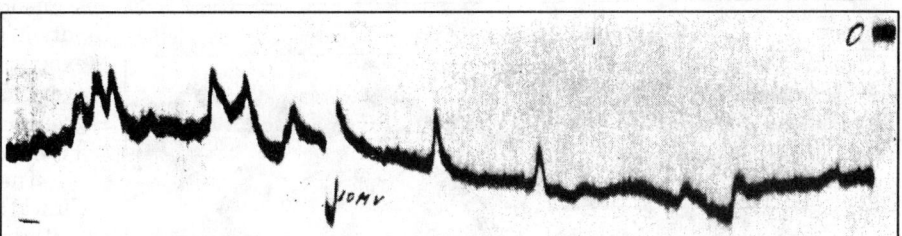

Figure 22. Orgastic excitation during masturbation

the ground potential. It continues to climb evenly, with steep rises in potential of about 10 mV. It is difficult to judge what relation the second major rise in positive potential, shown by the two peaks on the tracing, has to the first three sharp deflections due to the ejaculation. Since 2.3 mm. of tracing equals 1 second of time (accurately shown by the EKG complex), it appears that only the triple-peaked deflection corresponds to the ejaculation, while the other group reflects the post-ejaculatory penile spasms. The regularity of the intervals, and also the approximate height of the deflections (somewhat less than usual), attest to the biological nature of the phenomena. In addition, there is the falling off of the ground potential after its initial rise.

Of course, there are uncertainties due to technical difficulties and the unusual emotional demands made on the subject; but there is no doubt about the basic features of the phenomenon. The form of the electrical excitation, the rise and fall in potential, accords with what was expected from clinical experience. In principle (regardless of the potential height), the orgastic excitation curve must ascend and descend in equal amounts; the steepness of the ascending portion is not seen here. After successful ejaculation, the ground potential remains steady (horizontal, in the photo) at about 25 mV. We should note that the curve of orgastic excitation, at least in this case, lacks the deep negative deflections seen in the preorgastic friction tracing. It is confined to the region above the ground potential, for example, on the positive side of the base line.

The Technique of Indirect Leads. In order to achieve our major goal [of recording the coital excitation curve], while sparing our subjects' feelings as much as possible, we had to consider the feasibility of using indirect leads. This raised the following

question: if we attached the leads to a fingertip of each subject, could we separately measure the potential of two body surfaces in rhythmic friction with one another? This would give correct results only if: (1) the potential tracing obtained reproduced the form of the excitation coming from the test sites; (2) the attachment sites of the leads (the fingertips) did not move; (3) the ground potential of the two contiguous skin surfaces remained the same, regardless of the surface area in contact.

The following three electrophotos show tracing taken of:
1. The resting potential of two fingertips rubbing against each other (Electrophoto 23).
2. The pressure effect obtained by pressing a fingertip against the glass bottom of a vessel (Electrophoto 24).
3. The rise in potential resulting from the gentle, mutual, hand-stroking of two subjects (Electrophoto 25).

The experimental setup was as follows:

In the first photo, the EKGs of *both* subjects are superimposed on the tracing. The resting potential, as expected, starts off at about –20 mV. During the quiet interval [between the tests], the ground potential remains horizontal. The second photo shows several negative deflections, resulting from the heavy rubbing of a fingertip on the glass bottom of the electrolyte container. The third photo shows strong positive deflections, up to 20 mV—in other words, a 40 mV rise above the resting potential, resulting from gentle stroking. Direct observation showed that harsher pressure transformed the positive into a negative deflection—that is, it caused a fall in potential.

When the stroking stops, the ground potential returns to the resting state and a slow drop to the original resting potential is seen.

Figure 23. Contact potential of two fingertips

Figure 24. Rubbing of same fingertips on glass surface

Figure 25. Stroking of palm

Figure 26. Hand stroking alternating with pressure

Electrophoto 26 shows, in unique fashion, the antithesis of *pleasure* and *pressure*: two hands are alternately pressed together and stroked in sequence. The results are checked by direct observation; every single rise in potential corresponds exactly to a pleasant feeling [of being stroked]; every fall occurs during heavy pressure. The ground potential shows a slight rise, on a whole. Two female subjects were used.

The results of this experiment recall the clinical observation that during the sex act, gentle friction heightens pleasure, while harsh friction decreases it.

The following are the controls for our key experiment. Electrophoto 27 shows other respective potentials due to friction between:

1. Two fingertips, about −10 mV.
2. Two fingers, about −20 mV.
3. Two hands, about −10 mV.
4. Dorsal [outer] aspects of two fore arms, about −20 mV.
5. Ventral [inner] aspects of two fore arms, about −20 mV.

Encouraged by these irrefutable results, I photographed a pleasurable kiss between two individuals (Electrophoto 28).

We see the familiar effect of frictional excitation: steep peaks alternating with deep clefts.

Electrophoto 29 shows, "in slow motion", a greatly enlarged tracing of the frictional excitation. One centimeter on the horizontal axis corresponds to one second; one centimeter on the vertical axis equals about 3.3 mV.

The ground potential shows a rise, on the whole. We see that the various peaks of excitation show a basic similarity of form. However, the details are still to be worked out.

Electrophoto 30 shows the course of excitation during an unpleasant kiss with the same couple. The female partner shows visible malaise: the ground potential falls, and, at the same time, the frictional deflections grow smaller. At the end, a deep negative deflection is seen—sharp annoyance. This tracing was taken with rapidly moving film, as in slow-motion photography—one centimeter equals one second. The oscillations on the base line are artifacts of the oscillograph itself, as shown by the controls on inorganic substances.

From this we conclude: with minor exceptions, *the potential height shown by two quietly touching skin surfaces is independent of the surface area in contact*, provided that they are in an unexcited state.

On the basis of the foregoing experiments and controls, we used indirect leads to record the embrace of a naked couple, the male kissing the breast of the female (Electrophoto 31).

The ground potential registers a height of about 100 mV; the frictional deflections of the kiss amount to be about 10 mV, as before. The two EKGs are visible. The bodies reposed quietly together. The complete excitation process was no doubt disturbed by the conditions of the experimental setup, but, in spite of that, a level of +100 mV was reached.

From this, we may rightly draw conclusions as to the maximum reachable potential of full sexual excitation during an undisturbed sex act. There is no longer any

Figure 27. *Contact potential of various skin areas*

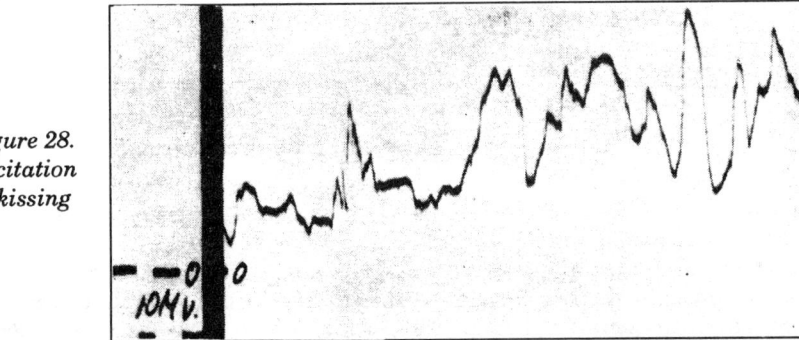

Figure 28. *Excitation in kissing*

Figure 29. *Kiss*

Figure 30. *Unpleasurable kiss (*annoyance)*

Figure 31. *Embrace of two naked bodies*

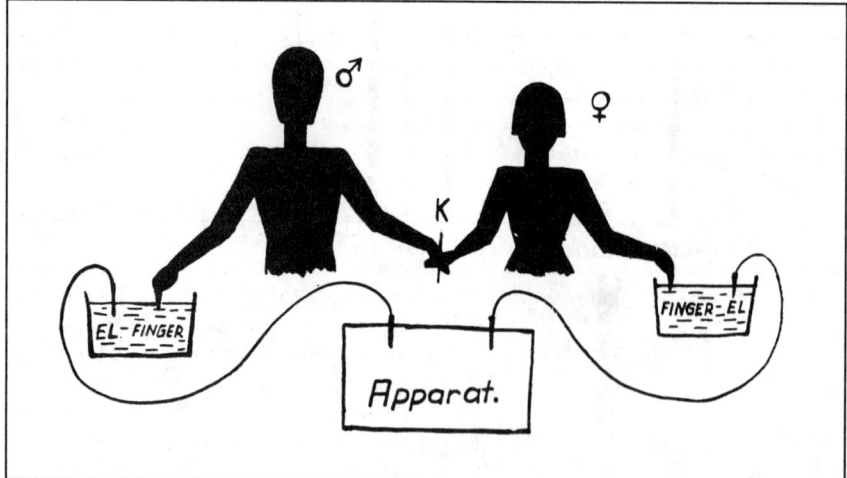

question of *whether* a process of electrical charge and discharge occurs in the sex act: rather, the problem is how to record such an excitation, in view of its strikingly high excursions above a photographic base line.

3. Results of Control Experiments

The electrical phenomena of the erogenous zones of the body would be far less meaningful if they did not specifically involve a process of biological excitation, that is, if the same phenomena were also to be shown by nonliving substances. On several occasions, I have alluded to control experiments on inorganic substances, which are summarized below:

1. Sources of error due to inadequate insulation.

Poorly insulated leads or electrodes may produce oscillographic deflections not originating in the skin sites being measured. For example, if the researcher or another individual collides with a subject connected to the apparatus, an immediate negative deflection is recorded. The degree of deflection varies with the person causing the movement. This source of error is easily spotted, since the previous potential level quickly reappears, and no such deflection shows up in the reruns. The condenser in the circuit was connected in such a way that any such source of error would produce a negative, rather than a positive deflection.

Poorly insulated electrodes invariably gave negative deflections, thus indicating a current loss. The electrode leads had to be firmly fixed; mechanical movement of the wires would show up in irregular bursts on the oscillograph once the circuit was closed.

Unless a Faraday case is used, the house current must be turned off or the apparatus is affected. The potentials are still measurable, but the tracing is not as sharp.

2. Could the phenomena reported here be artifacts of purely local effects around the electrodes?

For the *direct* leads, unpolarized electrodes of 0.1 N KCl solution were used.

The KCl electrodes were supplied by Doctors Hoffman and Lowenbach of the mental hospital at Dikemark. For the direct leads, a small rubber washer was attached to the skin, without pressure, and covered with a small watch glass, through which we fused a platinum wire coated with silver chloride. This served as the unpolarized electrode. When used properly, the electrodes gave readings of within half a millivolt of each. We introduced the KCl solution through a small

aperture in the water glass, taking care, of course, to avoid the presence of air bubbles.

The electrodes used for measuring the hand potentials were insulated with rubber and glass and shielded with a metal casing. Rubbing the electrode against the bottom of a glass container or heating the KCl solution produced no deflection on the tracing. Likewise, touching the KCl electrodes to the leads at various points in the hookup produced no variations in charge.

For the indirect [ground] leads, we used pure silver electrodes. If we placed them in KCl solution and closed the circuit, a swift negative deflection of variable intensity resulted. However, no significant deflection appeared when we wrapped the ends of the electrodes in KCl-soaked wadding, placed them on two KCl-soaked cotton pads, and immersed them in the electrolyte container.

3. Could variations in electrolyte concentration be a source of error?

At first, we used only KCl electrodes. However, since these proved irritating to mucosal surfaces, we subsequently changed to a 0.9 N saline solution. To rule out errors due to variations in the type of strength of solutions used, we repeatedly ran the following control experiments:

a. Silver electrodes wrapped in cotton soaked in 0.1 N KCl cause virtually no deflections, though exceptionally one gets a deflection of about –5 mV.

b. Similar results are obtained if cotton soaked in 0.9 N saline is wrapped around the silver electrodes.

c. If a more concentrated solution is used, the zero line remains unchanged.

d. With a more concentrated sugar solution, deflections of up to 10 mV may be observed.

e. If we pour concentrated saline solution on cotton soaked in 0.1 N KCl, deflections of between –5 and –10 mV appear.

If instead of directly immersing the electrodes, we connect them to various solutions through a cotton wick soaked in 0.9 saline, we get the following results:

NaCl (0.9 N):	no deflection
Concentrated NaCl:	–5 to –8 mV deflections
Concentrated sugar solution:	deflections up to –10 mV
Concentrated sugar mixed with concentrated salt solution:	deflections up to –10 mV

The fact that variations in ionic concentration seem to play an insignificant role is probably due to the use of a two-megohm resistance in the circuit between the electrode and the amplifier tube. This allows virtually no flow of current and measures only the electric potential. Thus, the basic features of the sugar- salt experiment are not obscured by the effects of concentration, even if we disregard the unmistakable biological phenomena.

4. *Can the aforementioned effects of pressure, tickling, and stroking be reproduced in nonliving substances?*

If we connect two electrodes together by means of a towel soaked in KCl or saline solution, we get a negative deflection of about 20 to 40 mV on closing the circuit. However, no manipulation of the cloth with an *insulated* material can elicit any deflection. On the other hand, if a finger is rubbed on the cloth, the typical "wandering" effects, etc., are produced. Thus if someone were careful about the experimental results on living substances, but less careful with the controls, he might, for example, press the silver electrode into the cloth with his finger and jump to the conclusion that "even the towel is 'alive'." (Electrophoto 32)

Figure 32. Control experiment with wet towel: pressure, rubbing, tickling

Figure 33. Control experiment with flashlight

If we increase the distance between the two electrodes on the cloth, the resistance is likewise increased, and the results remain negative.

In rechecking the experimental results, one can always easily disprove the findings simply by being careless. Thanks to one such "contradictory" experiment, a new problem arose, one for which we have not yet found a solution. We attached a catatonic subject to the apparatus and placed the differentiated [grid] electrode on the back of his hand. We then tickled it near the electrode with a piece of dry cotton and obtained the familiar "tickle effect." As a control, the cloth on which the hand lay was moistened with KCl solution, and we then tickled the cloth itself with the cotton—and obtained the same pattern of deflection! The problem seemed insoluble. Only on the following day did it strike me that during the control run the indifferent electrode had still been connected to the subject's leg. Thus a circuit of leg-body-hand-wet towel had been operating. This invalidated the control experiment. Furthermore, there still remained the important question of why the "tickle phenomenon" appeared, as though somehow the ability of living tissue to show this effect had been transferred to the electrolyte-soaked cloth. Meanwhile, the deflection caused by this "living cloth" remains unexplained.

5. With one exception, we were unable to elicit any potential rise in nonliving substances tested under the same circumstances. We must add, however, that this is true only in accordance with the control experiments performed up to now.

If two closed electrical contacts are brought together, no deflection results; if they are placed in solution, the potential shows a steep and rapid drop.

Deflections can be produced by rubbing the electrodes on a metallic substance, but such results are negative in direction, not reproducible, and completely arrhythmic.

If the electrodes are rubbed on a flashlight, positive deflections result. However, one immediately recognizes that they lack the rhythmic quality of the "wandering" obtained with living substances (Electrophoto 33). The increase in potential are arrhythmic and have a mechanical, angular appearance. Since the surface of the flashlight is charged electrically from within, there is a certain similarity to what occurs in a living organism. However, the tracings produced are quite different in appearance.

These control experiments demonstrate that excitation phenomena cannot be produced in nonliving substance.

6. It may be noted that the direction of the EKG varies up and down from one place to the next.

The direction of the cardiac complex is independent of the phenomena of sexual excitation. The potential rise caused by tickling is always the same (upward), regardless of whether the EKG points up or down. Controls show that the cardiac complex is positive when the left hand is connected to the cathode and the right to the grid. If the connections are reversed, the EKG points in the opposite direction. We cannot explain these findings at present, but they appear to be related to the polarity of the systolic electrical impulses. Undoubtedly, the potential variations reflect at the skin surface what is generated in the heart. Self-observations shows us that *each heartbeat is accompanied by a pulse of sensation* which we localize in the general cardiac region. This sensation is nothing but the onset of a feeling whose *fully developed* form we perceive as anxiety or pleasure. The details are still obscure.

7. If we connect the leads to a radio amplifier instead of the oscillograph, the potential variations will be transformed into sound instead of light.

The steady low hum of the amplifier disappears completely if the two electrodes are connected by electrolyte-soaked cotton; this corresponds to a negative deflection of the light tracing. With indirect leads connected to two touching palmar surfaces, a rhythmic sound results if they are rhythmically stroked together. Gentle stroking increases the intensity of the tone, while pressure decreases it. This corresponds completely to the light tracing on the oscillograph.

4. The Autonomic Center

Experimental investigation of skin potentials in pleasure and anxiety has supported our hypothesis that the process of excitation give rise to two opposite directions of flow of bioelectrical current: toward the *periphery* and towards the *center*. The question of the nature of the current may now be clearly answered. The sensation of streaming is not solely contingent upon the blood flow in pleasure and anxiety, but also depends on the transmission of electrically charged particles by the blood and lymph streams. It has long been known that ionic currents exist in the blood. The skin now turns out to be the peripheral site at which the electrical charges are deposited or withdrawn—the autonomic periphery, so to speak. The existence of the direction "toward the world", on which we based our sex-economic theory of the instincts, is clearly confirmed.

However, the nature of the direction "away from the world, into the self" has remained less clear until now. Where is the bioelectric current concentrated during anxiety? This brings up the question of the autonomic center.

Where in the body are the sources and storage areas of bioelectrical energy to be found? Our first hypothesis was—*the autonomic nervous system (primarily the celiac, hypogastric, and pudendal plexuses)*. I will shortly offer clinical support for this assumption. *The autonomic nervous system represents the generator, that is, the source, of the electrical energy of the human body.* The experimental investigations reported in the first part of this paper thoroughly substantiate this assumption. Now let us test to what extent it is supported by clinical facts, and how it enables us to comprehend hitherto unexplainable phenomena in neurotic and emotional disorders.

To do this, we must free ourselves from a preconceived notion that conventional thinking in neurology and medicine tends to foster. The term "center" usually refers to the cerebrum and its associated relay stations through which the nerve impulses are conducted. It would be premature to discuss in detail the appropriateness of such a use of this term. In any case, it involves the mechanical concept of the cerebrum as the true control center and source of all impulses transmitted to the rest of the body. The cerebrum is seen as the ruler, so to speak, of all of man's actions. However, recent work in neuropathology (especially that of Goldstein) has sought to bring forth a completely new concept that would seem to deprive the cerebrum of its hitherto dominant function. The discovery of the autonomic functions has excited the interest of all branches of medicine. Moreover, the essential workings of this system and its relationship to the psyche are being eagerly explored.

My formulation of the function of the vagal [parasympathetic] and sympathetic systems, the basic antithesis of vegetative life functions, is in complete accord with this newer direction and opposes on many counts mechanistic cerebral physiology. A lengthy discussion would be premature here, but we must make clear that the expression "autonomic center" implies much more than merely the "center" of the autonomic nervous system: it really connotes the center of all biophysiological and character-affective functioning in general. According to this view, the cerebrum—conservatively speaking—is only a specially developed accelerating and braking apparatus for the *totality of autonomic bodily functions*. This view is supported by the undeniable fact that the living organism shows an instinctive purposefulness long before the cerebrum is developed. In particular, the emotional processes, such as pleasure, anxiety, and anger, which have so greatly concerned us here, are by no means dependent on the existence of the cerebrum. Autonomic functions are phylogenetically older than those of the cerebrum. Thus the expression "autonomic center" has a much deeper significance than might appear at first glance. We must assume that cerebral functioning is also dependent upon autonomic functioning in general.

If we place a grid electrode on the epigastrium, about halfway between the umbilicus and the xiphoid process, the skin potential usually registers about −20 to −40 mV. If a finger is pressed into the abdomen near the electrode, there is a steady drop in potential of about 10 to 20 mV. *The same thing happens when the subject bears down as if at stool or inhales deeply.* One may object that the fall in potential is due to finger pressure on the skin. But, since deep inspiration produces the same kind of potential drop, this objection is invalid. When the subject exhales, the skin potential slowly rises to its previous level. During respiration, patients who are chronically held in the diaphragm and unable to exhale fully show lower and less clearly defined potential deflections than subjects with complete respiratory motility. This symptom warrants careful consideration. During inspiration, the diaphragm descends, compressing the organs beneath it; the abdominal cavity diminishes in volume, while the chest expands. During expiration, the opposite occurs; the chest contracts, and the abdomen expands. A second phenomenon points in the same direction. On deep inspiration, all vegetative streaming sensations subside completely in the upper abdomen. Conversely, on deep expiration, sensations akin to pleasure or anxiety appear in the upper abdomen or lower chest.

A glance at the organs of the abdominal cavity will clarify these experimental results. We see that two important organs lying beneath the dome of the diaphragm are mechanically displaced by the diaphragmatic movement. These are the stomach and the underlying *solar plexus*, the largest plexus of the autonomic nervous system. We have observed empirically that pressure reduces the buildup of electrical charge. We must further assume that the skin is continually being charged by a steady bioelectric current arising from a "still undetermined center." With pressure or anxiety, the charge on the skin decreases. In a state of pleasure, the bioelectrical charge reaches out like an animal to contact the outside world; in a state of anxiety, it pulls back. Now let us try to picture what happens to the viscera surrounding the abdominal and pelvic nerve plexuses when a person is in a state of fright:

1. The breath is drawn in deeply, and the shoulders are pulled up.
2. The abdominal muscles contract tightly.
3. The pelvic floor quickly pulls up.

Thus the abdomen behaves in anxiety like a creature that has something to protect. The walls press more closely on its contents. It seems obvious that what is being protected is the highly sensitive ganglia apparatus of the abdomen and the pelvis. The drop in abdominal skin potential upon compression or contraction of the abdominal wall can only be explained by the fact that an increased pressure is exerted on the plexus, which inhibits its bioelectrical activity. We will substantiate this theory in a later presentation of clinical data. Briefly stated: *it is now possible to understand neurotic sexual stasis, on a physiological basis, as the expression of the impaired functioning of the autonomic ganglia.*

5. Some Final Theoretical Conclusions

1. *Sexual excitation is functionally identical to the electrical charging of the erogenous zones.* The excitation during anxiety is associated with diminution of charge on the surface of the body. The concept of "libido" as a measure of "psychic energy" no longer remains a metaphor, but refers to [measurable] electro-energetic phenomena. In this manner, the sexual function falls within the general category of natural electrical processes.

2. The skin and mucosal surfaces maintain a *"resting potential"* (RP) that varies within certain limits in the same individual and corresponds to a non-excited state of the organism. The resting potential reflects a regular, continuous bioelectric charge on the surface of the organism.

3. The autonomic ganglia ("vegetative center"), together with the body's membrane-electrolyte biosystem, functions as the source of the electrical surface charge. The erogenous zones are endowed with a greater intensity of feeling and a higher charging capacity than other skin areas. In addition to greater excitability, they show a higher resting potential in general and a correspondingly greater range of oscillation when excited. Intense excitation, subjectively felt as mounting excitement or streaming sensations, corresponds to a state of higher electrical potential. Similarly, decreased excitation reflects a fall in potential. Specific feelings of pleasure or pain can be clearly differentiated from simple sensations of touch or pressure which are not associated with pleasure or pain. This accords with our clinical observation that states of sexual excitement or anxiety stand out clearly from any other kind of feeling both quantitatively and qualitatively. They can also be clearly differentiated from any other process by experimental means.

4. In its simplest form, pleasurable excitation manifests itself as a sensation of itching or tickling. The potential of an erogenous zone varies with the presence or absence of itching or tickling sensations. In the end stages of character analysis, some patients, for the first time, experience what they call "streaming," "sweet feelings," or "thrills"; these can be correctly understood as the preorgastic excitation or preorgastic rise in potential. The rise in preorgastic excitation is quantitatively identical to the upsurge of pleasure felt by the subject and to the soaring potential registered by the erogenous zone involved.

5. Passive mechanical congestion of a sexual organ will not cause any increase in charge over the resting potential. On the other hand, if the turgor and hyperemia are associated with sex play and feelings of pleasure, a clearly visible potential rise appears above the RP level. In other words, mechanical tumescence must be accompanied by an electrical surface charge in order for a pleasurable, that is, a "sexual" feeling to result. The positive findings of this experiment support the assumption that the transition from mechanical congestion to electrical charge is a specifically sexual-biological process. The first part of the orgasm formula is confirmed.

6. Sexual friction is a biological function stemming from the *alternation of charge and discharge.* The discharging is always connected with pleasure; the charging, then, is always pleasurable if it is followed by discharge.

7. When excited, an emotionally healthy subject, who is capable of orgastic and preorgastic sensations, can accurately describe the oscillographic tracing purely on the basis of his subjective feelings. *The intensity of the pleasure feeling corresponds to the quantity of electrical surface charge, and vice versa.*

8. The success of these experiments is of great significance for the theory of the body-mind relationship. For we have confirmed the existence of an orgastic and preorgastic potential and shown that the accompanying sensations exactly mirror the objectively measurable process of electrical excitation. We have in this manner demonstrated the functional identity and antithesis of the somatic process with the subjective pleasure-anxiety feelings. *The quantity of the surface potential and the intensity of the pleasurable or vegetative sensations are functionally identical.* There remains the deep question as to why nonerogenous sensations such as touch or pressure do not result in any potential rise.

9. Since only pleasurable vegetative sensations give rise to an increased surface charge, while pain, anxiety, annoyance, pressure, etc., cause it to fall, we must assume that pleasurable excitation is the *specific* process of all living organisms. Other biological processes show this also—for example, cell division, in which the cell shows an increase in surface charge coinciding with the biologically productive process of mitosis. Hence the sexual process would simply be the biologically productive energy process. Anxiety would be the antithetical basic biological tendency, which is akin to death but not identical to it.

10. If we assume that the orgasm is a fundamental manifestation of living matter, the orgasm formula of tension-charge-discharge-relaxation must represent *the general formula for all biological functions* and does not apply to nonliving processes. The heart, intestines, lungs, and bladder, as well as the single dividing cell, must, therefore, function according to this biological rhythm.

11. The economic regulation of sexual energy (that is, pleasure or electrical energy) and the sex-economic relationships between individuals now hold a new and deeper significance for the understanding of organ pathology and disease which must be interpreted as disturbances of the autonomic equilibrium.

As we weigh this series of crucial and far-reaching conclusions, we must guard against the danger of playing theoretical games and letting them take the place of sound clinical fact-finding and basic experimental work. The reverse danger is of equal consequence—that is, failure to back up the empirical findings with correct hypotheses and the revision of deep-seated but meaningless preconceptions. ■

Wilhelm Reich in Denmark (1933-1939)

by Ellen Siersted*
English translation by Karina Nilsson**

A man who didn't know Wilhelm Reich personally but who had read his books, said to me, "Write *the book* about Reich... he was a genius!" What is a genius? Reich himself said that he wasn't a genius but only a healthy human being.

He was a rare human being, the kind I wish all persons could be. He was warm and alive, interested in what was going on and easy to get into contact with. I don't mean to adore him—to put him on a pedestal. Reich surely would have asked that such a thing not be done, for he was against authoritarian attitudes. Naturally this didn't prevent us, who were going into treatment with Reich, from seeing him as an authority in his field. If we seemed hesitant of what Reich said, as often was the case, and we expressed our doubts or criticisms, he didn't become angry or get in a bad mood but he brought up our problem to talk it through with us and if we were right, he yielded to us. Reich was a very open and honest person, whom one immediately came to like.

How could Reich arouse such annoyance that he was chased out of both Germany and Denmark, as well as Sweden? And why should many of those who worked with him become "closed out" (among others, myself included), not only from family but also from many friends? This happened because the core of Reich's teachings involves the human body and the life in it; the physical and the mental as unity; sexuality and the feelings associated with it. What's *alive*. In this context people often are heard to remark how the healthy human doesn't even notice his own body.

Now, thirty-three years afterwards (1), I want to write something about the period when Wilhelm Reich lived in Denmark, as well as those years in Norway where I continued my contact with him. This narrative is written not only because of Reich's importance for persons who came to know Reich and his theories, but also because Reich, just during these years, became exposed to serious events which came to mean a lot to himself.

I will not go into Reich's scientific or political work or in any way defend him. Instead I want to give a picture of him so we will better understand what Reich was like when he came to Denmark. If I become subjective while writing about a person we like, this may then be read as a tribute to him.

---

1. This article was first published in Copenhagen in 1972.

* Ellen Siersted first met Wilhelm Reich in Germany in 1929. She was both a patient and student of Reich's character-analytic work, and helped him publish the *Journal for Political Psychology and Sex-Economy*.
** Permission to reprint First English Edition from the Reich Archive West, PO Box 60653, Palo Alto, CA 94306 USA. Copyright © 1977 by the Reich Archive West. First Danish Edition Copyright © 1972 by Ellen Siersted.

To understand why Reich's teachings—and thereby Reich himself— aroused so much annoyance we must consider the general attitudes to sexuality in Denmark and in most other countries, during the 1930s. Despite the many similarities to our world today, it looked quite different then.

Let us examine the purely middle-class, "bourgeois" milieu which, then as today, marked most of human society. The fixed pattern for most of the people was an engagement with the ring, which lasted until the man could support a family; after that, the marriage, which preferably would last a lifetime. Divorce was a scandal and so was having a child out of wedlock. The latter affected not only the mother but to the same degree, even the child. No one spoke about sexuality and many young women were married without even knowing how their bodies were built below the waist. One naturally didn't know anything about children, where they came from and so forth, except for the tales which friends repeated: It was said that the stork came with a little child if you just placed a little piece of sugar in the window!

Today, some forty years after the time of which I write, I see that it still is difficult to get truthful sex-education for children. Nevertheless, then as today, it was the youth who understood Wilhelm Reich and his work.

Denmark fortunately escaped the First World War (1914-1918). We heard about its starvation and its diseases, and the deaths in the mud-filled trenches. But we didn't have to look at it (nor did we have television to show us). Russia with its revolution was very far away and so was Germany. Here in Denmark there was much unemployment—but things seemed to be getting better so that we might again be able to live as well as we had before 1914. Quite surely, we knew that to the south of us, in Germany, a ridiculous man was going around places and yelling out and making the Germans extremely militaristic, but we felt that Germany was too weakened after the World War to be a danger to any other country.

These were mainly the views of the wide base of middle-class people in Denmark. I feel a little bit ashamed to think that most of us had lost our "scent" of history and we really didn't realize where we all were headed.

A small group of young persons perceived Europe's danger as early as the 1920s. You found these people within circles of academics and the arts as they had contact with Germany through their travels and their studies there. Most of them were communists and socialists without a party, and they gave out political-information pamphlets and held talks for workers, college students, and high-school people so as to open our eyes.

By the year 1930, refugees from Germany began coming to Denmark; most of these were the young, who had been working politically (this is to say, they were communists, etc.).

They spoke about persecutions, work-camps, Jews who had to wear arm-bands with a star to tell who they were... These things sounded unbelievable to the average Danish person. Only a short time later we heard about torture and gas chambers; we could not believe that anyone could get people to treat others in such a way... But we helped the refugees — "immigrants" they came to be called because this didn't sound so bad — with food, shelter, and the hope that it might not last too long before they could return home to Germany.

At that time we had in Denmark no trained psychoanalysts. The International Psychoanalytical Society (I.P.V.), whose chairman was Sigmund Freud, demanded that the psychoanalytic practitioner go through analysis with a person who had been acknowledged by the Society, before taking any patients in therapy. Among our young liberals was a group of persons who were especially interested in having a trained psychoanalyst come to Denmark. This group included a medical student (Tage Philipson), a student of political science (Jorgen Neergaard), and a doctoral candidate in political science (Erik Carstens), as well as myself. In 1933, this "Socialist Medicine Group" (Socialistisk Medicinergruppe) invited Dr. Wilhelm Reich up to Denmark to lecture. He was known as a famous therapist and teacher, with many years of work as a sex-political investigator behind him. He lectured at the Rockefeller Institute and aroused strong enthusiasm, and the group decided to ask I.P.V. if he could come to Denmark as a training analyst.

Tage Philipson wanted to take up psychiatry as a specialty after completing his medical studies, and he had worked with Dr. J.H. Leunbach in his sex-educational consultations. Jorgen Neergaard joined the group especially because of Reich's political views; and Erik Carstens (who formerly ran a free school in Switzerland) had worked with Jung and Piaget, and was interested in psychology and education. I was a journalist who had read with interest Freud's lectures and his dissertation about sexual theory, and as I wanted to know more about psychoanalysis, I joined the group.

I met Wilhelm Reich at a psychoanalytic meeting in Dresden, Germany, in 1929. He seemed to be a very serious person. He also was very disappointed, having returned from a trip in the Soviet Union, where he didn't find the personal freedom that he had expected.

Neergaard, Philipson, Carstens and I wrote to the International Psychoanalytical Society and requested having Wilhelm Reich come to Denmark as a training analyst. However, we got the reply that although Reich was a famous therapist, he was not suitable as a training analyst in Denmark. Instead, the I.P.V. sent Dr. J. Harnik up to us.

Dr. Harnik was a skilled and very empathetic analyst. Some of the younger students began their treatments with him and I, also, wanted to start. One day as Dr. Harnik and I sat in the sunshine on a river-bank in Copenhagen's "Krinsen," I asked him if he would take me in psychoanalytic treatment. He said no, "But if Wilhelm Reich comes, you go to him. He is very skilled but watch out—he works with dynamite in your private little 'kitchen'."

Harnik was a Jewish Hungarian whose wife and children still lived in Germany. Shortly after his arrival in Denmark he became ill: His anxiety for events in Germany and the fate of his family there became too much for him to endure.

In May 1933, Wilhelm Reich arrived in Denmark. He came shortly after the Nazi's assumed power in Germany. Reich, who on several occasions had been sought by Hitler's Gestapo, fled to Denmark. As with hundreds of other refugees in Denmark, Reich obtained a *permission to stay* (*Opholdstilladelse*) for a six-month duration, but with no permission to work here.

Jorgen Neergaard, Ellen Siersted, and Dr. Georg Gero.

Background: Reich in Vienna and Berlin

Wilhelm Reich was born on March 24, 1897, in the German-Ukraine part of the former Austro-Hungarian Empire. He was the son of a well-to-do farmer who owned about one thousand acres of land (Reich's grandfather had been a farmer also). Reich's parents were Jews but he wasn't given any Jewish religious upbringing and he never belonged to any religious belief-system. He read the Old and the New Testaments of the Bible purely out of scientific interest in the history of religion.

Reich's language was German. He received a private education and he lived at home on the farm where he eagerly took part in the husbandry including breeding and looking after the animals. He also was fortunate to have a private tutor who supported his interests in the life of plants and insects. In 1943, Reich wrote that as far back as he could remember he was familiar with natural living functions including sexuality. This surely was of importance for his wide biological understanding and for his biophysical innovations within medicine and biology, as well as for his own development.

From 1907 until 1915 Reich attended senior high school and in 1915 (his last year in high school) he was awarded the highest degrees. His main subjects were German, Latin, and natural science.

In 1914 his father died, leaving young Reich to manage the family's farm during the time of his final studies at the senior high school. In 1915, during the First World war, the farm was destroyed.

From 1916 until the end of World War I, Wilhelm Reich served as a Lieutenant in the Imperial Austrian Army and he participated in several battles at the Italian front.

After World War I, Reich studied (from 1918 to 1922) at the Medical Faculty in the University of Vienna. Students who were war veterans obtained the privilege to complete their studies in four years instead of six. In 1922, Reich became a candidate for Doctor of Medicine, having earned the highest academic degree.

During his medical studies Reich provided for his expenses by teaching introductory-course subjects to the younger medical students in Vienna.

In 1919, during his second year at the University, Reich organized a seminar in sexology for medical students, to make up for a deficiency in their medical education. Some twenty years later, a similar group of young Danish medical students was asking the same of Dr. J.H. Leunbach so that they might receive education in sex-information which they could not obtain at their university.

Reich went into analysis with Dr. Paul Federn for a short time, and thereafter became a member of the Vienna Psychoanalytical Society under the leadership of Professor Sigmund Freud. Reich studied psychiatry with Professor Wagner-Juaregg and biology with Professor Kammerer. For some time he also practiced at a clinic for speech disorders.

When Professor Sigmund Freud founded his Psychoanalytic Clinic, in Vienna in 1922, Reich was appointed Clinical Assistant and in 1928 he became the Assistant Director of the institution. He was also a Leader of the "Psychoanalytic Seminar" and a teacher at the "Psychoanalytic Training Institute" in Vienna, from 1924 to 1930. He instructed in clinical psychology and bio-psychiatric theory. Among his students at that time were several Americans who were to become Professors of Psychiatry and leaders of psychiatric clinics in the U.S.

Reich also taught psychoanalysis and character analysis.

From 1924, while working at Freud's Psychoanalytic Polyclinic in Vienna, Reich began his investigation into the social etiology of the neuroses. He also opened mental hygiene counseling clinics in the working districts, first in Vienna and later in Berlin, Germany. During this period he became an active communist, participating fully in the practical tasks demanded of intellectual Marxists in the 1920s such as sex-education and counseling, political lectures, and study seminars. By this work Reich came into contact with a totally different level of society than did most psychoanalysts at that time. He quickly realized how sexual deprivation and neurotic difficulty were great and widespread social problems which could not be resolved by individual therapy. Reich emphasized how the neuroses in the working masses made persons unable to fight and irrational in their struggle. Young workers gathered at his side and when he came to Berlin, Reich was a *primus motor* for the founding of the "German National Association for Proletarian Sexual Politics" (*Deutsche Reichsverband fuer Proletarische Sexualpolitik*), the western German Sexpol organization with almost twenty thousand members. Reich's 1931 "party platform" included the following demands:

1. Better housing conditions: Elimination of the housing shortage and high rents, as well as high taxes imposed upon the poor.
2. Abolition of all statutes against abortion, birth control, and homosexuality. Reform of the marriage laws.
3. Free distribution of contraceptive devices.
4. Social reform such as protection for mothers with children, and the utilization of radio, press, and the cinema for mass sex-education programs.
5. Sex-counseling and child-care facilities in all factories and locations of a certain size.
6. Abolition of all statutes forbidding sex-education.
7. Home visits for prisoners.

Leaders of the German Communist Party (K.P.D.) did not like Reich's ability to establish contact with the youth; they feared he would turn the young people's interests away from the purely economic views about socialism. When Reich tried to show how Marxist theory needs a psychological foundation, he was excluded from the Communist Party.

During this very productive period of his psychoanalytical and socio-political work, Reich wrote and published *The Sexual Struggle of Youth* (*Der Sexuelle Kampf der Jugend*), and *Sexual Maturity, Abstinence, and Marital Morality* (*Geschlechtsreife, Enthaltsomkeit, Ehemoral*), which are those of his books which came to be read first by people in Denmark. Shortly thereafter followed *The Function of the Orgasm* (*Die Funktion des Orgasmus*), *Character Analysis* (*Charakteranalyse*), and *The Mass Psychology of Fascism* (*Massenpsychologie des Fascismus*). These originally were written in German, with later translations into other languages including Danish and French.

Psychoanalysis was a young science which, despite strong "bourgeois" reactions and hard criticisms from physicians and psychiatrists, was beginning to make a good foothold in its practice of therapy. The core of psychoanalytic theory was (and is) Freud's clear definition about the child's sexual development, the libido theory, and the connection between repression of a child's sexuality and the subsequent occurrence and development of neuroses. Freud knew that the onset of the neuroses were connected not only to the repressed sexuality of the child, but also to the "fixation" of different developmental trends (i.e., the oral or the anal) which he always disclosed during therapy.

The mapping of the child's sexual development was a revolutionary development which aroused enormous anger in many circles: It was as if psychoanalysis was to soil the child's pure mind. Freud meant that the genital phase first came with puberty and that its foremost purpose was for propagation, and that it could be disciplined and sublimated. The demand for the purity of the female often cost her physical and mental health.

Psychoanalysis at that time employed a free association and the interpretation of patients' dreams to find which factors in childhood might have aroused anxiety for sexual feelings on the part of the child. During such psychoanalysis a patient might reach or remember the anxieties or anger he or she felt as a child.

Reich worked along these lines for several years but after becoming dissatisfied with the results, he began to work not so much with *what* the patient was saying, as *how*. The *manner* became an expression of the patient's character. If, for example, a man told how angry he was while at the same time wearing a calm and friendly smile, Reich became aware of the way in which that person was talking about his feelings. The calm and friendly smile was a protection against the repressed affections. Commonly, such a facade worked in both directions: It partially blocked the patient from feeling completely what he was experiencing, but it also hindered his awareness of the provocations which he was forced to endure from the world around him. In other words, the character works as an armor which both protects and inhibits the individual.

We have all seen persons who are stiff-headed, spiteful; who refuse to bend or take advice; and those who are anxious, as well as those who do not dare to admit their meanings; or those who always are polite and courteous. Naturally, everyone has his or her own character, whether they are neurotic or healthy. The difference is that a healthy person's character can adjust to circumstances when necessary. The neurotic character-armor is felt by the patient as something stiff — he feels himself as a boring person who in reality could have been someone totally different, but he cannot or does not dare to try. The work with the character-armor led consequently to the work with the muscle tension—the somatic aspect of the armor.

It was the above technique which Reich used in his therapy when he started to work with patients in Denmark. This technique led to a change in the relationship between the patient and the therapist. Reich didn't say anything behind the patient's back—he wished that the patient should have an unauthoritarian and human relationship with him. This certainly contributed to the fact that we who went for treatment with Reich, began to see him as a friend, as a person with whom one could have contact, and could trust.

Reich in Copenhagen

When Wilhelm Reich came to Denmark he moved first to Weber's Hotel on the *Vesterbrogade*, a principal thoroughfare in the center of Copenhagen. As he began to be visited by many individuals wanting to talk to him about coming for treatment or for education, and as his visitors increased in numbers, he was asked by the hotel management to find other lodging. The Danish writer, Jo Jacobsen, whom Reich had met while in Vienna, put her own small apartment (on St. Kjellsgade in the Osterbro district of Copenhagen) at his disposition.

Among the immigrants to Denmark came Reich's friend and student, the Hungarian physician George Gero, as well as some of the young communist workers from Reich's study-group in Berlin. They too, now visited him and together with our little Danish group we became of sufficient number to form a "study-group."

Hundreds of immigrants came drifting, unnoticed, into our Danish society but were continually observed by the police. However when Reich arrived, it seemed as if the Devil had come into a gathering of angels. "There came a man who undertook the easiest work of all: Sexuality." Furthermore, he was not spoken of as a real physician but as a charlatan; a demagogue who seduced the young to live in sin. And he wanted to provide training in psychoanalysis—an obscure science which we heard about from a group of Danish "analysts" who said that chimneys and table-legs were penis symbols, and who interpreted dreams about houses with balconies as being female symbols.

Just one day after Reich's arrival, Dr. Naesgaard (one of the "wild analysts") sent a young girl to Reich and asked that he diagnose her. Because Reich didn't have a Danish work-permit he refused to accept her for treatment. However, he wanted by means of several interviews to create a picture, so as to find whether her situation was suitable for later psychoanalytic treatment. As Reich refused to treat her, the girl attempted suicide. She was taken to Copenhagen Community Hospital's Ward Six (psychiatry), from which she was discharged two days later. But the psychiatrist in charge of Ward Six was in an uproar and denounced Reich to the Danish Police for having practiced medicine without legal permission. Reich was ordered to a hearing before the Police, who decided to let the matter of his work-permit and his *permission to stay* in Denmark be passed on to the Health Board for advisement.

Had we any earlier doubts, we now understood very clearly which way the wind was blowing, because the Health Board's medical consultants happened to be the psychiatrists George Schroeder, M.D., and Carl Clemmeson, M.D., both of Community Hospital's Ward Six! We who hoped to keep Reich in Denmark sent a petition to the Ministry of Justice, asking that Reich be granted permission to remain here and work.

In Norway was a group of psychiatrists and psychologists including Dr. Ola Raknes, Dr. Nic Waal (then married: Nic Hoel), Professor Harald Schjelderup, and the writer Sigurd Hoel. They had been in Berlin, Germany, and among various activities there, were under training with Dr. Karen Horney and Dr. Otto Fenichel. They participated in Dr. Fenichel's

> " Reich was a brilliant speaker. He had nothing to do with demagogy...He stood on the floor of the hall, closely facing his listeners... he spoke with them warmly and seriously about what was in his mind... and matters of concern to them. "

seminars on child analysis; later Dr. Fenichel fled up to Norway and kept working with them there.

When the Norwegian group heard about the difficulties with Reich in Denmark, Sigurd Hoel came to Copenhagen. He was an acknowledged writer and we hoped he could help us. Hoel, the painter Anton Hansen, and I went up to Justice Minister Zahle's office to discuss the matter. We were informed that the Justice Minister wanted to think the matter over. We knew this meant that he wanted to send Reich's application further along to the Health Board for advisement.

I went up to Professor Wimmer, who was the head of the psychiatrists in Denmark, and asked him to support us and thereby psychoanalysis. But Professor Wimmer said with a smile, "Freud is passé!" The year was 1933. The fact that psychoanalytic institutes had been established not only in Berlin and Vienna, but in London, Paris and New York, didn't seem to interest anyone, or persons seemed to know nothing about the matter.

Besides the students who were coming with Reich from Berlin, was our group of Danes who, despite the objections of the authorities, were visiting Reich in St. Kjeldsgate to enter into treatment or for training with him. To that address went Dr. Tage Philipson, who wanted to become a psychiatrist; the student statesman, Jorgen Neergaard, who wanted to be a sociologist; and also Dr. J. H. Leunbach.

Why I went for training by Reich, to this day I cannot explain other than to mention that it seemed to me that he was right in what he was saying and in what he was fighting for. Whatever I went into, I don't know, but I never have regretted committing myself totally into Reich's circle.

Whether we were to go into treatment or into training, we initially had to undertake a screening analysis so that Reich could determine whether it was of any use at all for one to go into analysis. At that time each of us made such a trial analysis, free of cost and lasting as a rule from two to three weeks. It was a way to provide a diagnosis. When my trial analysis was completed, Reich said that he thought I should practice child analysis and that the preparation should take two to three years. When I said that I couldn't afford his long and costly treatment, Reich answered that I could pay him back when I had the money.

Some of Reich's students from Berlin followed him up to Copenhagen, among others Dr. George Gero, a Hungarian physician and psychoanalyst; a young Polish scientist named Moteschitzsky; Walter Kolbenhoff, and several others. We gradually became a little group which created a work-seminar where we discussed Reich's theories. Most of the meetings took place at Jorgen Neergaard's pension "Home" on Gammel Kongevej in Copenhagen. Naturally, we who were working with Reich were afraid that his *permission to stay* of six months duration would not be extended. To further our program we invited the public to a meeting at Borop's High School (near the Palace in downtown Copenhagen). The meeting was led by Dr. Sven Hoffmeyer, not because he supported Reich's theories, but as a professional colleague; he felt that a scientist ought not to be prevented from obtaining a *permission to stay* in Denmark.

The large auditorium in Borops High School was packed, especially with young persons sitting not only on the seats but also in the windows and in the doorways. Reich was a brilliant speaker. He had nothing to do with demagogy; Reich didn't speak to the young to seduce them, but to shed some light on their problems and to explain to them about society's attitude about these problems. Reich didn't "hold forth"—he was not oratorical. He didn't stand up on the platform with a decanter of water, a drinking-glass, and a manuscript to read. He stood on the main floor of the hall, closely facing his listeners, and he spoke with them warmly and seriously about what was in his mind, what he was fighting for, and matters of concern to them.

Reich was not a tall man but he was agile and thin, with dark hair and strands of gray over his large, dark eyes. He seemed to be an extremely alive human being, who was easy to get in contact with.

Naturally we were anxious to find what the Danish press might write about our meeting, and what kind of influence this might have on the application for Reich's *permission to stay*. We knew that the Justice Ministry wanted to "pass the buck" to the Health Board, and that the final outcome rested there. On that Board were sitting Reich's adversaries, the psychiatrists George Schroeder, M.D. and Carl Clemmesen, M.D.

The Copenhagen newspapers wrote the following articles:

"GERMAN PSYCHOANALYST HAS BEEN PRACTICING HERE
and took payment for his consultations.

He therefore is denied *permission to a stay* when he brings our local 'analysts' into an uproar.

The Danish Psychoanalytic Society during the last few days by announcements in the newspapers, has invited the public to a meeting tomorrow evening at Borop High School with speakers such as Headmaster Erik Carstens, student mag. [editor, *Studentenbladet*, Copenhagen] Jorden Neergaard, and the Austrian psychoanalyst Wilhelm Reich, M.D.

Behind this 'appeal to the public' is a matter which for a long time has concerned minds in psychoanalytic circles in this town, and which we now want to lay open to a larger audience.

A school of psychoanalysts.

We have interviewed student mag. Jorgen Neergaard, who says:

Up to now, our local psychoanalysts have been working dispersed and only temporarily, without being able to take their position on the basis of a really authorized training program. Also, it has been very difficult to defend ourselves against persons who, with only a superficial knowledge about Freud's ideas, establish themselves as psychoanalysts. The Danish Psychoanalytical Society, which was established some months ago, has taken up the whole question in collaboration with the International Psychoanalytical Society.

It is our intention to establish authorized training for our local psychoanalysts. In accordance with the International Psychoanalytic Society's regulations. Such training takes three years and is terminated by a thorough examination by which we are assumed that the prospective psychoanalyst himself is mentally and sexually healthy. Obviously, if an individual suffers from mental inhibitions, he will not be able to achieve results with others. Therefore, such potential inhibitions must first be removed.

Dr. Reich denied *permission to stay* in Denmark.
Is the plan to establish a school for psychoanalysis here?

Yes, it is a plan which has concerned us for a long time— only we lacked the person who could lead such a school. Now, however, we have him: It is the famous Austrian psychoanalyst Wilhelm Reich, M.D., one of Freud's earlier co-workers. Dr. Reich has for the past few years been working in Germany but for some months he has been in this country and he is not unwilling to take up such work. He is an internationally known scientist, and it will be of great importance if we can keep him for Denmark. But you know, all over the world there is an intense struggle between those who believe in psychoanalysis and others believing in generally-accepted 'psychiatry;' this struggle seems to be breaking out like a bright fire, also here in Denmark.

In any case, during his stay here Dr. Reich has been an object for various troubles caused by a small circle of doctors who are opponents to his theories. It is said that he has taken patients without having a work-permit here, and for this reason a complaint has been sent to the Department of Health which quite likely will result in some kind of police case. The truth is that Dr. Reich has been overrun by patients but he hasn't taken anyone for treatment. Only on one special occasion did he, under pressure, engage in making a diagnosis and for that work someone pressed a payment to him. Quite obviously, the meaning is to make Dr. Reich suspicious in the eyes of the government, so that it will become difficult for him to stay here.

This plan has had unexpected success, as the Justice Minister some time ago and without giving reasons, refused to prolong his permission to stay, which expires within the next few days.

We see this as no less than a scandal; that a famous scientist is treated this way—and we are going to protest strongly against this. At the meeting tomorrow evening, all details of this matter will be explained and a protest resolution to the Ministry will probably be proposed.
What kind of doctors 'persecute' Reich?

Yes, I could mention a couple of names. To be mentioned in first order is the nerve-specialist, George E. Schroeder, M.D., Chief physician at Community Hospital's Ward Six, and C. Clemmesen, M.D., who is a reserve doctor at the same ward. We have invited them both to the meeting so they will have an opportunity to defend their behavior. It should be mentioned that we also have some physicians on our side. However, we also note that the meeting tomorrow will be led by the physician, Svend Hoffmeyer, of Slangerup."

Dr. Schroeder doesn't wish to comment.
Extrabladet addressed itself this morning to George A. Schroeder, M.D., and asked him for a comment on the matter. Dr. Schroeder answered briefly and easily: "*I wish not to comment on the matter and I am not going to participate in* the meeting tomorrow. *I see no reason why I, in front of the public, should deal with this matter.*

— Dr. Rank"

"AN OPEN LETTER
To Chief Physician Schroeder, M.D.
We have received the following contribution:

In the [above] interview with 'Extrabladet' today, you refused comment in public on your accusations of your famous foreign colleague, Wilhelm Reich, M.D. Is it that your behavior can't bear being tested before the public court? Or do you mean that it doesn't matter to the public, which weapons are being used in the scientific struggle in this country? Or how our foreign guests are being treated? If the answer in any case is a denial, why your silence?

In the following same interview, you refused to be present at the meeting at Borops High School on Friday evening, although this meeting would give you the possibility to debate openly your standpoint in the matter, 'Psychiatry versus psychoanalysis.' Are you staying away in order to escape eventual defeat? In the opposite case, on what basis?

I may speak only as a layman, but I mean that the public has to know about the conditions at issue. The question, whether the Danish inhabitants are closed out from a qualified psychoanalytic therapy by a single man's position of authority, is in no way unimportant. Furthermore, it will be of the greatest interest for the public to hear what psychiatry has to object about regarding this therapy, and whether the psychoanalytic side can meet these objections.
Kasterup, October 26, 1933.
Highest regards,
Martin Ellehauge, Ph.D.

As far as we know, the Chief Physician Doctor Schroeder, in a position as the Medical Director's Consultant, must in this kind of question necessarily take the position that his duty forbids him all newspaper polemic and meeting-debate concerning the decision-making.

— The Editors"

"FROM FASIONABILITY
TO MARTYRDOM
The psychoanalytic protest meeting
yesterday evening:

A *permission to stay* that was not extended.
Some forty years ago, the famous Vienna nerve specialist, Sigmund Freud, proposed a theory which in short states that different nervous afflictions are caused by traumatic experience which has no outlet but which has become repressed to the unconscious where it is now laying and is hurting the mind and the soul. Later Freud changed his theory by saying that these repressed complexes—which very often are several impressions and experiences—always have their origin in the sexual life. If it now succeeds, with the help of the 'mental analysis' to get these repressions welling up from the unconscious to consciousness, their affect is disarmed and the unhealthy person is on his way to recovery.

It would be a mistake to say that Freud's theory hasn't aroused attention: It has been both glorified and condemned and it has had its followers and its opponents, and it gradually became so watered down that it calmly and obsoletely drifted into the background.

But after World War I, Freud's psychoanalysis got a Renaissance. It was put forward as a special science, probably impelled by the same 'repressed complex' which in the church calls out for a reintroduction of the confessional. Probably compelled by the same drives, the young people have attached themselves to psychoanalysis to such a degree that many of its special expressions have become a part of their ordinary language.

Psychoanalysis at the moment is a fashion here, but yesterday evening it flared up even more: To a martyrdom.

The denied *permission to stay*.

The Danish Psychoanalytical Society invited the public to a meeting, to take place in the Borops High School meeting room, which became filled up. The Society holds the amiable objective to prevent cheaters and dilettantes who have no real psychoanalytic training, from taking persons under psychoanalytic treatment. The Society is very strict: One of our most hardworking practicing psychoanalysts, a PhD, who is very skilled in speaking and writing, we have nevertheless taken a stand against.

In order to get the necessary authorized training, leaders of the Society wanted to establish a school under the exiled Austrian sex-researcher and psychoanalyst, Wilhelm Reich, M.D. A hindrance has appeared however, as the government has refused to prolong Dr. Reich's *permission to stay*, giving the reason that he, by taking a patient into treatment, has violated the law of the country. This refusal changed the character of the meeting to a protest meeting and psychoanalysis to martyrdom.

Attempt to oppose free science.

Dr. Sven Hoffmeyer of the Slangerup Borough (Copenhagen) opened the meeting by saying that he did not take on the task to lead the meeting because he shared Reich's views (Dr. Reich started in this country by holding a strongly-colored communist lecture) but because he was against attempts to kill psychoanalysis by back-stabbing and thus oppose free science. He wanted, as does his colleague Dr. Moltved who writes in *The Danish Medical Journal (Ugeskrift for Laeger)*, to protest the use of a minor mistake to deport Reich. In these times, when so many intellectuals are being chased away from their workplaces, we in Denmark ought to grab the opportunity to gain from their knowledge.

The Chairman of the Society, psychoanalyst and political science PhD candidate Erik Carstens, gave a brief overview about the training given to psychoanalysts in other places, where they begin with a thorough analysis of the student under training. While it is not required that the psychoanalyst be a physician, Carstens considers it valuable that the psychoanalyst collaborate with a medical doctor to make sure that the patient is not suffering from any organic illness. It didn't make sense to him that the Society's carefully prepared petition about the *permission to stay* to keep Dr. Reich in this country, had been denied. To one of the Society's members, the Health Board's Consultant, Chief Physician Schroeder of Ward Six justified it by saying, 'why have new methods? The old ones are good.'

"The big politician burns books; the little one runs to the police.

After student mag. Jorgen Neergaard had discussed the radical importance of psychoanalysis for all of the sciences, it was Dr. Reich's turn and he was greeted with loud applause.

'I have had to promise not to talk politics,' he said, 'but it is difficult because science isn't floating freely in the room but is standing with both of its legs in society. It is a fact that books are burned and scientists have been fired—this is big politics. The little politician runs to the police.'

Dr. Reich went on say that science is two things: It can have a restrictive influence (this is the high, academic science) and it can be alien (as is psychoanalysis and sex-research). This is why the subjective motive for the denied *permission to stay* was unimportant to him; he perceived it as a symptom of the spirit of the times that some persons go in the front and lead forward while others lag behind and hold back.

Thereupon the speaker carefully took all his listeners by the hand, so to speak, and as a guide might lead through a museum, brought them into the work of psychoanalysis, pointing out its main wonders. A nerve-specialist is satisfied to put off the patient coming to him with anxiety feelings and a bad heart-beat, by a simple comment that this reflects some kind of neurosis. But the psychoanalyst will give his attention to the patient's sex-life and thereby find the reason for the neurosis in the sexual dysfunction.

Dr. Reich ended his lecture with the information that the psychoanalysts would not let themselves be hampered in their work, thus verifying what he in earlier situations had anticipated. Now he wanted to travel to Malmo (Sweden) and his students had to sail over to be with him. If Sweden wanted to expel him also, he would hire a ship and put himself in it, out in the channel between Denmark and Sweden.

Protest accepted.

After a brief discussion everyone voted in agreement to a resolution expressing protest of the Danish State's denial of a *permission to stay* to a scientist whom we have need for in this country, and especially protesting that this is denied to Dr. Reich in spite of the fact that his students, who are Danish men and women, have asked that he be given it."

"THE PATIENT WHOM DR. REICH 'TREATED' Why the psychoanalysts are angry at Chief Dr. Schroeder.

Dr. Reich came to this town as a tourist last May and has since then been getting money from Paris each month for his living. He seems, however, to have a clear notion as to why the Health Board has notified him, and he has written a tract describing his actual situation. This was handed out at the end of the meeting.

This situation concerns a young girl whom Dr. Naesgaard had sent to him, so he could make an analytic diagnosis. She suffered from serious depressions and several times had tried to commit suicide. After a short discussion with the girl, for which Dr. Reich did not get any payment, he told her that he could not treat her until his status was in order in this country. During the weeks that followed she telephoned him repeatedly and plagued him with questions about when he might take her into treatment. He then decided 'to diagnose her but to not treat her.' Since the end of June she came three times per week but treatment still was not begun—that would come when the question about the work-permit was settled. Three weeks later, in July, Reich stopped seeing her. Two days afterwards the sick girl made another suicide attempt and was admitted into Ward Six, from which she was discharged two days later. She telephoned immediately and said that her psychiatrist was very agitated: He had questioned her harshly and blamed the suicide attempt on the psychoanalytic treatment which they contended she had been exposed to.

Dr. Reich, however, explained that the doctors at the hospital had no basis for making such an accusation because first, they had to know that the patient had earlier attempted suicide; and second, at the most it could have been the interruption and not the meetings themselves that gave her reason to make a new attempt to take her life; third, the kind of patients we are discussing here (Diagnosis: Hysteric character with a strong schizophrenic element or onlayer) are known in mental hospitals in all countries, to be liable to attempt suicide before admission, during their stay, and after they are discharged.

It is thus Dr. Reich's hair-fine differentiation between opinion and diagnosis to which the Health Board has not wanted to yield. Unfortunately for him, the Health Board's Consultant, Dr. Schroeder, just happens to be the Chief physician on the ward where the young girl came in.

Within a few days Reich goes to Malmo, but then he has done so much for psychoanalysis in this country that it has gotten its martyrdom."

"THE PSYCHOANALYSTS ARE PREPARING FOR A FIGHT.
Your physician, Dr. Reich from Vienna, is denied *permission to stay*

The newly-formed 'Danish Psychoanalytical Society' called a meeting yesterday evening at Borops High School, and the large auditorium was filled to its last seat. The immediate reason for the meeting was the authorities' refusal to comply with a petition from the Society about a *permission to stay* for the Austrian psychoanalyst, Wilhelm Reich, M.D., who, as we have hoped, might offer training in psychoanalytic technique in Denmark so that practicing psychoanalysts may obtain international authorization. The Chairman of the psychoanalysts, PhD. candidate (polit.) Erik Carstens, clarified the aims of the Society and the leader of the meeting, Dr. Sven Hoffmeyer, stressed that the reason he led the gathering was to establish that the negative attitude which some of the contemporary nerve specialists took against Reich was not shared by all of the nation's physicians.

The next speaker was student mag. Jorgen Neergaard, Editor of the student newspaper, *Studenterbladet* (Copenhagen), who wants to see training in psychoanalysis at the University of Copenhagen.

Thereafter, Dr. Reich held a long talk in which he tried to show the great importance which psychoanalytic science plays for social hygiene, pedagogy, medical science, and culture as a whole.

After the meeting ended, members of the Society by a vote of all except two, decided to accept a resolution protesting the hindrance of a foreign scientist, a scientist for whom people have a strong need, by the refusal to permit him to practice in Denmark and especially the denial of Dr. Reich's wish for a *permission to stay* in this country.

— Ypsilon"

"October 28, 1933
PSYCHO-ANALYSIS

The authorities have had the splendid idea to refuse the German doctor Wilhelm Reich another *permission to stay* in Denmark after he performed psychoanalytic quackery on a young girl who later was admitted to the Sixth Ward. Thus the law about a foreigner's stay is being used to prevent 'quackery'.

This notification from the authorities has of course, generated a protest meeting. Protests are made every day. In this situation the protest comes from a society which calls itself the 'Danish Psychoanalytical Society.'

People will say that we refused science and research shelter in this country and that we chase the scientist away and prevent him from spreading knowledge and teachings to the thirsty youth.

But what has happened is the following: The authorities have successfully been able to use a paragraph in the aliens' law to prevent one of the German so-called sex-researchers from further confusing young men and women and getting students into this perverse pseudo-science about PLANKEVAERKS ("graffiti" -Ed.) — weird paintings and evil dreams.

Once upon a time there might have been a thought behind psychoanalysis, but as this soul-theory has developed, it has become a kind of scientific quackery which has nothing to do with science or with true psychology. When we become acquainted with the psychoanalytic literature, we find in reality that it is nothing but ancient locked-up books in new covers for the gentlemen. We 'came away from Venus' in fur and all that. Now we have sexual phenomena in 'scientific' dressings.

This could be a very good opportunity to use the statutes about the aliens' sojourn. But isn't it reasonable to consider whether this opportunity could be used to broaden the framework for the law against quackery? It is here we ought to do something."

"UGESKRIFT FOR LAEGER
(DANISH MEDICAL JOURNAL) 95th year.
Wilhelm Reich, M.D., denied
permission to stay in Denmark.

Psychoanalysis, which is one of medical science's newest branches, is under rapid expansion all over the world. In this respect Denmark lags far behind. At this moment there exists the possibility that psychoanalysis in this country can be brought onto the right track, as the Austrian scientist, Wilhelm Reich, M.D., who is one of the leading men in psychoanalysis, presently is here training Danish psychoanalysts. Now, however, the situation has become such that Dr.

Reich is refused extension of his *permission to stay*, brought about by a colleague who strangely enough has found it justifiable to use the foreign doctor's difficult situation in Denmark as a means to fight psychoanalysis. This strange way of dealing with scientific questions which, without a doubt, are of great importance for the development of psychotherapy, I wish to protest.

— George Moltved"

"PSYCHOANALYSIS OUTSIDE THE THREE-MILE LIMIT.
Dr. Wilhelm Reich, who no longer is permitted to remain in Denmark, spoke in Borops High School yesterday evening.

The newly-organized Psychoanalytical Society held its first meeting yesterday evening. It took place at Borops High School, where the auditorium was overcrowded when the engineer Erick Carstens gave the introductory speech. After the introduction which of course was polemic in nature, applied against the forces that have managed to banish the German psychoanalyst, Dr. Wilhelm Reich, from our country (A topic we mentioned in an interview yesterday with student mag. Jorden Neergaard, whose brief talk reprimanded the University's lack of interest for psychoanalysis — a subject which neither medical students nor philosophy students have the opportunity to learn the least about at the University of Copenhagen).

The dangerous Dr. Reich.
With that it became Reich's turn to speak. Without demeaning the introduction, it must be said that he was the more interesting speaker. A phenomenon, we dare to call him; a phenomenon and quite a magician. Immediately as you see him, it seems as if he could be a tailor's apprentice from the dark end of Copenhagen's 'Pilestraede.' Not overly dignified. But in the same second as he is let loose, not at the speaker's chair but as if moving around like a cat on agile paws, the metamorphosis happens: He becomes purely and simply a splendid orator. If we were living in the middle ages, we easily could understand that this man would be chased away from the country, for he doesn't have only the word in his power but he has his listeners 'nailed' to their seats, spellbound by the sparkling personality radiating out from his small black eyes. In a way, it must be said that he is a 'dangerous' man, who with both hands plucks the fruits from the 'tree of knowledge'. Some of the fruits were so 'green' when he served them, that several young girls had to be helped out of the auditorium in a hurry.

Mephistopheles with a warm heart.
What, then, did this dangerous man say? He showed by examples, totally disconnected but nevertheless pointing to a central idea of what psychoanalysis is about. He coquetted brilliantly against the 'barbarism' towards science which has made a Danish medical colleague 'run to the police' with the result that he now cannot get a *permission to stay* or a work-permit in Denmark. He picked the human being apart and put him together again in a new and surprising way; he juggled with the position of science in society and he balanced elegantly on the border of the forbidden land, the 'political matter' which he had promised neither to touch upon during his lecture, nor to participate in any other way.

A rain of well-turned sarcasms fell upon the doctor who reported him and didn't want to meet for a discussion with him, and he delivered heavy blows at the enemies of international science whom he identified as enemies of life.

Lastly, he touched upon the connections between psychoanalysis, sex-research, education, religion—and politics. He was like a Mephistopheles who with agile fingers was playing with all of the facets of the human spirit, but also a Mephistopheles with a warm heart and a streak of melancholy. He ended however, by declaring that now he was going to Malmo (Sweden) to find asylum, and if they should banish him there, he would hire a ship and continue his psychoanalytic teaching out beyond the three-mile nautical limit, a plan which has been spoken about seriously amongst his supporters.

After Reich ended his lecture, which brought him a thundering acclamation, a comical interlude happened when one person told about the 'bicycle thieveries,' declaring that he hadn't understood 'what the foreign gentleman said.' He took the psychoanalysis lecture to be something dealing with 'bicycle analysis'! Following this, we moved to a more matter-of-fact question-period.

The physicians and Dr. Reich.
The leader of the evening meeting was Dr. Hoffmeyer, who introduced himself by saying that he, in more than one respect, stood outside the circle of the psychoanalysts but that he had offered to serve as leader because he found it humiliating that we don't have room for a man like Reich, a foreigner, a homeless scientist who was trying to spread knowledge to the field of pure science.

Also by other means the physicians are letting their sympathies be known. In yesterday's Danish Medical Journal (*Ugeskrift for Laeger*), Dr. George Moltved has contributed a letter in which he firmly protests 'how one colleague has used the foreign doctor's difficult position in Denmark' to push Reich aside, even though his work may be of the greatest importance for the development of psychotherapy.

Resolution against deportation.
The evening ended with the gathering's acceptance of a resolution passed with all votes except two, protesting the Danish State's denial of a *permission to stay* to a 'foreign scientist whose work is of great use' and especially because Dr. Reich is denied such permission even though his students have appealed so that he may remain here. The resolution got several hundred names, with that of Professor Jorgen Jorgenson being the first."

Of those persons who decided Reich's fate, and with that the fate of scientific psychoanalysis in Denmark, none took the trouble to understand what psychoanalysis was about and who Reich is.

Before coming to Denmark, Reich and his writings were excluded from the German communist party and in an issue of The Daily Worker (*Arbejderbladet,* Copenhagen) dated December 1, 1933, his book, *The Mass Psychology of Fascism (Massenpsychologie des Fascismus)* was slashed to pieces. They called the book a back-stab at the Party's existing politics, "with a cowardliness that seems to be the author's most prominent characteristic...he tries in the book to obscure the real target of his attack on revolutionary politics." *Arbejderbladet* reproached Reich, saying that he, by stressing capitalistic society's repression of sexuality, mixed psychology into the political struggle.

Cowardice is the last thing of which Reich could be accused. He kept an openness which moved him from one controversy to another, and which forced him to flee from country to country, fighting for his ideas and his convictions.

While we were waiting for the reply from the Danish Minister of Justice, we continued our training-analysis under Reich. We worked in the technical seminar and in the pedagogical study-circle which we started in Copenhagen. This was composed for the most part of kindergarten teachers and young parents, who talked about the experiences and the problems they were having with the children. We took turns reading case-histories and their treatment, from issues of *The Journal for Psychoanalytic Pedagogy (Zeitschrift fuer Psychoanalytische Paedagogik,* Vienna). We read and discussed Bronislaw Malinowski's *Matriarchal Family and the Oedipus Complex (Mutterrechtliche Families und Oedipus-Komplex),* published by the "Internationale Psychoanalystische Verlag" in Vienna, and we read his *Sexual Life of the Savages.*

On October 3, 1933, the reply came from the Danish Minister of Justice, Mr. Zahle:

"MINISTRY OF JUSTICE, Letter No. 19294
Copenhagen, October 3, 1933.
Journal 3, K. 1933, Nr. 34-37

In an application sent here ,the Society inquired about work-and permission to stay for the Austrian citizen, Wilhelm Reich, M.D.
You are informed that no action will be taken in the matter which must remain in accordance with the decision made by the Minister of Justice on April 3, 1933, according to which said application cannot be approved.
—Zahle / Jacobi, Fm."

Reich moved to Malmo, on the southern tip of Sweden, and during the Winter of 1933-34 we began making trips by ferry across the channel for our training or treatment. Also, the technical seminar was being conducted in Malmo so we gathered there for it too. I don't remember just where these took place; only that it was not in a very good location and in the center of the city—we were close enough to be able to catch the last ferry home at night.

When the ferries with the analysands (the persons being analyzed) traveling to Malmo in the course of the day for treatment, passed our boat bringing us home from training, we used to wave to one another if we didn't feel too bad.

Treatment is often difficult to go through, at least when we are dealing with character-analysis. We have many ways to cover up our aggressions, anxiety, and depression. The posture, the expression of the face, one's voice. Everything covers up the real person in the form of a "muscle-armor." Mental excess was another point, which Reich always attacked.

As a therapist gradually succeeds in "loosening-up" only a few of the right muscles, the patient begins to feel life streaming through him and when experiencing this for the first time, it usually arouses anxiety. When Reich found that patients, by holding the breath, could stop these flowing feelings which he termed "vegetative currents", he included breathing exercises to facilitate his treatment. The patient relaxed and began to breathe out deeply and allowed the exhalation to pass the whole way through the body. This was experienced all over and especially in the genitals as a nice and living current which was not always of a sexual nature but a sensation of life and carnality.

The real goal in all of Reich's treatments was that the patient should reach a full orgasm, to a healthy sexual life, and therewith to achieve his full work potential. In contemporary society and with the rearing most persons have been exposed to, it is questionable whether there are any who can reach so far.

The goal of a therapist isn't just to pick the patient apart, but equally important is that the therapist support the positive aspects within the patient, in other words to understand how living and warm the patient can be after everything that inhibits life within him is removed, and to show this to the patient again and again.

When you participate in analysis, whether it is psychoanalysis or "vegetotherapy", you quite naturally get a definitive attitude toward the therapist, called an "uebertragung" (transference). In the beginning of the treatment the transference is positive but later it can become so negative that the patient himself becomes afraid of his own feelings.

Among his colleagues in the International Psychoanalytical Society (I.P.V.), Reich was known as a prominent therapist due to his ability, among other things, to make the patient aware of his negative attitudes. Also, the patient comes to the therapist with wishes and demands, without being aware of these, that the therapist become as a father or mother to him. If the patient becomes deeply disappointed in the demands which the therapist, quite naturally, cannot fulfill, he often breaks the treatment. Therefore, there were patients who left Reich, but there were always many new ones entering into treatment by him.

The words "character analysis" and "vegetotherapy" quickly became popular and were fashionable to characterize something which had nothing at all to do with Reich's technique. It could, in the hands of ignorant individuals, become a dangerous tool and under the best of circumstances, useless.

In addition to my personal analysis, my work in the technical seminar and my participation in the pedagogical study-circle, Reich required, because child analysis would be my specialty, that I should work for six months in a kindergarten and take part in Dr. Leunbach's sex-consultations and sex-guidance in the evenings when Leunbach provided these free services. Thereby, I and others came into contact with patients coming from a working-class milieu.

On March 30, 1934, Reich wrote the following to the Danish High Minister of Justice:

"Honorable Sir Minister of Justice:

On December 4, 1933, I left Denmark, after an application concerning extension of my 'permission to stay' had been refused in November, 1933. When I couldn't interrupt the work with several Danish scientists that I had taken on without hurting the people and the situation, I decided to take a stay in Malmo. My colleagues visited me regularly and spared no effort or travel-cost in order to be able to continue the work. On June 5, 1934, according to the law, I may return to Denmark as a tourist. However, some important physiological experiments have become necessary and Danish scientists have declared themselves ready to prepare and carry out these experiments. Both the forced necessity of this work and the trouble other colleagues have been exposed to due to my stay in Malmo lead me, Honorable Minister or Justice, to apply to you about the possibility that I, approximately four weeks before the stipulated calendar quarter, thus at the end of April or in the beginning of May, may return.

Respectfully yours,
Wilhelm Reich."

I don't know whether Reich got any answer to this letter but in any case, he returned to Denmark, to Sletten (at Humlebaeck, along the seashore to the north of Copenhagen).

In those years there used to be a series of small fishing villages almost in a continuous row, along the shore from the town of Helsingborg to Rungsted, Denmark. Here and there the Copenhagen people built themselves summer homes. At that time I had a little farmhouse in Humlebaeck, and when some of our group spent their vacations with me, Reich asked me to rent a house for him nearby. I located a beautiful wood-beam style home at the water's edge. There Reich lived during the summer of 1934 under the name, "Peter Stein." He wanted to be alone as much as possible since he, on one hand was expecting a visit from his family in Berlin, and on the other was preparing to take his position in the struggle which awaited him with his colleagues in the I.P.V. at the International Congress coming up that August in Lucerne, Switzerland.

Reich's lady-friend, Elsa Lindenberg, who had been a dancer in the Berlin State Opera, came up here to be with him. She was beautiful and politically a very brave young woman as she had been a co-worker in the Communist Party in Berlin and was active in the same "cell" with Reich.

Slettin, Denmark; summer 1934. Wilhelm Reich and his daughter, Lore.

Reich's two children, Eva and Lore, came visiting as well as did Elsa's mother and Elsa's little sister. From Oslo came Sigurd Hoel and Harald Schjelderup, who both were in treatment with Reich.

It was a summer full of work and play with the children. At times we gathered for seminars at Reich's house and on other occasions we had pleasant gatherings in my home.

Although Reich's situation, mildly speaking, was unstable (he had only a short-term "residence permit" and no place to emigrate to; he had no work permit; and he knew that his colleagues in Germany, including his former wife, Dr. Annie Pink Reich who also was a psychoanalyst, were working against him), I never heard him complain about his fate. We always had good contact with him. He was open and interested in what you were doing, how things were going and how your children were. The only time I saw Reich angry or indignant was when he met with dishonesty or cunning.

Slettin, Denmark; summer of 1934. Wilhelm Reich with daughters Eva and Lore.

Janne Woldbye, Wilhelm Reich, Eva Reich, Elsa Lindenberg, and Lore Reich.
To the extreme left is Dr. Fenichel. Slettin, Denmark; summer of 1934.

It is said that Reich was very hot-tempered. I experienced this only one time: It was when we were driving in his car from Copenhagen to Humlebaeck on a dark, rainy summer evening. The oncoming cars were driving with their high-beam headlights and the pavement was slippery. Reich was angry about the other drivers' ruthlessness and lack of consideration. Suddenly he stopped the car and asked in his native tongue, "Ellen, how do you say 'pig-dog' in Danish?" "Svinshund," I answered. Reich jumped out of the car and went into the middle of the road, yelling "Svinshund" as the next car with strong lights passed. Of course, they didn't hear him, but he got some fresh air!

That summer remains in my memory as a bright and good time. I feel that the reason Reich was so relaxed and calm was that his children and Elsa were with him and he felt he was surrounded by a circle of friends who not only wanted to learn from him, but who liked him as well.

During his last years in Germany, Reich had been trying to convince his colleagues in the I.P.V. that the present structure of society was the cause of most of the neuroses; and while he did enormous educational work himself, both by lecturing and by writing, his colleagues became more and more nervous about his membership in their Society. They meant that Reich was dangerous for their existence.

For the I.P.V. meeting that August in Lucerne, Switzerland, Reich announced a lecture, *Psychic Contact and Vegetative Current (Psychischer Kantakt und vegetative Stroemant)*. The reader may understand by my very brief summary of Reich's analytic technique and his socio-political attitude, that there was a great distance between Reich and most of the other psychoanalysts in the International Psychoanalytical Society. Dr. Fenichel, who was a member of I.P.V. and Reich's friend, traveled down from Oslo to influence Reich so that he might go more gently, and to make Reich aware that the consequence of his attitudes could possibly be that Reich would become excluded from the Society.

Reich did not want to yield his point of view. Later it appeared that the German Psycho-analytical Society had decided to exclude Reich one year earlier, but Reich and the others did not know anything; we only knew that they wanted to force Reich, "voluntarily", to resign from his membership in the Society — it would look better, that way!

In Lucerne, Reich gave his lecture on *Psychic Contact and Vegetative Current*. The atmosphere was cold and only a few of the young

Lucerne, 1934. Dr. Sandor Rado

psychoanalysts were really interested, but everything was decided ahead of time by the leading members within the Society.

That meeting stands out for me like a nightmare. Because I hadn't completed my training, I didn't attend the international negotiations, but the intrigues and the many small groups discussing Reich and his work, had a strong effect on those of us who still believed that when we became fully trained psychoanalysts, we too, on the whole would be "clear" about our reactions and the reasons behind them, and therefore able to overcome any irrelevant reactions on our part.

The effect of such an exclusion depends, naturally, on what kind of Society one is being excluded from. In I.P.V. were Reich's colleagues through many years — people he had worked together with and with whom

Lucerne, 1934. Dr. Eitingon and Dr. Ernst Jones.

Lucern, 1934. Dr. Alexander.

he, for sixteen years, had struggled for the cause of psychoanalysis. How strongly the whole atmosphere affected others besides myself, I realized when I saw how one of Reich's very close students, George Gero, burst into tears when Dr. Annie Reich and Dr. Sandor Rado declared that he had to choose between Reich and the I.P.V. George Gero came with Reich from Berlin to Denmark, and at that time he chose Reich.

The Norwegian group, constituting a segment of I.P.V. was represented at the International Congress by Dr. Ola Raknes, Dr. Nic Waal, and Professor Harald Schjelderup. They rallied to support Reich but members of the Danish group were not permitted to join with the Norwegian.

Reich in Norway

Neither the Danish Minister of Justice nor the Swedish Foreign Ministry wanted to renew Reich's six-month permission to stay. Neither wanted to give any reason for their refusals. Reich and Elsa Lindenberg moved to Oslo, Norway, late in the year 1934. Here he lived until August 1, 1939. His *permission to stay* was renewed several times in Norway but he was denied a permanent visa.

In Oslo, Reich gave lectures at the University of Oslo and found the opportunity to begin his investigations in the field of biophysics.

Reich had many Norwegian students. Many foreign psychiatrists, physicians, and educators, among others persons from America and England, came to be trained by him, and now we Danes started to travel between Copenhagen and Oslo, partly to continue our training and partly to participate in the seminars which Reich was leading, where different case studies were discussed.

We went up to Oslo once a month, usually remaining a couple of days each time. This short stay may seem extravagant but we traveled by what was called at the time, "third class" on the train, or "deck space" if we were going by boat. A few times we went over via Frederkishaben (Denmark), which was the cheapest route. In Oslo there were always places to stay in the homes of colleagues and friends.

Every minute we were in Oslo was used for discussion and consultations. We visited the laboratory which was put at Reich's disposal. He talked about his biophysical work, about the discoveries he had made, and he showed us in the microscope proof of the life he had found. I didn't fully understand his biological discoveries but his enthusiasm was very contagious and when I, both during my own treatment and with some of my patients whom I commenced to treat, got verification of his teaching about the muscle-armor and

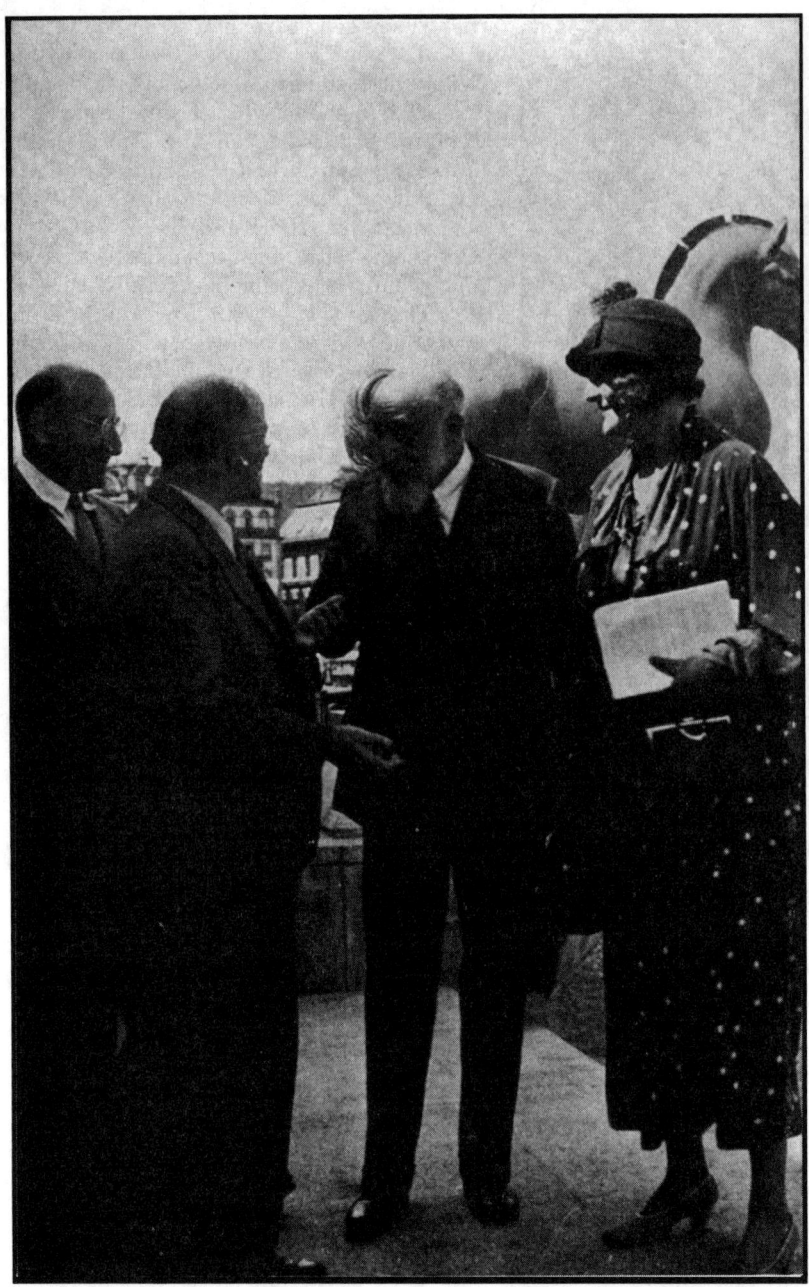

Lucern, 1934. Dr. Spitz, Dr. Eitingon, Prof. Federn, Princess Marie Bonaparte

is reflected in Reich's letters of that period.

Among the thirty-odd letters I received from Reich, it seems justifiable to quote a few which belong here so as to complete the picture of Reich as a public figure, in terms of world-wide interest in his work and his discoveries. His letters are very open and warm-hearted; if one asked him for advice he was always ready to help, but he didn't make persuasion nor did he try to impose his meanings on his readers.

Regarding the fight with Fenichel, he wrote:

"Dear Ellen:

Your letter made me happy, especially that your work is going well... The rest will come, and a little 'post-analysis' is not impossible.

...I am happy every time I hear about Gero and his work; he is a really fine child. They are tired of the fight up here—hope you will understand how dishonest Fenichel is towards me. If he had arranged for a meeting with me, if he openly had come with apprehensions, we probably would have been able to work together as we have been up to now. But he intrigues because he is afraid that the Norwegians will keep their promise about taking me into their Society. When he himself is aware of the danger, he doesn't have to agitate the others. Everyone was surprised. Both Gero and I made him aware of that. Now he's traveling around (in Germany) and making friends with the leading figures (in I.P.V.). I hate that kind of behavior. Well, I don't want to be bothered with him anymore. And you shouldn't either; only understand that this kind of thing happens.

Also, Ellen, try with a healthy attitude and a clear intellect, to put yourself in this fight... judge for yourself.

The best to you, yours,
Willy Reich"

the vegetative currents, I felt intuitively that Reich was on the right track in his biological work.

When some of us, very early in our training, began to have patients, they always were told that we had not yet completed our training and that their treatments were being controlled by Reich. Furthermore, each patient first underwent a regular psychiatric examination beforehand.

When Reich came to Oslo, several Norwegians who had been in training with Dr. Fenichel went over to Reich to learn his character-analytic technique. Instead of speaking out about this, Dr. Fenichel developed a very hostile feeling towards Reich. Earlier he had seen himself as Reich's friend, but after Reich's break with the I.P.V. (in which Fenichel remained a steady member), and with the intensified competition from the very vital Reich in Oslo, Fenichel decided to move to Prague, Czechoslovakia. But of course the struggle in Oslo also was introduced to us down here in Copenhagen, as

In November, 1935, Reich wrote:

"... I have much to do and big difficulties to overcome.

Why doesn't Gero ever write? Is it laziness or something else...? I believe it is advantageous to continue to be in contact with our work, because we constantly find very astounding new things. In the character-seminar we see clearly, that the person who has not gone through character-analysis, is quite incapable of understanding it. Our work is going well.

Write again soon, more and often. It makes me very happy to hear from you:

... Is the little house on the sea from last year perhaps still free? Can you find that out?"

Among the difficulties which Reich speaks of, are surely the rumors which his former colleagues in Germany (among others Dr. Fenichel and Dr. Annie Reich) spread, saying that he was mentally ill. And already in November of 1935 he was planning to once again spend the coming summer in Sletten, together with his children.

Because most of my colleagues were earlier in pure Freudian analysis before they started with Reich, I decided, in agreement with Reich, to travel to Berlin and go into analysis with Dr. Edith Jacobsen. She was a friend of Reich's and although she was interested in his techniques, she remained continuously a member of the I.P.V. Edith Jacobsen was a very sympathetic and warm person. I went to Berlin late in 1935 to begin treatment and I got one hour of analysis each day.

Berlin was gloomy. In the evening it was dark everywhere; there were no people except for the "SS" troops who were marching up and down in large numbers, obviously keeping an eye on things. For people in general, food was almost impossible to obtain. A standard dish was very fatty meat cooked with large chunks of cucumber. A vegetable-grocer in his cellar said to me, "Before this we had a good four-room apartment—now we have a little loft behind the store, and soon we will only have just four boards!"

One day, when I came to get my hour, Edith Jacobsen's housekeeper told me that I should meet Edith at a certain small restaurant. There Edith told me that the police were looking for her, and she asked if I could get her a sleeping-coach to Copenhagen that afternoon. All went well, and the very same evening we traveled to Copenhagen. I was so alarmed by the atmosphere in Berlin and by Edith's fate, that I couldn't sleep on the train but remained awake expecting the Germans to come and take Edith, but she, to my surprise, slept calmly the whole night.

Edith stayed with me in Copenhagen but was very worried about her brother, who was a physician also, and her elderly mother. They both were living in Berlin. After two weeks had passed, Edith wanted to return home. I tried to get her to wait a little longer. Dr. Fenichel, who had come from Prague, and Dr. Gero also, tried to get her to wait, but she wanted to set off for Berlin. She said that if I didn't hear from her within the next fourteen days, I ought to come back to Berlin again. When she didn't write I went down to Berlin and continued my hours with her. Without warning Edith was imprisoned. She was accused of giving money and clothing to help families whose provider was in prison or in a concentration camp.

It is natural that we wanted to help others who were closest to ourselves in their professions and their interests. I traveled back home immediately and went further on, to Oslo, to speak to Reich and the other colleagues. It was decided that I would return to Berlin and talk with a lawyer who was to free Edith from the prison. Again I returned to Berlin and talked to the lawyer who, obviously, offered hope and wanted to have lots of money. It was especially Reich and the Norwegian group who gathered money for the lawyer and paid for my travel back and forth to save Edith.

I traveled down to Berlin two times and met with the attorney in Berlin, but I came away with the impression that he wasn't especially interested in Edith's case. The last time I called, he had very little time because he was leaving for a hunting trip in the South of Germany.

During my analysis in Berlin, Edith put me up in a room at the home of a Jewish family which earlier had been well-off, but now was very poor. During my last visit to the attorney, I went to call on my former German hosts, but they also had been taken off.

We learned some years later that Edith had been released from the prison and had traveled via Switzerland to America.

Then began the work in Copenhagen again with the patients, the consultations, and the pedagogical study-circle, in addition to our travel to Oslo and the work there. On January 20, 1935, Reich wrote:

"Come to Oslo in February, but write in advance. Yesterday Philipson finally ordered the apparatus, (oscillometer-Ed.) 1300 Norwegian Crowns—1500 Danish 'Kroner' (Crowns)!!! It is the beginning! And within three years we will be able to state that Freud, long ago, had found how to measure the electrical power of sexuality! What do you think?

Tomorrow we begin the characterological seminar here. On Thursday the lectures begin for the students at the University!

Do you think we can protect the character-analytic method against being misused? It's already starting to become popular."

Reich planned to spend the summer of 1935 in Denmark in the same house he lived in at Sletten in 1934, and to have his children visit there. When the children weren't allowed to come, he decided to remain in Norway. He wrote to me that it was hard for him to be without the children, and that he was suffering because the rumor was spread within the Psychoanalytical Society in Germany that he was mentally ill. I believe that his great work capacity and his satisfaction in his work helped him to overcome the disappointment about his children and the former colleagues' behavior.

In Denmark we translated, collectively, Reich's articles in the *Journal for Political Psychology and Sexual Economy* (*Zeitschrift fuer Politische Psychologie und Sexualoekonomie*), issued by the Sexpol Publishing house in Copenhagen under various editorships: Sigurd Hoel, Dr. Ellehauge, and Ernst Parell (Wilhelm Reich). Naturally, we got many bad nicknames such as "Reichianare", "Reichwehr", etc., and the word "sexual economy" arouse many jokes by witty fellows.

When Gero and I came to Denmark together with Reich, I married him partly because I liked him and we had the same views about Reich, theories, and partly so he could get a *permission to stay* in Denmark. Many of the German emigrants who otherwise could only obtain the six-month obligatory permission to stay, married Danish women so as to be able to remain permanently in Denmark.

As of 1935, Gero clearly was beginning to sense the danger in following Reich's work, and there is no doubt that his earlier colleagues in I.P.V. were pulling on him, also, to leave Reich.

In a letter dated March 25, 1935, Reich wrote:

"Dear Ellen:
I have so much to do this week, that now is the first time I can answer your letter from the Third of March. I have the impression on the whole, that things are going well for you and this makes me happy. It is very sad that Gero has ceased to keep the situation between us open. His last letter was far from happy and it surprised all of us here. I hope the

situation doesn't develop so as to result in personal depression of any decisive importance. I have not demanded of anyone that he should confess himself to me, and I do not expect that of anyone. On the contrary, I hold the attitude that what comes not from the deepest conviction, is worth very little. I write this to you because it means much to me that I do not, on the basis of my objective work with people, become an enemy to persons with whom I have a very good personal relationship. I'm sorry if that condition cannot be maintained. I have finally realized how many problems with persons originate from their feeling of duty to support me, without in reality being able to or wanting to, and who therefore feel themselves suppressed by me and make affront towards me. I cannot do anything about the convinceability of sexual-economy and sexpol.

Write back soon, and have heartfelt greetings,
Your W. Reich"

In 1936 Dr. J.H. Leunbach and Dr. Tage Philipson were imprisoned, accused of performing abortions. Leunbach was sentenced to three months and Philipson was sentenced to two months in prison. When they came out, their right to practice (*jus practicandi*) was suspended five and three years, respectively.

When Leunbach left the Vestre Prison in Copenhagen, he was greeted by a group of young parents and other friends. Many had baby-carriages bearing the slogan, "I am a wanted child." We arranged a big party for him, together with many of the working women whom he had helped.

Shortly before Leunbach came out of prison, Jorgen Neergaard died in the hospital in Oslo. Since both men worked together closely with Reich and the others around Reich, I want to tell a little bit about them.

Jorgen Neergaard was born in 1910 and was the son of a military officer. As early as his high-school years, he was writing critical articles about literature for children and teenagers, for *Politiken*, a Copenhagen newspaper. He wrote about youth and its sexual problems; he criticized the museums which couldn't excite anyone because they smelled dusty and boresome. In 1932 he studied political science in Berlin and later became an undergraduate (student mag.) at the University of Copenhagen.

During his stay in Berlin, Jorgen Neergaard got a strong feeling for what Nazism was: "It is not enough to know how the Nazis behave," he wrote, "but one must also learn why they are like they are." And in a brilliant contribution to *Politiken* (published in the issue of July 19, 1932) he wrote: "Mr. Middleman is voting about the fate of Germany." He explained the premises for the state-election in Germany and he underlined that we in Denmark lacked perspective in dealing with political events. This lack of perspective meant that we in Denmark often saw Adolf Hitler as a farcical figure with a crowd of followers, because his whole performance seemed ridiculous to us.

Jorgen Neergaard was the Chairman of the Students' Society in Copenhagen and he was the Editor of the student newspaper, *Studenterbladet*. At an official meeting at "Weinold's Banquet Room" he was appointed by Dr. Martin Ellehauge and Svend Hoffmeyer, M.D., to a delegation representing the Students' Society in Copenhagen. In 1934 he, together with Mary Louise Begtrup (today Louise Roos) and the student of politics Erik Ib Schmidt (now Department Chief in the Danish Ministry of Education), traveled to Germany to get information about the trial against Ernst Thaelmann, and to obtain permission to visit a concentration camp.

The three young persons didn't get any further than to Warnemuende, at the German border. Their courage and enterprise, however, was ridiculed in the Danish newspapers. "B.T.," for example, wrote under the following headline:

"PJANK! (NONSENSE!)"

Denmark is a small country. We are only four million people. Statistically, we are only a drop in the milliard seas of the world, but thanks to a certain culture, a certain amount of common sense, it happens time after time that Denmark in the world framework comes to play a quite bigger role than would our population justify. All good Danes watch jealously over our influence on the world's problems—and when we know that this influence exists only due to our healthy common sense. We react strongly when "Sektorer" or womanly hysterics try to profit abroad on the Danish reputation— thereby undermining it. What is worse, we have in the latest years seen several examples of this—not lastly in the two big questions about India and the demilitarization—however, none of the ladies and gentlemen who run amuck in these discussions compare with the curious expedition which yesterday traveled to Germany but just as quickly was sent home from Warnemuende (at the German border). Three mentally-immature students who in all seriousness, went south in order to determine whether the trial against the Communist Thaelman was a pure criminal process or only a propaganda-farce. In a situation where passions are aroused to such heights, logical and non-emotional Denmark might perhaps soften a standpoint and perhaps save an offer because they are so unemotional. But if we, in the eyes of Germany, should give only the picture that members of the responsible academic circles in Denmark have not only lost their heads but are behaving as the lowest class of losers, then there can be no chance for the Danish voice of common sense to achieve the persuasion that could result from Danish tolerance."

Prior to the unsuccessful trip, Wilhelm Reich had come to Denmark and Jorgen Neergaard, quite naturally, joined Reich's circle.

Despite his serious disability — he had, since the age of eight or nine, a bone-marrow deficiency in both legs and he walked using two canes — Jorgen was very active, very extroverted, dedicated to people and current events. He surely was the one of our Danish group who was closest to Reich, and they no doubt meant very much to one another. When he was admitted to the hospital in Oslo, Reich visited him every day and he was with Jorgen when he died, on February 2, 1937. Arnulf Overland gave a very beautiful oration at Jorgen's funeral.

Jonathan Hoegh Leunbach was born in 1884. He was the son of a priest. He became a medical candidate in 1912 and served at various hospitals and went on study-travel to Berlin, and in Italy and Austria. He was a member of the Presidium of the World League for Sexual Reform.

Leunbach was very interested in social issues and he wrote articles on sexual reform in the Copenhagen newspaper, *Socialdemokraten*. He gave out a book about socialistic attitudes of life. A group of working women came to him and asked that he give lectures on sexual matters. He told them about birth control devices; about the diaphragm ("pessary") which women themselves could manage, and about its superiority over the condom (which at that time was the most well-known preventive means but also was the most expensive and the most unreliable device). Since the diaphragms needed to be fit so as to function preventively, the organization of the working women asked Leunbach to help and he founded the first sex clinic, on Linne Street in Copenhagen, in 1922. He provided free consultation two times a week, which offended many of his medical colleagues.

For many years Leunbach worked together with the Swedish sex educator, Elise Ottesen Jensen, who founded the Royal Swedish Society for Sexual Information (R.S.F.U.). During the summers she and Leunbach would drive into the great forests of northern Sweden where the men, working as loggers away from home for half of each year, would come back home and make children with their wives. Leunbach and Elise Ottesen Jensen traveled with their car filled with diaphragms: She gave the educational lectures and he taught the women how to apply the diaphragms for contraception.

Evidently, we cannot work in sex-education without abortion problems coming up, time after time. Leunbach was not the only physician in Denmark who performed abortions, but he said that he was the only one who didn't earn money for it. By his great interest in social problems, Leunbach quite naturally came into contact with Reich.

Leunbach (we always called him "Joyce") was a very fine and serene person. We were saddened by his death in 1955.

Reich was very interested in the abortion trial against Drs. Leunbach and Philipson. He wrote every week to the two "criminals" to ask how things were going. The court-case attracted a lot of attention. The National Socialist (Nazi) Party distributed leaflets and stressed that Leunbach was a communist and Philipson a Jew, plus a long list of all the crimes which had been committed by Jews in Denmark in the most recent years. The Nazi Party held a big meeting in Borops High School against the two "fetus-killers."

We and our circle of friends gathered signatures for the benefit of the "criminals", Leunbach and Philipson. The lists were filled with thousands of names of working women in Copenhagen. This occurred when Mr. Steincke was the Danish Minister of Justice.

Meetings were also held in Oslo regarding the Leunbach matter. Jorgen Neergaard, who was dying, stood up and participated in one of them. In a letter to me from Oslo he wrote how utterly weakened he felt, and how he wished to be in Copenhagen so he could explain to people about the background of Leunbach's work, and to combat the "garbage" which people get in the newspapers' treatment of the case. He sent me the manuscript of his little brochure, "Leunbach, did he get what he deserved?" and asked me to be sure to print as many copies as possible, preferably with pictures of Leunbach's "India countenance" (Leunbach's mother was from an East-Indian family). "It will go like lightning and thunder," he wrote, and he wanted to read the proofs himself. This, Neergaard wrote from Oslo on December 16, 1936. Jorgen Neergaard died on February 2, 1937, and Dr. Leunbach was

released from prison on April 11th of that year.

As early as February 15, 1935, Reich wrote that "within the character-analytic seminar it is clearly shown that a person who has not undergone character-analysis does not understand what it is about." The more he elaborated his technique, the more he alienated himself from the Freudian psychoanalysts and the more opponents he acquired within the I.P.V.

On the whole, Reich got many students in Oslo, both from Norway and from abroad. But there were some who became frightened and dropped out. Quite often they did this in a hostile manner, and despite the fact that they had been in training for several years with Reich and felt themselves to be tied with him in friendship, they became so hostile (because of their anxieties) that they did not even spare Reich from rumors, which they spread about him. When these became too much for him, Reich wrote on June 5, 1937:

"Dear Ellen:
I write this letter after a thorough discussion in the presence of professional colleagues, thus not only in my own name. It is to you and Philipson.
...I have never demanded or expected of you that you should break off your personal relationship with Gero. It would not occur to me to forbid you to talk with Gero as much as you want about our professional questions. I ask only... to tell as little as possible about our work, because one who is outside only can get a false picture by obtaining fragments of knowing, especially when he stands in association with an anxious, hostile, and insignificant middle-group...
My standpoint, as I presented it to my colleagues here yesterday and which they all supported, is the following: I have so far not undertaken to carry out repressions against the policy, which I.P.V. as an organization and its individual members are using against me and my work. What has happened does not worry me. You know that my opponents within I.P.V., and especially the Prague group, never have let it be an objective hostility, but also have gone deeply into my personal life to hold my children away from me and to spread the rumor all over that I am mentally ill. You yourself told me that you got this impression by Gero's talk at the Lucerne Congress with Rado and Annie Reich, and I understand much better now what you said to me then. While I have not been concerned about these matters so far, I must now take the standpoint that our work must be secured. I don't disturb anyone with my work, and I must not let myself be disturbed... Of course, I am ready to give all opportunities we may offer at my Institute, to any serious scientist who wants to learn about sexual economy and technique of the treatment of the neuroses, but if one gathers only fragments of knowledge about our work it can give a false picture. Under no circumstances can one force me to let persons take part in our work who do not belong to us, who don't want to learn our work, and moreover, who stand in asso-

ciation with a totally hostile group. It was therefore quite clearly expressed and decided yesterday that no person may work with us who is in contact with Fenichel. ...Our work is so difficult, so responsible, and so many-sided that we have to use all of our energies and all of our attention for our own sake. ...We are not an offshoot of psychoanalysis, not a variant, but a totally new scientific discipline. If Gero, as both Nic [Waal -Ed.] and I several times have come to agree, explicitly declares that he seriously wants to study sexual economy and the vegetotherapy developed out of character analysis, then we are at his disposal in the same way as we stand for any other person who wants the same.

....Warm greetings to you and Philipson,
Your Wilhelm Reich

P.S. As a private question: Write to me often please, if you fear that you personally also must break with Gero, if you follow through with your own decision about an objective demarcation. I assume thusly, that this was the basis for your letters.
In P.S. the main thing is written!!"

No doubt it hurt Reich, not only that Gero withdrew from him and his circle, but also that he did it in such a hostile manner. When Gero also alienated himself from me and criticized my work without objectivity, we separated.

Sigurd Hoel wrote from Oslo in a letter dated June 4, 1937:

"I have spoken with Reich and blamed him according to what you mentioned in the letter—that his anger preferably should be turned towards the place from where all the slander and the intrigues are originating. But he is not in a good mood nowadays—he just got the message that his daughter isn't coming up this year either—and he's presently contentious and belligerent. He has been disturbed by three lengthy, hostile, and also evil-minded articles by Dag Byrn in the newspaper, 'Arbejderbladet.' "

Reich invited a French scientist as a specialist in his biological work to come up to Oslo. He was Professor Roger du Teil, from the Natural Science Faculty at the University of Nice (France). Reich asked me to help du Teil, who was coming from Stettin (Germany) to Copenhagen; to bid him welcome on behalf of the group, and to arrange for the continuation of his voyage on the ship, "King Hakon," up to Oslo.

Professor du Teil obviously was a good choice and the news from Oslo was encouraging. Sigurd Hoel wrote, "Du Teil is fine!" Dr. Lottie Liebeck, a German psychoanalyst who fled to Norway and was working with Reich, wrote on August 4, 1937:

"Du Teil's visit influences everything nowadays. He is a marvelous man and we all like him. He is simple, natural, and very serious in his work. I don't think Willi could have found a better helper. It is a very positive time for Willi, the most positive time

since he left Germany. You know quite well how violently people have fought against him. Now he finally gets a verification that he is on the right track, when he himself in dark moments has doubted. — Every now and then we have parties, and this evening the French envoy is coming here and some local professional colleagues also — everything at the moment is influenced by du Teil."

The collaboration with du Teil became a big encouragement for Reich. Dr. Gunnar Leistiknow (Ph.D., polit.), who was interested in Reich's theories and often participated in the study-circles, wrote the following article in the March 3, 1938, issue of the Copenhagen newspaper, *Socialdemokraten*:

"SENSATIONAL SCIENTIFIC EXPERIMENTS

Can living creatures arise from inorganic material? Famous Austrian researcher stresses that they have found the proof. A theory which will mean a complete shakeup in biology — if it holds up.

A famous Austrian scientist, who, after being driven out from Germany, has been summoned to Norway by the University of Oslo, Dr. Wilhelm Reich, a few days ago sent out a work (*Die Bione*, Sexpol Verlag, Oslo) which will mean a complete revolution in biology and other natural sciences, if it reaches general acknowledgement.

Sensational experiments recorded on film.
Reich stressed that life here on Earth didn't arise once in the dawn of time, like one or another unexplainable monster, but that the transformation of inorganic material to organic life is a process which occurs daily, out in nature under certain definite mechanical pressure and electrical conditions. He stresses further that he has succeeded in showing the process experimentally in his laboratory and in recording it on file. The same is emphasized by the French biologist, Roger du Teil, Professor at the University of Nice, who has conducted control experiments in accordance with Reich's instructions and who, independent of him, arrived at the same results, results which have aroused lively interest at a lecture for the Academy d' Science (Paris) and which at this moment are being studied more closely at various French research institutions.

Before the Nazis' takeover of power, Dr. Reich was one of the best-known and inventive physicians and sex-researchers in Germany. As a trained psychoanalyst he was a student of Freud but he has been separated for many years from the psychoanalytic school. His research brought him, among other things, to a totally new view about sexuality, first and foremost as an electrical phenomenon. From this vantage point, Reich began his sensational experiments which he now reports.

To ground his views Reich, some years ago, began a microscopic study of amoebas and other single-celled creatures. Under high magnification, extremely strange changes were seen to occur gradually in plant fibers which were infused with the amoebas under investigation. They separated themselves into little 'vesicles' which tore themselves away from the plant matrix, gathering into small masses; within four hours they had taken such a form that they were impossible to distinguish from the amoebas! It is easy to make the assumption that all existing microscopic organisms originated from plant fibers in one or another uninvestigated manner.

The experiments were repeated with grass-straw and dried moss soaked in water. Here, also, the same thing happened. Now Reich tested with totally different kinds of preparations: A tulip leaf, a rose leaf, grass-straw, and plain earth. The results were amazing: After three days had passed, not the slightest thing had happened to the tulip or the rose leaf but from the grass-straw there had developed a mass of small creatures of different sizes and forms. What is most surprising is that the earth-crystals were on their way to separate into small 'vesicles' and small rods which moved freely between the crystals. 'I first thought I was wrong,' writes Reich, 'but additional, more carefully-performed experiments have excluded every doubt.'

It was easy to assume that organic spores of one kind or another had sneaked into the preparation, and that it was due to this that the swarming life had developed. For this reason Reich now changed by boiling his preparations from one-quarter to one-half an hour.

'This experiment got a completely unexpected result,' writes the German scientist. 'It appeared that the boiled preparation exhibited a much more rich and vigorous life than did the unboiled ones!'

Bions, as Reich calls these so-formed bacteria and amoeba-like creatures, or more correctly stated, preliminary stages or transient forms to living creatures, do not differ significantly from other single-celled animals. They are capable of moving, take nourishment to themselves, yes, even to reproduce themselves, and they can be grown in the same way as bacteria. As contrasted to the original material, it appeared that they also were electrically charged, according to Reich's assumption.

But isn't it likely that some spores from the air sneaked into the preparations after they were boiled? To test this possibility Reich made some experiments with dust particles from a vacuum cleaner but the amoeba and the bacteria seen were totally different in appearance and had characteristics which differed from those of the 'bions.'

To completely eliminate the 'spore-theory,' Reich undertook experiments with coke particles. How could spores come into the coke, which is distilled at thousands of degrees? But in the coke preparations also, the bions appeared.

Reich now started an experiment which ought to guarantee that every possible form of life or generative spore, which could be thought to exist beforehand, would have to be killed. Coke dust which was kept in a dry sterilizer continuously at a temperature of 180 degrees Centigrade, became incandescent in a benzine gas flame at 1500 degrees Centigrade until the cinders glowed red. This glowing-red coke was then mixed into a solution of autoclaved potassium chloride in a sterile solution of beef bouillon. 'To our astonishment,' Reich declares, 'something quite unexpected appeared.'

Immediately it was shown to be swarming with life as never before existed, neither in experiments using unsterilized materials nor with the boiled preparations. Photographic film recorded life which was possible to maintain through several generations of the so-formed bions. Experiments with incandescent soot and with ash from the central heating system boiled, led to similar results.

These and similar experiments, according to Reich, show the following: *Bions* are not created of spores which existed beforehand but are first developed when the incandescent mass comes into contact with the moist bouillon. We can hardly reject the notion that all recognized forms of spore species may have developed at the same time, at a time when Earth was in an incandescent condition. They may have been formed when the previously incandescent material came into contact with water.

Reich, who certainly is the first to apply the dialectical-materialistic research method which Marx and Engels shaped, to natural science, states that the research results which he now is explaining thoroughly in his book and can be replicated therefore by all biologists, will mean a complete revolution in biology and a whole lot of other sciences (also medicine) since we, from now on, no longer are able to keep up the commonly-held line between 'organic' and 'inorganic' but, according to Reich's notion, there exist lots of transition forms between 'life' and 'non-life'.

It will be exciting to see what science will say.

— Gunnar Leistiknow"

Despite Reich's occupation with his students, lectures, articles, and work in the laboratory, he was always ready to answer questions. When I wrote and asked him if he meant that I should take a sixteen-year old girl into treatment, he wrote in reply:

"You know that it is very difficult to give advice when the one concerned is not present. ...One ought not undertake any treatment during puberty, if there is no possibility for the outlet of the sexual energy that will be released; then it is better to wait until seventeen or eighteen years of age..."

In serious problems we didn't provide written sexual advice. If a couple was having difficulties we first talked with the spouse who had applied to us and after that to the partner, and if it seemed to us that they could improve then we asked them to come to us together for consultation. The reason for our caution was that the Copenhagen magazine, *Sex and Society (Sex og Samfund)*, which we at one time co-edited, was prosecuted for being pornographic. We first thought that it was the cover, which we ourselves didn't like, but it turned out to be the "mailbag" column which had irritated a man who thereupon wrote a letter to the Danish Minister of Justice (Steincke!) and mailed a copy of it to us. He wrote, "Honorable Minister of Justice: Someone is poisoning our young, our people, our country... etc., etc."

I was visited by two investigators from the detective corps, one older man and one younger (the younger was supposed to be a witness). It turned out that the older man who questioned me knew quite a lot about psychoanalysis, about Reich, and about the "Sexpol" movement. He realized that it wasn't pornography and he didn't think it would become a court case. He had underlined the questions which caused irritation: One about masturbation; a question from a transvestite; one about the enlargement of the penis, and another about beginners' difficulties. I could only answer that these were problems which meant a lot to many persons and that we who dealt with such problems couldn't see anything immoral in it. He gave me his telephone number, if we wanted to consult him, and said that as far as he could see, nothing was likely to happen to us.

Gunnar Leistikow (PhD., polit.), who worked at the newspaper, *Socialdemokraten*, discussed the matter with the editor and his colleagues, who were very sympathetic and advised him to speak with Justice Minister Steincke. Steincke was terribly insolent to Leistikow, saying among other things that he did not know anything about the matter and he hadn't seen the magazine but he would see to it that we got a court process on our necks; and if he lost our case he would get an opportunity to further strengthen the laws for punishment.

The above facts are extracted from my letter to Reich dated February 5, 1938. On February 7th, Reich replied:

"Dear Ellen:

I just received your letter which really has made me happy. It verified my feeling that in our work the people themselves are the worst servants of the police. Don't be worried. The more clearly and more openly you go in for the work, the easier you will have it. You can see how, up to now, not even a thing has happened to me.

We have no other tasks than to defend our work as physicians and educators.

Honestly, the title-picture appeared bad and pornographic to me also. We must be very careful. Regarding the 'mailbag' column, I will also advise that only typical, general questions should be taken up and not atypical and very individual questions. In such a movement as ours, perverse persons who are not serious or who are provocateurs, often are sliding in. First and foremost we have to help the ones who wish to develop their healthy sexual feelings. The sick cases belong in the sex-consultations. Among my fifty replies to questions published in "Sexualerrugung und Sexualbefriedigung", there is not a single one which can arouse apprehension. Remember, please, that the opposition every now and then have correct feelings, despite all the outrages in their way of thinking.

The majority of the people who deserve the greatest consideration, quite clearly want to know how to achieve a healthy love life, but do not want to be worried by the strange infantile fantasies of neurotics and perverts which only belong in the analysis-room.

I would not, for example, make public a question from a homosexual as whether he, during coitus 'a tergo,' should allow the sperm to remain in the anus or not, but would ask the man to come to the consultation. On the other hand, all questions dealing with prevention of pregnancy or premature ejaculation should be answered clearly and openly.

You will hear from us again, as soon as we know something. Du Teil's address is: Prof. du Teil, Centre Universitarre Mediterranean, Nice a. M., France.

I advise you strongly to hold du Teil outside of the social side of the matter. He doesn't want to have anything to do with it.

With my very warm regards,
Willi R."

Tyrifjord, Norway, 1939. Wilhelm Reich and Ola Raknes.

On July 4, 1938, he wrote that he and the colleagues in Oslo think that the latest issue of *Sex and Society* was terrible and that we shall take a stand against the magazine. We thereby withdrew from the collaboration with *Sex and Society*. The Norwegians protested against being listed as co-workers on the magazine. The protest was signed by Nic Hoel (Waal), Sigurd Hoel, Ola Raknes, Wilhelm Reich, Arnulf Overland, and August Lange.

In his first years in Oslo, Reich had a quite peaceful work-period but the slander and the intrigues gradually increased; psychiatrists and others of the same kind worked industriously to get Reich's *permission to stay* suspended. The weapons used against him were the same as the ones that had been used by the same category of persons in Denmark: They claimed that "Reich was not a doctor;" "he seduced children and youngsters;" "he was a quack;" etc., etc.

When, in 1938, Reich wrote the book, *Die Bione*, which was the result of one long year of laboratory work, the storm broke out against him. Reich wrote how he in his laboratory had observed lifeless masses' transformation into life—it aroused fury and fear within orthodox science and although Reich asked people to follow the development of his work in his laboratory, nobody came.

Nick Waal (earlier Nic Hoel), a wise and lucid physician, wrote to me in June, 1938:

"I have not followed the very culturization of the bions because I have too little time. But I myself have watched the experiments made by Reich and I have compared these with what appears under the microscope. You know that I have been serving for twelve months as a physician at the hospital (in Oslo) and as such have responsibility for both the laboratory and the microscopy—some swindle or charlatanism cannot be considered."

Sigurd Hoel wrote on November 16, 1938:

"Reich has gotten 'permission to stay;' I assume you know that? And under conditions which one would believe were taken from a satirical novel. With God's help it should be written... Down in Copenhagen I assume you saw the calmness after the final mental outbreak in Germany, more clearly than did we up here. Do you know what I am wishing? Let it be even worse—even worse but fast, fast, before the infinite elastic consciousness gets time to take that also. For the first time people all over the world start to understand that these big men in the world are really medically, mentally ill."

Besides the gradually greater circle of Norwegian, Danish, and Swedish students, Reich also had several English and American students in training. In 1938, A. S. Neill came to Oslo; he went into treatment with Reich and gave a lecture for the pedagogic circles of Norwegians and Danes.

In August, 1938, Professor Bronislaw Malinowski came from London to Copenhagen. He had been in psychoanalysis in Vienna. In our pedagogical study-circle we had reviewed in detail his theory about child-rearing in primitive societies and Reich was very interested in his work. Reich came down from Oslo. He, Malinowski, and many interested Danes spent a pleasant and informative afternoon and evening at my home in Copenhagen. Afterwards, Malinowski sent me his essay, *Culture* (London, 1931), bearing the inscription, "With kind remembrance of the evening of 5-8-38."

The work went on seemingly calmly, both in Copenhagen and in Oslo. This continued, despite the fights, but the pressure from the south was becoming steadily stronger and Reich, more than any of us, felt the coming Nazi danger. In the summer of 1939 I was again in Oslo and we went out on an automobile tour to Tyrifjord, Norway, where I took some candid pictures of Reich, Philipson, Raknes, and Elsa Lindenberg. Afterwards, Else took the camera so that I could be included in the pictures. Reich was serious and thoughtful and he had a totally different facial expression than that which can be seen in the photos I took of him in Sletten in 1934. (Photos at right.)

Some of Reich's American students advised him to leave Europe and they obtained a professorship in medical psychology for him at The New School for Social Research in New York City. On August 5, 1939, Reich wrote and asked me to get him a ticket for the "Pilsudski," which was to sail from Copenhagen to America on the 11th or 12th of August. He wanted to come by Copenhagen to say farewell to us down here. He wrote further:

"I need a Danish transit visa. The local Danish Consul asked the police in Copenhagen and although the discussion was only about an American visa, they imposed the conditions that I should obtain a Norwegian return visa. Then they would give me a Danish transit visa. A terribly narrow-minded stupidity when I have an American visa. Please will you both go and talk with them, and telegraph or write to me by airmail about what you can find? ...Tell the people that I am not going back to Norway but that I definitely am going to America.
Warmest regards, Reich.
I must travel to Copenhagen this coming Thursday at the latest, in order to catch the ship."

I spoke with the police, who said they would let Reich know via the Danish Consule in Oslo. On August 11, 1939, I received the following telegraph in English:

"DEPARTING TODAY 18 OCLOCK. KING OLAF. THEN PILSUDSKI. BE READY AT FRONTIER - REICH."

But later that day I got a telegram from Ola Raknes:

"REICH WON'T TRAVEL OVER DENMARK. POLICE DENY HIM TRANSIT VISA - OLA."

On August 29, 1939, Sigurd Hoel wrote to me:

"As the situation now seems, I believe you should take yourself and your own and come up and visit me and mine, here in Oslo. Despite everything, we up here are living a good part away from the anxiety-center. Copenhagen, on the other hand, is very close if the worst should happen. And remember, the worst of the worst will happen in the first days this time. Then it will become one or another form, but all the same again, anyhow. Despite everything, I don't believe in war. If it had come immediately, yes. But first this

Tyrifjord, Norway, 1939. Wilhelm Reich, Tage Philipson, Ola Raknes, Elsa Lindenberg.

Tyrifjord, Norge, 1939. Wilhelm Reich, Tage Philipson, Ola Raknes, Ellen Siersted.

development and then a one-week tug-of-war, and then war anyway. No, the world cannot be so crazy—not until next year!

But perhaps it is *that*, that I don't *want* to believe in anything so meaningless.

Reich has thus gone, and the group is sitting back, a little paralyzed but set up for the work, the magazine, and similar things.

Regards, your Sigurd."

Soon afterward I received a letter dated October 9, 1939, from Reich who was in Forest Hills, New York:

"Dear Ellen:

Many thanks for the letter and the report. I believe, like you, that the knowledge about the madness and the searching for a rational common sense for life and work, continually will break through more and more. And then people will want to meet us, absolutely. Especially, I warn you against fantasies for any form of leader. We will get enough responsibility to carry.

...I ask that you keep me thoroughly informed, preferably with each ship, about what Leunbach and the others will do if the war reaches Denmark. I myself am standing with one leg fully in Europe and I don't believe that I ever will be able to take it away. I wish you everything good, and please, write often.

Your Wilhelm Reich"

On December 7, 1939, I received another letter from Reich, a portion of which follows:

"Dear Ellen:

Since your letter of November 13th, many things have happened in Scandinavia and I'm very, very worried. Don't forget to keep me in touch, by means of each ship.

Do you believe that in all my life I must wander from place to place to make it possible for my students to become completely independent? Or can you give me some good advice?

...Do you believe that it can happen—that the distance and the events will separate me from my

European group? Sometimes I am afraid for that. We must keep the contact!
Give regards to your children and all friends!
Warmest regards,
Your Willy Reich"

In the beginning of 1940 I received the message that I was selected by the group in Oslo as a member of the "inner circle." I know that Reich, who was my teacher, had recommended me and I wrote to him how happy and at the same time, how afraid I was for having been selected. At the same time I sent him a Danish work, the first issue of *Sex-Economic Communications (Seksualokonomiske Meddelelser*, Copenhagen), entitled *Education for Life (Opdragelse til Liv)*. It was the initial result of a one-year program in the pedagogic study-circle.

On March 8, 1940, Reich wrote from Forest Hills, New York:

"My Dear Ellen:
I received your letter on February 14th and it makes me happy that you now belong to the inner circle. You are so well-oriented about the character of our work that I do not have to say anything, except for one thing: Please help us to not let anyone into our work with strained minds, who has not demonstrated the strength and courage to rebuild his character completely and in his inner being, to release himself from the so highly-esteemed values which now are governing the world. I will be very grateful to you if you can facilitate a better affiliation between the Scandinavian organization and the Institute in New York. I have not heard from Oslo since time immemorial.
With the warmest regards to you and yours,
Your Wilhelm Reich"

The next letter I received from Reich was dated May 29, 1941:

"Dear Mrs. Siersted:
It was good to hear from you. For a long time I have been worried, that one or another of our friends might jump off from 'too much,' if he doesn't keep up the contact with the clinical and experimental work. Therefore, I have decided that I will use two of this Summer's months to write about the area of my work, and send a copy over... A group of friends has formed here who, due to the first positive results in the treatment of cancer, is extraordinarily helpful. I am already sitting in the middle of difficult discussions with physicians, foundations, and so-called authorities.
I am waiting to get the promised clinical work from you soon.
...Please, keep in contact with me until the next general international congress. With firm regards to you and your children and all friends.
Yours, Willi Reich"

Reich was not aware that all letters, the ones from him and those from us to him, were being "opened" and censored by the *Oberkommando der Wehrmacht* (German Occupation Army); therefore we were not able to write to him about the people who had to flee to Sweden and the dangers for those of them who came back again.

During the Nazi occupation I had almost three times the work-load, because both Philipson and Leunbach were in Sweden, and I had to take over some of their patients. When they came home after the war ended, I made a break from my work as therapist.

I had not written about Reich's bion experiments (which I followed in Oslo) and his orgone teachings, partly because I do not feel competent to do so, even though I understand what it is about, and partly because Ola Raknes (in Oslo) has written a very instructive book about these matters: *Wilhelm Reich and Orgonomy* (Penguin Books, 1970).

Through character analysis and vegetotherapy you not only get a stronger feeling for your own body; you also get to see in your fellowman his or her often stiff posture, and to a certain degree, you acquire an ability to read part of their facial expressions. I utilized this technique in 1947 when Director Ebbe Neergaard of the Danish "Staatens Filmcentral" asked me, together with the press photographer Helmer Lund Hansen, to conduct a study about small children's reactions to motion pictures. The photos which Lund Hansen took of the children are so good that we can see every facial gesture and posture, and from Reich's theory I interpreted their reactions. The method is best applied to small children, i.e., children up to seven years of age.

If we want to ask about the importance Reich has had in Denmark, outside of the very close circle which worked together with him here for half a year, there is no comparison to his work in Norway, which continued for about five years.

The person who has had the greatest importance for Reich's teachings in Denmark is Dr. Nic Waal. Nic was a trainee of Reich; she was a very skilled therapist and was especially distinguished in her work with psychotic children. She had many Danish students and patients, and she gave lectures and conducted study-circles for psychologists and psychiatrists.

Nic Waal worked for one year as a guest at Professor Preben Plum's pediatric clinic (*Bornpoliklinik*) at the Royal Hospital in Copenhagen. She diagnosed children with the help of Reich's muscle test. While at Prof. Plum's clinic, she collaborated for a time with the psychologist, Bodil Farup. They undertook a study of fifty children from ten to twelve years of age, all of whom were suffering from asthma. Bodil Farup examined the children using the Rorschach Test; Nic Waal with Reich's muscle-test. Neither person knew anything else about the children other than their ages and that they had asthma. The results of the two different tests correspond fully with one another.

During 1952 and through 1954, Dr. Nic Waal and Dr. Ola Raknes traveled each month to Denmark for three days in Copenhagen, to train Danish psychiatrists and psychologists and to have seminars with them.

Nic Waal with a group of children.

Quite often I wonder how Reich could handle all that evilness that was turned against him, without becoming more angry than he at times became. First, when he came to America and discovered that the people there had no greater understanding than they had in Europe, it was as if it had become too much for him to bear and he wrote the book, *Listen, Little Man!* It is not a scientific, but a human document in which Reich points to what the little "average" person is doing to himself and how badly he treats himself. Here, Reich is not at all mild: He chastises the way in which we chastise the ones we like.

He wrote how the "Little Man" is so occupied with unimportant matters that he doesn't hear the children crying or see how unhappy the young are:

> "...When I think of your newborn children, of how you torture them in order to make them into 'normal' human beings after your image... In order correctly to handle the children's sexuality, one must oneself have experienced what love is."

Reich tells how the "Little Man" lays his woman to prove the man in him. But he, hearing about sex-economy, says, "Sex isn't everything. There are other important things in life." The Little Man does not know that sexuality is love and warmth, in Reich's view.

Reich's love for the young ones and the children, and his ability to understand them, is breathed into everything that he wrote. As to the warm and vital person Reich was, he had an empathy for the child, which ought to become of great importance for everybody who has anything to do with children.

In his 1952 interview for the Sigmund Freud Archive (transcribed and published in *Reich Speaks of Freud*, M.B. Higgins and C. Raphael, Eds., Farrar Straus & Giroux) Reich describes how the child is born with a certain amount of energy and how society takes hold of it and molds it. He asks whether anyone is able to direct the psychic energy in children, in the newborn and in the young, if society or the person keeps the libido out of the picture.

> "I may be wrong. I may be completely cockeyed. I don't think I am.." Reich tells, "...I began to try to understand it a few years ago. ...When a child is born, it comes out of a warm uterus, 37 degrees centigrade, into about 18 or 20 degrees centigrade. That's bad enough. The shock of birth...bad enough. But it could survive that if the following didn't happen. As it comes out, it is picked up by the legs and slapped on the buttocks. The first greeting is a slap. The next greeting: Take it away from the mother. Right? Take it away from the mother. This will sound unbelievable in a hundred years. Take it away from the mother. The mother must not touch or see the baby. The baby has no body contact after having had nine months of body contact at a very high temperature - what we call the 'orgonotic body energy contact,' the field action between them, the warmth and the heat.
> "Then, the Jews introduced something about six or seven thousand years ago. And that is circumcision. ...Take that poor penis. Take a knife—right? And start cutting. And everybody says, 'It doesn't hurt.' ...Everybody says, 'No, it doesn't hurt.' ...Circumcision is one of the worst treatments of children. ...They can't talk to you. They just cry."

Dr. Rene A. Spitz, the French pediatrician and psychoanalyst, states:

> "I find it difficult to believe that circumcision, as practiced in our hospitals, would not represent stress and shock of some kind. Nobody who has witnessed the way these infants are operated on without anesthesia, the infant screaming in manifest pain, can reasonably deny that such treatment is likely to leave traces of some kind on the personality. This is one of the cruelties the medical profession thoughtlessly inflicts on infants just because these cannot tell what they suffer."

Reich further stated:

> "This poor child, poor infant, tries always to stretch out and to find some warmth, something to hold on to. It goes to the mother, puts its lips to the mother's nipple. And what happens? The nipple is cold, or doesn't erect, or the milk doesn't come, or the milk is bad. ...It can't come to you and tell you, 'Oh, listen, I'm suffering so much, so much.' It just cries. And, finally, it gives up. It gives up and says, 'No!' It doesn't say 'no' in words, you understand, but that is the emotional situation."

In this manner, according to Reich, the person's biological system has become barren for a long time to come in the future. The children become from birth barren and cold; the child's will becomes broken. So long as infants are being hurt, nothing will be better. The individual therapy is of no use... the only thing that is worth anything, is the child.

If anyone wants to see Reich as an example of someone proclaiming free sexuality, he has failed to understand Reich. Reich stood in opposition to what he called the "glass of water" theory—that is, you sense your sexual need as uninhibited as the need to drink a glass of water when you are thirsty. Reich said, "Free Love" — and with that he stressed that with freedom, *responsibility* follows.

A.S. Neill said that Reich was one of the most moral persons he had met. I have never heard Reich tell an indecent story or bring evil slander. It was slander which followed him in Germany, Denmark, and Norway, and to a high degree in America.

Reich surely believed that he could work freely in America, where freedom occupies the seat of honor, and then the slander and the pettiness showed itself to be greater there than in any other place where he had been working. Persons went onto his property, they peeked in through his windows, and slandered.

If we want to ask why Reich also in America was declared to be mentally ill, we may recall that the rumor travels faster than man, and that his earlier colleagues in I.P.V. who already in 1934 said that Reich was a psychopath, fled to America several years before Reich arrived.

The problems of who the scientist was who initiated the American "Food and Drug Administration" accusations against Reich and the ban against his work with the orgone experiments, seems not to have been resolved in America. When Reich didn't behave according to the terms of the first prohibition, he was judged to be in contempt of court and his books and instruments were burned, and he was sentenced to two years imprisonment.

Reich died on November 3, 1957, in the Lewisberg Federal Penitentiary, in the State of Pennsylvania in America. ∎

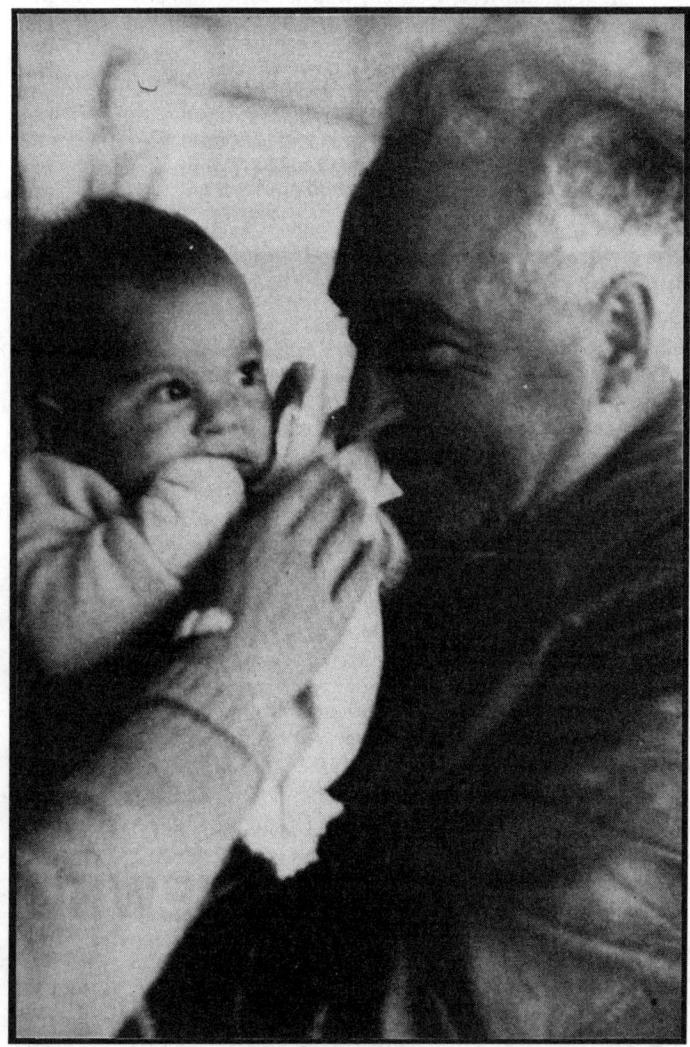

Reich with his son, Peter, in the USA.

A REPORT ON

THE JAILING OF A GREAT SCIENTIST IN THE USA, 1956*

Regarding the Resistance of Wilhelm Reich, M.D., to a Federal Injunction Abolishing Freedom of Scientific Research, Freedom of the Press and Freedom of Speech

by Lois Wyvell**

For resisting an injunction that abrogates freedom of scientific research, freedom of the press, and freedom of speech, Wilhelm Reich, M.D., was sentenced to two years in jail and fined $10,000 on May 25, 1956 in a federal court in Portland, Maine. This injunction, obtained by the Federal Food and Drug Administration (FDA), is no half-way measure: it is so bold in its sweeping, fascist liquidation of a new science — the monumental thirty years' work of a world-renowned scientist — that everyone seems to be stunned, unable to believe it; for everyone is fearfully silent. The newspapers have been strangely silent about this vital case that threatens the civil rights of every citizen and that should be especially interesting news to the newspapers since it contains censorship of the press.

To compensate in some small measure for this deficiency of the press, this communication is directed to all people concerned with their own civil rights as well as to those interested in orgonomy (the science of orgone energy) who have not understood the issues of the Federal Food and Drug Administration's case against it and its founder, Dr. Reich. And, it aims at refreshing the memory of those people who are indebted to Dr. Reich for a clearer understanding of Life and of the universe, for improved health and for all the great gifts given freely to the world by Dr. Reich through his discovery of and research with orgone energy (cosmic, primordial Life energy.)

General Statement of the Case

Wilhelm Reich, M.D., student and co-worker with Sigmund Freud for seventeen years, professor, scientist, inventor and author, internationally famous for his character-analytic therapy and for his discovery of orgone energy, was sentenced after a jury found him "guilty" of "contempt of court" for his refusal to obey an injunction ostensibly enjoining the distribution of the orgone energy accumulator and orgonomic literature referring to the accumulator in interstate commerce, but in fact enjoining orgonomic research and all orgonomic publications. After years of "investigation", the FDA could find no valid grounds on which to object to the distribution of the accumulator, so they based their case on an opinion that orgone energy does not exist. For Dr. Reich to have *contested* the injunction in court, would have been to grant the government the right to judge scientific research; and to *abide* by the injunction was as impossible as to abide by an injunction requiring the defendant to put his own hands around his throat and slowly strangle himself to death.

Michael Silvert, M.D., orgonomic physician, was sentenced to a year in jail for having allegedly disobeyed the injunction *after* the courts had ruled that the injunction did not apply to orgonomic doctors but only to Dr. Reich.

The case has been appealed and both doctors have been *temporarily* released on $15,000 bail each.

Keep in mind that the FDA "investigation" of the orgone energy accumulator began in 1947. This is how it happened:

Background

In 1947, Dr. Reich (who had long since left the medical field to do basic research in orgone physics and astrophysics) demonstrated the motor force of orgone energy. Medical orgonomy was quietly developing through the practice of about a dozen medical doctors who, after years of clinical and private practice in classical medicine, had extensive training in orgonomic medicine. The orgone energy accumulator, a simple arrangement of alternate layers of organic and inorganic materials, was being used carefully and effectively by these doctors in the treatment of various biopathies. The general principle of the accumulation of orgone energy from the atmosphere could be used in blanket form, in box form, funnel shapes, etc. Accumulators were constantly used by Dr.

Reich and other scientists in research in natural science. The orgone energy accumulator was also used by many laymen as a *preventative* measure against colds, etc., as an aid in healing burns and wounds quickly, without scars, and as a relief from the severe pain of burns, etc. Everyone who obtained an accumulator from the non-profit Orgone Institute Research Laboratories, Inc. was given instructions for its use and was informed that the accumulator was still in the experimental stage, that no claims of cures were made for it, and that they should be under the supervision of a medical doctor if they used it for any serious illness. To pay for the construction of the accumulator and to further orgonomic research, a contribution of $10 a month was requested but not required. None of this money nor the money from the sale of Dr. Reich's books by the non-profit Orgone Institute Press was ever paid to Dr. Reich. (On the contrary, Dr. Reich poured his own money into the research.) These monies were used exclusively to further research, to publish scientific books and journals on orgonomy, and to pay the very nominal salaries of a couple of office workers and laboratory assistants.

To repeat: In 1947, came this promise of an almost incredible power for good (or evil): the discovery of a motor force in cosmic orgone energy. This was also the year in which Dr. Reich's book, *The Mass Psychology of Fascism*,(1) became the most popular non-fiction book in the circulating department of the New York Public Library. This book is an analysis of the pathological basis of fascism, and it uses both Black and Red fascism as examples. Communists were certainly aware that this scientific book, more dangerous to them than bombs or congressional committees, had gained a wide audience.

Thus, it was not by coincidence that in April, 1947, two slanderous articles by a Communist free-lance writer, Mildred Edie Brady, were published: "The New Cult of Sex and Anarchy" in *Harper's Magazine*, and "The Strange Case of Wilhelm Reich" in the *New Republic*. (You may remember that in 1947 the staffs of most of the intellectual magazines were peppered with Communists, many of whom have since been exposed.) Both articles attacked Dr. Reich and his work by sneering insinuations and downright lies as well as by misleading half-truths, with no attempt at scientific repudiation, techniques typical of fascist literature. Brady *insinuated* that Dr. Reich was a sexual cultist and that he claimed cures and orgastic potency could be had from the use of the orgone energy accumulator. The latter article was picked up later by various organized enemies of orgonomy and published either verbatim with approval (*The Bulletin of the Menninger Clinic*), or used as a basis for more false statements about orgonomy, Dr. Reich and the orgone energy accumulator (*The Journal of the American Medical Association* in an article by the Council on Pharmacy and Chemistry). It was reprinted or paraphrased, either through malice or equally vicious ignorance by many others — the *McGill Daily*, Montreal; the *Saturday Review of Literature, Collier's*, etc.

The Birth of a Conspiracy

The clinical results of the use of the orgone energy accumulator had been published and submitted to the Surgeon General and the National research Council in 1942 and 1943, but not until the summer of 1947, after the Brady lies had been spread and embellished by kindred spirits, did the Federal Food and Drug Administration begin its "investigation" of the accumulator. The first FDA agent to make inquiries at

1. Orgone Institute Press, Rangeley, ME, 1946; Farrar, Straus, and Giroux, NY, 1969.

Orgonon, said that he was there because of the Brady article.

Documents published in *History of the Discovery of the Life Energy, Vol. A-XII-EP*, (2, 3, 4, 5) show, without need of comment, that the FDA action originated and was kept going as a conspiracy to kill orgonomy and to defame the discoverer of orgone energy. The people and organizations who joined this conspiracy named themselves by their letters and their publications, which anyone may read if the FDA has not destroyed all copies yet.

Thus the birth of a conspiracy: an organized political group (which Red fascism certainly is) produces the first big Lie, knowing that it will be picked up and used by those who are in sympathy with their purpose. It isn't necessary to get together in a dark room and whisper in order to conspire. The emotional conspiracy is composed of those individuals and organizations that aid and abet each other in furthering the deadly Lie to destroy that which they jointly hate: in this case, civil rights, orgonomy and Dr. Reich. It includes all those pharmaceutical and medical organizations, political groups, newspapers, psychoanalysts, newspaper reporters, Communists and judges who either instigated or upheld the fraudulent FDA "investigation" and the unconstitutional injunction. It includes the men within the FDA who carefully, consistently throttled the factual evidence in favor of orgonomy, and planted and cultivated only damning evidence. All silently know each other and act in an unacknowledged conspiracy.

Each new discovery has to fight for existence. The enemies are always the same, though given different designations in different ages. Orgonomy is confronted with three organized enemies:

1. *Political*: Communism and all politicians with fascist character structures. This, because Dr. Reich, in his *Mass Psychology of Fascism* (banned and burned in Nazi Germany and Communist Russia) and in other writings has analyzed the basis of fascism and hence given the world a tool for its destruction. Also, because fascism is in itself the antithesis of orgonomy.

2. *Those financially threatened by the discovery*: In particular the pharmaceutical industry. The development of a medical science based on *free* orgone energy which every man can in time use to *prevent* disease as well as heal burns and wounds, diminish pain, etc., without resort to medicines and drugs, threatens the profits of one of the biggest monopoly cartels in the country.

3. The organized status quo, such as the AMA, the Menninger Clinic and those professors and doctors and laymen whose comfortable rut, or whose prestige is threatened by a new discovery that may make them change, or that may prove their own life's work comparatively fruitless.

2. Reich, Wilhelm: *Conspiracy, An Emotional Chain Reaction*; Wilhelm Reich Biographical Material, History of the Discovery of the Life Energy, Vol. A-XII-EP, Orgone Inst. Press, Rangeley, ME, 1954.
3. Reich, Wilhelm: *Response to Ignorance*, Wilhelm Reich Biographical Material, History of the Discovery of the Life Energy, Doc. Sup. #1, A-XII-EP, Orgone Institute Press, Rangeley, ME, 1955.
4. Reich, Wilhelm: *Red Thread of Conspiracy*, Wilhelm Reich Biographical Material, History of the Discovery of the Life Energy, Doc. Sup. #2, A-XII-EP, Orgone Institute Press, Rangeley, ME, 1955.
5. Reich, Wilhelm: *Atoms for Peace Versus the HIG*, Wilhelm Reich Biographical Material, History of the Discovery of the Life Energy, Doc. Sup. #3, A-XII-EP, Orgone Institute Press, Rangeley, ME, 1956.

Orgonomy, as a new great truth, is unique in its fight only in the extent to which it touches on the core of Life in everyone, a *core* around which we have built up a stiff armor, the penetration of which we fear more than death. In its ultimate terms, orgone energy which is pre-atomic, creative, Life energy, is confronted by its Life-destroying enemies — the emotional plague, mechanism, mysticism, nuclear energy and *DOR*.

The FDA "Investigation"

The FDA "investigation" must be put in quotation marks because it was from the first no gathering of facts about the use of the orgone energy accumulator, but a spying and prying bent on trying to find or produce grounds for defamation. Its efforts in 1947 to establish grounds for sexual defamation and to claim the orgone energy accumulator was distributed for profit, failed. Though FDA agents throughout the country tried over a period of years, they could find no evidence from users of the accumulator that it was harmful, that it had been misrepresented, that it was connected with a sex cult or that it was used for personal financial gain. On the contrary, they obtained hundreds of statements from laymen and medical doctors about the benefits of the accumulator. *These they totally ignored in their complaint.* The truth they buried while they planted and cultivated fraudulent "experiments" and witnesses. The FDA's witnesses, no matter how well versed in electronics or atomic physics or classical medicine, are as ignorant as the judge in matters of orgonomy and as unable to judge it.

The FDA "investigation" apparently died out in 1950. It was revived a few years later and on February 10, 1954, a complaint was served on Dr. Reich and the Wilhelm Reich foundation enjoining the scientific work of Dr. Reich. For reasons stated below, Dr. Reich did not respond to the complaint.* On March 19, 1954, an injunction (Civil Action no. 1056) signed by U.S. District Judge John D. Clifford, Jr., Portland, Maine, was served on the defendants. Its prohibitions applied to Dr. Reich, the Foundation, Ilse Ollendorf, their servants, employees and "all persons in active concert or participation with them." The defendants were enjoined from distribution of the orgone energy accumulator in interstate commerce and all accumulators were to be disassembled and all printed matter constituting labeling of the "device" was to be destroyed by the defendant... *all on the grounds that orgone energy does not exist.* So might a government agency during Fulton's time, infiltrated by conspirators, have forbidden research in steam energy and claimed that it did not exist. Or, the early experiments in electrical energy might have been similarly prohibited and all mention of electricity banned, if a government agency had been permitted to issue an injunction stating that electrical energy does not exist and that all devices to demonstrate this energy were to be destroyed.

---

* Reich did prepare and submit to Judge Clifford a document *Response to Ignorance* which should be viewed as a proper legal response to the original complaint. Reich's *Response* was completely ignored by the judges, however. Indeed, the judges considered all technical and procedural matters which weighed *in favor* of Reich to be of virtually no importance whatsoever, while those which weighed *against* Reich were elevated to the level of "major consequence". Additionally, all the judges who presided over the Reich legal case knew they were approving the burning and banning of books — taken together, the facts suggest that the FDA and courts were out to "get Reich" no matter what kind of legal defense he would have offered. One is tempted to speculate that Reich also knew this. — J.D.

The following civil rights were clearly abolished by this injunction:

FREEDOM OF THE PRESS — ABOLISHED!

This injunction states that anything "which conveys the impression that the alleged orgone energy exists" constitutes misbranding; that any "photographic representation or suggestion with a caption, or otherwise, which conveys the impression that such is an actual photograph depicting the alleged orgone energy or an alleged excited orgone energy field" constitutes misrepresentation and misbranding of the orgone energy accumulator, even though they in no way refer to the accumulator, for it further orders that "all copies of the following items ... *which contain statements and representations pertaining to the existence of orgone energy* [and then they list these books: THE DISCOVERY OF THE ORGONE, Volumes I and II; THE SEXUAL REVOLUTION; ETHER, GOD AND DEVIL; COSMIC SUPERIMPOSITION; LISTEN, LITTLE MAN; THE MASS PSYCHOLOGY OF FASCISM; CHARACTER ANALYSIS; THE MURDER OF CHRIST; PEOPLE IN TROUBLE — all by Wilhelm Reich] *shall be withheld by the defendants" unless " such statements and representations, and any other allied material, are deleted."* (Italics are our emphasis.) In other words, works on orgone energy may be distributed if all statements about orgone energy are deleted.

Books having no word about the accumulator were thus banned and many books and periodicals listed to be destroyed because they contain the words "orgone energy." The FDA declared that this energy does not exist, and that therefore the mere mention of the words "orgone energy" constitutes labeling of a "device" even though the text is purely concerned with orgone biophysics, sociology or astronomy. Only fascists and psychopaths so flagrantly abuse rationality. It expresses the fascist's wholesale contempt for reasonable people and democracy — which they thereby challenge with the smug assurance that they won't be fought.

Books written before orgone energy was discovered (*The Sexual Revolution, Character Analysis,* etc.) were banned as constituting labeling of the orgone energy accumulator. Among the books to be *destroyed* (not only banned) is the one published in 1947 on the FDA campaign against orgone biophysics. Can censorship of the press go further?

The same books that were banned and burned in Nazi Germany and Communist Russia — books dealing with fascism, not with orgone energy — are now banned in the USA on the totally irrational charge that they constitute labeling of a "device" that isn't even mentioned!

FREEDOM OF SPEECH — ABOLISHED !

This injunction states "That the defendants {must} refrain from, either directly or indirectly, in violation of said Act, disseminating information pertaining to the assembly, construction, or composition of orgone energy accumulator devices to be employed for therapeutic or prophylactic uses by man or for other animals." Thus, Dr. Reich cannot *talk* about the construction of orgone energy accumulators, nor can anyone who is ever "in concert or participation" with Dr. Reich. Does not this make clear the fact that this injunction aims to stop orgonomic research altogether? Obviously, since the orgone energy accumulator *can* be used therapeutically on men and animals, to speak about it at all becomes contempt of court. And, since to the FDA, the very words "orgone energy" constitute labeling, the injunction may be interpreted a few years hence so that anyone who talks about orgone energy is in contempt of court.

THE RIGHT TO SEARCH AND QUESTION — ABOLISHED !

"With the freedom of religion goes the freedom to question." This interpretation by Judge Curtis Bok has been the interpretation of the courts of this country, and protects the right to do scientific research. This injunction assumes that the FDA, a department of the government, has the right to judge scientific truth and curtail scientific research. The FDA in its complaint and injunction claims specifically that orgone energy does not exist, and it is directed towards the defendants and anyone participating with them — in other words, *no one* may work in the field of orgonomic research. For how can one work with cosmic orgone energy without being in concert with Dr. Reich, without talking about it or writing about it or using devices to concentrate it?

The injunction states that the defendants and those in concert and participation with them are "perpetually" enjoined and restrained from the enumerated acts mentioned — making, talking or writing about orgone energy accumulators. So, if it stands as law, it will be a useful tool for future blacklist roundups.

FREEDOM FROM UNREASONABLE SEARCHES AND SEIZURE — ABOLISHED !

This injunction states "employees of the Food and Drug Administration, at reasonable times, {shall} have access to and {shall} copy from, all books, ledgers, accounts, correspondence, memoranda, and other records and documents in the possession of {or} under the control of said defendants, including all affiliated persons, corporations, associations, and organizations at Rangeley, Maine, or elsewhere, relating to any matters contained in this decree." What is the purpose of this particular fascist outrage? It is two-fold:

First, to obtain access to Dr. Reich's unpublished formulas in orgonomic research. Dr. Reich has said that part of the motive of the conspiring group within the FDA (most probably Communists after the immense power that the use of orgone energy as a motor force and in cosmic engineering promises) was to get his unpublished work, the "Y" factor of the orgone energy motor which he did not reveal, etc. We ask those people who were incredulous and thought Dr. Reich must surely have imagined this, to read the above paragraph again and then to think. After destroying the accumulators and all of the publications relating to the orgone energy accumulators, and especially since the FDA *claims* to believe that orgone energy does not exist, why do they want to *copy* from Dr. Reich's memoranda and documents? They also want to copy from the correspondence and records, and that leads to the second obvious motive:

They can glean from these records and correspondence a black list: the names and addresses of all people who are interested in orgonomic work. This is the clearest warning that if this injunction isn't declared unconstitutional, Dr. Reich's jail sentence is only the beginning of the persecution. Everyone even remotely connected with orgonomy is threatened. Every patient whose case history is in the files is threatened as well as all those people who have bought orgonomic literature. Since when in the USA has the government agent had access to the private case histories of medical doctors to *copy*? The FDA agents tried to get hold of these private case histories during the investigation, and since every orgonomic physician not only refused to divulge the name or illness of any patient, but refused with angry protest against such an outrageous demand, the FDA conspirators had to wait until they could arrange an injunction to give them access to the doctor's private files.

The injunction also takes away our right to refuse to be questioned outside of court, for it states that "any such authorized representative of the Secretary of Health, Education and Welfare (read "representative of the FDA" which is a department under the Secretary) *shall be permitted to interview* officers or employees of the defendant, or any affiliate, regarding such matters ..." Must we now submit to being "interviewed" (read "interrogated and intimidated") by these FDA agents? Shall we have to admit these spies to our homes to have access to and copy from all books, ledgers, accounts, correspondence and memoranda?

If the fascist group in the FDA and the groups behind them, can get by with the jailing of a great and internationally famous scientist like Dr. Reich, who has done only good to this world of men, and get by with destroying his books and prying into his private records and correspondence, they can most easily extend that word "affiliated with the defendant" to include anyone who as ever so much as bought a book on orgonomy or used an orgone energy accumulator. One of their first acts in the "investigation" was to try to get hold of the mailing list of the Orgone Institute Press — to be used later to wipe out everyone who even knows of the existence of orgone energy. This is our Munich — USA, 1956 ! (And if you think this is fantastic, please stop for a moment and *remember* Hitler's Germany — the murder of hundreds of thousands of men, women and children in gas chambers only a few years ago; and Stalin's Russia with equal numbers of human beings worked to death and starved to death in slave labor camps. That wasn't only yesterday! That is today. For fascist character structure has not changed and it is not without its ardent and powerful representatives in the USA.)

The orgonomic physicians have been unable to contest the injunction in court, which they have tried to do on the grounds that it interferes with their right to practice medicine as they see fit. So far, their case has not been admitted to court for the court rules that the injunction does not apply to medical doctors, even though they are using the orgone energy accumulator for treatment of their patients. The court, at this moment, *supposedly* refuses to consider them "in concert" with Dr. Reich. However, Dr. Michael Silvert, acting on this ruling of the courts, has been sentenced to a year in jail. So, let no one be mislead by the court's evasive decision. So long as this injunction remains in effect (which will be forever if it is not declared unconstitutional), it is a federal law, and it is not only subject to reinterpretation, but *it is a dangerous precedent for further suppression of civil rights by government injunction.*

Dr. Reich's Reply

Dr. Reich could not enter the court as a "defendant" against the complaint or the injunction obtained by the FDA because, in his words, "such action would, in my mind, imply admission of the authority of this special branch of the government to pass judgement on primordial, pre-atomic cosmic orgone energy." This has been the factor most difficult for many friends to understand. They say: since every charge in the complaint is false, why not simply go to court, trust in the justice of our democratic law, and prove that orgone energy does exist, that the orgone energy accumulator was never misrepresented or inaccurately labeled, and that its distribution was a costly effort rather than a profiteering racket? The answer is that the courts can not and must not judge scientific truth. To contest with the FDA as to the truth of orgonomic research, theoretical or applied, would be to grant a dictator's power to the government. THE GOVERNMENT MUST NOT EVER BE THE FINAL AUTHORITY ON MATTERS OF SCIENTIFIC RESEARCH OR RELIGIOUS BELIEF! That is the core of democracy. Such authority vested in the government is the core of all dictatorship. It IS dictatorship. That is what happened in Russia under Stalin. Dr. Reich, by not making the fight *in court* that the conspirators arranged for him, is not only protecting orgonomy, he is protecting our basic civil rights ... at the risk of his own freedom.

Knowing from the history of thousands of famous cases in the past thousands of years that no religious or scientific truth can be proven in court, and that the defender is always condemned along with the new truth; and knowing that the United States Constitution provides for protection of every citizen's right to search for truth and write about and speak about his findings and beliefs, Dr. Reich was unwilling to give up these rights by replying to the injunction in court.

But Dr. Reich did reply in several ways. First, he wrote a letter to Judge Clifford and sent him his published RESPONSE (3) which was widely circulated. He kept Judge Clifford informed of his activities and why he could not conform to the injunction. (Perhaps Judge Clifford finally understood the significance of the injunction he had signed, for when the case finally came to trial, Judge Clifford was replaced by another man, Judge Sweeney.)

Second, Dr. Reich published documents (*photographs* of the documents, not type-set copies) proving *his* case against the FDA. These documents substantiate everything Dr. Reich wrote about the case and everything that has been said in his report. Dr. Reich has spread his case out before the world: his lifetime of work is published in his many books that are circulated throughout the world; his contentions about the Communist instigation of the FDA "investigation" are proven by published documents; and Dr. Reich's side of the case is clearly presented in *History of the Discovery of Life Energy, Documentary Supplements Nos. 1 and 3*. (3,5) Being a scientist and strictly non-political, he published clean, clear, reasoned argument based on factual, documentary evidence.

Why have none of the newspapers and magazines picked up and repeated the facts of such a vital and newsworthy case, as they picked up and spread the Brady lies? The news sources have been informed of each step in this case, but have maintained a strange silence. Only the local Portland papers and the *New York Times* gave brief accounts of the trial and sentence. *Time Magazine* printed a mangled report, stating that the jail sentence had been suspended. The effect of this was, as it undoubtedly was meant to be, that the people who would be seriously concerned about a jail sentence believed that it was just a matter of a fine and that they need do nothing.

Implications and Perspective

With the usual fear and hatred toward a knowledge that transcends our own, today as in the past, we have attempted to destroy a new science that exposes the limits and inconsistencies of our efforts to achieve a solution to the problems of mankind. With all our theories of the universe and matter, society and the individual, we have failed in all our endeavors to relieve the suffering and misery that surrounds us. Mass murder in nuclear warfare and enslavement of whole nations is still tomorrow's promise. Starvation and drought, and insanity and the sexual misery of all the people of our planet are to most of us mysteries before which we are helpless. And yet, today, in the USA, a new science that offers a fruitful method of research into these mysteries, has been brutally thrust aside and condemned.

Medical orgonomy, based on knowledge of Life energy, has found the basis of social sickness in the individual's disturbed energy economy and thus offers a way to work toward individual health and a sane society. Orgonomic physics has discovered the relationship between cosmic pre-atomic energy and nuclear energy, offering a way to work toward counteracting deadly nuclear radiation. Cosmic orgone engineering has turned the course of hurricanes and made inroads against drought, offering a practical method of developing weather control. All of this work has been stopped by an order of the court. This new science, embodied in the person of the great scientist Wilhelm Reich, has been silenced.

With all its contempt for truth and human liberty, that awful fettered thinking which sent great men to the cross and the stake, gave its verdict. And this verdict will stand as a law of the land, as a huge breach of the Constitution of the United States, a threat to the liberties of every citizen, unless public opinion is informed and the voice of the people is heard. A voiced public opinion is our only weapon, and, despite opinions to the contrary, it is still effective in the USA today. "In 1953, American public opinion against book banning was so outspoken that the State Department revised its policies", states Supreme Court Justice William O. Douglas in *An Almanac of Liberty*.

That is why we who write and sign this communication are sending it to you — to inform you, hoping you will think about this deeply, urgently; talk about it and write about it to congressmen, commentators, editors, lawyers, judges, educators and all individuals and organizations who can be effective in speaking out against this evil abridgement of civil rights and fascist persecution of good men. We are not affiliated with Dr. Reich or the Wilhelm Reich Foundation, nor are we representing them. We are terrified by a government injunction which, if allowed to stand, abridges most of our civil rights, and we do not want orgonomy to be stifled or Dr. Reich or Dr. Silvert to be jailed. ∎

---

3. *Response to Ignorance*, Ibid.
5. *Atoms for Peace*, Ibid.

AN EYEWITNESS REPORT
of the
BURNING of SCIENTIFIC BOOKS
in the USA
1956

by Victor M. Sobey, M.D.

The following letter is printed as a supplement to A REPORT ON THE JAILING OF A GREAT SCIENTIST IN THE USA, 1956, Regarding the Resistance of Wilhelm Reich, M.D., to a Federal Injunction Abolishing Freedom of Scientific Research, Freedom of the Press and Freedom of Speech, by Lois Wyvell. It speaks for itself.

Dear Miss Wyvell,

I had meant to write to you after I received "The Report", in order to ask for some additional copies. It seems that people have reacted quite a bit to the report, but like everything else, if they can't see this fight as a tangible struggle in their lives, they just go back into their daily routines until someone pushes them again.

Yes, I saw the books burned. It hurt a great deal for awhile, but then I compared this loss to the destruction of an airplane or battleship in war and realized that this is just what we are in.

On August 22, I called Dr. Silvert just to talk. He told me that the next morning the F.D.A. agents were to order the press to remove for destruction all the literature that came under section 6 of the injunction, as follows: Catalogue Sheet, Physicians' Reports, Application for the Use of the Orgone Energy Accumulator, Additional Information Regarding Soft Orgone Irradiation, *Orgone Energy Accumulator—Its Scientific and Medical Use, Orgone Energy Bulletin, Orgone Energy Emergency Bulletin, Internationale Zeitschrift fur Orgonomie, Emotional Plague versus Orgone Biophysics, Annals of the Orgone Institute, Ether God and Devil,* and *Oranur Experiment.* He asked me to attend, and I said I would be willing to come.

I arrived at the stockroom at 7:30 a.m. on August 23. Present were Dr. Silvert, Martin Bell, Miss Shepard, myself, and two F.D.A. agents, a Mr. Ledder and a Mr. Conway. All the expenses and labor had to be provided by the Press. A huge truck with three in help were hired. I felt like people who, when they are to be executed, are made to dig their own graves first and are then shot and thrown in. We carried box after box of the literature. No accurate check was taken of the amount, but it filled the truck.

Toward the end, Mr. Conway stopped Dr. Silvert to tell him that the New York office of the F.D.A. had received information from Dr. Milstead of the Washington office that it was their opinion that the literature of Section 5 of the injunction should also be applied to Section 1,2,3, of the injunction. Dr. Silvert asked if this meant that these books should also be burnt and the agent shrugged his shoulders and said that "this was their opinion." So again they were laying a trap. If the Press decided to destroy the books of Section 5, then the F.D.A. could say they were blameless, because the Press agreed with their opinion. If the press didn't destroy the books, the F.D.A. could serve the press with a complaint for not complying with the injunction, and then everybody is in court again.

After loading was completed, the truck went to the Gansevoort Incinerator at Gansevoort and Hudson Streets. It dumped its load of books into the fire, and it was done.

My one regret is that I did not think of taking pictures, but I didn't really believe it happened until I started to put it down in this letter to you. ...Of course you are free to quote all or any part of this letter.

Might I also suggest that you do not lose the true issue here; the burning of these books is not the whole issue but is only one aspect in the murder of the truth.

Sincerely Yours,
Victor M. Sobey, M.D.

Reich being escorted to prison, March 1957.

Why is Reich Never Mentioned?*

by R.D. Laing**

It is as though he had never existed. Few medical students, if any, will have heard his name so much as mentioned in medical school, and will never come across him in their textbooks. It is not that his views are less scientific than many of those taught today — which are no more scientific than those clinical dogmas of even 50 years ago that we are now pleased to ridicule or patronize.

Reich's proposals as to the *social* influences on the functions of sympathetic, parasympathetic and central nervous systems, and on our biochemistry, *are* testable, but are never tested, as with much else that is really important — Lemert's work on the conspiratorial nature of the social field of people who think there is a conspiracy going on; Scheff's work on admission procedures to mental hospitals; Jourard's work on bodily contact, for instance. Exciting to "laymen", perhaps noticed by professionals, seldom pursued. If one insists on referring to them, one is becoming tiresome.

Not one person, as far as I know, in any institution in this country is doing a single piece of research even to disconfirm any of the detailed findings or hypothesis of the above gentlemen, including Reich. Professions institutionalize ignorance, and turn ignorance into a claim for status. Reich was arrested by the FBI as a suspected Nazi spy. He was actively persecuted while alive, and is conspiratorially ignored now he is dead. More ought to be done on the sociology of attempts to destroy heretics without a trace. How can we tell when they are successful? Many psychiatric textbooks are largely concerned to screen out information that only advanced students can be trusted to know about, when they, it is hoped, will be so brainwashed theoretically, or hooked to professional practices, that no one can do anything about it (if we had more staff, more money, etc.) The textbook becomes a burial ground. Intellectual ancestor worship. Seldom read after a few years, but there are always new ideas that are dying or can be killed and buried.

Reich has been written off professionally for years. But — somehow or other — patients, perhaps, who must be as daft as him, keep on reading his books. Suddenly it is going to be discovered that we have known all along everything that is worthwhile to know of what he said — the rest can easily be consigned to the convenient dustbins of psychotic ideas. The true dustbins of history are the textbooks. Try reading the textbooks of 30 to 40 years ago and compare them with Reich's work at that time. Reich is still *alive*. There is no a priori reason to suppose that what survives through history is the truth. More likely we have not much else to go on than the lies that those who win the power game pass on.

The true story of Reich's split with the inner psychoanalytic circle is still a closely kept secret, and will now probably never be known. Why? The dynamics of that group are likely to be as instructive as the theories that emerged from it. More than 50 per cent killed themselves or allegedly went mad, or both. Ernest Jones's official story is less credible than many fairy stories. Reich has penetrating insights into the European patriarchal family but, like Groddeck, he seems to have formed a primitive transference to Freud, without fully appreciating the whole group scenario.

Although Wilhelm Reich's presence still hovers — ridiculous, menacing, pitiful, according to projection — walled off "outside" the orthodoxy of psychiatry and psychoanalysis, there seems to be a quiet reevaluation going on among the younger people of all ages. Even his later work on what he called biophysics cannot be so glibly consigned to cranksville as it was even ten years ago. The more I know at first hand of what Reich was talking about, the more seriously I take him.

Reich began in the twenties as a psychoanalyst, with a particular interest in sexology. He was a distinguished member of Freud's circle in Vienna. Gradually his views took shape out of his own clinical experience. They ran the following course, as recounted by him.

He formed the impression that *all* his patients suffered from a disturbance of genitality. This was not always manifested in obvious frigidity or impotence, but always entailed an incapacity for total orgasm with full gratification. This was not obvious because many people did not (and do not) know what total orgasm is, so they did not know what they were missing. Orgasm, as Reich described it, is a serpentine undulation of the whole body, a giving in, a surrender, reaching an acme followed by complete dissolution of pre-orgasmic tension.

It is generated by a free flow of bioelectric energy, and is resisted by practically everyone to some extent by means of chronic tensions in the skeletal muscles. From head to foot, according to Reich, we are all encased in a sort of muscle armour, that *is* our character. Its main function is to avoid pleasure. It kills gratification and life. We have developed this lethal anti-gratification equipment in childhood, learning to keep a stiff upper lip, holding our head high, chin up, back arched, shoulders rounded, diaphragm rigid, pelvis dead, afraid even to breathe freely, especially to expire.

After some years Reich gave up the techniques of psychoanalysis. He came to regard the exclusive use of talking as

---

* The following article appeared in *New Society*, March 28, 1968 under the title "Liberation by Orgasm."
** R.D. Laing was a controversial British psychologist who pioneered the innovative and humane treatment of schizophrenics, and emphasized the social and family origins of the illness.

often a collusive way for both analyst and patient to remain trapped in their character armour. He moved to direct efforts to disarmour the person by various methods of relaxing the muscles.

In doing this, the imprisoned serpent-power was mobilized — sometimes, as he describes it, in ways that would frighten anyone who did not have real trust in the basic forces of life. Character armour maintains in frozen preservation all through life the original conflicts which occasioned its formation in the first place. When loosened, the first impulses to be released may not look too nice.

The biopathy of this state of affairs leads directly to many physical functional and structural ills, and the latter, especially cancer, gained increasing attention from him towards the end of his life. The culmination for Reich of his life's work was the discovery of a type of biological and cosmic energy, and the investigation of its particular energy field.

The best single introduction to Reich is *The Function of the Orgasm*, now in paperback. *

Whether or not one agrees or disagrees with this or that of Reich's theory and practice, it is inescapable that he was a great clinician, with an unusually wide range. His account of his therapy with schizoid and schizophrenic patients will enlighten in some ways anyone involved in this enterprise. He understood the mess we are all in — hysteric, obsessional, psychosomatic, *homo normalis* — as very few have done. Yet one will look through a hundred journals in the Royal Society of Medicine without coming across one mention of him. Why is he *never* mentioned?

He assaults our narcissism in almost unforgivable ways. Freud was cool. Reich is uncool. He tells us that *homo normalis* is a sort of bladder, often dried up, sometimes overtaken with convulsions, longing and terrified to burst, whether through penetration from outside, or explosion from within: terrified to live freely, which would be to love; with an insane fear of being destroyed and at the same time with a senseless readiness to die, to destroy what he fears; fearful of almost everything, most of all, himself; psychically turned inside out, persecuting righteously his persecutors outside himself, none other than his own projections of evil.

It is easy to dismiss statements of this kind as wild and untestable by the canons of science, which Reich claims for them. I do not think it is justified. The signs and symptoms of what Reich called the endemic emotional plague are as evident as the signs of the bubonic plague would be. The extent to which Reich is ignored cannot be explained rationally, and invites an explanation along his own lines — viz, the plague is no respecter of professional boundaries, and psychiatrists suffer from it as much as anyone else. One of its symptoms is an inability to see that one suffers from it.

Some people do see it, but are still subject to it. They are liable to be diagnosed as schizophrenics. *"There must be a potent reason why the schizophrenic is treated so cruelly and the cruel homo normalis is honored so crazily all over this planet."* Indeed. *"The neurotic and the perverse are to the*

---

* Published by Farrar, Straus, and Giroux, N.Y., 1968. Available from Natural Energy Works, PO Box 864, El Cerrito, CA 94530.

schizophrenic, as far as their feelings of life are concerned, as the miserly shopkeeper is to the big scale safe cracker." *"A few cases of the schizophrenia, well understood instead of 'shocked', would, in the long run, save society countless millions of dollars."*

"It seems too much to expect such foresight. It is known that mental institutions are, in reality, jails for psychotics, with little medical care, scarce funds, and in most of them, no research at all." Written in 1948, true today, as the more enlightened and honest superintendents, staff, and patients of mental hospitals continue to testify. [And still true in 1993! — Editors]

Reich asks us to imagine a parliamentary debate on puberty, to suggest to us how divorced from the facts of life politicians are, who at the same time make it their business to regiment even our biochemistry. He would not have been disappointed in the debates in the Commons and Lords last year on the new dangerous-drug legislation. Political and war correspondents are possibly pretty tough, but they still seem to get frightened when a general or leading politician seems actually to believe his own nonsense. Then watch out. We have got used to the idea that the majority of people will believe what they are told. The danger is that the politician might *stop* being cynical.

Freud felt there was nothing to be done about it. Our civilization was founded on repression, and societal repression was interlocked in alliance with part of the biological constitution of each of us. Reich was more optimistic. He does not explain why man has turned against himself in the first place, but his work contains rich detailed documentation of *how* he has, and he did seem to be able to disarm a number of very heavily armoured characters. He has left us a vivid record of part of his adventure. We would be wise to study it with care. I for one have been instructed. ∎

Wilhelm Reich, 1952

The Biophysical Discoveries of Wilhelm Reich*
by James DeMeo, Ph.D.**

I'm going to speak on the biophysical work of the late Dr. Wilhelm Reich. For approximately 20 years, I've been engaged in experimental reproductions of different aspects of Reich's work, and specifically the controversial discoveries he made on the orgone energy. *Orgone* is his term for what is more generally known as the *life energy,* or *lebens-energie* in the German language. This term, *life energy,* is more widely known than Reich's *orgone,* although orgone is a quantified, scientific term and if you're interested in this idea of a life energy — a specific energy associated with living organisms that's different from other forms of energy — you will not find anybody who has done as much quantitative scientific documentation on this principle than Wilhelm Reich. The following is only a thumbnail sketch of Reich's biophysical work.

Reich was a student of Sigmund Freud; in fact, he was being groomed as Freud's successor: he was responsible for the training of all the younger psychoanalysts in the Vienna period of Freud's work. He fell out of favor with psychoanalysis, for several reasons. Reich discovered the sexual orgasm played a more central role in human health and psychic processes than the more conservative analysts were willing to admit. He also took a strong public stand against Hitler, writing a book on the *Mass Psychology of Fascism.*(1) This book correctly identified the Nazis as psychopathological at a time when many other analysts were trying to get along with them. Reich was forced to flee from Germany; first to Denmark, then Scandinavia, and eventually to the United States. He set up a laboratory and research facility in the United States approximately in 1940. His research on the whole question of the emotional energy, the sexual energy or the *libido* of Freud, (which he found to be a *quantifiable* energy force in the body), led him ultimately to discover the orgone energy. The orgone is a very specific energetic force at work in all living creatures.

Reich's work, more than anybody else of that period or today, precisely connected the psyche with the soma. We hear a lot of talk today about "mind-body relationships", but Reich's work really provides a solid foundation to the connection between mind and body. Reich identified a specific emotional, bioenergetic *movement* of energy, where an individual expands outwards towards the world in states of pleasure, or contracts away from the world in states of anxiety.

A person might be fortunate to have a childhood free of significant pain and trauma, in which case their emotional *capacity* to tolerate pleasure and expansion would be preserved. A person can also be conditioned emotionally into a state of chronic anxiety or chronic contraction, much like chronic punishment turning a friendly dog into a cowering or aggressive animal, which is not only an emotional phenomenon, but something bioenergetic, expressing itself in body posture, manner of speaking, and the whole character of a person. The capacity of each individual cell to energetically pulsate, to expand and contract, is also affected by these emotional or bioenergetic considerations. Bioenergetic contraction, Reich said, is instilled all the way down to the plasmatic cellular level; it's something that gets *into one's protoplasm.* Here, we're dealing with an energetic force which links emotions with the somatic aspects of the body in a very direct and straightforward way.

Reich was able to objectify the movement of energy within the body. During expanded states of pleasure, there is an emotional-energetic, and plasmatic-muscular movement from the core, or center, towards the periphery of the organism, outwards, *toward the world.* Conversely, the movement is from the periphery towards the core, or *away from the world,* during states of anxiety, as following trauma or punishment. He objectified this energetic movement through the use of sensitive millivoltmeters. Reich was a pioneer in the measurement of bioelectricity. Much of the discussion about bioelectricity as it is articulated today, has roots in Reich's early experiments. A book by Reich titled *The Bioelectrical Investigation of Sexuality and Anxiety* (2) describes his experiments on this subject. Reich made extensive bio-electrical measurements of the skin surface potentials of humans under different emotional states. He was one of the first, if not *the* first to objectify human emotion in this way; he actually constructed his own millivoltmeter, which was not then available off-the-shelf as we can get them today. He firstly identified a bioelectrical current in the body, but later argued that bioelectrical theory was insufficient to explain the power and qualitative variations of the emotions. He concluded there must be some other energy force involved.

Reich later became interested in studying ameba under the microscope; he was intending to measure the bio-electricity of the ameba during states of expansion and contraction. While undertaking these experiments, he ran into a big puzzle and controversy in the field of microbiology. To study ameba, he had to "grow" them, by putting dead moss and grass in a dish of water. According to orthodox thinking, the ameba spores will swell and grow in the culture dish. However, when Reich observed the moss and grass in the microscope, hour after hour, he couldn't see any spores "growing". What he did observe and later photograph through time-lapse photogra-

---

1. Farrar, Straus & Giroux, NY, 1970.

* Transcribed from a presentation to the *Cancer Control Society* [2043 N. Berendo St., Los Angeles, CA 90027, (213) 663-7801], Annual Meeting, Pasadena, California, September 1992. The Cancer Control Society was formed to present natural healing methods directly to the public .
** Director of Research, Orgone Biophysical Research Laboratory, PO Box 1395, El Cerrito, CA 94530.

---

2. Farrar, Straus & Giroux, NY 1982.

> " ...the origin of the cancer cell in the human body has a parallel to the origin of the ameba in the world of nature. In both cases, it's the loss of the primary life energy from tissues which initiates a process of tissue disintegration. "

phy, was the grass undergoing a process of swelling and disintegrating, breaking down into microscopic vesicles; the vesicles would later reorganize themselves into motile ameba. In other words, the genesis of ameba and other protozoans in the natural world of soils and grass not only occurs from parent cells dividing into new daughter cells (as is the standard biology textbook description). The process also occurs through the vesicular breakdown and later reorganization of decaying plant and mineral materials. Dead, decaying vegetation disintegrates into tiny vesicles Reich called *bions*, and the bions then reorganize themselves into completely new protozoans which can then swim off to multiply. The control procedures and tests Reich subjected this particular observation to are quite sophisticated and have been reproduced many times.

The parallel to this natural bionous process in human disease is that under states of immune dysfunction — or as Reich called it, emotional stagnation and energetic depletion, oxygen suffocation and premature putrefaction of the tissues — the body's own cells disintegrate into the same tiny vesicular bions, which then reorganize and form into motile protozoan cancer cells. As Reich said, the origin of the cancer cell in the human body has a parallel to the origin of the ameba in the world of nature. In both cases, its the loss of the primary life energy from tissues which initiates a process of tissue disintegration. This is a very controversial idea, but it has support from a number of different directions.

The bions have been observed by other scientists both before and since Reich's time. The bions were called *microzymas* by the French microbiologist Antoine Bechamp, who was opposed by Pasteur. Gaston Naessens, the Canadian microscopist has called them *somatids*. Dr. Enderlein in Germany calls them the *protids*. There's a similarity between Reich's bions and Virginia Livingston's *progenitor cryptocides,* and this relationship has been acknowledged by her student, Dr. Allen Cantwell. Cell-wall-deficient bacteria, symbiotic bacteria as discussed by some of the soil bacteriologists, mitochondria and chloroplasts (sub-cellular organelles), mycoplasmas, viruses and retroviruses, all have similarities to Reich's bions.

Reich's discovery of the bion has some similarities and parallels to other cutting-edge research in cancer today, but also some differences. For example, Naessens' somatids, Enderlein's protids, and Livingston's *progenitor cryptocides* are not considered to be, as far as I know, derivable from the breakdown products of one's own cells; nor are they considered to be derivable from nonliving sources, as Reich demonstrated with the bions. Bions could be derived from coal, sand, soot, or iron filings even when those materials were heated to red hot, glowing conditions and then immersed into sterile nutrient broth solutions.(3) Bions could be formed and even cultured through such sterile techniques. From the viewpoint of Reich, with the origin of the cancer cell, we deal with the issue of *biogenesis* itself, the origins of life. This is one of the reasons why I believe that not only Reich, but this whole field of bacterial-viral *pleomorphism* is such a controversy. It threat-

ens to change not just one little aspect of biology, but the entire view of life and the disease process.

Reich emphasized the need for very high microscope magnifications and the use of *living* preparations, not dead and stained preparations, because when you kill the preparations, you can't observe either movement or process. Bions are shaped like a robin's egg, about one micron in diameter with a distinct blue, glowing character. They pulsate, move about, and often clump together to form higher protozoan organisms. Reich and other scientists have made time-lapse movies of the bions forming and organizing; and you can see the bions coming right off of the crystals of earth or out of decaying plant tissue. Earth, which has been boiled and autoclaved for a long period of time and then viewed under the microscope under sterile conditions, will often show clumps of bions forming new membranes around themselves. The bion clumps then roll and turn inside the membrane and eventually a completely new organism is formed. The blue color is also very important: Reich later identified the blue color as the specific color of orgone energy.

Dr. Reich's books *The Bion Experiments* (4) and *The Cancer Biopathy* (5) provide extensive documentation of his discovery of these processes, which other scientists have replicated. Reich's original time-lapse photographs of the bions are on display at the Wilhelm Reich Museum. The American College of Orgonomy in Princeton, New Jersey also gives seminars to clinicians and doctors on Reich's bion and cancer discoveries. Many papers have been published on the subject, including very high quality and revealing microphotos. In my view, there is no longer any question, scientifically, as to whether the bions exist or not; or about Reich's description of the processes involved. The problem is that it contradicts so much of what is in the standard biology and medical textbooks concerning the origins of cells.

Another parallel area of work Reich undertook was to observe *living* red blood cells, and he was one of the first scientists to do so systematically. He was among the first to describe a particular type of degenerated red blood cell, with the spiked form. I believe it's now called the "Burr" cell by hematologists. Reich called it the *T-spike cell.* (Figure 2.) He observed that healthy red blood cells, when put into a physiological saline solution at body temperature, will degenerate and decay very slowly because, in a healthy person, the red blood cells have a strong energy charge which allows them to retain their structure longer. With a good microscope, you can actually see a blue-glowing energy field around the "red" cells. Red blood cells are blue in the light microscope and they will retain the form of a "donut" for a long period. (Figure 1.) But a person who has cancer or other degenerative illness will, even before any visible signs of cancer or disease are apparent, exhibit a large percentage of red cells rapidly degenerating towards the T-spike form. A specific *Reich Blood Test* was developed, as a way of assessing the bioenergetic vitality of blood and the disposition of a patient towards cancer or other degenerative illness.

---

3. Electron microphotos of bions from iron dust are published on the page immediately following this article.

4. Farrar, Straus & Giroux, NY 1979.
5. Farrar, Straus & Giroux, NY 1973.

Reich's discovery of the orgone radiation itself was made in the process of observing the blue energy fields of bion cultures made from sterile beach sand preparations. The energy radiation of the sand bions was particularly strong; it could fog unexposed film, still kept in its wrapper, and impart static charges and magnetic fields to ordinary rubber or metal items left nearby. The sand bions would irritate the eyes of workers who observed them too long with the microscope, and Reich reported a tanning effect upon the skin. To better study this unusual radiation, Reich placed sand-bion cultures in special metal-lined cabinets which he felt would capture and amplify it. The experiment was successful, but to his surprise, the radiation effect persisted in the metal-lined cabinet even *after* the bion cultures were removed. This experiment led to the discovery of the orgone energy, or the life energy, as both a biological and solar-atmospheric phenomenon. Reich later refined the special metal-lined cabinet, and called it the

Figure 1. Reich Blood Test: energetically strong and healthy red blood cells.

Figure 2. Reich Blood Test: Energetically weak and disease-prone red blood cells.

orgone energy accumulator. When you sit inside of an accumulator, it actually has a charging-up affect which most people can readily feel. It's not a fantasy, but a real energetic force which has objective influences upon human physiology. The accumulators were used experimentally by Reich in the 1940s and 1950s as a therapy for diseases considered to be the product of a low energy level.

Malignant cancer is considered one of the low-energy diseases, or *biopathies* (using Reich's term), where the body tissues have been deprived of adequate energy, due to a chronically contracted life situation related to the patient's emotional and sexual history. And I should mention that poor respiration was part of the cancer equation discovered by Reich: cancer patients tend to have not only a resigned, unpleasurable sexual life and poor outlet for strong emotion, but also tend to be shallow breathers. Aside from therapy to address deeper-lying emotional and sexual factors, one way of helping such an individual was to have the person sit inside of the accumulator, to increase the life-energy charge of the tissues, and help them to expand: the breath would begin to deepen; the focus of the eyes would become brighter and sharper, and the skin surface would feel warmer. Over time, people treated in the accumulator would increase their energy level and this could also be seen in the healthier blood picture in the Reich Blood Test. This effect was researched clinically by Reich and his associates, and more recently by physicians in the USA and Germany.

Let me briefly review a few of the other experiments Reich was doing. He made x-ray photographs of the orgone energy coming off the hands of a subject. Some of you know that you can put your palms close together and feel an energy field in between. Subjectively, you can feel something when you move the hands gently towards and away from each other. Reich made x-ray photographs of this phenomenon, which is the basis of the so-called "x-ray ghost". It has never been fully explained by the radiologists, but Reich demonstrated the charge build-up between the hands could block the beam of the x-ray with a smoke-like phenomenon. It appears like smoke being "blown" into the x-ray image. But, of course, it's not smoke — it's an energetic phenomenon — but the critics don't study it, they just dismiss it. They don't care what it is; they just call it the "x-ray ghost" and ignore it, but that's not a scientific approach. Reich believed this phenomenon was the orgone energy in a concentrated and excited form. He later constructed orgone accumulators the size of entire rooms in his laboratory in Rangeley, Maine. He would take glass vacuum tubes with a very deep vacuum, and charge them up with orgone energy by placing them in a strong accumulator. The tubes would exhibit the same bluish coloration as the bions. Reich was a very careful scientist and he didn't want to make any statement about what was going on without re-searching it and testing it with controlled experiments. He was not content just to say it "looked like" life energy of a blue color was coming off the bions, or only that one could "feel" it in the accumulator. He made photographs of the energy, went on to isolate it in the vacuum tubes, and demonstrated that it had the same blue color. This is fairly good proof of the original line of reasoning, as Reich called it: the "red thread" which led to his discoveries during the 1940s and 1950s.(6)

6. Documentation on these points is covered in various issues of Reich's research journal, *Orgone Energy Bulletin*; copies available from the *Wilhelm Reich Museum Bookstore* (address follows).

> **" There was as much as *six times* the normal growth from seeds sprouting inside the orgone accumulator as seeds in the control group. This is not a minor, subtle difference — it's quite powerful. "**

A lively group of people worked with Reich in Rangeley, Maine. He was training physicians in his methods of diagnosis and therapy and giving workshops and seminars to scientists from the USA and overseas. However, in the 1940s, long-standing antagonisms against Reich's work surfaced in a vicious journalistic smear campaign. As Reich noted at the time: it's totally frustrating to see lies appearing in print, and the truth has to come limping behind on crutches. The truth of his work never received the same press attention as the Big Lies of the hostile journalists and doctors. The Food and Drug Administration became involved, and they perpetrated a serious fraud upon the American court by literally concocting a "case". This was later very clearly documented in the book by Professor Jerome Greenfield, *Wilhelm Reich Versus the USA*,(7) which was researched by using the Freedom Of Information Act to review FDA files. On a technicality, Reich was sentenced to two years in federal prison. He died in prison before his sentence was up. The FDA obtained a court order to ban and burn every single book of Reich's that had the word "orgone" printed in it. Almost all of Dr. Reich's books and research journals were burned in incinerators in the late 1950s and early 1960s.

People ask the question of how far the FDA will go today towards assaulting new research findings, such as with the recent SWAT-Team invasion of Dr. Jonathan Wright's clinic in Washington. I'll tell you how far they'll go: they will burn books, and if they thought they could get away with it, they would take every speaker at this conference off to jail. If you think I'm exaggerating, you haven't studied history. This business of the FDA invading natural healing clinics at gunpoint is a very serious matter; very serious, indeed.

At Dr. Reich's trial, he kept insisting on the scientist's right to do research, and he said, "A scientist even has a right to be wrong, and not be hung by the neck for it." Nonetheless, he insisted that he *was right*, but the court would not allow any of his evidence to be presented. As you know from the cases discussed at this conference, this kind of legal assault is going on all across the United States now, with judges and courts ignoring the intent and spirit of the law, and shredding the Constitution. The mainstream press and television don't provide much information on these assaults, but the truth does often appear in the alternative press.(8)

The burning of Reich's books was not complete, however. Most have been reprinted, and are available in many libraries. I have written a book called *The Orgone Accumulator Handbook* (9) which describes the discoveries of Reich with updates on more recent research. The Food and Drug Administration case against Reich is described in this book, and it gives a complete bibliography of research papers, as well as instructions on how to build accumulators. Very few medical physicians in the United States are going to touch the orgone accumulator due to ignorance, hostility, or potential legal problems. However, that's not a problem because it's simple

enough to privately build and use. Anyone can take the plans in my book, and go to a carpenter and have one built. Or do it yourself; it's very simple. Where a lot of people have *speculated* about, or merely *postulated* the existence of a life energy over the years, Reich's discoveries made the life energy concretely available to the average person. And you don't have to be a medical specialist, or engage in metaphysical exercises in order to use it effectively. This is something which, if people want it, they can build it and use it on their own.

Figure 3. The orgone energy accumulator.

I should emphasize, I am not a medical doctor. My doctorate is in environmental science and geography. Most of my research has gone in the directions of environmental questions, but the medical aspects have always interested me. I have lectured and undertaken research in Germany where many clinicians openly work with Reich's approach. In Germany, it is completely legal for a doctor to use orgone energy accumulators in the treatment of cancer patients. I have met with many of these physicians, and they openly acknowledge the powerful, life-beneficial somatic effects of the accumulator. Orgone accumulator therapy of cancer patients often restores lost energy, appetite, the will to continue fighting the disease, and analgesics (pain killers) can be greatly reduced or eliminated. Regarding my own research, I have treated seeds and plants experimentally with the accumulator with very positive results. In Figure 4, the seeds on the right were charged up inside of the accumulator. The seeds on the left are the control group. There was as much as *six times* the normal

---

7.   W. W. Norton, NY 1974.
8.   See the article addressing continuing FDA police raids on natural healing clinics, in this issue of *Pulse*.
9.   Natural Energy Works, El Cerrito (CA) 1989.

Figure 4. Seeds on right were charged in an orgone accumulator. Seeds on the left are the control group. (10)

growth from seeds sprouting inside the orgone accumulator as seeds in the control group.(10) This is not a minor, subtle difference — it's quite powerful. We're talking about a natural energetic force which enhances the growth of tissues in a powerful manner.

This expansive, growth-stimulating influence has also been successfully demonstrated in wound and burn healing experiments. I was once a laboratory assistant for Dr. Richard Blasband at the Elsworth F. Baker Research Lab in Pennsylvania. Baker was a student of Reich and I worked with Blasband on mice experiments, charging up cancer mice in accumulators. In that work, we routinely delayed the onset of the tumors, or caused slower growth of the tumors in the orgone-treated mice. I assisted in wound healing experiments where it was very obvious that mice were healed faster with the accumulator.

The orgone energy accumulator is very simple to make, and the instructions are readily available. Reich's original *Orgone Energy Bulletin,* and more recently, *The Journal of Orgonomy,* and *Pulse of the Planet* have carried many research papers on the treatment of plants, mice and humans, in controlled studies showing that the orgone accumulator has a powerful somatic influence. Perhaps, someday, Reich's orgone accumulator experiments with cancer patients can be openly undertaken again in this country, and the orgone accumulator will become a more widely used tool for healing. My speaking time is up. Thank you very much. ∎

---

10. DeMeo, J.: "Seed Sprouting Inside the Orgone Accumulator", *J. Orgonomy,* 12(2):253-258, 1978.

RESOURCE LIST

The American College of Orgonomy:
    PO Box 490, Princeton, NJ 08542
    Publications: *The Journal of Orgonomy*
Natural Energy Works: PO Box 864, El Cerrito, CA 94530
    Publications: *Orgone Accumulator Handbook* ,
    and other titles on sex-economy and life energy
Orgone Biophysical Research Laboratory:
    PO Box 1395, El Cerrito, CA 94530,
    Publications: *Pulse of the Planet,* various books
The Wilhelm Reich Museum:
    PO Box 687, Rangeley, ME 04970,
    Publications: *Orgonomic Functionalism,* and xerox
    editions of Reich's out-of-print books and journals

SUGGESTED READING

By Wilhelm Reich, M.D. (Farrar, Straus & Giroux, NY)
    The Bioelectrical Investigation of Sexuality and Anxiety
    The Bion Experiments: On the Origin of Life
    Children of the Future
    The Cancer Biopathy
    Ether, God and Devil; Cosmic Superimposition
    The Function of the Orgasm
    Listen, Little Man!
    Mass Psychology of Fascism
    The Orgone Energy Accumulator, Its Scientific and
        Medical Use
    Orgonomic Diagnosis of the Cancer Biopathy
    People in Trouble
    The Sexual Revolution

Electron Microscope Photographs of Bions from Iron Dust
(20,000 power magnification) Captured by Stephen Shanahan, Melbourne University.

These remarkable bion photos come from Stephen Shanahan, a biophysics student at Melbourne University, Australia. The bion preparations show a number of very life-like qualities, such as: double cell walls, fissioning (reproduction), bridging (conjugation?) nucleated features and "organelles". The preparations were made as follows: iron dust was heated to white-hot, glowing incandescence over a torch. The glowing hot iron was then, using sterile techniques, immediately immersed into a sterilized solution of brain-heart and KCl nutrient solution, in keeping with Wilhelm Reich's protocols on the bions.(1) The solution was then prepared and photographed using an electron microscope. In one of the photos, a bion appears to be developing out of a "nest" of iron material. A video of these same preparations demonstrated very vigorous "Brownian" movements, which Reich (and Brown) attributed to the life force (orgone) contained within the solution. Many thanks to Steven Shanahan for sharing these photos with us.

1.   *The Bion Experiments*, Farrar Straus & Giroux, NY 1983.

Three Mile Island Revisited *

by Mitsuru Katagiri ** and Aileen Smith

Almost four years have passed since the [1978] near meltdown at the Three Mile Island (TMI) nuclear power plant, an event which scared Pennsylvanians and people of neighboring regions in North America. A tremendous amount of investigation has been done by various government agencies and other research groups, often more or less funded with government money. Yet, most of the local people's immediate concerns remain untouched in spite of the fact that this should be a vital subject of research.

In the official reports and analyses, no words were written on the rather unique experiences many people had at the time of the accident and its aftermath. A considerable number of residents complained of a funny metal-like taste in their mouths, a burnt metal-like odor, dryness of the mouth and throat, or a sunburn-like sensation on their skin. There were people who even had irritation and tearing of the eyes or tightness of breath. Nausea and diarrhea also are to be counted among the symptoms occurring at the time.

In addition to the people's own experiences during the days of the accident, there were a number of sudden deaths of adult animals and a rush of stillbirths and newborn deaths among the domestic animals in the vicinity of the plant. Then, through the following months hundreds of cats died from unknown illnesses. And now, three and half years after running into stillbirths and C-sections, a local veterinarian is witnessing a threefold increase of cancer in pets and livestock.

Why have these episodes not been taken up by, or caught the interest of, the country's health experts? Is this another case of the traditional cover-up elaborately maneuvered against the local ranchers' complaints in Utah and Nevada, or the Marshall Islanders' suffering from weapons test fallout? Or is it just a built-in insensitivity of today's health scientists, whose highly systematized methodology is too alien for such bizarre local episodes?

There is, however, one well ascertained fact. A standard argument pervades and is openly spoken about within the American scientific establishment. The argument goes as follows. *"The local farmers' and veterinarians' allegations were scientifically discredited and claims of symptoms by humans should be considered, rather, in the realm of psychology."* This

is a perversion worthy of extensive socio-clinical study, for there is an apparent pathological complexity involved here. Scientists have even failed to consider atmospheric phenomena which many local people observed, and which could have logically been expected to occur due to the radioactive releases.

Becky Mease is a thirty-two year old nurse who works in Pennsylvania's state capital of Harrisburg, and lives in Middletown with her husband Dave and four year old daughter Pam.

Her family, as well as many other families, went through a traumatic series of events during and after the March 28, 1979 accident. In the summer of 1981, Pam was diagnosed as having cataracts in both of her eyes, and the parents were told that the condition was caused by juvenile rheumatoid arthritis. The doctor said he had never seen a child's eyes so inflamed that it scarred down the lenses of the eyes. Becky asked him if that could have anything to do with radiation from TMI. He looked at her and said, *"Becky, I'm not going to say it wouldn't. I'm not going to say it did either. But I'm not going to rule it out."*

The following is an excerpt from an interview with outspoken Becky about her family's experience of the accident. In October 1982, we talked to the Meases at their mobile home which sat about four miles north of the power plant that was still purging radioactive gases into the environment.

Becky Mease's Story

I guess it would have probably been about 9 o'clock when I first started to taste it, because I was driving home from Harrisburg in my car. It was really warm and I had the car windows rolled down. Probably on the expressway somewhere around the Keystone Drive-In. You know where the Harrisburg East Mall is? Probably somewhere around in there, because by the time I got home, it was bad enough that I came in the door and said to Dave, "I have a funny metallic taste in my mouth, really strange." I didn't even associate it with the accident, to tell you the truth.

It was late that Wednesday evening, like 11 o'clock, and we were watching the news. They said everything was under control. I said to Dave, "You know, this is really funny. I have this terrible metallic taste." When I get my teeth filled, you can taste the filings for a while. I said the only other time I had this funny metallic taste was when I was working in the operating room and they'd come in and take a lot of x-rays of the patient who was there for surgery. You're in such a confined area, even though you are behind the lead screen. The x-rays bounce off the walls and the ceiling. And for a couple of days afterwards you'd have this metal taste in your mouth.

* Reprinted from *Kyoto Review*, 16:6-15, 1983, and 17:24-39, 1984. Part II of a series. Part I appeared in *Pulse of the Planet* 3:26-38, 1991; that article includes a comparison between Wilhelm Reich's prior discovery of radiation-induced atmospheric *oranur,* and the unusual biological and atmospheric phenomena described here.

** Mitsuru Katagiri is Dean of Academic Affairs, Kyoto Seika University, 137 Kinoty, Iwakura, Sakyo-ku, Kyoto 606, Japan.

Thursday, it got worse. By Friday we were just all filled up. We couldn't get enough to drink because of this metal taste. We just kept drinking, trying to get rid of it. Five and six times a day, I mean it, I would go in and scrub my teeth because you'd think there would have to be a way that you could get rid of it. But it just wouldn't go away.

And Thursday night. Dave works in the body shop. I said to Dave, "Did you spray some primer today?" "No," he said. 'Cause you know what primer's like, an off-colored red, like a rust color... that they spray on cars. When I drained the water out of the bathtub, there's this rust-colored orangey, rust-colored red around the tub. While we were evacuated, they said (on a national TV news show) that one of the ways that you would know if your water supply had been contaminated is that around sinks and tubs you would see this rust-colored red . That was Thursday night. That was before we even heard anything from the media about how bad it was.

And Pam had been at Joyce's on Wednesday and Friday. And they were outside playing. They were out playing in the grass and 8 months old, she was crawling around. And of course Thursday, they gave the all clear signal, you know, from the accident Wednesday. Thursday they said there was no problem, that everything was under control. So I imagine, that we were outside pretty much on Thursday too.

I was at work Friday morning. Then I heard this on the radio, you know, that there had been another accident. I was crazy.

We evacuated Friday. A friend and I and Pam were parked out on the expressway, waiting for Dave who had gone back to the house to pick up a few things for Pam. We sat out there and we saw this haze out over the area and around Three Mile Island. And you could just see like this thick, heavy... Looked like smog. I don't know if that had anything to do with the accident or not. But it was just a funny orangeish type haze. Had a — this is going to sound trite — had a glow to it, you know what I mean. Not just a normal smoggy haze around here, which when we do have one is usually more blue colored from the steelworks. I know that sounds funny.

We were sitting on the expressway. We got on, then pulled off to the side of the road right where it starts to incline a little bit. And on this inclination, if you look out over there, you could see Three Mile Island, the cooling towers and what-not. It's up, a little bit higher than we sit here (at home). You could see the haze here, but it wasn't as distinguishable as it was when you pulled down the road because we were sitting more down on it. It's like one of the cocktails that you mix, you know, where you get different layers. I'm sure it reached out past us, since we sat down in a little valley right in there. Yeah, you could see it (even here). It was like there was a fire three blocks away, but you couldn't see the fire itself. All you could see was the orangey smoke. But it wasn't as obvious as when we were sitting out there (on the expressway).

I can give you an exact time. That was 4:30 in the afternoon. Because I looked at the clock when we left. It was really kind of funny. I knew that we may never come back, I looked at the clock and I thought, "4:30 in the afternoon...this might be the last time, you know, I'm ever in my own home." It was really, quite a scary thing, to tell the truth. And I knocked on doors. I told people, I said, "Look at the sky." I said, "You can taste it. You must get out of here." Do you remember? A lot of them laughed at me. They said, "You're crazy, you're completely crazy." I think it was more that they felt it didn't mean anything. But then a lot of people did pick up and go. In fact the man across the street came home from Baltimore where he worked, took his wife and left.

And then we went to Ocean City, Maryland. I wanted to get over 250 miles away. I just drove in panic.

About two days later, Pam got violently ill. She had projectile vomiting. Anything we put in her would just come right back out again. She had no means of sustaining any nutrition she took. We started to feed her with an eye dropper, and she couldn't even keep that down. And we took her to the hospital down there (in Ocean City) and they made all kinds of tests, and they said they couldn't find any bacteria, any foreign organisms that could be causing this. So they made us go to a Civil Defense station.

We had an old '66 Pontiac, great big tank of a car. And this was the car we had that was last in here, and they ran the Geiger counter over the car and it just went completely crazy. And they told us to go wash everything down. It went like nuts when it went over my pocketbook too. They looked at us like we were crazy when we asked them to do it. And we explained to them why. (So) they knew where we were from and they just stared at it and said, "Wash everything."

This had to be the middle of the next week like I'd say the Wednesday or Thursday after the accident. 'Cause we got down there early on a Saturday morning. Pam got sick Sunday or Monday.

As a matter of fact, on the receipts they had given me for Pam, they put "Possible to Probable Radiation Sickness." So when I went to the insurance company, you know, GPU's (General Public Utilities, the parent company of the Three Mile Island power station) insurance company, and they said that was absurd. So they tried to call down there and talk to the doctor. Well, I don't know what happened. By this time the doctor had said, "Well we couldn't find anything else, and we considered the area. That was the only other thing. Because the symptoms were identical to what radiation sickness would be."

First it started out with the diarrhea. That afternoon, if you tried to put anything in her stomach, she'd have this projectile vomiting. That went on for three or four days. And the diarrhea, the severe diarrhea, lasted 'til we were home (three weeks later). The other couple was with us. It got to a point that it took four adults to take care of this one child. One person would start the adults to take care of this one child. One person would start the tub water, somebody else would get the rags somebody else would grab a pad, and we had it down to a science. Because it happened so often. Her behind was so raw that we just let it lay on diapers. Didn't even put them on after a couple of days because her rear end looked like...red. Well, it bled. She couldn't... it was... open. You know, after so much of it, it just opened.

(Pam had a) low-grade fever. Nothing extreme. Like a 100 degree - 100.5 degree, which for a child is not very high. And she had the fever more in the morning than at night, for some reason. She became very dry, but that was because she was getting dehydrated. Her lips were cracked. Her cheeks were real red and like flaky.

When I worked in the operating room years ago, I developed a skin rash. They put me through all kinds of allergy tests and nothing would show up; no definite reaction to anything. And I couldn't figure out how all of my life, why at 19 years of age , I would develop this rash when I had never had it before. Well, when we got down to Maryland, my hands and feet were so raw that I had to sit in the tub and soak because I'd walk and my feet would crack. My fingers were cracked the whole way across. The lady that was with us didn't have anything at the time. But three months after the accident happened, she fell and she broke a shoulder, so she went and had an x-ray, and she broke out in a rash all over her body after the x-ray.

Thursday, her husband Dave started getting a headache. And Friday morning he woke up with a terrible sinus condition and his headache got worse to the point where he felt nauseous. Becky had a soreness of the nose, too.

Right after the accident, our noses were sore for a long, long time. You couldn't even stand to touch the outside of it because of this crack right here (between the nostrils). And our gums bled, like maybe a week or so afterwards. They had started to get sore with the taste in the mouth. They got sore, they got purplish. And when you brush your teeth, they'd bleed.

We were playing cards down at the motel in Ocean City, (we were down there for almost three weeks) and this was a while after we went down. This was the last motel we were in. And we were playing cards one morning about 3 o'clock. And I said, "You know, that taste has really finally gone away." And everybody said, "Yeah, it is." And within the next day or so it was gone, but we had it for a good while when we were down there. That's how, for sure, I know that we didn't go down there and it was immediately gone.

When they vented the Krypton (in the summer of 1980), the biggest, the largest purge, we woke up on a Saturday morning. I had sent Pam to Philadelphia to my parents when I knew they were going to purge the Krypton. And then again, we got the metallic taste. So I went first to the Environmental Protection Agency which is down in one of these little plazas in Middletown. I said, "Does anybody in here have it?" Because by this time I'm obsessed, you know. I didn't want to think I was crazy, you know. "Well, we don't. We've never heard of anything like that associated with radiation." I said, "I'm sorry, then you're the one that's crazy." Then I left. Then I went down to the NRC (Nuclear Regulatory Commission) office which is around the corner from the Environmental Protection Agency. I went storming in there and I said, "I taste that metallic taste again! What are you guys doing?" "Now, what's the problem here." And I said, "You cannot bluff me." I said, "I tasted it during the accident, and I taste it again." I said, "It tastes like I either have a mouthful of braces on my teeth, or I just had every tooth in my mouth filled and the fillings are all crumbling, you know." He laughed and he said, "We haven't many complaints of that, but I guess it could cause it." (Becky laughs.)

I guess the most frustrating part is trying to convince people. Because they all want to down-play everything so much and... for the all-mighty dollar. Save the dollar and the heck with everybody else. They'd just try to dismiss these things that people say they feel, they taste. I know there were a lot of people that had the taste; several of the patients that come in our office.

Every time they vent, even times that they didn't make a big deal about it...would do it, and then later say on the news that they purged "x" amount of Krypton or whatever, the patients would say, "I bet they're venting down there again because I have that taste."

I remember Doris, and Carol finally admitted (that they did have the taste). I think what happened, people didn't associate it necessarily with the accident, o.k.? Then when they started to purge, and a lot of people got the same taste back again, then they thought, "Oh, this really may be connected with what's happening." Because the girl at the corner finally said, "Yeah, tastes funny around here again. I bet they're shooting something off at the island." So after a few times of it, people just kind of learned to associate one with the other. At first, as a matter of fact , at first, a lot of people said it's fear. Your mouth is dry because you're scared.

Since the accident, I bet one out of every four of our patients has a sinus condition. And that's not an exaggeration. I would say we have about 350 active patients, I mean patients that come in once or twice a year at least. In fact, one patient has asthma. Summer before last when they would vent, you could tell. She'd be in the very next day for a cortisone injection because her asthma was so bad that she could hardly breathe. Sometimes the doctor would give her adrenaline one day and a couple of days later a small injection of Kenalog, an anti-inflammatory agent, to keep her going. Anybody that was asthmatic, after they'd vent, their asthma would get worse. And I associate all of that with bronchial sinuses.

Right after this (accident) happened and different patients would come in, the doctor would say, "Gee, it's funny. We had them really stabilized on this anti-hypertensive. Now all of a sudden, it's gone whacky." I said, "Well, I told you why." And he'd say, "Now, come on Becky." He wouldn't believe any of this. So I had gotten charts out for him and pointed out everybody that this had happened to. When I gave it to him collectively and showed him, he said, "Maybe we've got something there." I said, "Hold on, look at the sinus conditions that are coming in here." I said, "People that never complained of any of this before are having such terrible sinus headaches that they couldn't even see straight." "Well," he says, "you probably have something there." But to get a doctor to commit themselves...

And last year is the first year since the accident that we had crickets. There were no crickets [for four years]. I'm one that's nitwitted for sound, like in the summer. I like to lay back in bed and go to sleep at night and wait for the crickets and the honeysuckle. That's why I noticed it. I said, "Dave, you know, we don't have any crickets anymore." And last year, come about the first of September, the crickets came back again. The first time since the accident that I had heard them.

THE DAYS AFTER :
BIKINI 1946
THREE MILE ISLAND 1979

In the context that "the public's right to information during the emergency was not well served," the President's Commission on the March 28, 1979 Accident at Three Mile Island wrote:

In considering the handling of information during the nuclear accident, it is vitally important to remember the fear with respect to nuclear energy that exists in many human *beings. The first application of nuclear energy was to atomic bombs which destroyed two major Japanese cities. The fear of radiation has been with us ever since and is made worse by the fact that, unlike floods or tornadoes, we can neither hear nor see nor smell radiation. Therefore, utilities engaged in the operation of nuclear power plants, and news media that may cover a possible nuclear accident, must make extraordinary preparation for the accurate and sensitive handling of information.*

There is a natural conflict between the public's right to know and the need of disaster managers to concentrate on their vital tasks without distractions. There is no simple resolution for this conflict. But significant advance preparation can alleviate the problem. It is our judgment that in this case, neither the utility nor the Nuclear Regulatory Commission (NRC) nor the media were sufficiently prepared to serve the public well.

Implicit is this statement is the mythical dichotomy that prevails in our society: The experts can understand radiation but laymen can't.

"Significant advance preparation" might likely mean teaching people the knowledge of radiation as something that can only be detected by scientific equipment. Such a world of "scientific" language is put against the "ignorance" and fear of the general public. It is a small number of experts against the mass of lay people.

Honestly speaking, don't we become a little confused upon reading this Commission's report? Wasn't the accident brought about in the first place by that "scientific" language? And wasn't that an event where the inability of this approach became overt in catastrophic proportions? How can one rely on this dichotomy of a few experts against the powerless people?

On the contrary, we have even come to think that the laymen's view that radiation is something dreadful and beyond understanding should assume authority. Especially when people have experienced an event on their own, why shouldn't we take their account as something of primal importance? Actually, there was an opportunity for the local residents' voice to be listened to. In May, 1982, a referendum appeared on primary election ballots in three counties neighboring Three Mile Island. It asked whether or not voters favored the restart of TMI Unit One which was not involved in the accident of March 28, 1979.

Voters in the three counties voted overwhelmingly against the restart (by 5-2, 2-1, and 4-3 margins). But the referendum carries no legal weight. Legally it is the NRC that judges whether to reopen the other nuclear reactor on Three Mile Island. It indeed is a strange set up that the NRC is not bound by the results of this referendum. Isn't this the picture image of technocracy?

The technocracy appears in many ways. Scientists in the human and social sciences have been researching this accident. They researched the general public, the people without knowledge, the public who by definition do not have direct decision-making powers regarding this accident. Much of the research was about public awareness. The results of the studies show, for example, that psychosomatic symptoms indicating anxiety were found to be greater near Three Mile Island. Young mothers and women pregnant during the accident were found to be the most concerned and anxious. Looking at the results one can say, "Indeed." The research gave objective measurement to the mothers' fears. In itself that is a worthy insight. The results, elegantly produced, are

the culmination of considerable effort on the part of the social scientist. But, we would like to say a word about this. Even if the experts didn't make their appearance here, isn't this a social reality that is already understood by general common sense? This is not a society in which mothers can express their fear publicly only if it passes through the filter of the experts, the medium of the social scientists. Let us say that we go to some unknown planet and there we study the behavior of beings unknown to us. The beings appear on the monitor screen. They have strange behavioral characteristics. Scientists observe these characteristics and translate them into our planet's language. Three Mile Island is a different case from this. It is we human beings who created the nuclear power plants and the fears of this accident were experienced by us or our neighbors. We speak the same language.

Those social psychological studies that resemble market research in their methods have not helped us understand the society which produced this crisis. At most they ended up in market research of a product called nuclear power. Should this be the function or role of our present day sociology or psychology? So much statistical research has repeatedly bombarded the area, but almost none of them were intended to have sensitivity in picking up the people's own stories as told by them.

———————————

Bill Peters and his wife Darla lived at their home on Big Spring Road in York County, Pennsylvania at the time of the accident. Big Spring Road is located up against an elevated ridge northwest of Three Mile Island. It is a country road that winds through a wooded area and some fields. Many of the houses on it are suburban type homes built by people some of whom work "in town," in Pennsylvania's capital Harrisburg or on the West Shore across the Susquehanna from Harrisburg.

We talked with the Peters at their home 6 miles from the power plant on January 7th and 31st of 1983. Bill, 46 at the time of the accident, owned and operated an auto body shop adjacent to his home. He had been silent about the accident until that past fall when he started to talk publicly about it. Emphasizing that he is an auto-racer and "no sissy," he told us the following:

We heard on the news Wednesday morning (March 28, 1979) that there was a minor mishap or something like that down at Three Mile Island. It was nothing that even concerned us. We kind of even laughed about it.

Thursday, we were in the garage working. It's a large garage and I have large doors that a tractor trailer type truck could back in. Well, my son and I, we were in there working all day on Thursday. We weren't outside. We had the doors open 'cause the weather was warm. We were inside working. We went up about 9:30, 10 o'clock at night and took a shower. I had come out joking. I said, (Laughs) "I got a sunburn!" you know. That was Thursday evening. And we were joking about it. We really didn't think it was anything really that bad. It looked like we got a mild sunburn at the seashore. Anything that was exposed. 'Cause, we had T-shirts on and right where your arms went, it looked like the way you look if you were electric welding. You probably don't know anything about this, but when you electric weld and you don't have yourself covered up, you'd get burnt, you'd get red. It's similar. And this is what you look like.

Friday, I was redder; like you were laying in the sun the first time you go out in the beginning of the year, and you'd get red. That's what it looked like. Friday morning, we were joking. Nobody wanted to say anything... We were getting this hot feeling in the throat. And you were tasting, it tasted like you were burning galvanized steel with a torch, you know, or welding it. This is the kind of taste you had in your mouth. This is exactly what it tastes like. It made you half sick. Sometime in the afternoon on Thursday we had started tasting it. And it kept getting stronger and stronger. My son-in-law, he came home Friday from Hershey and he says to me, "I taste something." My daughter was working at the hospital, and when she came home, said she was tasting it, and they lived right down the road here. And nobody would really admit what they were feeling, 'cause everybody thought we were imagining it. It was nerves or something like this.

Well, you felt hot down in your chest. Friday morning I got up and I had blisters, little bitty white blisters on my lips and in my nose. And then also I got diarrhea real bad. I had it that weekend real bad. And you felt half sick in your stomach, half nauseated. See, that could have been from nerves too. I mean nerves would do that to you. And from that time on, it would seem like I was having trouble with my bowels up to about... oh, man, about two or three months ago, I guess it was. I was having problems. Not as bad as it was then.

Friday, March 30, 1979 most of the local people learned for the first time the seriousness of the trouble at the island. Around 9:30 WHP radio of Harrisburg announced to the area people to get ready for evacuation. Children were ordered to get indoors at local schools. All the windows were shut.

So, we started to leave Friday morning. And we went down the road. And we were talking, and guys on the CB, truck drivers saying there's a lot of people leaving. And they were telling people that anybody that was leaving, evacuating on account of TMI, they better get back and get everything because you might not be coming back. Then I got scared. Then panic started.

So, we turned around and came up. We were planning on going for a couple of days. So we came back up the road, and got back home. I guess it was about 1 o'clock when we started loading all our business records, our trophies, our painting, pictures, any keepsakes we could have. All our tools. We had three truckloads of stuff we left with, pick-up truck loads.

So, while in the process of leaving, the Fairview Township police come down the road, and he hollered, "Bill, get the hell inside." He says, "I mean it. Get inside. Don't breathe this air." He said, "Close your doors and windows." So I waved to him. I said, "Yeah... Keep going. (Laughs) I'm getting out of here. I'm not staying." So we kept loading. This is about 3 o'clock in the afternoon. And this is when, I think, we got the worst of it.

So we left here, it was about 4 o'clock, 4:30. And we went up to my father-in-law's, that's up off the Gettysburg Pike, off of Route 15, outside of Mechanicsburg. We stayed up there Friday night and Saturday during the day. And they started talking on television about evacuation. That's all they talked about on television. He's close to the Turnpike, so I went down to the Turnpike. There were State police down there and there were people working at the toll booths and I said, "How bad is it?" "Well, I'll tell you what. If you can get out of here, you better get." So I went back. We left. It was about 9 o'clock that night.

We got my mother, and a friend of my mother's and mine, and we got my father-in-law, my brother-in-law, my son-in-law, and daughter, and my son. And all of us...we all left. From up there we went down to Virginia. We got in the Virginia line, I guess about 11 o'clock, 1:30 that night. I called this campground and I said, "Would you have any spots available?" They said, "Take a spot." And we got down there. I guess it was about 1 o'clock in the morning when we got there. So this guy says, "Yeah, probably a lot of your friends and neighbors are down there."

When I got up Saturday morning (before they evacuated to Virginal) my lips were burnt more. And they were blistered. I couldn't blow my nose, it was sore. I never had this before.

Sunday morning I was blistered more. You know, how you get sunburn blisters. (But) I never got blisters in the sun. I never did. I never had blisters on my lips before then. Down in your throat was really hot. It's like you couldn't drink enough. My chest; it was like putting hot towels on you, except the heat came from inside. This is something you can't explain. It's just like you were burning up inside. And you just wanted to drink. I don't know if my getting sick with this heart condition was related to the accident, but that burning feeling in the chest was located right over where that valve went wrong.

Now, it didn't affect everybody the way it did me. Now, my son, he was like that. My wife stayed in most of the time. She got a little bit. She could taste it, and got a little hot, but she didn't get like I did.

We were gone seven days. We had a 4 year old male German shepherd. He was healthy when we left. He knew how to take care of himself because we go to Florida every winter normally, and he would stay in the garage. We had food prepared. We had 200 pounds of dog chow, Purina Dog Chow, separated out in boxes. I had ten 5-gallon cans of water that he always used. Same cans he ever used. And, we left a window cracked in the garage, and he had a mattress in the back. When we came back, he was laying on his mattress dead. And his eyes were burnt white. Both eyes were burnt white. He didn't eat any food, hardly any food. He drank a whole 5-gallon can of water, and he threw it up all over the garage. He was dead a lot more than a day. We walked in, we were sick. And you could still taste this like a burning galvanized steel, metal.

Darla: The mobile home (across the street above the present home) was all shut, the windows were shut and everything. When we came home, outside you couldn't taste it. When we opened the door and walked in, then you could taste it.

Bill: It made you almost half sick.

We had five cats out in back. And four of them were lying dead with their eyes burnt out, burnt white, just like they were burnt bad, you know. One cat was in the back of the box, in the cat box back in the corner. And her one eye was burnt. She was blind. She lived six months after that, then she died. There might have been more than that. We had kittens. The three kittens. And they were dead too. We had milk and we had water for the cats, the same as we did with the dog. And it was in a fenced-in area where no other dogs or animals could get in. There was water enough to last them for a month. And there was food enough to last them for a month. It was under a porch where it's protected from the weather.

> **" I was starting to mow, and I started chopping up birds. All kinds of birds. No one kind in particular. I had that (5 ft. hydraulic) bucket ....half full of dead birds...That's when I got scared. And I was scared ever since."**

I washed the garage out. We washed everything out in the mobile home too. She washed the walls down. And we washed all our clothes.

Right about the second or third week of April, I guess it would be., it could be the last week of April, we were going back to work, and you know, you kind of even forget about the whole thing. And I was starting to mow, and I started chopping up birds. All kinds of birds. No one kind in particular. I had that (5 ft. hydraulic) bucket, I would say a quarter to a half full of dead birds that I dumped down over the bank and covered them up back there before I could cut the grass. And that's when I got scared. And I was scared ever since.

That summer, the walnut trees were starting to bud; there were no walnuts on the trees. The leaves left the walnut trees. It looked like winter. That's how it looked all year with the walnut trees, they looked like palm trees. Super big.

There were eight walnut trees in all. None of them had leaves on that summer. Darla thought the leaves came out to about the size of one inch, then stopped and fell off. Bill thought they had just stayed as buds and then fell off. Darla says, the next year's leaves were maybe twice as big. Those that would usually be four inches were eight inches. Six-inch leaves were nearly a foot.

That whole summer (1979) 'til about August there were no flies, no mosquitoes, no nothing up there. You'd be outside eating and there would be no flies. We got other cats and we had our other dog. There were just no flies around, and there was no flies, no mosquitoes, no bugs! (Laughs) It was just unreal. Like 4th of July, you'd be out there eating and there were no flies. You'd have a barbecue.. ..there were no flies. They came back about August. And there were no birds up there at the time either. I mean none.

I've lived here all these years, I don't need those kind of statistics. I mean, maybe it's not TMI. Maybe it's something from the Depot; they were putting chemicals in the air. I don't know what it is around here. But all I know is that I don't like it when you look out the window and you don't see.. I mean it's crazy I know.. but you don't see any birds. There's two birds that come up across here and that's it. And this used to be loaded with birds, 'cause we had birdfeeders around. You go down the road two miles, you'd see all kinds of birds and pheasants and stuff. You go out to my mother's in Lemoyne (an urban area on the West Shore) and she has hundreds of them in her backyard. This is what I don't like. I walk or run a mile every day; down over here, down there where we walk. It's a year and a half since we've been walking down that road and running, and I haven't seen a bird, I haven't seen a pheasant, I haven't seen anything. No rabbits. There's one or two little scrawny squirrels. And that's it.

I had the Audubon Society come over. They were over here on Saturday (January 1983) and they just couldn't believe it. They were out here with their binoculars and looking around. They were out here about two and a half hours. I called them and told them about this. I got tired of it. I wanted to know in my own mind too if I'm over-reacting or something like this.. I mean, if everything is all coincidence.

I had to have this valve put in (the heart). I got the effects I feel from that (accident), but I can't prove it. I had to have the operation in December (1980). In the meantime, the day I came home from the doctor.. when they told me I had to have this it was November 17th.. and we had a real, real good German shepherd dog. She was 6 years old at the time. She died that night. And they said, I don't know why they said.. " we don't know what caused it." People told me that they thought she had cancer, you know. And we took her to the vet and he said her stomach turned, and when they opened her up to do an autopsy it was just stuffed full of.. I don't know if it was cancer or what it was. But this was the same time my valve got bad.

There seemed to be some other people on Big Spring Road who became ill around the same time Bill Peters was diagnosed as having a heart problem. Many of them died in subsequent months. The number of people who had died since that fall of 1980 was rather striking to us. Excluding empty homes and newcomers after the accident, we counted a total of 21 households along the road. Among these 21 households, we learned, eight persons had died within just about one year. Their ages ranged from the 30's to 80's; two of them in their 50's, three of them 60's and one 70's. And at least seven of them turned out to be persons who did not evacuate at the time of the accident. Besides those people who died, we counted three additional cancer patients from the 21 households. It is no doubt natural that this unusual experience of a neighborhood has made the Peters seriously worried.

The NRC guy was here. He stood out here and said, "I was in the center of the plume and the plume was nowhere up near here." He says it was down farther down the road. But he was down the road. How does he know it wasn't up here. Nobody ever checked! He's telling me that I imagined my lips got blistered, I imagined that our dog and cats died, that there was no walnuts on the trees! That this couldn't have happened. And there were no dead birds up there. He says if it was that kind of a thing, you couldn't live here now. He says the people around here couldn't be living here. I say, "Well, not too many are living here right now!" you know.

I'd like to know from somebody.. I mean, what's your personal opinion? If you think I'm foolish, if I'm over, over cautious or overdoing the whole thing. Right now, myself, I don't think there's anything wrong with living here. I mean that's the way I feel in my own mind. You know, I think the damage has been done, if there was a damage, it's been done.

On the other hand, Bill feared that numerous problems could happen at the damaged reactor on the island. And they were still not seeing many birds around. Bill asked us, "What would you do?" Darla: "If you lived here for twenty years, would that situation make you want to leave? Or would you feel it's safe to stay?" We couldn't answer them.

A few weeks after our second interview, they sold their house and moved to Florida. However, they still seem undecided. In a Christmas card we received from them in December 1983, they wrote that they are now planning to live in Florida only half of each year, spending the rest of their time in a new house they are building on Big Spring Road.

We have met many people more or less like the Peters who experienced extraordinary things following the March 28 accident and yet cannot be sure about the meaning of their own experiences. Some are afraid that they might be called psychologically abnormal if they speak up. Others clearly remember odd events but do not feel they are important enough to speak about. Five years, however, might not be enough time for people to have created some effective form of language with which they can integrate their experiences of the accident with their social values — "to prove it" to themselves, thereby replacing the dichotomy that the expert can understand but the layman can't.

Three Mile Island is not an isolated case. Since Hiroshima and Nagasaki there have been other groups of people who encountered radiation hazards. Often it took them many, many years to convince themselves and others about the things that happened to them. One of these groups is the atomic veterans.

It is now common knowledge that tens of thousands of soldiers participated in atmospheric nuclear testing at close distances. Some of these atomic veterans have created an organization called the National Association of Atomic Veterans (NAAV) and are speaking up as victims of nuclear testing. NAAV has been in existence only since 1978. It is not just military secrecy that caused the gap in years between the original events and the voicing of these experiences.

During the NAAV annual convention of 1982, we had the opportunity to speak at length with Anthony Guarisco who is in charge of one of NAAV's major projects, Reconstruction. The veterans are recalling their experiences and reconstructing the events that happened to them with their own hands. Anthony currently suffers from ankylosing spondilitis, a degenerative bone disease in which the spine gradually fuses together. His life today consists of that condition and fighting the Defense Nuclear Agency through working on Reconstruction. Anthony participated in the maneuvers at Bikini in the summer of 1946, when the first and then second nuclear bomb after World War II were exploded. He was a 19 year old sailor at the time. His realizations today do not originate from figures recorded by dosimeters or "information" provided by the government or the media. At the time he was not even issued a dosimeter, and the indication on it could not have possibly taken into account his experience.

The government and experts were not able to do anything regarding the radiation and radioactivity that the bombs spread. Neither were they able to understand or predict what kind of effects this would have on people. And when people began to speak up and say they were affected, the countermeasures the government took were to lie and hide the truth. But what happens to the unforgettable experience of the flash, the shock wave and other overwhelming things which followed? Undoubtedly, these personal experiences form the core of the atomic veterans' understanding and identity of themselves as victims. These men have gone far beyond the myth, that "the experts" can understand radiation but laymen can't.

Thirty-seven years ago at Bikini, Anthony's ship, LST 388, was about ten miles away from the blast when the first bomb was detonated. They were told to face away from the blast, close their eyes and put their arms over their faces. The first thing he was aware of was a reddish brightness within his head.

Within 6 hours they went back into the lagoon to beach the ship again up onto the island which was about one to two miles from the point where the detonation had taken place. They came in from the ocean and went through the target area where 70 target ships had been put up at anchor. They could feel the heat coming off the battleships and cruisers which hadn't sunk but had burnt or twisted superstructures. Besides the burning smell, they noticed a metal-like taste. The air had a grayishness. The sky above was clear, but a gray haze was in the area; it was not a haze from the water. Anthony described the weirdness he noticed in the air.

The air was really different.. It was just like there wasn't anything alive in it. And when I would talk to somebody, my voice sounded kind of flat. Like it didn't carry right. And when somebody would talk to me, it was like I didn't hear his voice right. It was like more shallow or hollow or something. It was like you were inside of a big dome. Like they put a glass dome over you, and there was no movement of the air. The water in the lagoon, for the first time in the months that I had been in that area, it was like a piece of glass. There was no wave to it. And even when we beached up onto the beach, the only action there was what came from our ship.

It tasted to me as if somebody had put some dust in my mouth, like maybe dust from a foundry. Like someplace where they grind a lot of metal. It tasted almost like that. I could taste it to this day. If I think about it.. I can still taste it. It's weird. I never lost it.

And that night, was the first night that I had ever been on that island where the mosquitoes and insects never bothered me. Before that, even with the extensive DDT spraying they

Atomic bomb test in the lagoon at Bilkini atoll.   U.S. Naval Historical Center *would drive you crazy in that place. But that night, not a thing. And it never was the same after that.*

In 24 days, he and the other crew members of the LST again witnessed another nuclear bomb. Two weeks later, they were ordered to go to Kwajalein Island. Anthony Guarisco started getting sick. He said it was like having a severe case of influenza. He had headaches, nausea, throwing up, diarrhea. He was weak. A rash broke out all over. The rash would burn and become itchy a little. Then it would settle down in 15 or 20 minutes. This rash would last a couple of days at a time. He remembered some other people having the same thing and that they thought they had a cold, even though there were times he urinated with blood.

Five or six months later, he was aboard a destroyer. When he would look at the gyro-compass he noticed his vision was blurred, and he began to lose his visual sense of distance. About the same time, his teeth loosened up, especially the ones on the top. A couple of months later, they started to tighten up again but they never got as tight as they once were. From then one he would always make sure he broke a piece of bread before he put it in his mouth.

After being discharged from the Navy, he went to Chicago and got a job as a taxi driver. He started having trouble with his ankles. One day when he woke up he found his feet swollen and they hurt. He was hospitalized for about two weeks.

But after this, almost for ten years he thought he had no serious problems except once in a while he would feel a little rash, just a little twinge of a feeling in his body, like a hot flash; and except for the fact that his back started bothering him, and that his ankles would always feel kind of tender.

Then he started having a growth below his right knee. And then he got seriously sick again and was hospitalized in Kingman, Arizona. They said that there's nothing wrong with him that they could see. But they were concerned about his neck. The diagnosis was ankylosing spondylitis.

Anthony Guarisco told us that for years he had never told his experience of the atomic bombs to others. His father died without Anthony telling him. His wife was the first person he told, and that was eight years ago — about 30 years after his mission to Bikini.

I told her about Bikini, and she just couldn't believe it. That was when I was really starting to have trouble with my back and I was putting things together that maybe, maybe.. it was connected to Bikini. And then even when I was beginning to think that, I'd say, "Oh, no.. that isn't right, because I don't think the government would do that." It was a hard thing for me to accept that because I truly do love my country, to this day I love this country. By the time we were realizing what was happening, we were all systematically going through that latent period which I believe was 15 years, at least for me it was about 12 to 15 years. And then when the process of my degenerative bone condition started, it's so gradual, it's just so gradual that you know, it takes another 12 to 15 years to realize that this has been happening to you for thirty years. *It takes thirty years for it to manifest to the period where you could say, "That is it, this is what bothered me."*

It was midnight when Anthony finished telling us his story. The second day of the convention lay before us. We decided to escort him back to his hotel room. As we walked down the hallway of the Howard Johnson's Motor Lodge towards his room late that night, we told him about what some of the people living near Three Mile Island experienced during the March, 1979 accident. We told him about the metallic taste.

Anthony stopped for a moment, and then with his cane in one hand and his stiff back, he slowly turned his whole body around to look at us and, quietly but startled, said, "Oh.. Is that so."

We had known that our comment would take him by surprise. But unpredicted was the impact his reaction had upon us. For we had before us this man who after thirty years had at last come to grasp the meaning of what had happened to himself. ■

U.S. Naval Institute Reference Library

OROP ISRAEL 1991-1992:
A Cloudbusting Experiment to Restore Wintertime Rains to Israel and the Eastern Mediterranean During an Extended Period of Drought.*

by James DeMeo, Ph.D.**

Background to Israel Cloudbusting Operations: Drought and Water Crisis in the East Mediterranean

During a normal rainy season, from two to four major cyclonic storms may push east across the Mediterranean Sea and make landfall in Israel each month. However, the winter rainy seasons for all years since 1988 had been subnormal. Few cyclonic storms entered the area during these years, and all the nations of the Eastern Mediterranean had been suffering from drought. This, in addition to a lack of adequate water conservation methods in virtually all nations of the area, led to a progressive decline in groundwater reserves and a lowering of the level of Israel's primary reservoir, Lake Kinneret (Sea of Galilee). By mid-January 1991, when a third year of drought was imminent, the level of Lake Kinneret was at a 60-year record low.(1) The lake supplies roughly a third of Israel's agricultural and domestic water needs, the other two thirds coming from groundwater and wells — however, with scanty rains, groundwater had also been rapidly drained by both Israeli and Palestinian farmers. A similar incessant exploitation of remaining groundwater reserves had been under way in neighboring Jordan, Syria and Lebanon. Salt water intrusion was increasingly affecting coastal wells due to overpumping inland, and salt springs threatened to further contaminate sweet water supplies, even in Lake Kinneret. The lake itself was also losing fish stock, due to drying up of lakeshore breeding grounds, and tourists were staying away. To make matters worse, severe dwindling of water supplies in the region promised to fuel regional disputes between Israelis and neighboring Arab states, given the dependence of both upon the limited waters of the lake, and the related groundwater supplies. Newspapers and television commentators painted a grim picture and openly quoted both Arab and Israeli leaders regarding the likelihood of war over dwindling water supplies.(1,2)

The water resource situation had been building to a crisis point over many years, partly due to the drought, but also due to a combination of social factors: population growth in every country of the arid region, increased use of irrigation agriculture, and failure to use existing water resources in a conservative manner. In 1988, for example, drought in the horn of Africa led to a dwindling of water in the Nile River. This brought Lake Nasser nearly to its absolute low red line, after which no more water would have flowed downstream through irrigation canals or into hydroelectric turbines. Some years before, with the Nile river reaching the point of exhaustion, Egypt actually threatened war with the Sudan and also Ethiopia, if either nation went ahead with plans to dam or divert Nile waters upstream. Water diversions in Eastern Turkey and Syria similarly produced hostile reactions from Iraq and Jordan, both of which stood to lose. Water-rights issues also partly underlie the Arab-Israeli conflict. Both sides have attacked water pumping stations allegedly diverting water from their own settlements. Syria once attempted to block the Golan Heights headwaters of the Jordan River, which supplies 25% of Israel's water supplies, and this threat was a factor in the outbreak of the 1967 war. By the end of that war Israel gained control of the Golan Heights, insuring a steady flow of Jordan headwaters. Israel has continued to challenge the Syrian and Lebanese governments over possible diversions of Jordan River water, and all three nations have unsuccessfully attempted to assert authority over the mostly untapped water resources of the Litanni River in Southern Lebanon. Control of water resources has historically been a hot, fighting issue for every nation of this arid region, and the current drought situation had inflamed them all the more.

Regarding this particular drought, rains had been scanty for most of the Eastern Mediterranean, from Cyprus south to Africa, for three years. Strict water rationing had already been established on Cyprus, where domestic water was delivered to most homes for only two hours a day. By early 1991, water delivery on Cyprus was restricted to *two hours per week*.(3)

1. Williams, D.: "Taking a Stroll on the Parched Sea of Galilee", *New York Times*, 15 Jan. 1991.

* Condensed from a *Special Report* of the same title.(8) Previously published (with color photos) in the *Journal of Orgonomy*, 26(2):248-265, Fall/winter 1992.
** Director of Research, Orgone Biophysical Research Laboratory, PO Box 1395, El Cerrito, CA 94530 USA.

Funding for this project was provided by a grant from the Fox Foundation. A heartfelt thanks to Richard J. Fox for his generous support and encouragements. A note of special thanks and appreciation also to the members and friends of the Hellenic Orgonomic Association, who undertook coordinated field work in Greece and Cyprus. Thanks also to various persons in the USA and overseas who helped with crucial logistical support, information, research data, and other small and large helps: Lydia Axelrod, Richard Blasband, Schmuel Cantor, Theirrie Cook, Madeleine Gassner, Pinchas Rimon, Moshe Tal, and Yoash Tsiddon.

2. Goell, Y.: "Mideast Faces Withdrawal Symptoms, Water Shortage", *Jerusalem Post*, International Edition, 5 Nov. 1991; Anon. Editorial, "Peace Talks at Water Level", *Jerusalem Post*, International Edition, 2 Sept. 1991; also as quoted from CNN television report on water issues in the Middle East, Summer 1991.
3. Personal communications with several residents of Cyprus.

In spring of 1991, I was contacted regarding the serious drought situation in Israel and asked what the possibilities were for increasing rains or restoring the normal rainy season to the region by using the technique of cloudbusting. After some preliminary analysis of the situation, the possibility of success in Israel appeared to be high, an assessment based not only on my own past successful experiences with the cloudbuster in the deserts of the American Southwest, but also on the equally positive results of cloudbuster experiments in Israel undertaken by the associates of Dr. Walter Hoppe in the 1960s and 1970s (4), and by Dr. Richard Blasband of the American College of Orgonomy in 1983.(5) Both Hoppe's and Blasband's experiments were followed by significant rainfall increases, although to my knowledge no attempts were made at long-term applications of the technique. Hoppe left Israel in the 1950s to establish a clinic in Germany, while Blasband resides permanently in the USA. Blasband was one of the first individuals in the USA to undertake controlled studies evaluating Reich's biophysical findings (6), and he has led a team of researchers on the issue of cloudbusting. His cloudbusting work in Israel was followed by major rains over all of Israel. Also of significant note were the 1963-1964 cloudbuster tests by Israeli meteorologist Gad Assaf, who observed significant decreases in the 500 mb pressure surface over the region after cloudbusting, as compared to the objective barotropic prediction.(7) These positive experiences by others provided a solid foundation for my feeling that the present drought could be reduced or completely ended through cloudbusting.

After reviewing climate conditions for Israel, it was determined that two attempts would be made to use the cloudbuster, first in November 1991, and second in February 1992. It was hoped that the cloudbuster would complement the natural tendencies towards rain that would take place at the onset of the wintertime rainy period. Based upon prior experiences with the cloudbuster in Greece and California, which have similar "Mediterranean" climate types (winter rainy season, summer dry), it was anticipated that successful cloudbusting in the latter half of November would produce a higher than normal quantity of December rainfall, with beneficial effects that might last into January 1992. The second operation in late February was timed to follow what we anticipated would be the end of any persisting effects from the November cloudbusting. Or, if the November operations were a total failure, February gave a second chance. As everything was being planned from offices in the USA, the actual dates of

operations were determined months in advance of the arrival of the research team in Israel. Other than simple climate data and a few informal, and often contradictory, opinions of meteorologists given in newspapers, there were no certain long term forecasts for the region — the vast majority of long-term forecasts are, in any case, not particularly reliable. Several months before the onset of the winter rainy season, for example, one Israeli forecaster predicted a wetter-than-normal rainy season based upon dusts from the eruption of Mount Pinatubo in the Philippines. However, this same volcano was being cited by forecasters in California, where we lived, to predict a drier-than-normal year. Other forecasters in Israel whom we met with privately were predicting another dry year.

Logistical planning for OROP Israel got underway as early as July 1991, when letters and memoranda were drafted and sent to various sponsors, volunteers and observers of the Israel experiments, outlining how the operations would proceed and the specific results which were anticipated; these are reproduced in the published *Special Report*.(8)

The November 1991 Cloudbusting Operations in Israel: From Drought to Heavy, Repetitive Rainstorms

According to our plans and specifications, a small but powerful cloudbuster was constructed by a private engineer and machine shop in Israel. It was operated manually, mounted on a truck during transportation, but removed and set on the ground during operations. Figure 1 is a photo of this cloudbuster, set up and operating on the shores of Lake Kinneret (Sea of Galilee). It was given the name *Sabra*, which is Hebrew for *native of Israel*. The atmosphere depicted in this photo is representative of the widespread hazy, dorish conditions we observed upon arrival in Israel, on the 12th of November 1991. The horizon is nearly 100% obscured, to the point that mountains on the other side of the lake, only a few kilometers away, can hardly be seen. On that day, Israeli television announced that Lake Kinneret was down to its lowest point in history, only 2 millimeters above the red line, due to drought and heavy water demands. In Figure 1, the low water level is made apparent by the position of the dock at the far right side of the photo.

After our arrival, several days were required for making final preparations for the work, and also to check out the cloudbuster for mechanical problems. By the 15th of November, and prior to any work with the cloudbuster, the Israeli meteorological service announced the onset of an episode of *Sharav* or *Hamsin* winds, which blew from the interior deserts westward, towards the Mediterranean. This was an upsetting problem for us to encounter, as we knew from past experience that such desert winds would work *against* any increase in moisture and rains which the cloudbusting might bring. Indeed, we had specifically planned the first operations for late

4.   Rosen, R.: "Report on Cloudbusting Operations and Rain Fall", unpublished report; anon. "News and Comment: Weather Control in Israel", *Creative Process*, III (1):2, 1963; Greenfield, J.: "Between orgonomy and Jewishness", *Energy and Character*, 7(3):58-59, 1976; Gassner, M.: "Orgonomy in Israel: Yesterday and Today", *Offshoots of Orgonomy*, 10:53-57, Spring 1985.
5.   Blasband, R.: "Summary Report of Orgonomic Weather Control Operations in Israel, 1983", unpublished report.
6.   See the citation list at the end of this document, and the author index for listings in *Bibliography on Orgone Biophysics*, Natural Energy Works, PO Box 864, El Cerrito, CA 94530, USA, 1986.
7.   Personal communication, letter from Gad Assaf to James DeMeo, 12 Feb. 1979.

8.   DeMeo, J.: *OROP Israel 1991-1992: A Cloudbusting Experiment to Restore Wintertime Rains to Israel and the Eastern Mediterranean During an Extended Period of Drought*, Special Report, Orgone Biophysical Research Laboratory, PO Box 1395, El Cerrito, CA, 94530 USA, 1992.

*Figure 1:
Cloudbuster Sabra at work
on the shore of Lake Kinneret (Sea of Galilee), Tiberius, Northern Israel, on
November 17, 1991. Opera-
tions had been underway
for around one hour at the
time this photograph was
taken. Note the heavy dor
layer in the background
horizon and the low level of
water, as compared to the
photo in Figure 3, taken
several months after rains
were restored to the region.*

November with the expectation that, by that date, the desert atmosphere would have naturally moved south, as is the usual case in November. Given the Sharav, we anticipated a delayed response to the cloudbuster. By November 15th, the weather over Israel had developed a hardened, desert-like character, similar to more arid summertime conditions. While it was difficult for us to predict just how responsive the atmosphere would be to the cloudbuster, the presence of the Sharav suggested a delayed response, at best.

Starting late in the evening on the 15th of November, and periodically until November 24th, cloudbuster Sabra was moved and operated from one location in Israel to the next, from Kfar Blum in the north to Eilat in the south, according to the schedule given below. Additional cloudbusting was simultaneously undertaken by members of the Hellenic Orgonomic Association in Greece and on the Island of Cyprus, as coordinated by long distance telephone and directed by myself. The operational plan of action was ambitious and bold, but adequate to the task, and necessary given the severity of the crisis situation being confronted. Weather conditions in Israel and over the Mediterranean were constantly monitored for any signs of change in the weather situation, through a variety of methods:

1. The USA-based WeatherFax company provided timely weather maps, via long-distance fax;

2. The Israeli Meteorological Service at Bet Degan and the Rainfall Augmentation Branch at Ben Gurion Airport provided telephone updates on weather conditions, and on several occasions we visited the facilities to view the satellite images or obtain weather data;

3. We constantly monitored English language weather forecasts from various radio and television stations in the region, notably the BBC broadcasts from Cyprus.

4. Most importantly, through our own network of personal contacts in the region, in Israel, Greece, Crete and Cyprus, we could obtain on-the-spot descriptions of both prevailing weather and orgone-energetic conditions in the atmosphere.

Information gathered from these various sources was correlated on the weather map and integrated with our own observations, as made in the field during the cloudbuster operations. In this manner we were able to develop a reasonably precise and timely picture of then-current weather conditions — from both classical meteorological and orgone-energetic viewpoints — for the entire eastern Mediterranean region.

OROP ISRAEL, OPERATIONS TIMETABLE, 1991:

Nov. 12: Cloudbuster team arrives in Israel. Preparations get underway. Heavy Dor.

Nov. 13-14: Preparations continue. Cloudbuster mounted on rental truck. Sharav winds develop, dorish conditions increase.

Nov. 15: Cloudbuster trucked to Kfar Blum, in northeast Israel. OPERATIONS BEGIN, set up late PM on the Jordan River. Cloudbuster also set into operation on Crete, late PM. Winds respond, but dor infestation is thick.

Nov. 16: Work continues at Jordan River site, Kfar Blum. Dor lessening to west, continues thick to east. Additional small cloudbusters set up in Athens and Thessaloniki, Greece. Orgone (jet) streams active over region.

Nov. 17: Cloudbuster moved from Jordan River site to Lake Kinneret, at Tiberius. Sharav decreasing. Dor significantly less to west. Rains over Greece, with new storms entering central Mediterranean. Cloudbusters in Greece are shut down.

Nov. 18: Operations ended in Tiberius with move to Tel Aviv on the Mediterranean Sea coast. No work undertaken in Israel today; cannot find suitable draw site. Cloudbusting continues in Cyprus.

Nov. 19: Operations resume at noontime in Tel Aviv, at coast. Thick dorish "marine layer" is present. Fog, stratus and light drizzle by late PM. New fronts on weather map. Rains forecast.

Nov. 20: Move from Tel Aviv to Ein Geddi, on the Dead Sea. Set up by late PM. Heavy dor.

Nov. 21: Move from Dead Sea site south to Eilat, on Red Sea. Continuing dor busting. Cyprus work also continues. Significant rain fronts near Italy, slowly moving east.

Nov. 22: Continuing work at Eilat. Storm over Italy slows, is now a "cut-off" low pressure.

Nov. 23: Long drive back to Tel Aviv, set up on Mediterranean Sea. Rains now in Greece, but not Cyprus. Tremendous dor is being mobilized, pushing ahead of storms. All workers in Greece and Cyprus are overworked, dorized, despondent; operations are completely ended in those locations. Only *Sabra* continues operations in Israel. Set up only by late PM in Tel Aviv.

Nov. 24: Operations continue at Tel Aviv until 7:00 PM, when ALL OPERATIONS END. Satellite images indicate strong superimposition developing over eastern Mediterranean, as "cut-off" low migrates slowly eastward, towards Cyprus, Lebanon, Israel.

Nov. 25: Storm in Mediterranean still holding together, with rains in Greece, Turkey, Cyprus.

Nov. 26: More dor pushed into Israel, ahead of approaching storm. Meteorologists still do not forecast any significant rain, as they expect storm to deviate northward.

Rains began falling in Israel on November 27, as the storm arrived at the coast, and rains continued for the next week. Good to heavy rains also fell across Lebanon, Cyprus, and Turkey, ending only around December 7th. A 50-year rainfall record was broken in Israel. It is significant to note this was the very same storm which was previously observed as a Mediterranean weather front near Italy on November 21, and which developed into a "cut-off low" which moved east towards Greece on November 22. That storm even went "retrograde" (temporarily moved westward) before finally moving eastward again towards Crete and Israel. The storm's path was unusually far south as contrasted to the path of other storms throughout the drought period.

This rainfall episode, of November 27 to December 7 is plotted on the Percentage of Normal Precipitation map given in Figure 2.(9) Israel, the West Bank territories, and northwest Jordan received the greatest portion of these rains, from 200 to 400 percent of normal. By December 7, some Israeli and Jordanian regions had received nearly 90% of the normal annual rainfall. The mountains in Turkey, Cyprus, Syria and Lebanon received unexpected heavy snows, and several rivers in the mountains of Cyprus were flowing with water for the first time in years.(9) It was, indeed, a major shift in weather conditions, from the previously droughty and stagnant conditions, to a wet and moving, highly animated atmosphere.

After this major breakthrough of rains, a pulsatory pattern of rainfall was established in the eastern Mediterranean Sea, far beyond anything expected or previously observed by members of the cloudbusting team. A second storm passed through the Eastern Mediterranean, including Israel, after December 8th. By December 15, the level of Lake Kinneret was up 60 cm from the red line! Rains were also still progressing in Turkey, Cyprus, Lebanon, Syria, Jordan, Israel and Egypt. New storms pushed into the area with heavy snow after December 31st; Jerusalem received a record 16" of snow, while 24" fell in Amman Jordan. Additional storms pushed into Israel and across the entire Eastern Mediterranean through January and February 1992 as well, making the planned second phase of operations completely unnecessary.

9. Global Climate Highlights Feature Map, *Weekly Climate Bulletin*, USDOC/NOAA, Washington, D.C., for week ending 7 Dec. 1991.

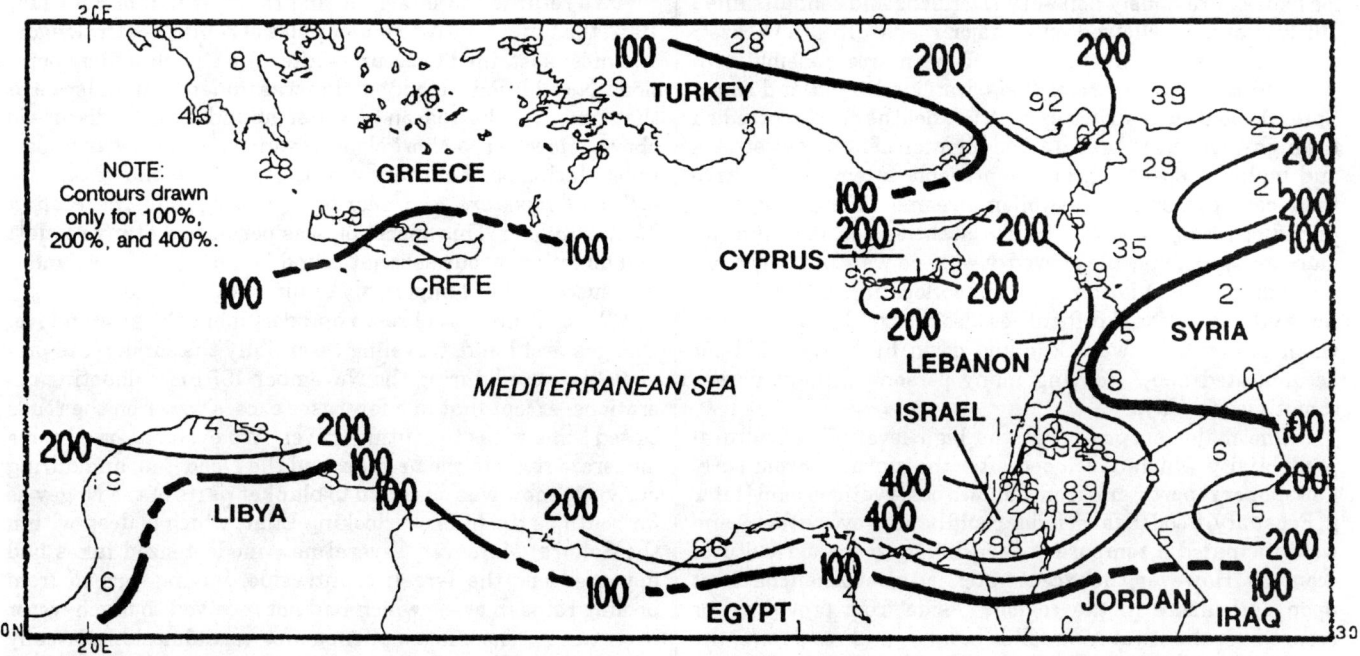

Figure 2: Percentage of Normal Precipitation Map, Eastern Mediterranean, Nov. 27 to Dec. 7, 1991, showing rainfall contours for the first major storm to enter Israel shortly after the onset of cloudbusting operations.(9) This exceptionally heavy rainfall episode began only 10 days after cloudbusting operations were initiated, and only a few days after those operations ended. The storm which brought these rains had developed in the western and central Mediterranean as a "cut-off low" on approximately Nov. 21-22, during the cloudbusting operations. It slowly moved eastward, intensifying as it approached the coast of Israel. Six additional episodes of moderate-to-heavy rainfall entered Israel after this storm, from mid-December through March of 1992, and these are identified on the graph below, in Figure 4.

> " The impression...was of the sudden release of an incredible accumulated atmospheric tension, with an associated shift of climate back towards what probably existed prior to the original desertification of the Saharasian region several thousand years ago. "

While virtually all reservoirs, rivers and lakes of the region would fill to capacity, and the water shortages of the area would be completely wiped away within a few dramatic months, our research team had not anticipated the strength of the storms which subsequently developed in the eastern Mediterranean, nor the exceptional, even historical quantities of rainfall and snow which fell across the area. Indeed, in my 15+ years of working with the cloudbuster in drought and desert regions on three continents, I had never before witnessed such a powerful response to cloudbusting — the impression gained was of the sudden release of an incredible accumulated atmospheric tension, with an associated shift of climate back towards what probably existed prior to the original desertification of the Saharasian region several thousand years ago.

The local populations in most cases celebrated the arrival of those storms, and endured the inconveniences and disruptions of daily life due to heavy rains without complaint; the water was, after all, a badly-needed resource. In some cases, however, people were not well prepared for the magnitude of the temporary weather changes. For example, drainage systems in some cities had been poorly maintained, and were overgrown with brush, while in others, officials had ignored the prior warnings of hydrologists and urban planners, allowing people to build homes in low-lying, flood-prone areas. When the heavy rains came, traffic often came to a stand-still for hours. Previously bone-dry river beds and conduits filled quickly, and overflowed onto major roads. In a few cases, where homes and businesses had been irresponsibly constructed down in dry river beds, water collected and sometimes flooded such structures. A few deaths also occurred on the highways due to the fatal combination of rain-slick streets and highway speeding, or when people attempted to drive their cars through rain-swollen streams. For the general period of rains, however, traffic fatalities declined in a net manner, as most people slowed down, and were possibly more alert due to alleviation of prior suffocating dorish conditions.(10) Additional difficulties also occurred in a few areas when power lines were knocked down by heavy winds or accumulated snow, leaving many persons without power, sometimes for days.

One major surprise was the high level of agricultural productivity which developed after the storms. From early newspaper reports, and from our own observations made later in February, flooded farm fields could be seen everywhere, and we anticipated a temporary devastation to the agricultural economy. However, the excess water had a net beneficial effect upon agriculture in the region. Aside from providing for secure irrigation water supplies in lakes and reservoirs, the excess water flushed away years of accumulated soil salts, replenished subsoil moisture supplies, greened pasturelands, and benefited many crops which had just begun to sprout in the fields. Orchards which had been previously abandoned due to inadequate rains or salinized irrigation waters, and which had died back to leafless twigs and barren stumps, in some cases began to bloom again with unexpected vigor and

fruit production. While some farm animals, chickens and fruit trees were lost to episodes of freezing conditions, the abundance of fruits and vegetables was so great only a few months later that prices in the Israeli markets actually declined by 14.3%, producing a 23-year record drop of -0.4% in the cost-of-living statistics.(11) This price decrease was not due to cheaper agricultural imports, as Israel is a net exporter of fruits and vegetables in the region. However, I do not wish to paint a completely rosy face on these weather changes. In other areas, such as Egypt, Turkey, and Lebanon, greater difficulties were experienced from the winter storms. There was, additionally, a complicating factor in the analysis of these strong storms: a very ambitious Israeli government *cloudseeding* program, employing seeding aircraft and several dozen ground-based seeding generators, was constantly underway during every single storm cycle, even during the heaviest of downpours and flooding. It was ended only in late February, after widespread public protest. While the cloudseeding was not a factor in bringing about the end to drought in the eastern Mediterranean (they were seeding also during drought years), it did appear to contribute significantly to the flooding problems, once the cloudbusting had eliminated the energetic barrier to the Mediterranean storms. These problems, as well as operational details and characteristics of the drought-breaking storms, have been more fully discussed in the *Special Report*.(8)

We returned to Israel during the first half of February 1992, the time of the *fifth* major pulse of rainfall — the longest and most sustained to occur — after the cloudbusting operations. No additional cloudbusting was undertaken in Israel at that time, for the reason of water abundance, as discussed above. However, a short cloudbusting operation was undertaken during our February visit to *slow down and reduce the influx of moisture and energy streaming into the eastern Mediterranean*. This operation was performed at my request and direction by our associates and helpers in Greece, and it was successful in temporarily diminishing the rains.

We continued to observe and document the ground-level changes first hand, traveling essentially the same route previously covered during the November 1991 cloudbusting operations, except that in a few cases excess water on the roads closed some areas to routine travel. We even observed some moderate rains in the area around the Dead Sea, and during our visit, snow was observed to blanket parts of the Negev as far south as the hills overlooking Eilat, which is deep within the Sahara. Moreover, several new modest-sized lakes had appeared on the Israeli countryside, having formed from pooling rains in areas which had not received so much water in centuries. These latter phenomena were almost historically unique, we were told. Besides the spectacle of the rains and storms themselves, the most incredible and remarkable two aspects we observed on this February trip were:

1) The complete absence of any hazy, dorish qualities to the atmosphere. The air was not only cool and crisp to breathe and walk in, but it was absolutely transparent, allowing unrivaled views of surrounding snow-capped mountains and

10. *Jerusalem Report*, 26 December 1991.

11. *Jerusalem Post*, 27 June 1992, p.21.

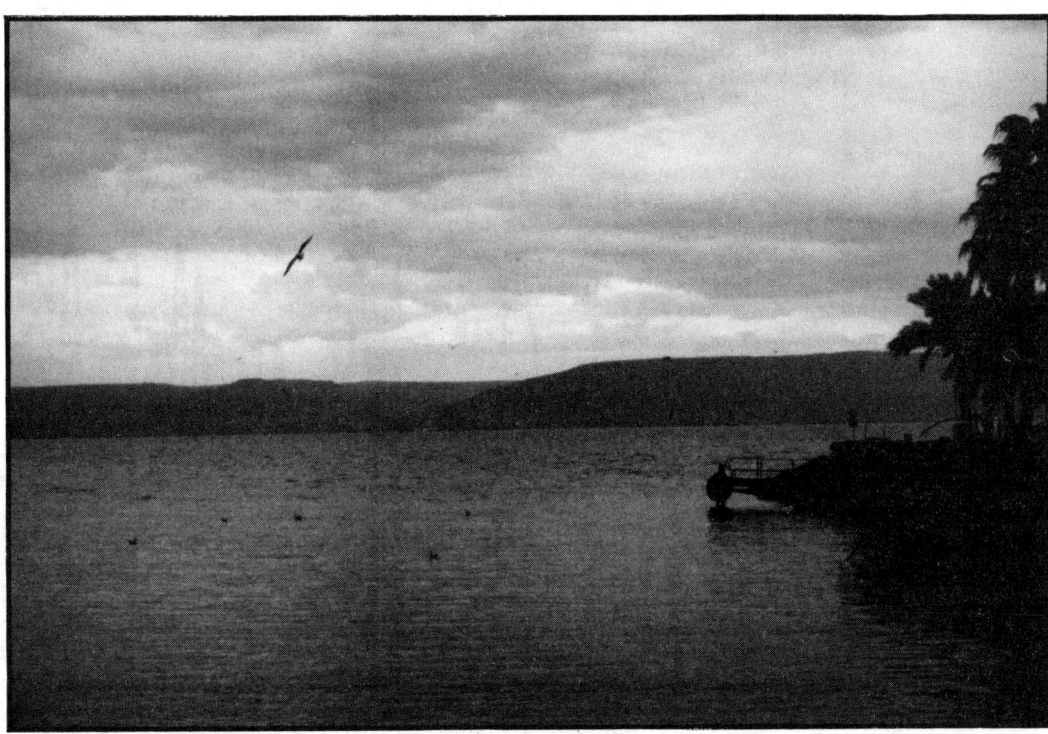

Figure 3:
Lake Kinneret (Sea of Galilee) under sparkling and transparent atmospheric conditions in early February 1992, after several months of good rain. Notice the clearly-observable mountains in the background, the sea birds, the moving environmental conditions, and the increased height of the water level as compared to the conditions in late November, seen in Figure 1.

hills. Figure 3, for example, is a photograph taken in early February 1992, from the same cloudbusting site on Lake Kinneret as given in Figure 1. The difference in the quality of the atmosphere, its greater transparency and crispness, as well as the increased height of water in the lake are immediately apparent, as are the mountains on the other side of the Lake, which could hardly be seen the previous November.

2) The vegetation-barren areas of the Negev Desert, and those regions surrounding the Dead Sea, were in the process of greening up with grasses and blooming with flowers. In particular, formerly dry wadis (river beds) in the desert areas had greened up and bloomed significantly, with new streams and waterfalls on the landscape. These were extraordinary observations, quite rare, and most beautiful to behold (Figure 5). By March 1992, the blooming of flowers and grasses in the formerly-barren areas of the desert were so spectacular that special bus expeditions were being organized by Israeli travel bureaus, so that people could see the highly unusual phenomenon for themselves.

By the time we left Israel on February 12th, the rains had eased up, to everyone's relief. Only one more pulse of rain came into the region after our departure, in late February. By the first of March a total of six major pulses of rainfall, each from five to ten days in duration, had passed through the eastern Mediterranean. Through January and February, with the dramatically increased rainfall and surface water runoff, the level of Lake Kinneret continued to rise dramatically. The precious excess water was being pumped from the Lake into previously depleted groundwater aquifers using every available pump. On February 9th, the Deganya Dam, which controls water flowing from Lake Kinneret south towards the Dead Sea, was opened, allowing even more water to drain away. In spite of the pumping and opening of the dam, by the end of March, Lake Kinneret was brim full. This raised a fear of flooding to the coastal cities around the lake, such as

the resort town of Tiberius, and so an unprecedented decision was made to keep the Deganya Dam open, allowing even more water to flow into the Dead Sea. It was originally believed that the dam would be open only for a few days, but the waters continued to rise so rapidly that the dam remained open for six full weeks, the longest opening period on record. So precious was the water flowing into the lake that planners had delayed the decision to open the dam. Even a special net placed across the opening of the dam, to keep the Lake's fish population from being swept downstream, was removed to allow a more rapid outflow. The dam was finally shut in late March, after a record 6 weeks opening, but pumping out of the lake into groundwater aquifers continued. Flooding of coastal towns did not occur. By May and June, the lake was still receiving such great quantities of surface runoff from surrounding areas, that it was still close to its maximum level. It had proved to be the wettest winter rainy season ever recorded, since record-keeping began at the turn of the century.(12) Figure 4 presents a graph of daily precipitation values for 13 measuring stations in Israel.(13) The period of the November 1991 cloudbusting operations to bring rain and end drought are marked, as is the short cloudbusting operation to reduce rains, undertaken in February in Greece.

Weather over the eastern Mediterranean remained several degrees cooler than the climatological average for the spring and summer months of 1992, and rare late spring and summertime rains swept parts of the region. The following quotations underscore the highly unusual nature of these

12. *Jerusalem Post* Int. Ed., 15 Feb. 92, p.11
13. Data from *Agroclimatological Summary*, Bet Dagan Climate Center, Israel, weekly reports dated October 1991 through March 1992. The 13 weather stations were: Acre Farm, Ein Ha Haresh, Bet Dagan, Negba, Dorot, Besar Farm, Matityahu Farm, Kibbutz Ramat-David, Netiv Ha Lamed Hey, Beersheva, Kefar Blum, Massada, and Tirat Zvi.

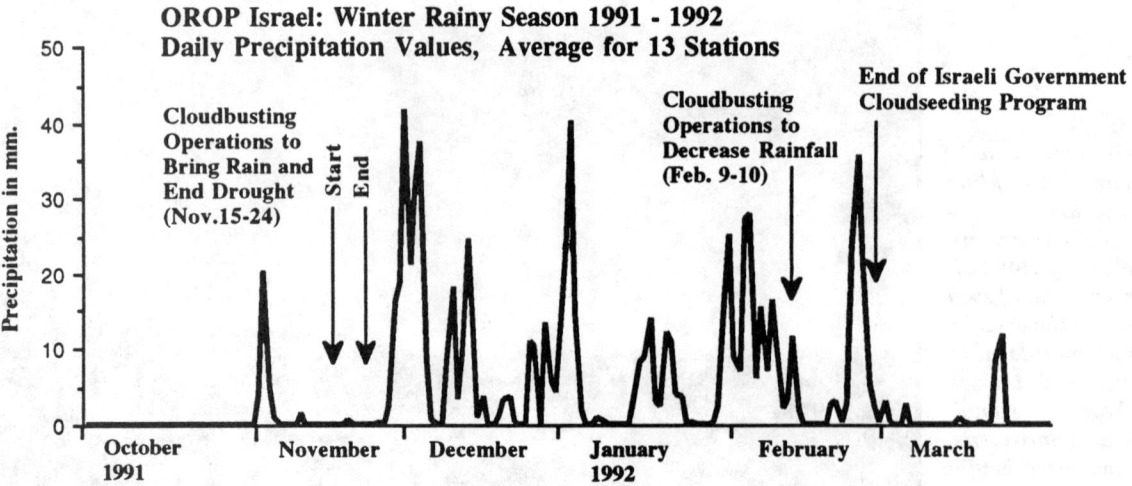

OROP Israel: Winter Rainy Season 1991 - 1992
Daily Precipitation Values, Average for 13 Stations

Cloudbusting
Operations to
Bring Rain and
End Drought
(Nov.15-24)

Start
End

Cloudbusting
Operations to
Decrease Rainfall
(Feb. 9-10)

End of Israeli Government
Cloudseeding Program

Precipitation in mm.

October 1991 — November — December — January 1992 — February — March

Figure 4: Daily Precipitation Values, Average for 13 Stations in Israel, for the period from 1 October 1991 to 31 March 1992. The periods of cloudbusting operations are marked with arrows, and roughly six major pulses of rainfall can be identified on the graph. Only the first of these rainfall episodes, that of Nov. 27 to Dec. 7, is plotted on the map in Figure 2, above.(13)

wintertime rains. Figure 5 shows the highly unusual desert-greening which took place in the harsh environment surrounding the Dead Sea.

Feb. 15: News Report: "Its official. The current and far-from-over winter is the wettest in a century in Jerusalem and Tel Aviv, where there hasn't been so much rain since records were first kept in 1904." 75 cm of snow on Mt. Hermon, the heaviest snowfall in 140 years. "In the Golan Heights, snow is considered a blessing... Mt. Hermon is composed of eroded limestone, which absorbs water into its many crevices. The melting snow trickles down into multi-year reservoirs, which feed the head-

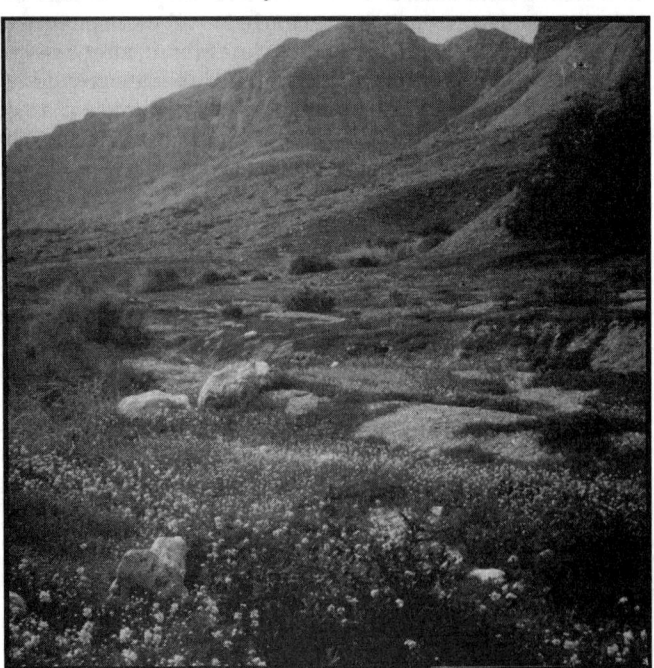

Figure 5: Greening of desert landscapes, in formerly barren, rocky regions; a sea of wildflowers on the edge of the Dead Sea, around 10 February 1992.

waters of the Jordan river, providing the only source of water to the Kinneret during the summer." (*Jerusalem Post* Int. Ed., 15 Feb. 92, p.11)

April 11: News Report: "The hills are alive again. The winter's rains transformed the face of the Judean Desert... Never in all their winters had they seen their familiar pasture so transformed. From the craggy heights where it starts just east of the Judean Hills to the clifftops overlooking the Dead Sea, the desert was carpeted with flowers and grasses. Asher, a veteran guide for the Metzoke Dragot desert tour company, had never seen anything like it either. 'This winter has been unlike any other'." (*Jerusalem Post* Int. Ed., 11 April 92)

June 17: News Report: "Meanwhile, the water level in the Kinneret is remaining at virtually its maximum mark. This is the first time since the national water carrier was opened in 1964 that anybody can remember such a high water level in the Kinneret in the middle of June. The lake yesterday stood at 208.91 meters below sea level, just one centimeter from its maximum high-water mark." (*Jerusalem Post* Int. Ed., June 17-18, 1992)

"As a result of the unusually wet winter, we have had a glorious spring with lush growth everywhere and significant reserves of water both above ground and underground. The Jordan is still extraordinarily high for this time of the year."
(Personal Communication, P. Rimon, Kfar Blum, 19 May 92)

"It's the nicest spring ever in Israel. Flowers are all over the Negev, and people go to look and can't believe it!"
(Personal Communication, L. Axelrod, Tel Aviv, May 92)

POSTSCRIPT, January 1993. News reports from Israel indicate that the following winter rainy season, of 1992-1993, is also an exceptionally wet one for the entire eastern Mediterranean, even though no additional cloudbusting has been undertaken. The drought did not return, and appears to be ended completely for the foreseeable future. ∎

HIV is Not the Cause of AIDS:
A Summary of Current Research Findings

by James DeMeo, Ph.D.*

In the last issue of *Pulse of the Planet* (3:106-108, 1991) I reviewed a book by Michael Fumento, *The Myth of Heterosexual AIDS*. Fumento's book summarized evidence gathered by various scientists to the affect that there never was, nor is, a "Heterosexual AIDS Epidemic" taking place, either in the USA or overseas. Fumento documented how the Centers for Disease Control (CDC) had doctored the epidemiological data, unscientifically "adjusting" it here and there, in order to have it support a previously formulated and "politically correct" conclusion: that everyone, including relatively monogamous heterosexuals, and even non-drug-using heterosexual teenagers, were "at risk for AIDS". Fumento's criticism of this position was attacked even before the ink was dry, and his book was suppressed and sabotaged both by national book distributors, and by his publisher, who came under attack by homosexual activist groups. Fumento himself lost his job, and was subject to harassment and death threats by these same groups, who — as demonstrated in his book — have glaring sex-political agendas and economic motivations.

In this article, I wish to add reinforcing, additional evidence on this same issue by presenting findings developed by Dr. Peter Duesberg, a pioneer in retrovirus research and Professor of Cell Biology at the University of California, in Berkeley. Duesberg is a top-notch scientist who has brought forth important criticism of the HIV hypothesis of AIDS to the podium of science. His research findings came to my attention around 1990, demonstrating that AIDS cannot be caused by HIV (or any other virus) and therefore is, as the term "AIDS" originally implied, an *acquired, non-infectious immune system deficiency*. Duesberg's most recent 77-page paper on the subject appeared in a British research journal (*Pharmac. Ther.*, 55:201-277, 1992), and contains 17 pages of citations to the published scientific and medical literature. This article will summarize some of that evidence, and provide additional historical notes. For detailed citations to the published scientific literature, I refer the reader to the original works of Duesberg and his supporters, listed at the end of this article. If the reader is skeptical of my statements here, they must "go to the source" and review those citations prior to dismissing this summary of criticisms of the official HIV = AIDS propaganda.

To begin, use of the term "AIDS virus" is completely suspended, as it presumes AIDS is an infectious disorder for which a viral causation has been identified. Neither supposition has been proven; both remain hypotheses. The diagnostic terminology "AIDS" does not by itself imply causation; it merely indicates severe immunological break-down and deficiency within an individual. We must also be clear about the differences between the *virus* HIV and the HIV *antibody*; these are not the same thing. This clarifying discipline in terminology is necessary, precisely because so many television and newspaper journalists, and many scientists and science

editors as well, have abandoned rigor in their terminology, critical review, and research.

AIDS remains a problem mainly for individuals engaging in identifiable and preventable high-risk behaviors which, over time, deplete and destroy the immune system. These factors include: promiscuous and unsanitary anal intercourse and anal object-penetration and trauma in association with the party-swinger, bath-house, anonymous-sex lifestyle; the associated or independent chronic use of aphrodisiac sexual stimulants, psychoactive drugs, amphetamines, alcohol, antibiotics and other immune-system depleting substances (legal and illegal); and malnutrition. To this list must be included also the taking of deadly, poisonous medications, such as AZT — a DNA chain terminator — which all by itself will produce the same "wasting" symptoms attributed to AIDS.

I. The Virus HIV

The claim that the virus HIV causes AIDS is *an hypothesis* which is not supported by facts or evidence; an hypothesis which has demonstrated no usefulness for predicting or explaining the epidemiology of AIDS.

A) The advocates of the HIV hypothesis suggest HIV is significantly different from all other viruses in that the presence of *antibody alone* is sufficient to predict the future development of deadly AIDS symptoms. In all other diseases, however, the presence of antibody in the absence of active virus is a clear sign that the individual's immune system has been exposed to the virus, but successfully responded to it, and defeated it. One is considered "immune" for development of the disease, or from further exposure to that infectious agent. With HIV, however, we are asked to suspend this well-known immunological response, and believe that the presence of antibody alone is synonymous to a death sentence.

B) HIV=AIDS advocates counter that the virus goes into "hiding" within certain cells of the body, and remains dormant for many years until such time that something triggers them into activity, after which symptoms appear. However, they fail to demonstrate this part of their hypothesis; the "hiding places" have not been demonstrated to any degree of significance. In fact, this absence of demonstrated "hiding viruses" was a major stumbling-block to the general theory of viral causation of diseases. The viral hypothesis of AIDS likewise suffers from this difficulty.

C) The HIV hypothesis of AIDS does not satisfy Koch's postulates for the identification of a pathogen as the causative agent for a particular disease. These postulates have very successfully guided microbiological research for the last 100 years. They are:

1) The organism must occur in each case of a disease and in amounts sufficient to cause pathological effects;

2) The organism is not found in other diseases; and

3) After isolation and propagation in culture, the organism can induce the disease in an inoculated host. Failure to develop symptoms after inoculation is a sign the organism is not the active agent of the disease.

*   Director of Research, Orgone Biophysical Research Lab, PO Box 1395, El Cerrito, CA 94530

The HIV hypothesis fails on all the above counts. There are many examples of people suffering from AIDS symptoms, but who do not show traces of HIV. There are additionally a large number of people in whom traces of HIV have been identified (virus or antibody), but who remain symptom-free for years. This difficulty has prompted some "HIV Fundamentalists" to assert that HIV is unique in the world of viruses, that Koch's postulates don't apply to HIV. Every year, the group of people identified as "HIV antibody positive" gets larger, partly because of expanded HIV testing programs, but also because so many previously identified antibody-positive people remain alive and healthy. Many have lived over 10 years without developing the predicted AIDS symptoms, or other health problems. And so, the CDC is continually redefining and lengthening the "latency period" for development of AIDS symptoms. For each year that passes, the latency period is extended by around one additional year. Not only does HIV "hide" in the body, it "sleeps". This is, of course, an unscientific attempt to salvage an hypothesis which fails to accurately predict observed pathology or epidemiology.

D) HIV is a difficult and inefficient virus to transmit from one organism to another, either accidentally, by sexual means, or even through deliberate injection. Many attempts have been made to infect primates with AIDS diseases through direct injection of HIV — when so exposed, primates may develop typical antibody responses, but do not sicken and die. Around 150 chimpanzees have been injected with HIV by the National Institute of Health, in a program which began ten years ago, and all are still healthy. Needle-stick injuries in hospitals, where hospital workers are accidentally exposed to HIV-infected blood, also fail to demonstrate any cases of AIDS. The virus simply does not "infect" so easily, and even when it does, produces only the well-known antibody response, but not the symptoms of AIDS.

E) HIV does not readily or quickly kill the t-helper blood cells, which act as its host. It appears to infect those cells only with great difficulty, and once having infected them, lives quietly and uneventfully within those cells for their normal lifetime, without proliferating significantly to other cells and tissues. As Duesberg points out, this is the precise nature of a retrovirus, which does not kill its host cell, and leads a rather quiet existence in the organism. By contrast, viruses which produce deadly symptoms proliferate rapidly, infecting many cell types, and they kill the infected cells, thereby producing acute symptoms. Active virus is spread widely in such a virus-sickened organism and is not difficult to identify or locate. HIV does none of this, and for this reason, Duesberg suggests it is probably a perinatally-transmitted retrovirus which has been within a small percentage of the human race for generations, but without any associated pathology. HIV was observed for the first time only in recent years, because the technology to identify and search for retroviruses was developed in recent years. In a few cases, evidence suggests HIV might produce mild flu-like symptoms within 24-48 hours after infection to a new organism, but after that it has no additional affect upon the individual.

F) Duesberg points to the fact that, before the retrovirus HIV was discovered, and before AIDS was identified and proclaimed as an infectious disorder, people in high risk groups were dying of the same disease symptoms and were diagnosed quite differently. Before AIDS, these same symptoms were diagnosed as candidiasis, tuberculosis, pneumonia, syphilis, anemia, dementia, sarcoma, and other diseases or infections well-known to attending physicians. Today, the diagnosis of "AIDS" is made whenever any of 25 different disease symptoms appear in the presence of active HIV or HIV antibody. If they display symptoms and have traces of HIV in their blood, the physicians says they have "AIDS"; if no traces of HIV are found, they are diagnosed as having one or more of those original 25 diseases. Duesberg points out the incredible potency attributed to this one virus, HIV, which is said to produce such widely varied symptoms — and yet, as discussed above, laboratory studies of HIV suggest its hidden nature, its non-toxicity, and its difficulty of transmission.

G) The HIV hypothesis of AIDS is rooted in the general viral theory of diseases. However, historically, viral theories of disease have generally failed to bring forth either cures or advancements in treatments. This is particularly true for cancer and other degenerative, immunologically-related disorders. Funding for virus research had precipitously declined over the years. But AIDS changed all that. HIV was announced, not at a scientific meeting, but rather at a Washington D.C. press conference. In April 1984, Margaret Heckler, then Secretary of Health and Human Services, announced "The cause of AIDS has been found", and then introduced Dr. Robert Gallo, who presented his "discovery of the AIDS virus" to a story-hungry press. This political event was eventually overshadowed by the fact that Gallo had misrepresented "his" discovery of HIV—in fact, he had acquired his samples of HIV on loan from the real discoverer, Luc Montagnier of the Pasteur Institute in Paris. A prolonged legal battle ensued regarding who would retain lucrative international patent rights to HIV-antibody testing, the so-called "AIDS Tests" which cost from $15 to $50 each. Both the French and American governments got into the legal dispute, backing their respective scientists. Later, in an out-of-court settlement, both Gallo and Montagnier agreed to split the royalties, and a new "official history of the discovery of HIV" was written and distributed, expunged of all unpleasant references to the unethical stealing of ideas, or the legal dispute. Fortunately, Gallo was later exposed and no credible individuals in the scientific community supported the "official history". However, Gallo has never been censured for his unethical conduct; he collects new awards and medals nearly every month, and his laboratory is very-well funded by tax dollars. By contrast, Duesberg, the major vocal critic of the entire shabby affair, has been censored and isolated for his criticisms, his research funding terminated. As hundreds of millions of public dollars are being shoveled into the research laboratories of the HIV=AIDS researchers, and into generally ineffective and counter-productive "safe sex" educational programs, no advancements in the treatment or prevention of AIDS has taken place. The HIV Hypothesis of AIDS has produced no public health benefits, and is a total failure, but it is quite a gravy train for a lot of special interests!

II. Epidemiology of AIDS

As mentioned in my prior review of Fumento's book, there is no epidemiological evidence demonstrating an "AIDS epidemic" is taking place outside of recognized high-risk groups. The high risk groups are certainly suffering badly from very serious *disease symptoms*, but the questions remain: Are the disease symptoms displayed by these groups a product of exposure to HIV infection? Or are they the product of more commonly known infectious diseases, overlapping and opportunistically flourishing within individuals whose behavior, lifestyles, malnutrition and medications have badly weakened them, leaving them exceptionally vulnerable and wasted?

A) Homosexuals and bisexuals engaged in promiscuous "party-swinger" lifestyles remain the largest at-risk group for the AIDS syndrome. Here, one can speak of a group with a collective pool of shared body fluids, suffering from chronic, multiple low-grade infections. Minor epidemics of sexually transmitted diseases (STD's), including syphilis, gonorrhea, and herpes, as well as hepatitis have occurred within the gay communities in the USA. Bowel, bladder and urinary infections related to contamination are common (eg, the "gay bowel syndrome", the "drips", etc.). Chronic exposures to both infectious materials and organisms, and correspondingly high rates of exposure to antibiotic medications, may become an integral part of the gay man's lifestyle, with a great toll upon health and immune system functioning. Even before the discovery of HIV and identification of "AIDS", the bath-house, anonymous-sex lifestyles of gay men, who were increasingly coming "out of the closet" in the larger cities, became a public-health nightmare. And this "lifestyle" includes the concurrent widespread and abundant use of various immune-depleting drugs, both legal and illegal. Interviews with gay men and symptomatic AIDS patients demonstrate the widespread use of cocaine, amphetamine, marijuana, alcohol, sexual stimulants, aphrodisiacs, and amyl or butyl nitrites ("poppers"), often taken in various mixtures. From all of these factors combined, one can readily see how a severely damaged immune system could result. Again, it is an _Acquired_ _I_mmune _D_eficiency _S_yndrome. In particular, Kaposi's sarcoma has been identified as a by-product of nitrite exposure, even before the era of AIDS, and has specifically been linked to the use of the over-the-counter "poppers" — this particular drug is a sphincter dilator, allowing the individual to tolerate the insertion of a fully erect penis, or even another man's fist ("fisting" techniques) into the anus. These vigorous assaults to the passive-receptive homosexual are correlated with tearing of rectal tissue, or even fistulas, all of which further breaks down protective barriers to infection.

B) Illegal injection drug users whose social condition and lifestyle includes frequent bouts with addiction, malnutrition, and the introduction of foreign substances into the bloodstream, are also at risk for immune system depletion. Generally, the life experiences of such addicted people are those of poverty and neglect of personal health and hygiene, and the introduction of foreign substances into the blood stream by injection as a commonplace, every-day affair. Over the years, these groups also suffer and decline immunologically. Duesberg properly points out the incredible naivete of the so-called "clean needle" propaganda programs, which provide antiseptic needles by which unsanitary immune-depleting substances can be injected into the bloodstream. The cocaine, amphetamine or heroin which an addict injects might be harvested by hand in Asia or South America, be packaged and processed in dirt-shacks, thick with insects and soil, and likewise handled in unsanitary conditions by dozens of possibly sick people en-route to the USA, where it is purposefully cut with additional unsanitary materials of various sorts, in back-room or basement laboratories, etc. — but for some reason, we are told that AIDS will be prevented if these people only inject such "junk" with a clean needle! Clearly, there is no science behind such politically-motivated assertions. There are good arguments for assisting drug addicts and decriminalizing illegal drugs, but "combatting HIV infection" is not one of them.

C) HIV-antibody positive individuals may also suffer a health risk from *AIDS medications* routinely administered by physicians uncritical of drug-company propaganda. There are, for example, large numbers of HIV-antibody positive individuals who have for years remained completely free of any symptoms for AIDS or any other significant disease. When treated with medications like AZT, however, these people are observed to sicken and die from "wasting disease" in short order. The question is, do they die from HIV-induced AIDS, or from toxic AZT? Regarding AZT, it was an experimental cancer chemotherapy drug, but was withdrawn from testing and never approved for public use because of toxic side effects. Indeed, *AZT is a DNA-chain terminator which suppresses immune-system functions and produces many of the same symptoms attributed to HIV!* According to Duesberg and his associates, nobody who has been treated with AZT has lived for more than around one year. Worse, no truly controlled studies have ever been performed with AZT, and so nobody knows for certain if the thousands of symptom-free but HIV-antibody positives who took the drug and died, died because of "HIV-induced AIDS" or because of AZT-poisoning. Many of the young people, and various Hollywood celebrities who were paraded on television talk shows, who preached the "safe-sex" and "sex can kill" propaganda to audiences, and who themselves later died from "AIDS" were treated with AZT from the very beginning, even though they showed no signs, or few signs of ill-health at the start of their program of AZT ingestion. Some examples: Arthur Ashe, the heterosexual tennis professional, and Kimberly Bergalis, who supposedly "caught AIDS" from her Florida dentist — Bergalis had only a minor yeast infection at the start of her AZT program. In typical fashion, the news media focused upon and widely broadcast the details of their gradual degeneration and painful deaths, which exhibited all the classic symptoms of AZT poisoning. Meanwhile, Duesberg and other critics of AZT were routinely censored from media exposure, insuring the public heard only good things about AZT and the "progress in treatment of AIDS".

D) Hemophiliacs and immune-suppressed infants are often identified as an "at risk" group for AIDS. But by definition, these are groups who already suffer from major health problems. Hemophiliacs receive multiple intravenous transfusions over the course of the years, repeatedly exposing them to foreign blood products, and other powerful medications may be given. Likewise with immune-suppressed infants, whose mothers were often drug-addicted and malnourished. Not all of these individuals, indeed only a small proportion, may be HIV infected — indeed, the proportion of HIV infections among hemophiliacs or immune-suppressed infants has never been greater than what exists in the general population at large. Additionally, it has not been demonstrated that HIV infections occur more frequently among acutely ill hemophiliacs or immune-suppressed infants than among those not so acutely ill, and who recover to a reasonable state of health. Again, the health problems of such acutely ill hemophiliacs and infants has never been demonstrated to be caused by HIV.

E) Generally, heterosexual promiscuousness has no correlation to AIDS, and itself is not a risk factor. Studies of prostitutes in Nevada brothels, which forbid anal intercourse or the use of drugs, demonstrate the absence of HIV infection or AIDS-like symptoms. However, street prostitutes in large cities, such as New York, are often found to suffer immune system damage, not from sexual promiscuity, but rather from drug usage, malnutrition, and other factors related to life on the streets. Drug usage and associated malnutrition is also the mechanism for immune system depletion among groups whose "risk factor" is often, for lack of information, misidentified as simply "heterosexual HIV transmission". These groups include lower-income inner city populations with higher levels of drug usage, malnutrition, and other immune-damaging correlations. It would be incorrect to say that race, ethnicity, and immigration status play a role in the risk for AIDS, and likewise incorrect that "heterosexual HIV transmission" is the mechanism by which their immune systems became depleted. The "risk factors" borne by some racial minorities and immigrant groups are the same as those identified above for the racial majority of non-immigrants: behavioral, lifestyle, dietary and environmental.

F) The "AIDS epidemic" in the USA and Europe is fundamentally different from that of Africa, giving the appearance of two completely unrelated epidemics. In the USA and Europe, it is primarily males who are affected, either as homosexuals or drug addicts; no other virus or sexually transmitted disease is so selective as this. In the USA and Europe, "AIDS" is identified through disease symptoms long known, observed and recognized by physicians in those nations (plus HIV traces, of course). By contrast, African AIDS is composed of disease symptoms different from those observed in the USA or Europe, but typical of those long observed by physicians in Africa. The African epidemic also afflicts roughly equal numbers of males and females. In the USA and Europe, the epidemic is not primarily affecting the weakest members of society, such as infants and the elderly, who usually are among the first to fall from infectious illness. Rather, HIV is touted as affecting mainly the biologically strongest, young adults in their 20s and 30s. Again, these sex-selective, age-selective, and geographically-skewed epidemiological differences are not characteristic of other microbe-borne diseases.

G) In Africa, there is little money for public health measures, and so the expensive HIV-antibody test, or "AIDS test" is infrequently administered. The diagnosis of "AIDS", as accepted today by the World Health Organization and other public health bodies, is often the mere presentation of symptoms of the various AIDS-correlated diseases. Through such creative book-keeping, vast numbers of people in Africa are said to be dying of unproven and undocumented AIDS. Traditional mortality factors at work in Africa, which have taken a terrible death toll over the centuries (famine, malnutrition, pestilent parasites, infectious organisms, and widespread African STD's,) are ignored in this rush to classify the problem as a malady caused by the single virus HIV. The epidemiology of AIDS in Africa certainly provides no supporting evidence for the HIV hypothesis, and in any case, cannot be used to make any meaningful predictions about the future health of Americans or Europeans.

H) In the USA, deceptive statistical manipulations have inflated the numbers of HIV infected individuals and AIDS deaths. Firstly, the CDC early got into the habit of classifying HIV-positive individuals according to political, and not scientific criteria. For example, immigrants testing positive for HIV often would not acknowledge their homosexuality or illegal drug use. Drug use is a deportable offense for immigrants, and many foreign nations have much stricter social taboos about homosexuality. Therefore, these groups routinely had fewer *reported* homosexuals and drug users, inflating the "unknown" category. When the general public began to associate this "unknown" factor to specific nationalities, prejudice developed, and for social reasons, entire groups were simply reclassified into the "heterosexual HIV transmission" category. Revised figures were then released by the CDC, showing an upward spurt in the numbers "infected with HIV through heterosexual contact." The newspapers would then routinely announce "a dramatic surge in the numbers people infected with AIDS by heterosexual transmission", with extrapolations out to the year 2000 suggesting the entire world would be infected: eg, "everyone is at risk". Only a few journalists, like Fumento, would report the real reasons for the "increase".

I) The definition of what constitutes AIDS has been constantly expanding, with more diseases being added to the list with each passing year. Today, not only are tuberculosis, pneumonia, syphilis, herpes, anemia, dementia, Kaposi's sarcoma, and other long-known diseases often lumped under the banner of AIDS, but problems such as chronic fatigue syndrome and yeast infections are being redefined as having a background in HIV infection. These latter two problems afflict women in high proportions, and their reclassification as "AIDS indicators" have unscientifically inflated the "heterosexual risk" category. When such new disease classifications occur, by magic the numbers of "infected AIDS victims" balloons, all without solid epidemiological evidence or proof. The news media, of course, reports these new figures with the usual drama and lack of critical scrutiny.

J) The correlations between active HIV, HIV antibody and the disease symptoms of the above individuals in the "high risk" groups have never been proven to be more than *spurious*

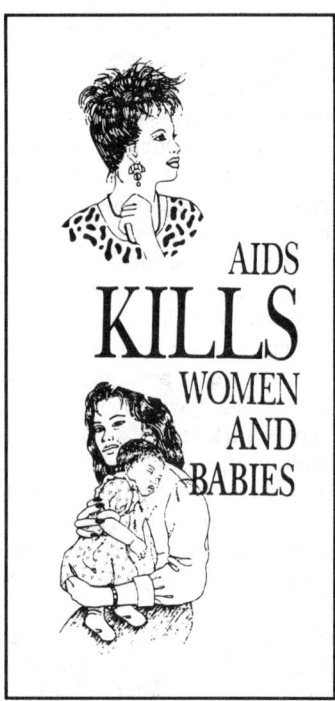

AIDS misinformation pamphlet distributed in the lobby of a California county public health facility; no other prenatal or birth control information besides condoms was displayed.

AIDS KILLS WOMEN AND BABIES

> **"...condoms...shift birth control practices *away from* methods which are under control of the female...they reduce reliance on better methods of birth control, they work to increase unwanted pregnancy...sexual anxiety and displeasure."**

correlations, lacking in attributable causal characteristics. This is true for all the various "AIDS diseases", wrongly attributed to HIV. These same diseases appear in the general population both with and without evidence of HIV exposure. Furthermore, HIV antibody is present among large segments of the overall background population, without evidence of any associated disease pathology — excepting for when these a-symptomatic individuals are scared by the AIDS propaganda machine, into a program of AZT medication. *To prove that HIV is the cause of AIDS, and make HIV=AIDS more than a speculative hypothesis, it would be necessary to show the presence of HIV among patients with AIDS diseases whose personal history did not include: 1) chronic male homosexual activity with associated chronic drug abuse and antibiotic dependency, 2) massive ingestion or injections of legal and illegal drugs, and 3) use of toxic medications, including AZT. Likewise one would have to show that HIV was absent among groups of healthy, a-symptomatic individuals.* In spite of the millions which have been spent on AIDS research, such a study has never been undertaken. Duesberg's arguments have fallen on mostly deaf and stubbornly arrogant ears. And without funding, neither Duesberg nor his supporters could undertake such a controlled study themselves. Research funds today flow only in the direction of the HIV Fundamentalists.

III. The Politics of AIDS

A) The advocates of condom distribution programs have no credible scientific evidence to support the stated goals of their social engineering. Studies on the safety and efficacy of condoms firstly suggest the inability of condoms to prevent the passage of virus-sized particles. This is particularly true for the thinner-walled varieties. In addition, the failure rate of condoms is a major concern not addressed in these programs. Thick walled condoms are better in resisting breakage, but thin-walled varieties are more desired, given the more natural feeling during intercourse. However, thin condoms tend to break more readily, and all condoms tend to reduce sexual pleasure. The consequences of these facts are: there is a lot of compromising involved when condoms are used. They may de-excite a man, causing temporary loss of erection and slippage of the condom; or they may break. The effectiveness of condoms even for birth control is not so good — next to the rhythm method and "withdrawl", condoms are a frequently-cited method of "birth control" employed by women visiting abortion clinics.

Given the absence of evidence to link HIV with AIDS, and the generally poor track record of condoms, a question is raised as to the motivations for the condom propaganda. Two elements come to mind. Firstly, condoms very definitely shift birth control practices *away from* methods which are under control of the female and therefore are more likely to be workable and successful, such as the pill or diaphragm — therefore, to the extent they reduce reliance on better methods of birth control, they work to increase unwanted pregnancy. Condom propaganda and distribution also appear designed to increase sexual anxiety and displeasure. Condom activists

rarely address the associated reduction of sexual pleasure, and generally distribute the devices as part of hysterical "safe sex" educational programs. The safe-sex activists I have come into contact with displayed an arrogant disinterest in any facts or evidence which would conflict with their eagerly-delivered "sex can kill" warnings to schoolchildren.

Fumento points to a growing suspicion among adolescents towards these "sex-educators" — increasingly, schoolchildren simply don't believe them, concluding (properly so) that all the talk about AIDS in schools are big lies designed solely to frighten them out of having sex. A telling fact is that, before AIDS, most of the condom activists had little or no interest in matters of public health or sexual hygiene counseling. Likewise, the overwhelming majority are totally ignorant of, or blatantly hostile towards the findings of the AIDS critics, such as Peter Duesberg. In the San Francisco area, we routinely see more extreme examples of this "condomania": billboards simultaneously promoting condoms and homosexuality — naked-to-the-waist homosexual men kissing or embracing, with a short sentence about "safe sex" below. These public "educational programs", well-funded with tax money or donations from pharmacy companies, studiously avoid any mention of risky immune-depleting behaviors or the effects of poppers or other drugs; they have done little or nothing to slow the incidence of immune-system damage among high-risk groups. AIDS is actually increasing today among younger gay men in large American cities. Concurrent to this increase, we also observe an increasing number of unwanted teenage pregnancies, as the basics of birth control and sexual hygiene education are being displaced by the distinctly sex-negative propaganda of the condom pushers.

B) In the early 1990s, Burroughs-Wellcome Pharmaceutical, the manufacturer of AZT, was shaken under growing criticism of the drug. New studies demonstrated no benefits to AZT users, but documented negative health effects. Burroughs-Wellcome therefore proposed to reduce the dosages — Duesberg's critique of this proposal was, simply, with less poison, the patients would take a bit longer to die. The general response of the Official AIDS Establishment to Duesberg and other AIDS critics can be surmised from the following report, which is fairly typical of the way Big Science treats the voices of dissent:

Dissent at the Berlin AIDS Conference

Despite over 6,000 presentations, nothing useful came out of the IX International Conference on AIDS (Berlin 7-11 June 1993). The prevailing mood was one of despair and confusion.

Hopes placed in Jonas Salk's experimental vaccine, to be given to those already "infected" with HIV, were shattered when his presentation showed that the vaccine did nothing. [Newsday medical writer Laurie Garrett noted that of the 9000 people at the AIDS conference listening to Jonas Salk, some "had cellular telephones and were calling their stockbrokers on Wall Street straight from the hall"]

Some drama was provided by Wellcome Pharmaceutical's frenetic efforts at "damage control", in the wake of the Concorde Trial [showing AZT did not help patients]. Wellcome sponsored satellite symposia, gave free lunches, and published advertisements, but to no avail. The

Concorde researchers stood by their findings — that AZT had no benefits for asymptomatic, HIV-positive individuals — and Wellcome shares continued to fall.

In one way Berlin was a breakthrough. For the first time at an international AIDS conference, there was a presence of AIDS dissidents, who came to Berlin from North and South America, Africa, India, and most European countries. During the week of the conference, the English-language version of Fritz Poppenberg's film, "The AIDS Rebels" was shown. AIDS critics stood outside the conference center (ICC), with signs and leaflets denouncing the "AIDS Lie" and the "rat poison, AZT". On Berlin's Open Channel TV, 9 hours of AIDS-critical programs were aired, produced by Peter Schmidt and Kawi Schneider. For one day, AIDS critics had a table inside the ICC itself.

At the first press conference (6 June), journalists asked conference organizers why no alternative voices were represented — for example, Peter Duesberg. Habermehl said that Duesberg had not submitted an abstract, and that alternative voices were represented by ACT UP [a homosexual activist group]. Journalists were not satisfied, and pointed out that the conference had issued speaking invitations to members of ACT UP and Project Inform, and to the discredited AIDS expert, Robert Gallo.

Later on the 6th, ACT UP held a poorly attended press conference. Most of the 300 ACT UP members had the 950 DM [$600] entrance fee waived by the organizers. Many had travelled to Berlin, staying in hotels with swimming pools, with all expenses paid by Wellcome. An ACT UP representative from London admitted that his group had received L50,000 [$75,000] from Wellcome.

The same day, a television program attacked the "Duesbergians". A representative of the leading AIDS organization, Deutsche AIDS-Hilfe, said that nobody should listen to AIDS critics, and showed a slick new, 30-page pamphlet, "All a Lie? Arguments to AIDS Criticism". Finally, the woman narrator referred to AIDS critics as "rotten eggs" and the camera showed a close up of a splattering egg.

At a press conference on the 7th, representatives of the World Health Organization and the World Bank discussed vast amounts of money being allotted to "AIDS Prevention". For example, $250 million has been lent to Brazil, so that the population can be informed about condoms and "safe" needles.

At a press conference on the 8th, Joan Shenton of Meditel Productions of London, asked: Was it not time to re-appraise the basic AIDS orthodoxies, including alleged heterosexual spread? Martin Delaney of Project Inform, a California group that is funded by Wellcome and other pharmaceutical interests, angrily confronted Shenton and shook her by the wrist. Delaney, who is not a scientist, was a featured conference speaker. Robert Laarhoven, a representative of the Dutch Foundation for Alternative AIDS Research (S.A.A.O) and a journalist for the Dutch magazine CARE, asked Habermehl whether the invitation to Robert Gallo was issued before or after he had been found guilty of "scientific misconduct". Habermehl declined to answer; Gallo became angry, and yelled at a reporter, "Don't bother me!"

Beginning at noon on Wednesday the 9th, Robert Laarhoven set up a literature table, with reprints of Rethinking AIDS. All afternoon the table was a gathering point for AIDS critics. I had expected hostility, but it was just the opposite — people were keenly interested in hearing our ideas.

On Thursday the 10th, the AIDS Empire struck back. Robert Laarhoven was approached by conference officials, police, and a member of the border control. His press pass was confiscated and he was threatened with deportation from Germany for having committed "criminal trespass" — placing copies of Rethinking AIDS on an unauthorized table. Many other groups had put literature on tables in the same area, but the conference officials were not concerned about them. Earlier in the week, the S.A.A.O. had applied for permission to put copies of Rethinking AIDS in the press release area; their request was denied.

In front of the ICC, Christian Joswig and Peter Schmidt were attacked by several dozen members of ACT UP, who destroyed signs, burned leaflets and attempted to destroy camera equipment. Conference officials witnessed these acts, and then ordered the victims of the assault to stay at least 100 meters from the ICC. Officials took no action against the attackers from ACT UP.

Also on the 10th, 100 ACT UP members destroyed a booth belonging to AIDS-Information Switzerland. They chanted obscenities, smashed panels, destroyed displays and chairs, and tore up literature, before covering the remains of the booth with 30 rolls of toilet paper. The Swiss group's sin had been to criticize condoms.

At the final press conference on Friday the 11th, a dozen media people passed out a press release, "Offenses Against Free Speech". I asked Habermehl if he would apologize for those offenses against free speech for which he personally was responsible, and if he would rebuke ACT UP for their violent attacks on the rights of others. He said he would not. The moderator refused to allow other known AIDS critics, like Joan Shenton, to speak.

If future AIDS conferences want to call themselves "trade shows", let them. But if they claim any affinity with science, they had better show a lot more respect for free inquiry.

(John Lauritsen, Rethinking AIDS, 1(7):2, July 1993)

Two years ago, the *Group for the Scientific Reappraisal of the HIV-AIDS Hypothesis* came into existence, as a result of an effort to get the following four-sentence letter published in a number of prominent scientific journals. The letter today has nearly 400 signatories, at least half of which hold advanced degrees (Ph.D., M.D., etc.). To date, the letter has still not been published in those journals:

"It is widely believed by the general public that a retrovirus called HIV causes the group of diseases called AIDS. Many biomedical scientists now question this hypothesis. We propose that a thorough reappraisal of the existing evidence for and against this hypothesis be conducted by a suitable independent group. We further propose that critical epidemiological studies be devised and undertaken."

Group for the Scientific Reappraisal of the HIV/AIDS Hypothesis.
2040 Polk Street, #321
San Francisco, CA 94104

Duesberg and his supporters, who today number in the hundreds, have typically been banished from official conferences and symposia on the AIDS question, particularly in the USA. Major scientific journals, such as *Science* and *Nature*, have published seriously flawed studies purporting to demonstrate that illegal drugs are not the causative factor for AIDS, alongside of condemnations of Duesberg and other AIDS critics. The editors of these journals have often refused to print pointed criticisms of the studies which demonstrate where they are flawed, and likewise refused to allow letters of rebuttal against the personal attacks. (The 11 March 1993 Commentary in *Nature*, by Ascher, et al., "Does Drug Use

Cause AIDS?", and associated 16 April 1993 Editorial in *Science* are cases in point -- both were seriously flawed and attacked Duesberg by name, but no published critique or rebuttal was allowed.) It is Big Science at work, in an unholy collusion with Big Medicine, Big Government, and Big Media. Some HIV Fundamentalists have even called for the forced silencing of AIDS critics, on the grounds that they are "confusing the public" and "causing deaths" by getting in the way of the AZT medication, HIV vaccination, and safe-sex programs. While these same conference gatherings and research journals will invite comments from homosexual activist groups, and spotlight the discredited Gallo and other HIV/AZT millionaires, Duesberg and the AIDS critics are forbidden access to the podium, and threatened or physically attacked.

Fortunately, there is growing public knowledge of the circus atmosphere, pseudo-science and vested interests at work behind the HIV hypothesis of AIDS, and the public has generally become better educated and skeptical of the new poisons being peddled by doctors and pharmacy companies. A new AIDS criticism group, "Project AIDS International" has been formed, apparently for the main purpose to bring criminal charges and class-action lawsuits against officials of Burroughs-Wellcome Pharmaceutical. The allegation is made they knew AZT was both highly toxic and worthless against AIDS, and continued to promote it even after thousands of people began to sicken and die from the treatment.

The above facts are testimony to the general death of science and critical science journalism in the USA. Where is the independent news media? Where are the independent scientists and scientific scholarly societies? The answer is, they are all emotionally contracted and too intellectually incapacitated to effectively deal with this burning sexual issue, or they have been bought off, threatened into silence, or fired from positions of public influence. A deep culture-wide emotional anxiety and paralyzing anti-sexual hysteria has silenced most people on the AIDS issue — they simply parrot what comes through the television or newspapers. A cadre of loud and vocal anti-sexual zealots now dominates the discussion. Their political agendas have been publicized, and sometimes written into law. Nearly everyone, from right-wing conservatives to left-wing radicals, has fallen lock-step into brainless nodding approval of the public anti-heterosexual brainwash. Also, there is a tight collusion of moneyed special interests controlling academe, medicine, politics, and the press. Dissenters to the "Official Truth" that "HIV causes AIDS" have been effectively silenced. This collusion of emotional and economic factors have dovetailed to barricade rational public discussion and debate on the issue.

The Big Lie of the "heterosexual AIDS epidemic" satisfies the most deep emotional fears and hatreds of gratified genitality in the average individual. The emotional component is the only factor which explains how and why this disastrous lie has become a new Official Truth, why to question it publicly is to risk social isolation or attack from "believers" — and why the mythology has worked to reinforce the most pleasure-fearing and censorious aspects of human personal relationships and social contact. "AIDS" was the emotional plague's deceitful response to an un-focused and chaotic, but *potentially* healthy sexual revolution, and it has been a most effective deceit, of sweeping, global proportions.

There is no valid scientific proof or even suggestive evidence to support the huge public investment in the hypothesis that HIV causes AIDS. As Duesberg says, the HIV hypothesis fails to explain or predict the epidemiology and pathology of AIDS. It is a failed hypothesis which has cost thousands of lives, and billions of wasted dollars. The HIV hypothesis of AIDS is not supported by science, but is rather maintained by big money pharmacy investments, by political hardball tactics from groups with clear political agendas, and by a lot of bad science, often undertaken by those who profited handsomely from the carnage. The campaign to inform the public that "HIV causes AIDS" and "everyone is at risk for AIDS" is, bluntly, a Big Lie, and should be openly exposed and corrected at every possible level. ∎

REFERENCES

- Adams, Jad: *AIDS, The HIV Myth*, St. Martin's Press, NY, 1989.
- Bethel, Tom: "The Cure that Failed: Did the AIDS lobby know what it was doing when it pressed the government to approve AZT?" *National Review*, 10 May 1993, pp.33-35.
- Duesberg, Peter: "AIDS Acquired by Drug Consumption and Other Non-Contagious Risk Factors", *Pharmac. Ther.* 55:201-277, 1992.
- Fumento, Michael: *The Myth of Heterosexual AIDS: How a Tragedy has been Distorted by Media and Partisan Politics*, Basic Books, NY 1990.
- Fumento, M.: "Teenaids, the Latest HIV Fib", *New Republic*, 10 August 1992, pp.17-19.
- Rappoport, J.: *AIDS, Inc.: Scandal of the Century*, Human Energy Press, San Bruno, CA, 1988.
- Root-Bernstein, Robert: *Rethinking AIDS: The Tragic Cost of Premature Consensus*, Free Press, NY, 1993.
- Harman, Robert: "The Emotional Plague and the AIDS Hysteria," *Journal of Orgonomy*, 22(2):173-195, Nov. 1988.

Postscript: Controlled scientific studies have recently been undertaken on the Western Blot and ELISA "AIDS tests", demonstrating a very high rate of false-positives among both sick and healthy people who have never been exposed to HIV, but who have, instead, previously experienced general *immunological stress* of various sorts. These "AIDS tests" often yield a "positive" result if the tested individual has previously been exposed to other viruses and microbes, foreign blood proteins, and/or excessive toxic illegal or legal drugs, including excessive antibiotics. These new studies further prove that *AIDS is not an infectious disorder and has little or no relationship to the virus HIV.* See articles in: *Biotechnology*, 11:696-707, June 1993; and *J. Infectious Diseases*, 169:296-304, Feb. 1994.

Information & Publication Sources:
- *Group for the Scientific Reappraisal of the HIV/AIDS Hypothesis*, 2040 Polk St., #321, San Francisco, CA 94104, FAX 415-775-1984. Reprints of Dr. Duesberg's paper, cited above, are available for $15. This Group also publishes the monthly newsletter *Rethinking AIDS*, $20 yearly.
- *HEAL: Health Education Aids Liaison*, PO Box 1103, Old Chelsea Station, New York, NY 10113, Tel: 800/ 410-4325.
- *Project AIDS International*, 8033 Sunset Blvd., #2640, Los Angeles, CA 90046. FAX 213-857-0334. Educational work on the AZT scandal.
- *Natural Energy Works*, PO Box 864, El Cerrito, CA 94530. Books and videos on AIDS mythology.

In 1994, Dr. Peter Duesberg will have his own book published on the AIDS question and the political reactions to his work.

Anti-Constitutional Activities and Abuse of Police Power by the U.S. Food and Drug Administration and Other Federal Agencies

by James DeMeo, Ph.D.*

In recent years, there has been an upsurge of police activities in the USA, the nature of which most Americans would more readily associate with repressive dictatorships. We Americans have been educated to believe that democracy, due process, assumed innocence-until-proven-guilt, and Constitutional protections against illegal search and seizure are the laws of the land. On paper, these protections are there; but in reality, these basic Constitutional rights and freedoms have been gradually and steadily eroded away by new laws, judicial rulings, and bureaucratic decrees. One of the lesser-known but more significant leaders of this assault on American freedom has been the US Food and Drug Administration (FDA).

Background to FDA Police-State Activities

As early as the 1950s, the FDA was engaged in aggressively spying on health-care providers who employed medications and approaches which were not considered "acceptable" by mainstream orthodox medicine. Notably, it was and has been the American Medical Association (AMA) which has dominated ideas within the medical community, as well as nearly all legislation related to health care. If the AMA dislikes a particular health care approach, they work to banish such methods within hospitals, and to suspend the medical licenses of any doctor who employs them. They have often been able to rely upon state licensing boards and legislatures, and even the US Congress, to pass laws outlawing natural healing methods and the non-MD practitioner (such as midwives, herbalists or acupuncturists). Failing here, the AMA and friends in the drug industry have relied upon their allies in the FDA to aggressively assault the advocates of natural treatment methods.

Many new health care discoveries have thereby remained "underground", never being allowed to flower productively in the light of day. Inexpensive, non-toxic and unpatentable natural healing methods have never been seriously or honestly evaluated by the AMA-FDA-pharmaceutical-dominated medical establishment. Instead, policemen have been called in to simply arrest and jail the offending practitioners, seize their files, mailing lists and other property, burn their books, and otherwise trample the US Constitution into the dirt.

—Dr. Royal Raymond Rife was crushed when his new microscopical techniques demonstrated the pleomorphic nature of viruses and bacterium.(1)

—Harry Hoxsey's successful herbal formulas for the treatment of cancer, used in dozens of clinics across the USA in the 1950s, were stomped into oblivion by an enraged FDA, after Hoxsey refused to sell his formula to Dr. Morris Fishbein, then president of the AMA.(2)

—Max Gerson's dietary immune-boosting treatments for degenerative disease were criminalized by the FDA at the very time he published scientific evidence and clinical reports on their effectiveness.(3)

Today, none of these treatments are *openly* used in the USA, but only in clinics south of the Mexican-California border. The FDA also attempted to ban and burn Rodale's *Organic Farming and Gardening* magazine as "advertising literature" not covered by the First Amendment; many vitamin companies were advertising in it, and Rodale claimed — to the annoyance of the chemical fertilizer and drug companies — that the vitamin and nutrient values of plants were increased by use of natural-organic farming methods, thereby improving human health. The FDA lost that case, but Rodale was forced to spend a fortune in legal fees to defend his right of free speech.

Probably the most significant and blatant example of FDA aggression and anti-Constitutional activity is the case of Dr. Wilhelm Reich. The Reich Legal Case surpassed the Scopes Monkey Trial in legal and historical significance, as it clearly marked the willingness of the US courts to condone the censoring of speech, the burning of books, the unreasonable seizure of property, and the willful ignoring of written documents presented to judges. Reich may not have been what one could call a "model legal client", but the willingness of the US courts to incarcerate him, burn his books, and in general treat him like a criminal, demonstrated how far legal technicalities and procedural issues had replaced the *original intent* and *spirit of the law*. Certainly, all the various judges who reviewed Reich's case and ruled against him, from the local and district court judges to the US Supreme Court judges, *knew they were agreeing to censorship of speech and to the burning of books.*

The judges also demonstrated no interest in any of the technical/procedural issues which would have weighed in Reich's favor, such as the fact that the prosecutor was himself Reich's former personal attorney, or that Reich had submitted documents (his "Response to Ignorance") to the lower courts which were, essentially, thrown into the trash. Indeed, the deep significance the courts gave to procedural technicalities in his case was exclusively to those matters which worked *against* Reich. Clearly, they were out to "get Reich", no matter what. On the basis of legal technicalities, his many books and research journals were burned in incinerators by court order, and both Reich and a co-worker, Dr. Michael Silvert, were sentenced to over a year in prison. Reich died in prison, while Silvert committed suicide shortly afterward. Other FDA violations at the time included the warrantless invasions and searches of the homes of people peripherally associated with

---

1. Barry Lynes, *The Cancer Cure that Worked: Fifty Years of Suppression*, Marcus Books, Ontario, 1987.

* Director of Research, Orgone Biophysical Research Laboratory, PO Box 1395, El Cerrito, CA 94530.

2. Ken Ausubel, *Hoxsey: How Healing Becomes a Crime*, Mystic Fire Video, Malibu, California, 1987.

3. Max Gerson, *A Cancer Therapy: Results of 50 Cases*, Gerson Institute, Bonita, California 1990.

Reich. In one such case, a home was searched and Reich's books were confiscated from private bookshelves. School teachers and doctors who worked with Reich were fired from their jobs, in a manner reminiscent of the more purely political repressions of that time, the McCarthy period.

The Reich Legal Case has been discussed in detail elsewhere,(4) and so will not be repeated here, but its importance lies in the fact that the FDA was able to commit severe anti-Constitutional actions, indeed, *murderous* actions, against an internationally-known and respected scientist without so much as a peep of protest from the various academic "scholarly societies", "civil liberties" or "free speech" groups, etc. This lack of significant social protest was an encouragement and green light of approval to nearly every federal agency wanting to shape public or private behavior to one or another government policy. While blatant *political repression of politicians* has declined over the years, with increasing protections afforded to *political speech*, the political repression of unorthodox scientific discoveries related to health and sickness has not declined at all. In fact, *repression of non-political speech has increased*, especially when it is linked with concrete marketplace activities which conflict with official government policies or big business monopolies.

In the years since Reich's death, Constitutional protections against illegal seizure of property, assumed innocence-until-proven-guilt, and due process of law have been flagrantly violated and trampled into the dirt by the FDA leaders and field agents, who are increasingly teaming up with other arms of the federal bureaucracy to increase their power. Numerous medical pioneers have been assaulted and personally destroyed, in a manner so blatant and aggressive it makes Reich's treatment by the FDA appear almost gentle by comparison. The FDA's police-state activities are taking place all across the USA, but little of it is being reported in the mainstream media — or if so, generally with biased justifications given for the FDA actions, that "the FDA is combatting health fraud" or "medical quackery". Here, the reader will be informed of more recent assaults by the FDA against the natural health movement.

The AMA-FDA-Pharmaceutical Cartel

Increasingly, health care decisions in the USA are being mandated by small cadres of "specialists" who decide whether this or that medication will be made legal and available to the American public. Where scientific evidence once was the criteria for extended use of a new medication, such decisions are today being made more on the basis of the profits which can be made from a particular medication — too many of the top physician-bureaucrats working in the FDA, National Institutes of Health (NIH), American Cancer Society (ACS), etc. are themselves often drug-company millionaires, with personal stock holdings or investments in the companies whom they

regulate. Drug companies provide large sums to political campaigns so as to definitively influence legislation, and to various medical institutes, to "research" their products. Their full-page color advertisements for new drugs in medical journals essentially pay for those publications. Pharmaceutical companies are one of the highest profit margin industries in the U.S. who do not have to account for the often extreme prices they charge - higher than anywhere else in the world. Drug company money plays a powerful role in shaping health policy, the approval process for new patent drugs, and publishing (or censoring) research findings about the effectiveness or side-effects of those drugs.

Additionally, nearly every major medical organization and medical society in the USA, to include many governmental agencies like the FDA, NIH, and ACS, expend significant sums of money each year to fund unfactual, even slanderous propaganda against relatively inexpensive natural healing methods, which might otherwise substitute for the expensive and often toxic medications and surgical procedures pushed by the medical-pharmaceutical cartel. "Quack-busting" groups, such as the National Council Against Health Fraud, team up with various medical societies, licensing boards, and the FDA to efficiently snoop upon and "police" the medical community, making sure that only the most orthodox medical treatments will prevail. Word quickly spreads, through the medical gossip system, if a doctor does not prescribe the usual drugs or treatments. Any doctor employing vitamins, herbs, nutrition, energetic medicine (homeopathy, orgone accumulator), chelation therapy, or any other progressive, innovative or unorthodox treatment can expect great pressure from these groups, up to and including visits from aggressive, gun-waving "health-care" policemen.

Similar, or even more aggressive treatment is meted out to midwives, herbalists or to other health care providers who lack the MD degree, and employ methods which compete with the entire lucrative doctor-hospital system. A doctor or midwife who is today labeled a "quack" in the newspapers can expect as bad and unfair a treatment as did a "witch" in the Middle Ages. The quite telling consequences of this anti-scientific pogrom against the new and unorthodox health research findings are that a higher percentage of people are dying from degenerative illness today than in the 1950s, while cancer cure and survival rates are essentially unchanged from when the multi-billion dollar orthodox "war" against cancer was initiated.(5) Like the "wars" against crime, poverty and drugs, the "war against cancer" has been a huge, expensive flop, benefiting only the over-bloated cancer industry — today more people are engaged in the "treatment" of cancer than those who die from it in a given year. Obviously, the attitude that "war" is necessary to solve a social or health-care problem is itself part of the problem, and not part of the solution.

Increasing Use of SWAT Teams and Seizure Laws

One clear consequence of the widespread "war" approach to social problems has been the growing use of police Special

---

4.   Jerome Greenfield, *Wilhelm Reich Versus the USA*, W.W. Norton, NY 1979; Lois Wyvell, "The Jailing of a Great Scientist in the USA", *Pulse of the Planet* #4, 1993; James DeMeo, "Author's Preface", *The Orgone Accumulator Handbook*, Natural Energy Works, El Cerrito, CA 1989

5.   J. C. Bailar & E.M. Smith: "Progress Against Cancer?", *New England Journal of Medicine*, 314:1226-1232, 8 May 1986.

Weapons and Tactical (SWAT) teams to enforce bureaucratic decrees by federal agencies, even those agencies one normally does not associate with "law enforcement". In recent years, the farm journal *Acres, USA* (6) has exposed numerous examples where individual farmers, who were making legal challenges to US Department of Agriculture (USDA) rulings about crop quotas or loan-security arrangements, had their homes, land and farm equipment *seized* at gun-point by the USDA. A few farmers have been shot dead. Legal and constitutionally-protected citizen opposition to federal government policies has been met by increasingly aggressive and militant reactions by policemen, armed with machine guns, flak jackets, concussion grenades, and even tanks — the message is, *Obey, Or Else!* The USDA, Bureau of Alcohol, Tobacco and Firearms (BATF), Drug Enforcement Agency (DEA), and US Forest Service (USFS) have all developed well-armed "security forces" which flagrantly defy the Constitutional ban against the use of military forces for domestic law enforcement. Hundreds of millions of dollars in property, to include homes, automobiles, cash in bank accounts, and other personal and business property has been seized by these various agencies, who often work in coordination with the FBI, Internal Revenue Service (IRS), US Customs Service, and US Postal Service.

The various "War on Drugs" seizure laws have allowed these various government agencies to seize the property or cash money of any citizen, based upon *mere suspicion* that the property or money was acquired from sales of illegal drugs. A citizen whose property which has been seized must post a significant cash bond to the courts (a percentage of the value of the seized goods), and then go to court and "prove their innocence" to the judge before the property is returned. Failing to do so, the "law enforcement" agencies which made the seizure are then allowed to auction off the seized properties and keep a percentage of the money for "internal use"! For example, there was the case where a large fishing boat was seized by the DEA during a "routine" US Coast Guard inspection, when one of the deck hands was found to have marijuana cigarettes in his pocket. The seizure of the expensive fishing boat destroyed the life's work of the boat-owner captain, who was held responsible for the concealed actions of one employee.

Then there was the case of Willie Jones, a hard-working gardener who paid cash for an airline ticket, not knowing that airline ticket agents often provide "tips" to policemen about travelers who pay for tickets with cash. The assumption is that anybody buying an airline ticket with cash is a drug dealer! The cops confronted Jones, and confiscated $9,600 he was carrying for purchase of shrubbery for his landscaping business — he was flying to a gardening convention to purchase plants for next year's work. Although the cops "arrested" his cash, Jones was never charged with anything, and he did not have additional money to go to the courts to "prove his innocence". So the cops just kept the money. Jones observed "I didn't know it was against the law for a 42-year old black man to have money in his pocket!"

In another remarkable case, two gardening supply stores, along with inventories and bank accounts, were seized by DEA agents after an employee advised undercover agents how grow-lights might be used for indoor cultivation. Marijuana was implied, but never mentioned explicitly — but so what! The DEA felt the selling of *grow-lights* was contributing to the drug trade, so they raided the stores. Now, this is, purely *legal stealing,* where the activities of the cash-greedy federal agents

6. *Acres USA*, PO Box 9547, Kansas City, MO 64133.

and judges is not supported by anything written in the Constitution, nor by any other moral or rational premise. Indeed, in fully 80% of the cases where assets are seized by the US government under the forfeiture laws, *no one is charged with a crime of any sort.*(7)

Even the US Environmental Protection Agency has gotten into the act, of creating its own police force SWAT teams; they recently raided an insectary which was legally challenging the need to obtain "EPA permission" to sell lady bugs to organic farmers. In another recent disgusting example, when the National Park Service (NPS) wanted to purchase a large plot of land adjacent to a National Park in southern California, the elderly owner, Mr. Donald Scott, refused to sell. Angered, NPS officials, teamed up with the IRS and DEA, went snooping for dirt on Mr. Scott, "to see" if he was growing pot on his property. One of the NPS agents then conveniently volunteered that he had seen "pot plants" when flying overhead many hundreds of feet in a helicopter (!), and somebody else received an "anonymous tip" that Mrs. Scott was seen purchasing items in town with hundred-dollar bills. With this fabricated "evidence", they raided Scott's rural mountain home with SWAT teams and gunslingers, with the expectation that — if drugs were found — they could confiscate his home and land, and whatever money he had in the bank, which would then become the property of the various "law enforcement" agencies. As they burst in on Scott's mountain home early in the morning, Mrs. Scott screamed with alarm at the sight of guns being pointed at her by strangers. Still dressed in pajamas, Mr. Scott jumped up from his bed with a pistol in his hand to defend his wife against intruders. With his pistol pointed to the ceiling, he was shot dead in his own home by the cops, at the very moment when he was complying with police orders to put the gun down. *No drugs of any kind were found on the property. The entire raid was staged purely for the purpose of stealing the man's land, and placing it on the auction block!* (7)

These are just a few incredible examples, from *hundreds to perhaps thousands* of similar cases, of federal assaults upon ordinary citizens who were never charged with a crime, as more political powers and guns are accumulated into the hands of our unelected federal bureaucracy. And, of course, there were the events in Waco, Texas, where an unruly fundamentalist religious group was needlessly assaulted by swarms of federal and state police, and Bureau of Alcohol Tobacco and Firearms (BATF) agents armed with automatic weapons and tanks, leading to nearly 100 deaths (including over 20 children).† The incident at Waco was undertaken for allegations which were no more severe than what has been routinely *certified and documented* as occurring within more established religions (such as child sexual abuse by Catholic Clergy). By contrast, no Catholic church or school has ever been invaded by BATF or Health and Human Services (HHS) agents, snooping out "alleged child sexual abuse" at the point of a gun. A recent Congressional investigation into the Waco massacre suggested the allegations of "child sexual abuse" had been concocted, after-the-fact, by Attorney General Janet Reno, to justify her approval of the shockingly aggressive raid.

7. *SF Chronicle*, 25 June 93; *Contra Costa Times*, 5 June 93; *Bay Guardian*, 2 June 93; *Pacific Sun*, 12 March 93.
† A videotape "Waco, The Big Lie" (*American Justice Fed.*, 3850 S. Emerson Ave., #E, Indianapolis, IN 46203) shows flame-throwing equipment on the front of the tanks which assaulted the Waco compound, casting serious doubt upon the "official" version of events.

> **" The percentage of Americans attracted to natural healing methods is growing and threatens the economic monopoly of...the AMA-FDA-Pharmacy cartel, which has for many years dictated health care approaches used in the USA with an iron fist."**

These examples are only a few from many, of clear and growing evidence of the *decline of respect for Constitutional principles and due process of law*, not by ordinary citizens, but rather, *by out-of-control, power-hungry government leaders and bureaucrats*, stimulating the growth of an American Police State. Increasingly, these various federal police forces are coordinated through larger and larger computer data banks on ordinary citizens. With poverty and homelessness on the rise, with more and more of the public wealth, lands, resources and means of production owned and controlled by fewer and fewer people, and with new reforms blocked by both political barriers and bureaucratic immobility, it is not surprising to see an increase in social chaos and crime. But the public clamor has unfortunately *not* been to address the root causes of crime, or even to hold the guilty federal leaders accountable for their autocratic, indeed fascistic, conduct. Rather, with the news media nearly silent about these various assaults upon democracy and freedom, the cry from Washington, DC is for even more police "protection". And so, new legislation is making its way through Congress, supported by both conservative Republicans and liberal Democrats, to grant even more police powers to the various federal agencies, and frighteningly, to centralize their activities under a single anti-crime umbrella. This is the background against which the AMA-FDA-Pharmacy cartel has turned up the heat against health care reformers, midwives, physicians employing natural healing methods, and vitamin and herb companies.

Growth of Natural Healing Methods in the USA

According to a recent study in the *New England Journal of Medicine*(8) about a third of all American adults use unconventional medical treatments, such as chiropractic, therapeutic massage, relaxation techniques, special diets and megavitamins. Americans are increasingly attracted to non-toxic natural healing methods, as an alternative to the cut, burn and poison methods of allopathic medicine. In recent years, there also has been increasing evidence that vitamins and other items advocated by "health food nuts" do indeed work to prevent degenerative diseases, and to promote recovery and remission from severe illness. Health reformers are increasingly advocating natural healing methods, including natural childbirth, home birth, breastfeeding of infants, and organic fruits and vegetables Vitamins A, B, C and E in moderate to high doses are increasingly being found to reduce one's risk of heart disease, cancers, and other degenerative diseases. Indeed, the National Institute of Health, in response to growing pressure from the public, recently opened an "Office of Alternative Medicine", and has started to fund investigations of natural healing methods.(9)

The percentage of Americans attracted to natural healing methods is growing and threatens the economic monopoly of Big Medicine, the AMA-FDA-Pharmacy cartel, which has for many years dictated health care approaches used in the USA

with an iron fist. This appears to be *the* major reason for the intensification of the FDA's vicious and murderous war against the natural health movement. The Director of FDA, under both the Bush and Clinton Administrations, is Dr. David Kessler, a powerful bureaucrat who epitomizes what Wilhelm Reich meant by the term *HIG* (Hooligan In Government). Kessler has intensified efforts by the FDA to control what is said, published, used or sold in all aspects of health care in the USA. He has established a "snitch" telephone hot line whereby "responsible doctors can call in and report any of their colleagues engaged in unacceptable, unorthodox, or deviant medical practice".

A blatant double-standard is applied: natural health advocates are assaulted for legal technicalities or for no reason at all, while big pharmacy and surgical device companies can literally get away with murder. Nutritional supplements with proven benefits are banned without evidence of any public health hazards, while synthetic pharmacological drugs or horrific surgical devices which have never been proven effective are approved in spite of demonstrated deadly side effects. Even when evidence is found that the pharmacy companies completely fabricated their FDA-approval data, out of thin air, nothing is done; the FDA turns a blind eye in such cases. Some examples: The FDA has received over 5,500 complaints against Aspartame (NutraSweet), which was legalized amid controversy regarding the capacity of this substance to alter brain hormone balances; some 9% of the complaints today involve serious neurological effects, including seizures. A recent major study by UCLA researchers of 109 patent-drug advertisements found 81% to be "inaccurate, misleading and even dangerous."(10) A General Accounting Office report found that 51.5% of patent drugs approved by the FDA between 1978 and 1986 had "serious post-approval risks" not disclosed on originally-approved package inserts, including "heart failure, myocardial infarction, anaphylaxis, respiratory depression, convulsions, seizures, kidney and liver failure, severe blood disorders, birth defects and blindness".(11)

In spite of these and many other deadly problems associated with costly "FDA-approved" patent drugs and medical devices, you never read about a major pharmacy company being raided with SWAT teams, their bank accounts seized, with offices, laboratories and homes of officers being raided and ransacked at gun-point, or their drug inventories being confiscated and impounded. Nor has the FDA taken any actions against the blatant advertising of drugs within medical journals publishing papers purportedly evaluating the efficacy and safety of those same drugs. But such repressions and police actions are being taken against natural healing clinics and smaller laboratories all across the USA, for doing nothing more than manufacturing, selling or prescribing vitamins, aloe vera, herbs and other non-toxic food substances. Witness the following recent examples:

---

8.   Eisenberg, et al; *New England Journal of Medicine*, 328:246-52, 1993.
9.   *Health Federation News*, March 1993; *SF Chronicle* 16 Feb.93, 18 May 93, 13 Sept. 93)

10.   *Health Federation News,* March 1993; *SF Chronicle* 16 Feb.93, 18 May 93, 13 Sept. 93.
11.   GAO/PEMD 90-15 *FDA Drug Review: Post Approval Risks* 1976-85, p.3, 28 April 1990.

1) 1987; Ft. Lauderdale, Florida: Based upon a perjured search warrant, the Life Extension Foundation, a non-profit organization supplying supplements to low income individuals, is raided by armed FDA agents and US Marshals. Breaking down the doors, the agents spent 12 hours seizing every nutrient product, file, and newsletter they could get their hands on, including many personal affects of owners and employees. Even telephones and computers were "ripped from the wall". Four years later, another raid took place, after the Foundation relocated to Arizona. Employees were intimidated into thinking they had been "shipping illegal drugs" (*vitamins!*), but no charges were filed against anyone. The raid took three days to complete. Requests for the return of property were consistently refused. Lawsuits against the FDA are in progress.(12)

2) 1990; Mt. Angel, Oregon: Nine FDA agents, 11 US marshalls, and 8 heavily armed Oregon state police raid Highland Laboratories, kicking in both front and back doors. Over an 11 hour period, virtually everything except tables and chairs is carted off to waiting trucks, including many items not listed on the search warrant, at a total value of $37,000. Nobody was informed about the grounds for the raid, the "supporting affidavit" being suppressed by the court. The seized property was taken to an undisclosed location. Mr. Kenneth Scott, owner, and other Highland employees were threatened with violence if they attempted to enter the company premises, and the daughter of the owner was held "in house arrest" for 12 hours at a location several miles away. Highland subsequently reopened, and hired a separate outside mailing service to satisfy FDA requirements. In response, the FDA raided the mailing service, which was a small business run out of the home of a woman in another town. Finding nothing there except mailing equipment and business records, FDA agents threatened to confiscate the woman's checkbooks and cash, failing to do so only after being begged not to. When she asked them "Why are you doing this?", the agent replied "Somebodies got to do it!!" Because of the raids, the owner of the mailing firm subsequently closed her business, and refuses to file charges out of *fear of government reprisals*(!!). No charges were ever filed by the FDA against anyone, nor has any of the seized property been returned. The FDA still has not given anyone reasons for their outrageous tactics, which were designed simply to put the firm out of business.(13)

3) 1990; El Cajon, California: The FDA attempts to railroad Sissy Harrington-McGill, 57-year old owner of a pet food store, for violation of a proposed "Health Claims Law" because her literature stated vitamins would help keep pets healthy. Her store was raided and ransacked without a search warrant. When her day in court arrived, Harrington-McGill requested a jury trial — the judge refused her request, dictating that he alone would judge the case. She was tried and convicted of violation of the Health Claims Law, *even though it had not yet been passed by the US Congress at the time the FDA raided her, or at the time of her trial or conviction.* Ms. Harrington-McGill repeatedly informed the federal judge of this fact, but he ignored her complaint. For this first-time misdemeanor "violation" of a non-existing law, she was sentenced to 179 days in prison, with a fine of $10,000. She was led away in chains and

served 114 days in prison before being released after the U.S. Congress refused to pass the "Health Claims Law". Lawsuits against the FDA have been filed. (14)

4) 1990; Reno, Nevada: The Century Clinic, which employs chelation therapy, homeopathy, nutritional and natural therapies, is raided twice by FDA and Postal Service inspectors and other government agents. During the first raid, a 14 page list of items was confiscated even though the warrant itemized only three short paragraphs of materials for seizure. Virtually all equipment, supplies, files, mailing lists, computers and records were taken during a 16 hour ransacking of facilities. No charges were filed. Century Clinic then recovered, rebuilt their facility and sued the FDA for return of the seized property. The FDA responded with a second raid, this time involving searches of the persons, homes and vehicles of Clinic owners and employees. Patients in treatment at the time of the raid were treated rudely, ordered about, and interrogated. Many were not allowed to leave without giving names and addresses. Cash and checks were also seized, along with another 14 pages of inventory. Again, *no charges were filed against anybody!!* (15)

5) March, 1991; Tijuana, Mexico: Four armed Mexican police, without warrants or charges, kidnapped Jimmy Keller from his office at the St. Jude Hospital, and took him to their headquarters. There, six men in blue jeans and work shirts who refused to identify themselves (later identified as bounty hunters for the US Justice Department) seized him and forced him to cross the border to the USA. There, Keller was arrested by the FBI on 12 counts of wire fraud — Keller had made telephone calls across interstate lines to attract people to his Mexican clinic. Following the illegal kidnapping of Keller from Mexican soil, without extradition, he was jailed in Texas, his bond set at $5 million. He was later convicted and sent to a North Dakota prison for two years. Keller ran a very successful cancer treatment clinic, which he founded after using natural methods to cure himself of "terminal" cancer. His own cancer had been unsuccessfully "treated" 25 years earlier by orthodox cancer specialists who amputated his ear and mutilated his face. Following the horrific surgery, Keller's cancer returned and metastisized. He investigated natural healing methods, cured himself, and then began helping others to do so.(16)

6) 1991; Texas: The alternative medical clinic of Dr. Stanislaw Burzynski, an emigre from communist Poland, is raided by FDA and Texas Department of Health agents, following public announcement that Burzynski's successful, unorthodox methods will be evaluated by the National Cancer Institute. Until then, Burzynski had worked quietly for 15 years without any complaints or trouble with the law.(17)

7) 1991; San Leandro, California: NutriCology, a nutrition supplement company operated by Stephen Levine, Ph.D., a molecular geneticist from the University of California at Berkeley, is raided by 12 FDA agents. Levine spends $500,000 over the next year to fight three different FDA injunctions, all of which are thrown out of court. No complaints were ever made about the firm.(18)

12. *FDA Versus The People of the United States*, Jonathan Wright Legal Defense Fund, Citizens For Health, PO Box 368, Tacoma, WA 98401 206/ 922-2457, FAX 206/922-7583.

13. *FDA Versus The People...* ibid

14. *Body & Soul*, 8(4):6, June 1992; *FDA Versus The People...* ibid.
15. *FDA Versus The People...* ibid.
16. *FDA Versus The People...* ibid.
17. *FDA Versus The People...* ibid.
18. *FDA Versus The People...* ibid.

> **" The FDA alliance has destroyed the lives and work of numerous medical pioneers... usually *without any charges being filed*. They simply... seize and impound office and laboratory equipment, mailing lists, computers, files, bank accounts, etc."**

8) 1992; Kent Washington: The unlocked door of Dr. Jonathan Wright's natural medical clinic was kicked in, while FDA agents wearing bullet-proof vests with drawn guns, pushed into the room, shouting at everyone to "Freeze! Put up your hands!" The raid was in reaction to a recent FDA ban on a contaminated batch of B-vitamins in another state. Wright was not connected to that particular incident, and did not ever use contaminated vitamins. No matter. Workers were held at gun-point and his office searched, while computers, mailing lists, books and files were hauled away in a large truck. Patients were generally treated like criminals. The FDA Gestapo agents spent 14 hours at the clinic, searching through everything. Dr. Wright is internationally known for his work on nutritional medicine and preventative health approaches. At the same time, down the street, the For Your Health pharmacy was being raided in a similar manner. This pharmacy serves preventative health doctors in the Kent area. As of mid-1993, none of the impounded equipment, computers or files have been returned, and *no charges have been filed against anyone*. (19)

9) 1992: San Diego: David Halpern and several of his family members, as well as the Presidents of three British and one German vitamin companies, are charged with 198 counts of "conspiracy", "smuggling" and "violation of the Food, Drug and Cosmetic Act" for importing banned nutritional supplements which are freely available, over the counter, in Britain and Germany. The indictments carry a potential prison term of 990 years in prison.(20)

10) 1992: Texas: The FDA, working behind the scenes, prompted the Texas Department of Health (TDH) and Texas Department of Food and Drug to undertake raids upon over a dozen large health food stores. Over 250 different products, an arbitrary list some 88 pages long, was forcibly seized from shelves. The list includes flaxseed oil, effervescent vitamin C, various herbs, Sleepytime Tea, aloe vera, and zinc products. Following a public outcry, and restraining reactions from Texas politicians, the TDH Gestapo officers threatened one of the ravaged health food store owners in the manner of a Mafia extortionist: "Don't talk to the press, or we'll come down on you twice as hard". No justifications were given for the inclusion of any of the products on the seizure list, no charges were filed, and none of the products were ever returned to the stores. (21)

11) 1993: USA: Nearly 40 different natural healing clinics, health food stores, and vitamin manufacturers were raided in May and September, in armed commando-style assaults by combined agents of the FDA, DEA, IRS, US Customs and US Postal services. Details on these more recent raids are difficult to come by, but it is reported that, besides seizing various stocks of vitamins, herbs and other nutritional supplements and compounds (such as shark cartilage), IRS officials seized both personal and company bank accounts, along with automobiles, computers, office equipment, and other valuables. Mailing lists of customers and patients were of particular interest in the seizures. The homes of the company owners and employees were also raided, without search warrants. SWAT teams, armed with machine guns and flak jackets, participated in some of the raids. The Post Office, in turn, acted to illegally block the mail of some of the companies, effectively shutting them off from communication with the public and leaving them without funds, mailing lists, or other resources necessary to mount a proper legal defense.

As before, *no charges were filed*. Some shocking examples of Gestapo tactics occurred. At the home of one employee, dark-dressed men with guns demanded entry, but the scared individual refused to let them in; instead, she went to the bedroom to dial 911 for the local police. The door was smashed down and she was shoved to the floor with a gun put to her head. In another case, a breast-feeding mother employed at a raided firm was roughed-up and handcuffed for 11 hours while FDA agents ransacked her home. These latter raids included the clinic and offices of Dr. Kurt Donsbach, author of many self-help nutrition-oriented books widely sold in health food stores. Donsbach's home was also reportedly raided, and his personal bank accounts seized. Also raided were the USA distributors of German-made Neiper Products, formulated by the internationally-known and respected Dr. Hans Neiper, who operates a successful clinic in Germany, and sponsors the popular health-science magazine *Raum & Zeit*. Many ordinary citizens were manhandled and threatened with death by gun-pointing government agents during these raids, all for the "crime" of manufacturing, distributing, selling or prescribing vitamins, nutritional supplements, and related natural health products or methods.(22)

The above are only representative examples from a very long list of similar FDA abuses of power in recent years. The FDA clearly has become the attack-dog tool of the AMA and pharmacy industry, and many FDA field agents are on record as stating that the agency is out to "destroy the health food and nutritional supplements industries". And that is precisely what they are trying to do. FDA Director Kessler wants to control not only the marketing of products, but also what is said in speech or print about health matters. He has vowed to "crack down" even on scientific meetings and conferences which present findings "unacceptable" to FDA policies, and this is no idle threat. Kessler and the FDA are the closest thing to a domestic Gestapo-type police force in the USA, and their power is growing; new alliances are being cemented between the FDA, IRS, DEA, FTC, Customs and Postal Services, HHS and other government agencies, to "combat the growing menace of health fraud".

The FDA alliance has destroyed the lives and work of numerous medical pioneers, as outlined above, usually *without any charges being filed*. They simply arrive at the offending clinic and home of the pioneer, break down the doors, shove

---

19. *Seattle Post-Intelligencer*, 7 May 92, 11 May 92; *FDA Versus The People*...ibid.
20. *FDA Versus The People*... ibid.
21. *FDA Versus The People*... ibid.

22. *Sarasota Eco Report*, July 1993; *Am. Preventative Medical Assn.*, PO Box 2111, Tacoma, WA 98401, 206/926-0551, FAX 206/922-7583.

guns into the faces of everyone present, seize and impound office and laboratory equipment, mailing lists, computers, files, bank accounts, etc., carting everything off to a warehouse where it is dumped. Even personal funds in a bank account are "impounded" (*stolen!*) by these government thugs, whom we may assume are, like DEA agents raiding a crack house, using drug-seizure laws to *keep a percentage of whatever they steal!* Amazingly, *none* of the major political parties have displayed alarm or interest in these FDA assaults. It has all been done with the full knowledge and approval of top politicians (Reagan, Bush, Clinton, Gore) and Justice Department officials (Janet Reno). Virtually *all* of these politicians have consistently been sent letters of protest by the lawyers, friends, patients and co-workers of the various clinicians or small businesses who have been raided — to my knowledge, nobody who has been raided by the FDA has ever received a friendly note or a helpful response from any of our political Royal Family. These power elites either agree with the FDA, don't care about natural health matters, or are completely isolated from what is going on in the real world by layers of bureaucracy and "helpers", who censor the the pleas for help from their mail and telephone calls.

The FDA raids demonstrate *a serious erosion in the principles of government by law, due process, liberty and justice.* For health matters, at least, we now have *government by iron-fisted bureaucratic decree, with only the facade and illusion of law.* Originally, the FDA was formed under the mandate of the Pure Food and Drug Act which simply required that products be accurately labeled as to what their contents are and to actually contain those ingredients, which is a necessary regulation in order for consumers to make informed decisions. However, this simple mandate has grown into a bureaucratic monster which has decreed itself the sole judge, jury, and prosecutor (with its own hit squads) on matters of medical efficacy. Since Reich's time, and through the 1960s, 1970s and 1980s, the FDA has consumed millions of taxpayer dollars to wage its war against natural approaches to health care. The result is that our health care system is one big gigantic expensive mess, rife with official fraud, and a holocaust of victims due to the toxic and deadly side effects from ineffective "approved" drugs and horrific surgical mutilations. Nature, science, and compassion have been thrown out of the house of modern medicine, and the doors and windows have been barred shut, with armed guards posted outside.

The Congressional Battle

In spite of the damage done to many individuals, clinics and small businesses, the natural health movement continues to fight back, through legal means and by pressuring their elected representatives to restrain the FDA. But the FDA has its own supporters in Congress, and wants even more power and authority, so that it can go out and even more thoroughly "search and destroy" the natural health movement. New legislation has been offered into the US Congress which would grant the FDA the more complete and sweeping police powers it wants. These new Congressional bills are the Regulatory Enforcement Amendments for the existing Nutritional Labeling and Education Act (H1662, H2597, H3642, S1982, S2135). Their sponsors are long-time FDA supporters and recipients of pharmaceutical PAC "donations" Rep. Henry Waxman (D-California), Rep. John Dingell (D-Michigan), Sen. Edward M. Kennedy (D-Massachusetts), and Sen Howard Metzenbaum (D-Ohio). The proposed legislation would grant to the FDA:

– power to set arbitrarily low potency levels for vitamins and foodstuffs, and to forbid the sale of any vitamin or foodstuff which contained levels higher than the FDA mandates.

– power to forcibly censor advertising of health claims in magazines and books.

– power to embargo and destroy any imported product without proving its threat to the public health

– power to issue its own subpoenas and to undertake *warrantless* searches, seizures, and electronic surveillance, based upon *mere suspicion*, without the need for court approval.

– power to set its own punitive fines against anyone who fails to obey their demands — up to $250,000 for individuals, and $2 million for businesses.

– power to dictate to the Federal Trade Commission new regulations for censoring health claims in television and radio programs and advertisements.

– power to pay informants a reward, up to $250,000, for reporting on suspected violators of FDA regulations.

Other related legislation has recently been proposed (SS732, S733, H940, Sen. Edward Kennedy sponsoring on behalf of the Clinton Administration), which would establish a "national registry and tracking system" for the vaccination of all infants and children, a prelude to the notorious "Smart Card" or "Health Identity Card", with total control over health care decisions by a centralized medical Big Brother. These bills mandate "social workers" to essentially become the new "health care police", calling upon every home in America, door to door, to "investigate" whether or not every child in residence would have all "mandatory vaccines". If not, the child might be blocked from enrollment in school, or the parents charged with "child abuse", and the child forcibly taken away by the state for adoption. Already, legal attacks for "child neglect and abuse" have been mounted by social workers and medical authorities against parents opting for home-birth, and against parents refusing to inoculate their children with potentially dangerous experimental vaccines.(23) Even breast-feeding mothers have had infants ripped from their arms, being charged with "child sexual abuse", by power-drunk "social workers", who did not approve of breast-feeding beyond two years.(24)

Coupled with the new, national health insurance initiatives, we rapidly approach the creation of a politically-directed, centralized network of "health spys" and "health police", whose ultimate goal would be to root out any and all forms of natural health care, self-responsible health care, or anyone who would exhibit signs of independent-mindedness or "disobedience to authority" regarding basic matters of child-rearing, sexuality, education or health. This is reminiscent of the *KGB-neighborhood-spy* systems of the communist nations, and the *religious police* of the fundamentalist Muslim nations. It is a clear and present danger to our democracy, given the fact that Americans today are prone to grant to

23. Regarding the vaccine issue, see: Neil Z. Miller, *Vaccines: Are They Really Safe and Effective?*, New Atlantean Press, NM, 1993; Editors of Mothering: *Vaccinations, The Rest of the Story*, *Mothering Magazine*, PO Box 1690, Santa Fe, NM 87504.
24. The average age of weaning, world-wide, is around 3.5 years. See the case of Denise Perrigo in New York, discussed in *Birth Gazette*, Spring 92, p.11-12; also discussed in Sex-Economic Notes, *Pulse of the Planet #4*, 1993.

given the fact that Americans today are prone to grant to white-coated "doctors" the same uncritical, unquestioning obedience as once was given to black-robed priests during the witch-burning period of history, or to communist-party functionaries during the Stalinist purges. Science, particularly medical science, is today the New Religion of *Homo Normalis*, and the witch hunt against heretic disobedient unbelievers is gathering steam.

Opposing the above FDA-AMA-Gestapo legislation is the Health Freedom Act (S784 and H1709) sponsored by Sen.Orrin Hatch (R-Utah) and Rep. Bill Richardson (D-New Mexico). This bill would restrict the FDA on some of the above matters, preserving the rights of Americans to make their own essential health decisions — regarding vitamins, herbs and food supplements, at least. There additionally are a few states, such as Alaska and Washington, which have passed specific legislation to protect natural health-care methods, though it is not clear that these laws do anything to restrain the FDA, which is governed by federal legislation. Rep. Henry Hyde (R-Illinois) has also sponsored the Civil Asset Forfeiture Reform Act of 1993 to restrain the "long arm of the law", and place the burden of proof on the government in asset seizure cases, where it belongs.

These latter laws to restrain government power are a start in the right direction, but in fact do not go far enough to curb the persisting abuses. Wilhelm Reich's suggestion, that judges, prosecutors, and government officials who plot to throw innocent people into prison should themselves be imprisoned, is the kind of strong medicine necessary to prevent our social situation from spiraling into even more despotic conditions. Clearly, a Congressional Investigation with public hearings and testimony should be initiated in Washington, DC, to allow hundreds of ordinary citizens the right to come forward and tell their stories about US government hooliganism, in full light of day, and where the "mainstream" news media could not so easily ignore it. A Special Prosecutor should also appointed by the President, to investigate the blatant Police State activities of the FDA and other governmental agencies. FDA Commissioner Kessler should immediately be fired and investigated for his role in these abuses. All FDA leaders, field agents and lawyers, AMA officials, and prosecutors and judges who plotted, approved, or directed the invasions of clinics, laboratories and homes of medical pioneers, carrying out the massive seizures of property where nobody was ever charged with a crime — those individuals should receive stiff fines and jail terms, with compensation paid to those whose lives and work was destroyed by power-drunk bureaucrats. Even those now-elderly FDA officials, prosecutors and judges who presided over the burning of Reich's books should be held fully accountable for their past abuses of power. These and other concrete steps must be undertaken if we are serious about our Constitution and Bill of Rights, and if the words "Land of the Free" are to have meaning beyond that of a mere slogan, recited mindlessly at political rallies.

Clearly, unless our social reformers and health-care pioneers are allowed to move from the present suppressed "underground" situation, and practice their arts openly in the social marketplace, free from constant FDA-police harassment, there will be no real health reforms or pioneering health breakthroughs to reach the general public. The battle lines are drawn, but the outcome is not clear or certain at all. Hanging in the balance is nothing less than the future of our remaining democratic and social freedoms. ■

Health Freedom & Natural Health Organizations

- *American Preventative Medical Assoc.*, PO Box 2111, Tacoma, WA 98401, 206/ 926-0551, FAX 206/ 922-7583.
- *Cancer Control Society*, 2043 N. Berendo, Los Angeles, CA 90027, 213/ 663-7801.
- *Citizens For Health,* PO Box 368, Tacoma, WA 98401 206/ 922-2457, FAX 206/922-7583.
- *Committee for Freedom of Choice in Medicine*, 1180 Walnut Ave., Chula Vista, CA 91911 619/429-8200.
- *Foundation for the Advancement of Innovative Medicine*, PO Box 338, Kinderhook, NY 12106.
- *Independent Citizens Research Foundation for the Study of Degenerative Diseases*, PO Box 97, Ardsley, NY 10502.
- *Life Extension Foundation*, PO Box 229120, Hollywood, FL 33022 800/841-5433, 305/966-4886.
- *Natural Health Care Alliance*, 1348 LaPlaya Ave., #2, San Francisco, CA 94122 415/ 731-8115.
- *National Health Federation*, 212 W. Foothill Blvd., Monrovia, CA 91016, 818/ 359-8334, FAX:818/303-0642.
- *New England Health Freedom Coalition*, 105 Main St., Brattleboro, VT 05301, 802/257-9345, FAX 802/ 257-0652.
- *Nutritional Health Alliance*, PO Box 267, Farmingdale, NY 11735 800/ 226-4642, 516/ 249-7070.
- *People Against Cancer*, PO Box 10, Otho, IA 50569, 515/ 972-4444, FAX: 515/ 972-4415.
- *People for Pure Foods*, 433 Main St., Half Moon Bay, CA 94019, 415/ 726-8110, FAX 415/ 712-8008.

Organizations Against Seizure Laws

- *Forfeiture Endangers American Rights*, 265 Miller Ave., Mill Valley, CA 94941, 415/ 380-9108, FAX 415/ 380-9208.
- *Freeman Education Association*, 8141 E. 31st St., #F, Tulsa, OK 74145
- *Fully Informed Jury Association*, PO Box 59, Helmville, MT 59843,Tel: 406/ 793-5550, 314/ 997-8588.

The Constitution of the United States
Bill of Rights, 15 December 1791

Amendment 1: Congress shall make no law ... abridging the freedom of speech, or of the press...

Amendment IV: The right of the people to be secure in their persons, houses, papers, and effects, against unreasonable searches and seizures, shall not be violated...

Amendment V: No person shall be ... deprived of life, liberty, or property, without due process of law...

The USA *CORE Network*

An informal, cooperative group has been formed to share pertinent weather information and coordinate cloudbusting operations in the USA, the *CORE Network*. Every member of the group has significant, long-term interest in orgonomy and the work of Wilhelm Reich, though with varying degrees of practical experimental and field work experience. Following many years of cooperative work, the first formal meeting of the Network was held in August 1992, in Ashland, Oregon. The minutes of this meeting were published in the *Journal of Orgonomy* [26(2):237-247, 1992]. Cooperative cloudbusting work undertaken by members of the *CORE Network* since 1990 have been followed by correlated, often significant rainfall increases on the West Coast, particularly in California. Significant work was undertaken during the 1992-1993 rainy season, a highly critical time because of extremely scarce water resources. Cloudbusters were employed from San Francisco to Seattle. The rains following those operations were quite significant and gratifying, and the California drought is now completely ended. By early summer 1993, significant snowpack had accumulated in the mountains, and all state reservoirs were at near-to-full capacity. See the Publications Review section of this issue of *Pulse* for a listing of relevant papers on this work. Additional materials, including an in-depth data analysis of the 1992-1993 West Coast rainy season, will be published in the future.

OROP Israel 1991-1992

Following years of drought in the semi-arid regions of Israel and the eastern Mediterranean, water supplies as of the summer of 1991 were nearing record low conditions. Open war over scarce water supplies was a distinct possibility. A plan was developed to construct and use a Reich cloudbuster in Israel to end the drought. This work was undertaken in November 1991 by James DeMeo, assisted by Theirrie Cook and by operators in Greece with the Hellenic Orgonomic Association. The expedition was also greatly assisted by Madeleine Gassner and Lydia Axelrod, both long-time residents of Israel. Ms. Gassner formerly worked with Dr. Walter Hoppe, one of the first individuals to bring knowledge of orgonomy to both Israel and Germany. The results of the Israel cloudbusting operations were quite impressive; it was overall a very humbling experience, as strong rainstorms pushed across the region. By Spring 1992 the drought was completely ended, with all reservoirs in the region at full or near-to-full capacity. Deserts throughout the region were blooming into grasses and flowers, in a nearly unbelievable profusion which people had seldom seen before. A summary on that work is published in this issue of *Pulse*, and a more detailed *Special Report* on the Israel experiments is now available from the Orgone Biophysical Research Lab (price: $20, overseas $25.), PO Box 1395, El Cerrito, CA 94530 USA.

Orgonomic Project Waldheilung 1989-1993

The experimental forest-healing (Waldheilung) research project continues in the region of Berlin, with support from observers and members in other parts of Germany and Switzerland. Just over three years of work have taken place, under the direction of James DeMeo, using a single small cloudbuster in the Berlin region and a second one in the western part of Germany. The project was first conceptualized and undertaken in 1989; since that date, the atmosphere over the Berlin region of Germany has exhibited a clearing and more refreshing characteristic, noticeable to everyone participating in the group. The operations have mainly been confined to periods of dense smog and atmospheric stagnation in the wintertime months. In the years prior to the first operations, it was routine for several smog-warnings or smog-alarms to be issued each year by the Berlin authorities, after which children would not be allowed outdoors to play and automobile driving in the city center would be prohibited. Since the operations began, not one smog alarm has been issued for the Berlin region, and the beneficial influences to air quality may cover a larger area than just Berlin. The overall effect on trees and the pH of rainwater has yet to be quantified, and at the moment, funds are being sought for an analysis of Berlin air pollution data. More information will be published about this project as it becomes available. [DeMeo, J.: "CORE Prog. Report #25: Two Year Research Summary", *J. Orgonomy*, 25(2):175-190, 1991; DeMeo, J.: "Research Progress Report", *Pulse of the Planet*, 3:110-116, 1991.]

Shasta Reservoir filled to capacity after a winter of good rains.

OROP Namibia 1992-1993

With cooperative assistance and support from the members and friends of *Orgonomic Project Waldheilung* in Germany and Switzerland, two cloudbusting expeditions were undertaken in the African nation of Namibia (formerly South West Africa). Following the ending of a decades-long civil war, peaceful conditions have continued in Namibia, today considered one of the more stable and democratically-oriented nations in Africa. Unfortunately, a ten-year water deficit, with critical drought from around 1989, had threatened the economy of the entire southern part of Africa. Namibia, South Africa, Botswana and Zimbabwe were all suffering from drought and facing possible food shortages. At that point, Bernd Senf of Berlin, a primary worker in the Waldheilung Project, initiated a fund-raising effort to support cloudbusting in Namibia.

James DeMeo was asked to organize and lead the expedition; other participants included Theirrie Cook and Donald Bill, from the USA, Bernd Senf of Berlin, and Manfred Metz, an agricultural consultant with knowledge of Namibia. After many months of planning two expeditions were undertaken, in November 1992 and February 1993. The November expedition was primarily dedicated to construction and preliminary testing of a new cloudbuster in Namibia. It was given the name *!Nanus*, a Bushman word for rain (the exclamation point is pronounced with a kissing sound). Minor rains followed short operations in November, which is considered the "small rainy season". The February operations were timed to coincide with the "big rainy season", though no "big rains" had taken place for years. The operations in February 1993 were more ambitious and significant rains fell afterward; in fact, rains in February, March and April were significant across much of the southern part of Africa, and a major drought and crop-loss disaster was averted. The operations team was very fortunate to meet with individuals in Namibia who had been familiar with Reich's work for more than a decade, and an assistant observer-apprentice came along for the entire series of February operations. With instructions, this individual continued operations independently in subsequent months. Rainfall data for the entire period of operations has not yet been analyzed, but field observations suggest a strong correlation between cloudbusting work and the onset of the greatest rains. For example, the figure below presents daily precipitation data for one rain measuring station close to where the cloudbuster was stationed for the months of February and March of 1993. A *Special Report* on the Namibia cloudbusting operations is under preparation, and will probably be available to the public in 1994; summary articles will also be published.

Daily Precipitation Values, from one measuring station close to the operating cloudbuster !Nanus. Dates of cloudbuster operations are marked with a dark bar at the bottom of the graph.

Cloudbuster !Nanus on the shores of a reservoir in Namibia, Africa, with rainstorm on the horizon. A drought of several years duration was greatly diminished following several weeks of field work, undertaken by the workers from the USA and Germany.

Cloudbusting is not "Weather Modification"

Over the years there has been a tendency for cloudbusting to be called "orgonomic weather modification", and other terms which imply that the primary function of cloudbusting is to *change* the weather in a specified manner, to *make* the weather do this or that. The Editor of *Pulse* wishes to suggest this terminology be henceforth dropped completely from the lexicon of orgonomy. Reich's impetus in the development of the cloudbuster was not to "modify" or "make" anything — rather, it was to *restore the lost property of atmospheric pulsation.* Cloudbusting is a technique to *remove obstacles in the way of natural atmospheric functioning,* to restore the lost principle of *atmospheric self-regulation.* The context is similar to the goal of Reich's therapy, to help the individual function in a more free, self-regulated manner. When armor or atmospheric stagnation sets in, one might attempt to *assist* or help nature to function as it would normally, had not the armor or atmospheric stagnation developed.

Regarding atmospheric functioning, part of the difficulty is the term "cloudbusting" itself, which implies to many people the "busting up of clouds". Or it implies "cloud*burst*", the triggering of rains from a given cloud. Both of these are possible with the cloudbuster, but neither are primary goals of the technique.

While grappling with these terms, the Editor of *Pulse* came to observations about words and language. It is far easier to come up with descriptive terms or synonyms for cloudbusting which imply "doing something" *to* the weather: modification, alteration, change, perturbation, and so forth. Related words which imply the outright stopping or interfering with natural processes are even more abundant: suppression, repression, containment, stop, halt, end, terminate, kill, discontinue, squash, quell, calm, quiet, silence, etc. But try to come up with single words which say, clearly, *assisting a natural function to function more freely,* or *restoring a lost natural function,* or *setting free a natural impulse formerly bound up and repressed.* Here, one finds the English language fails entirely, as do most other languages. Perhaps the Trobriand Islanders or Minoans had such words, but we just don't know. And so, we continue to use the word *cloudbusting,* but also search for descriptive terms which avoid the implications of "controlling the weather", and acknowledge the *restoration of free movement of formerly blocked life energy.*

Another reason to cease using the term "orgonomic weather modification" is the fact that the cloud*seeders* do use the "modification" terminology — they also start from the basic assumptions that space is empty, without any primary energy, and that both nature and the universe are *dead.* Meteorologists have no acceptance of any principle which comes close to atmospheric self-regulation, and indeed have been hot to criticize the use of concepts which come from the world of biology, such as *homeostasis* or the *Gaia theory* of Lovelock. By contrast, orgonomy came from the world of the biological sciences, with an emphasis upon self-regulatory processes. We therefore should strive to avoid the "control-make" terminology of the armored world.

Effect of an [Orgone] Energy Accumulator on Phosphorus Availability

T.M. Lai and D. D. Eberl, U.S. Geological Survey, Denver, CO. "An energy accumulator was constructed with alternative layers of metal and organic materials according to Reich's hypothesis. A mixture of soil and water was kept in a tube within the accumulator for a period of time to investigate its effect on P availability as measured by a chemical extraction method. Available P content increased up to 30% as compared with a control after the soil was kept in the accumulator. The longer the soil was kept in the accumulator the greater the quantity of available P. Adding organic matter and K to the soil increased the effect of the accumulator on P availability. Different materials used to construct the accumulator influenced the effect of the accumulator on available P. The mechanism of this effect needs further study". (*Abstracts, 80th Annual Meeting,* American Society of Agronomy, 1988, p.240.)

Healing Dead Lakes with Life Energy?

A German researcher, Roland Plocher, appears to have developed a special new method for revitalizing the waters in toxified or oxygen-depleted lakes and streams. Plocher has attributed his discovery to the more basic research findings of "Wilhelm Reich, Nikola Tesla and Rudolph Steiner", but the apparatus he employs is clearly of his own making. A thin sheet of aluminum about two feet square is impregnated with a white powder. An apparatus similar to a film projector is then used to project the "homeopathic information" of oxygen into the powder. The aluminum sheets with powder and oxygen-information are then rolled up and placed inside hollow plastic pipes, which are then bundled together in groups of four, weighted with a concrete block, and immersed down into the dead lake or pond. By the miracle of life energy processes, the lake comes back to life, and becomes capable of supporting fish and other oxygen-breathing creatures. Or so is the claim made by the unassuming Plocher, who has been quietly selling his services to satisfied farmers in Germany and Switzerland for several years. Switzerland recently ran him out at gun-point, however. He was apprehended by police who took all his cash and belongings, drove him to the border and told him to never return. All "unofficial", of course. German television recently ran a special on Plocher's work, complete with interviews from many satisfied farmers and lake owners. We will try to bring more on this fascinating subject in the next issue of the *Pulse*.

Over the last years, a number of unusual observations have been made which add additional support to the early observations of Reich, on long-distance energetic-atmospheric reactions to low-level nuclear radiation and nuclear bomb testing. Following are some specific, telling examples.

The Oakland Wildfires of October 1991

The Spring 1992 issue of *Journal of Orgonomy* (1) carried a paper by James DeMeo describing research undertaken in 1990-1991 on the California drought, with a "Special Note on Underground Nuclear Testing and the Oakland Wildfires" that bears repeating here:

Weather Response to Nuclear Testing

In prior articles, I discussed a possible connection between underground nuclear bomb testing in Nevada to weather changes in the Western US.(2) A graph was published showing changes in 500 mb pressure over Nevada and Montana in 1990, with a generalized association with nuclear tests. Nuclear testing appeared to have increased atmospheric pressure in the upper atmosphere, a possible factor in the expansion of high-pressure drought conditions in the West. Unusual weather events in 1991 also expressed a strong correlation to underground nuclear bomb tests, and the following preliminary observations can be reported.

Following the heavy rains of California's Miracle March in 1991 (described in the original *JO* article), spring and summer conditions were cool and cloudy; it appeared that, after five years of drought, a normal rainy fall and winter season would occur. We attributed this partly to the strong persistence of March rains, and also to gentle stimulating draws being made periodically with a small cloudbuster in the Hayward area and from the Tomales Bay site. However, such pleasant conditions did not last.

Between May and July of 1991, France exploded a total of six nuclear bombs at its underground test site at the Mururoa Atoll, near Tahiti. The US had also exploded four by the end of July, with a fifth underground nuclear bomb exploded on September 14. That particular bomb had to be delayed several times, due to erratic and shifting wind patterns. A sixth nuclear bomb was exploded on September 19, in a special horizontal tunnel for testing of high-energy beam weapons of the "Star Wars" program. These two nuclear tests signaled an end to the cool, cloudy conditions in the West. Late September and October were characterized by hot, sunny conditions which built up to high, record-breaking temperatures in a few places. The first major forest fires of the year broke out in Washington, Oregon, and California. DORish conditions again prevailed across the state, high pressure returned, the jet stream moved north into Canada, and drought appeared to be entrenched once again.

1. DeMeo, J.: "Core Progress Report #26: California Drought of 1991-1992, With a Special Note on Underground Nuclear Testing and the Oakland Wildfires", *J. Orgonomy*, 26(1):49-71, Spring/Summer 1992.
2. DeMeo, J.: "CORE Progress Report #25: Two Year Research Summary — The American West, Greece, and Germany", *Journal of Orgonomy*, 25(2):175-190, 1991; DeMeo, J.: "Research Progress Report", *Pulse of the Planet*, 3:110-116, 1991.

Outbreak of Bad Winds and Wildfires

On October 18, 1991, another underground nuclear blast took place in Nevada, the most powerful one of the year, measuring close to 150 kilotons of explosive power. A 4.8 magnitude earthquake was generated in the test region. Within a day, heavy oranur conditions set into the Great Basin, expressed as raging desert windstorms. One windstorm pushed west, from the Central Valley towards the Pacific Ocean, a phenomenon called the Santa Anna winds, or plainly, "bad winds". They are hot, very dry, with relative humidities of about 10%, and can reach high velocities. They rapidly dry out vegetation, which will fuel dramatic wildfires if sparked. One such fire did occur in the hills above Oakland, California, on October 19. The flames were extinguished, but irresponsibly allowed to smolder overnight. The next day, October 20, the fierce Santa Anna winds appeared, and caused a dramatic flare-up of the fires. The winds fanned the embers into gigantic flames, which fed upon the dry vegetation and wooden structures, creating a massive urban/suburban firestorm.

I watched this fire from my front porch, in silent horror, as it moved across the hills, burning one home after another about five miles from where I live. Nobody, including the firefighters, ever expected it to get as large as it did. By early afternoon it was clear that a major disaster was in the making. Flames were widespread across the hills, and a thick column of smoke rose to several thousand feet, blotting out the sun. The firefighters and many news reporters at the scene kept blaming the Santa Anna winds. "We can't keep up with the flames! They're moving too fast!" they exclaimed, nearly in a panic.

One fireman openly moaned about the recent change in weather, wishing aloud for the moist sea breezes and heavy clouds which had characterized the region prior to late September, before the last nuclear bomb tests. According to the fire fighters, the fire would "lie down" with moist ocean wind, but would "rise up" and flare with the dry desert winds. Indeed, they appeared to describe a major energetic difference between oranur wind and the cooler, moist life-energy winds, which were previously coming in from the ocean. After hearing this, it was clear that we could do something to assist with the cloudbuster. Local weather reports held no hope for rain, and the weather maps were free of frontal activity along the West Coast, except far to the north, near Seattle. It was unrealistic to expect that cloudbusting could bring rains within the next few hours, given the prevailing cloud-free, widespread high-pressure conditions. However, it did seem possible to restore the moist ocean winds and fog which often move directly eastward from the mouth of San Francisco Bay towards the Berkeley and Oakland hills. Such cool, moist fog was a more typical condition for the area now gripped in desert winds and massive fires.

Emergency CORE Operation Initiated

By 11:00 PM on October 20, the day of the big fire, the cloudbuster was set up and operating at the water's edge, near the Oakland hills. All pipes were directed low to the horizon, west towards the Golden Gate and the opening of the Bay to the Pacific Ocean. Within minutes, a gentle, westerly breeze developed, with increasing humidity. We could look east to the Oakland hills and see a thousand ghostly lights, each of which was a burned-out remnant of someone's home. While the night-time had seen a decline in the fires, if the Santa Anna desert winds returned in the morning, each of those points of light would blaze up and become a source for another raging inferno and wildfire. By 3:00 AM of the 21st, with cloudbusting continuing, a brisk westerly sea breeze had developed. Operations were then ended.

By sunrise, the fire was still not completely contained, but the Santa Anna winds did not return. Instead, cool moist air with blankets of thick fog firmly pushed into the Bay area. The fog banks thickened over the course of the day such that by late afternoon they appeared more like rain clouds than fog. And, indeed, by late that day, a light drizzle did fall in a few places around the Bay. This was just what the fire fighters needed. By sunset on the 21st, about 36 hours after the fire began, it was completely contained and under control.

Only then did the real shock of what happened become obvious. With the fires out and smoke clearing, the hillside looked as if it had been hit by an atomic bomb. Nearly 4,000 homes and apartments were completely destroyed by the fire, and perhaps 40 or more persons died in the flames — the full number of dead was never firmly established due to the complete destruction of most of the homes. The total damage was estimated at close to $2 billion, one of the largest and most costly urban fires in US history! This event shocked me deeply, seeing it all so close up, and knowing about the possible link between the nuclear bomb testing and the weather changes along the West Coast. The only bright spot was the observation that the cooler, wetter conditions were reestablished after the cloudbusting operations. Thick clouds, cool fogs, and several new fronts with gentle to moderate rains pushed into coastal and interior California starting on October 22. These rains completely drenched the smoldering embers of the burned-out homes, and also extinguished other forest fires around the state. The weather had changed considerably for the better.

Deadly Oranur Winds Continue

Another episode tied to nuclear testing occurred only a few weeks later, in a strikingly similar manner. On November 26, a joint American/British underground nuclear bomb test took place in Nevada, with a 4.7 magnitude earthquake. Heavy oranur winds were again triggered, such that, by November 29, wind damage had occurred in various places. On that same evening, dust storms developed in the Central Valley, not too far from the same area where the Oakland fires took place. One major dust storm created blinding, zero-visibility conditions along major interstate highway I-5. The zero visibility and "normal" high-speed driving combined to create a massive automobile accident involving 130 vehicles. Some 35 people were killed and more than a hundred were seriously injured.

Did the underground nuclear tests actually *cause* the observed "bad winds"? Or were the events purely coincidental? I believe the oranur phenomenon, discovered by Reich (3), provides an adequate explanation for the observed atmospheric effects which developed on the heels of underground nuclear bomb tests: these nuclear explosions drive the orgone into a frenzied oranur condition. Oranur eventually dies off, to become deadened life energy, or deadly orgone, *DOR*. Both oranur and DOR conditions are inimical to the pulsatory energetic processes which govern clouds and rain; consequently, the qualities of stagnant energy in the desert areas of the West may be significantly increased by underground nuclear bomb tests. The desert atmosphere expands afterward, creating droughts in bordering areas. These ideas are developed from the writings of both Wilhelm Reich (3, 4) and Jerome Eden (5), as well as from my own field observations cited above. I have also endeavored to search out evidence from other workers, completely independent of Reich and orgonomy, who have observed similar unusual energetic phenomena associated with nuclear bomb tests or nuclear energy (6-15). Reich and his followers are not alone in observing unusual phenomena associated with nuclear energy, or long distance environmental reactions to underground nuclear bomb tests which violate classical theory. However, virtually every researcher investigating connections such as these has been censured and attacked for suggesting that the influences are real. We are forced to wonder how big a disaster will finally be required for people to wake up and take these issues seriously. ∎

3) Reich, W.: *The Oranur Experiment, First Report (1947-1951)*, Wilhelm Reich Foundation, Maine, 1951; partly reprinted in Reich, W.: *Selected Writings*, NY: Farrar Straus & Giroux, 1960.

4) Reich, W.: *Contact With Space*, Core Pilot Press, NY, 1957.

5) Eden J.: "Drought Relief in the Northwest", *Journal of Orgonomy*, 6(1):98-103, 1972; "UFOs, Dor, and Drought in the Northwest", *Journal of Orgonomy*, 7(2):246-253, 1973; "OROP Schweitzer Basin", *Journal of Orgonomy*, 13(1):140-145, 1979; "Operation Firebreak", *Journal of Orgonomy*, 13(2):261-267, 1979.

6) Berkson, J.: "Examination of Randomness of Alpha Particle Emissions", *Research Papers in Statistics*, F.N. David, ed., Wiley, NY, 1966.

7) Emery, G.: "Perturbation of Nuclear Decay Rates", *Annual Review of Nuclear Science*, Annual Reviews, Palo Alto, CA 1972.

8) Anderson, J. & Spangler, G.: "Serial Statistics: Is Radioactive Decay Random?" *J. Physical Chemistry*, 77:3114-3121, 1973.

9) Eugster, J.: "Radioactivity in the Simplon Tunnel (Switzerland)", *Physikalische Blatter*, 23, Jahrgang Heft 6, 1967.

10) Shnol, E., et al.: "Macroscopic Fluctuations with Discrete Structure Distributions as a Result of Universal Causes Including Cosmophysical Factors", and Udaltsova, N.V., et al.: "Possible Gravitational Nature of Factors Influencing Discrete Macroscopic Fluctuations", *Geo-Cosmic Relations, The Earth and its Macro-Environment*, Proceedings, 1st International Congress on Geo-Cosmic Relations, Amsterdam, Netherlands, 19-22 April 1989, G.J.M. Tomassen, ed., PUDOC Press, Wageningen, Netherlands, 1990.

11) Dahlman, O., et al: "Ground Motion and Atmospheric Pressure Waves from Nuclear Explosions in the Polynesian Test Area Recorded in Sweden, 1970", *FOA 4 Report*, C4461-26, 1971.

12) Katagiri, Y.: "Three Mile Island: The Language of Science Versus the People's Reality", *Pulse of the Planet*, 3:26-38, 1991.

13) Kato, Y.: "Recent Abnormal Phenomena on Earth and Atomic Power Tests", *Pulse of the Planet*, 1(1):5-9, Spring 1989.

14) "Lightning Increase After Chernobyl", *Science News*, 312:238, 10 Oct. 1987.

15) Whiteford, G.: "Earthquakes and Nuclear Testing: Dangerous Patterns and Trends", *Pulse of the Planet*, 1(2):11-21, 1989.

Report on Nuclear Accident, at Tomsk, Russia, 6 April 1993

The following paragraphs are extracted from memos circulated within the USA *CORE Network*, giving stark testimony to the intensification of widespread, hemispherical atmospheric oranur from recent nuclear pollution.

"MEMO: To CORE Network,
From Dr. Stephen Nagy, 10 May 1993:

Record high temperatures were set today in Seattle, Olympia, Portland, Stockton, and Fresno. Winds gusted to 47 miles per hour through the Klamath Basin, reducing visibility here to three miles at times because of dust. More dramatically, the sky changed abruptly, from this morning, when it was soft and dappled with clouds, to later in the day, when the clouds were dissipated completely at times, to be replaced by dark DOR clouds on the western horizon. Through the day I have been parched, a dry sense in my mouth, a feeling of being out of contact and headachy, and many people were observed to be irritable. After months of soft pulsation in the atmosphere, the change is dramatic and shocking, and cries out ORANUR. American Peace Test at (702) 386-9831 reports that the last US nuclear test was on Sept. 23 [1992], and the last test worldwide was Sept. 25 at Lop Nor, China, with a yield of 5 to 30 KT. Their report was last updated on April 29... Another possibility of the current dramatic change is the gradual downstream effect of the radiation blast in Siberia in the week of April 9. Apparently a tank at a nuclear waste depot exploded near Tomsk, with uranium and plutonium salts released into the atmosphere. In the week ending April 23, record high temperatures were recorded in Beijing, rising to 90°, making it the hottest April day since 1949. Frightening electrical storms developed in the Sichuan province on April 25th, spawning large hail that killed 12 people and destroyed thousands of homes in Chongqing, a major industrial city on the banks of the Yangtze. (*Earthweek*, weeks of April 9, 23, and 30) It seems possible that the oranur cloud has now crossed the Pacific. Please let me know of observations at your locations."

"MEMO: To CORE Network,
From Dr. James DeMeo, 18 May 1993:

Regarding Stephen Nagy's prior memo on oranur along the West Coast, he is absolutely correct here. Following the nuclear accident in Russia (April 9th) I received telephone calls from contacts in Germany, indicating a drought/heat wave and oranur crisis there following the accident, with unusual easterly winds blowing from Russia towards Germany. Over the next several weeks, that area of oranur migrated eastward around the globe, and finally arrived in California during the first 10 days of May. The feeling on the West Coast, which nearly everyone in the Network noticed, was similar to that of a nuclear bomb, with high air temperatures, cloud-free conditions, incredibly rich blue skies with a milky quality near the horizon, and wild angry winds. In fact, a number of wildfires developed in the hilly areas east of Los Angeles, reminiscent of conditions in early 1992. Thankfully, a cut-off low developed in the Pacific, sending streamers of moisture and clouds inland over the next days, and so the oranur crisis here was short-lived. It continues in Europe and Asia, however."

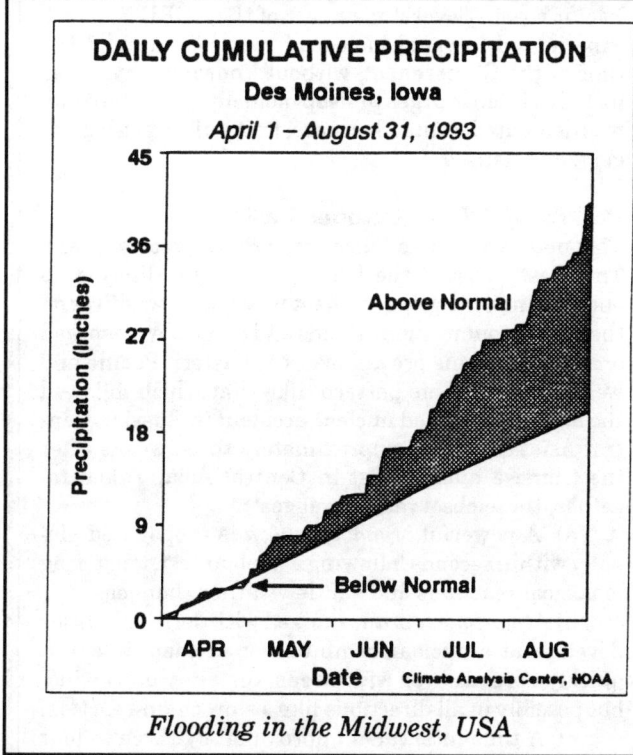

Flooding in the Midwest, USA

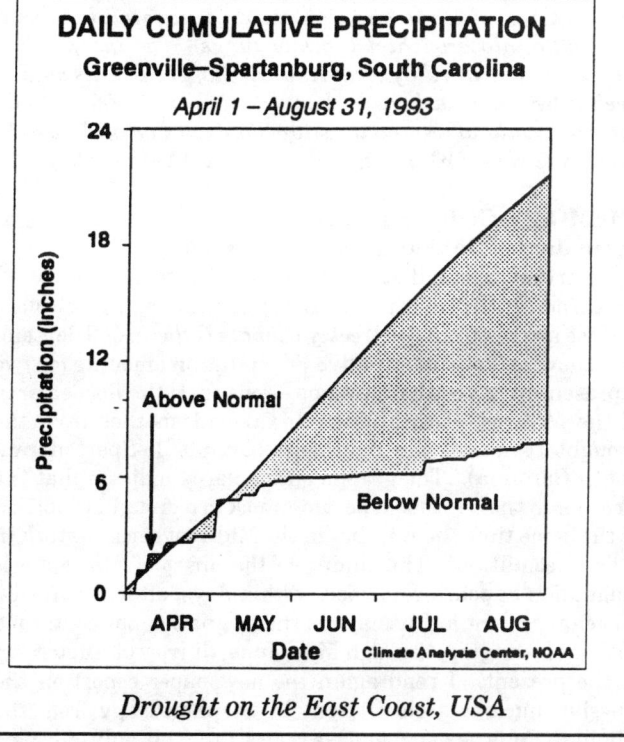

Drought on the East Coast, USA

Following the 6 April 1993 nuclear accident in Tomsk, Russia, sharp precipitation contrasts marked the Midwest and Eastern USA, and other places in the Northern Hemisphere. Massive floods occurred with droughts lying just to the east of flood areas, in both North America and Asia, suggesting a block in global atmospheric flow patterns.

"Earthweek, 14 May 1993:

An awesome sandstorm, which swept through China's Gansu and Ningxia provinces and Inner Mongolia for several days, killed at least 43 people. Many of the victims drowned when the 'black wind', as farmers called it, swept them into canals. The wind turned day into night as it whipped up sand and pebbles. Crops were buried by vast quantities of sand, and 300,000 head of cattle were smothered by the whirling cloud of earth. The leading edge of the sandstorm looked like a half-mile-high wave that came crashing down as it advanced across the Gobi Desert."

"Scientists: Russians Erred at Nuclear Site.

MOSCOW (AP) Scientists say Russia's government has grossly underestimated the contamination from last month's radioactive waste explosion in Siberia, the ITAR-Tass news agency reported. The April 6 accident was the worst in the former Soviet Union since the 1986 explosion and fire at Chernobyl, which killed 31 people and spread radioactive contamination over a wide area. The explosion near Tomsk contaminated about 46 square miles of land. Much of the area, about 1,700 miles east of Moscow, is covered by dense forest and is uninhabited. Authorities had said the explosion at the Siberian Chemical Complex posed no immediate danger to the health of people living in the area. But a non-governmental commission made up of local environmental officials, independent experts from Russia's Ecology Union, and scientists from nearby Krasnoyarsk have found "extremely high levels" of beta-ray radiation in soil around the area... The commission focused on farmland and private plots around the village of Georgiyevka, the news agency reported. It said the biggest danger was posed by radioactive dust particles — known as "hot particles" — that could be stirred from the ground or other surfaces and breathed in. The commission compared the "hot particles" to the residue around Chernobyl. It said they could cause fatal diseases if they settle into bronchial tubes or lungs. The independent report was disclosed by local Altai Radio, ITAR-Tass said, a week after local authorities banned work on 1,200 to 1,500 acres of farmland around the site of the explosion of Tomsk-7."
(*Herald & News*, Klamath Falls, Oregon, 13 May 1993)

"MEMO: To CORE Network,
From James DeMeo, 14 September 1993:

Further to our discussions about the hemispherical effects from the April 6th nuclear accident in Tomsk, Russia, I enclose a xerox from the *Weekly Climate Bulletin* of 8 September, showing daily cumulative precipitation amounts for two representative weather stations — one from the flooded area of the Midwest (Des Moines, Iowa) and another from the drought region of the Southeast (Greenville-Spartanburg, South Carolina). The graphs on the xerox indicate that the weather in the Southeast became stuck in a drought condition at the same time the weather in the Midwest became stuck in a flood condition. The timing of the onset of atmospheric stagnation appears very soon, within days, after the April 6 nuclear accident in Russia, and the stagnation has continued without letting up, through May, June, July, and August, up to the present. I read again the newspaper report on the Russian nuclear accident sent by Stephen Nagy from the Klamath Falls newspaper; this report probably only tells part of the story. I have other reports now in hand of massive nuclear accidents in Russia within recent years, suggesting that the problems there are far worse than anyone here could

imagine. I enclose a few relevant items [see the Nuclear Notes section reporting events in Russia in this issue of *Pulse*]. Recall my last mailing with the *Earthweek* and *Global Climate Highlight* maps for these recent months, indicating other major floods in the Northern Hemisphere, with droughts immediately to the east. This suggests the atmospheric stagnation is hemispherical in nature, having attached itself to the surface possibly at several places. If the situation continues, it may be that the only thing which will break it up will be some cloudbusting work in the Southeast, similar to that undertaken by John Schleining, Bob Morris and myself, back in 1986. As suggested in the last batch of maps, the complex of nuclear facilities in South Carolina is the central location of the Southeastern drought, and this appears to be the place where the North American stagnation is anchored."

An End to the Moratorium on Nuclear Testing

On October 5, 1993, the Chinese broke the world-wide moratorium on nuclear bomb testing. According to the Testing Alert Network Hotline (702/386-9831), the bomb was set off at the Lop Nor test site at 2:00 AM, GMT (6:00 PM Pacific Time) with a strength of <90 Kilotons, producing a local earthquake of 5.8 magnitude. It was detected by 71 seismic stations around the world. Following this test, the Clinton administration has issued instructions for the Department of Defense to resume nuclear testing in the USA, probably by next spring. France is also expected to resume testing in the Pacific, and so we can expect more disturbed weather and a possible Spring 1994 return of the drought on the Pacific coast. Several members of the CORE Network experienced unusual biological reactions around the time of the Chinese test, without knowing why; these included intense urges to sleep moments after the bomb was detonated, contactlessness, irritability, aching fingers, and nausea.

POSTSCRIPT, **27 October 1993:**
This note is added as *Pulse of the Planet* goes to press. The West Coast of the USA, primarily California, is once again in the grips of a heat wave, with wildfires on the hills consuming grasslands and homes. Widespread *oranur* conditions prevail over the eastern Pacific and western USA. This pattern, like that which followed the above-mentioned nuclear accident in Russian Central Asia, developed approximately three weeks after the Chinese nuclear test in Central Asia. Taken together, these observations suggest:

a) A powerful *orgonotic shock* is propagated globally within seconds following a nuclear test, triggering biological reactions and subtle weather changes.

b) *Atmospheric oranur* mixed with dorish qualities develops at a nuclear bomb test or accident site, but quickly spreads over wide areas, certainly downwind, but possibly in all directions like a slow chain-reaction.

c) A time interval of approximately three to four weeks is necessary for atmospheric oranur to travel from Central Asian nuclear test or accident sites to California, a distance of some 8,000 miles.

Wilhelm Reich Lecture Series

An evening class on "The Life and Works of Wilhelm Reich" was presented during the Spring and Summer months of both 1992 and 1993 at the Ft. Mason Conference Center in San Francisco, California. The class was instructed by James DeMeo, Ph.D., with guest lectures given by Marilyn Milos, R.N., Richard Blasband, M.D., and Joseph Heckman, Ph.D. The class covered the entire life and work of the late Wilhelm Reich, M.D., with significant discussion given to new research which corroborates Reich's findings. The course was attended by 20 to 30 individuals each evening, from around the San Francisco Bay area, and also occasionally from greater distances. Video documentary materials were presented on Reich, his family and co-workers, and laboratory demonstrations were given: The millivoltmeter was discussed and demonstrated, orgone accumulators and orgone blankets were presented and constructed during the class, and microscopic demonstrations of the bions and Reich blood test were given. The course will be repeated during Spring and Summer of 1994, on Thursday evenings. Cost will be $60 for the entire series, or $6 per class, payable at the door. Contact James DeMeo at the OBR Lab after January 1994 to receive more information and details. (PO Box 1395, El Cerrito, CA 94530 510/ 526-5978)

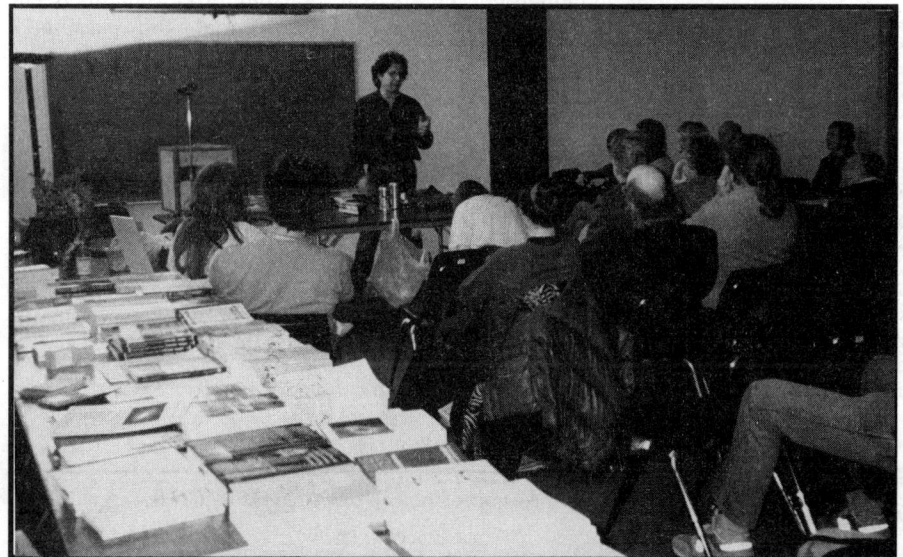

Wilhelm Reich Lecture Series, led by James DeMeo, Ph.D.

Introductory Workshop on Bions and Biogenesis

In June 1993, the Orgone Biophysical Research Laboratory hosted a one-day introductory laboratory workshop on Reich's bion and biogenesis findings. The workshop was led by Grier Sellers, C.A., who has years of experience in replicating aspects of Reich's work. Sellers formerly worked as a research assistant at NASA Ames Research Center, with Adolph Smith, Ph.D., on projects paralleling Reich's biogenesis work. Sellers was also a former organizer and participant in the West Coast Orgone Energy Workshop, an informal group which met regularly in San Francisco for years to discuss and replicate

Reich's findings. This year's Bion and Biogenesis Workshop was attended by around 12 individuals, including many professionals. It was a lively event which will be repeated in 1994. Contact James DeMeo at the OBR Lab after January 1994 for more information and details on the 1994 event. (PO Box 1395, El Cerrito, CA 94530 510/ 526-5978)

Proposal: A West-Coast Research and Educational Center

A new Research and Educational Center will be developed by the Lab in 1994, and financial support is being solicited from individuals and foundations. With the growth of working projects and public educational efforts, the present facility in El Cerrito, California is overcrowded and outgrown. Most of the Lab's analytical equipment is now in storage to make room for books, archived material and environmental data acquired during numerous field expeditions. New lab equipment has also been acquired for microscopic and spectrophotometric analyses, but with no space for set-up. Educational programs have also grown, and outside facilities must be rented for workshops and classes. The new Center will remedy this situation. The work of the Laboratory falls into the following four categories:

1) Environmental Field Work: This includes Desert Greening field operations in Arizona, California, Israel and Namibia, Africa, forest-healing research in Germany (*Orgonomic Project Waldheilung*), and work with the *CORE Network*, as described above. Additional projects may develop overseas in 1994, in the horn of Africa and Mediterranean regions. Together with responsible workers in the USA, the Lab has been contributing to the *CORE Network* in various ways. The new Center will allow better coordination and data analysis, and provide additional space for real-time display of weather maps and satellite images.

2) Laboratory Research: A new project is being drafted for study of the energetic properties of water (water structure), and also for analysis of the bionous characteristics of various soil and sand samples gathered over the years. Microscopes with video recording capabilities and spectrophotometric equipment have been acquired, but space is required for the undertaking. A student's lab is also needed. Another important requirement is a laboratory facility at a higher altitude, above 2500' elevation in the forested zone, where more sensitive and highly-charged orgone energy experiments can be undertaken. This has not been possible so far, and there currently is no functioning orgonomic laboratory facility in the world which is set up to replicate these high-charge aspects of Reich's original work. The new facility being planned will allow such work to proceed, in coordination with apprentice and educational functions.

3) Educational Activities: Our course *The Life and Works of Wilhelm Reich* and the lab-hosted workshop on *Bions and Biogenesis* will become yearly events. Working laboratory space is needed for these and other workshops. The research undertaken at the new Center would form the basis of educational functions, as it does within the university. Additional courses will be offered to fulfill the requests of many students who have requested the opportunity to study.

4) Publishing: Four issues of *Pulse of the Planet* have been published, along with a detailed *Bibliography on Orgone Biophysics*, and the popular *Orgone Accumulator Handbook*. Several *Special Reports* have also been completed: *OROP Arizona 1989* and *OROP Israel 1991-1992*. A *Special Report* is also in preparation for the Namibia, Africa 1992-93 Desert Greening research, and likewise, the work undertaken on Forest Healing will soon be published.

The above listing is an impressive record of accomplishment, about which we are most gratified. With development of the new Center, even more can be accomplished. A total of $300,000 is being sought to purchase land with existing facilities in the area of northern California — this is an environmentally clean region, with sufficient altitude to allow the development of a suitable orgone research facility. There are dozens of small ranches and farms within this price range, with several houses and outbuildings on 20 to 50 acres of land, which can be converted into the necessary facility. Several such places have been identified and surveyed. The new Research and Educational Center will provide space for: a Working Laboratory, a Student's Laboratory, an Environmental Monitoring and Weather Lab, a Library and Reading Room, a Typesetting Layout and Printing Room, a Tool and Fabrications Workshop, a Metal-lined Orgone Energy Darkroom, a General Office and Reception Room, a Classroom or Lecture/Seminar Room, a Rooftop Observatory, and a Guest Facility, with sufficient land for privacy and later expansion of facilities.

A 42-page proposal document is now available, outlining the details and rationale for the development of the new Research and Educational Center. Anyone interested in supporting, or learning more details about this proposed Center may write in or call to receive a copy. Donations (tax-deductible) of any amount will be greatly appreciated. Contact: Orgone Biophysical Research Laboratory, PO Box 1395, El Cerrito, CA 94530 USA, telephone 510/ 526-5978 (voice or fax).

3rd International Symposium on Circumcision
May 22-25, 1994, Washington, D.C.

The Symposia is sponsored by the National Organization of Circumcision Information Resource Centers (NOCIRC), covering genital and sexual mutilations of children, and broader issues relevant to the health and well-being of the infant and child. Speakers include Marilyn Milos, James Prescott, James DeMeo, Fran Hosken, George Denniston, James Snyder, and other clinicians and researchers on the topic of infant and child genital/sexual health. To be held on the campus of the University of Maryland, University College Conference Center. For additional information and a brochure, contact NOCIRC, PO Box 2512, San Anselmo 94979. 415/ 488-9883.

Educational Field Expedition to Santorini (Thera) and Crete

In Summer of 1993, at the invitation and sponsorship of the Hellenic Orgonomic Association, James DeMeo led a field expedition to various field sites and ruins of the ancient Minoan culture, which occupied the islands prior to c. 1600 BC. The Minoans were a peaceful society, exhibiting characteristics of unarmored genitality prior to the invasion of their island home by patristic mainlanders and the subsequent catastrophic explosion of the volcanic island of Thera. Thera is today a nearly vanished island, with only a crescent-shaped remnant, renamed Santorini. The ancient ash-covered city-site of Acrotiri on Santorini was explored, and the group also hiked to the smaller central volcanic cone and crater of the island, which had re-built itself from smaller lava eruptions over the centuries. There, sulphurous steam vents of the sleeping volcano were observed.

On Crete, the museum at Heraklion was a major highlight of the trip. This is where most of the artifacts and colorful wall frescoes of ancient Minoa were gathered. Other field sites were explored, such as the Minoan central administrative centers ("palaces") at Knossos and Phaistos. The trip included many shorter expeditions by boat to other sites and beaches, and it was an expansive and enjoyable educational adventure for the entire group, with a glimpse into an ancient world of sanity and happiness. A second educational, exploratory expedition is planned to these same islands in summer 1994 and interested students (young or old) may apply to participate. We wish to express a heart-felt "Thank You!" to Dr. Theodota Hassapi and other members of the Hellenic Orgonomic Association for making this exciting educational event possible.

Minoan Frescos from Knossos, Crete.

Towards Healthy Children of the Future

A special book sale organized by Lou Hochberg raised a seven hundred dollar honorarium for Eva Reich, M.D. Eva has spent most of her professional life traveling worldwide as an educator working with others towards the goal of self-regulation for children, and establishing gentle birthing clinics. Eva lives sparingly on a small farm in northern New England, growing much of her own food. The event was held during the Wilhelm Reich Lecture Series, San Francisco, to honor Eva Reich's many life-positive efforts and achievements.

The Deadly Innocent Nature of Gossip

STORY: *There once was a chicken who lost a feather from its wing. Upon seeing the feather float to the ground, the chicken exclaimed "Oh, I've lost a feather! But that's OK, because I'll grow two new ones in its place, and be even more beautiful!" The chicken was overheard by two other chickens who were standing behind the barn. Alarmed, they ran off and told the story to their friends. "Did you hear! Someone lost a bunch of feathers from their wing!" Oh, how the other chickens were alarmed to hear this, and they all ran off to tell the story to their friends. "Did you hear! Several chickens lost all their wing-feathers!" And so the story went round and round the barnyard, until the sun set and everyone went inside to sleep. In the morning, the first chicken, who lost the feather, came outside and stretched her wings. "Did you hear!" said another chicken standing nearby. "Hear What?" said the first chicken. "Well, several chickens lost all their feathers yesterday, and froze to death during the night!" "Oh, how terrible!" said the first chicken, who ran off to tell her friends!*

The moral of the above story is that rumor and gossip is not a reliable source of information. Reich was killed by such poisonous gossip, which formed the basis of various "articles" written about him by plaguey journalists, and from there, the "investigation" by the FDA. He also warred against gossipy tendencies within his own circle of associates, and even wrote several articles on the subject. One, titled "Truth Versus Modju: A Necessary Appendix on Social Pathology" (1) dealt mainly with the pestilent character, the trouble-maker who sets out purposefully to interfere with rational, work-democratic human interrelationships.

Another, titled "The Deadly Innocent Gossip of the Plague" (never published) appears to equally apply to the "social" gossip, the individual who "innocently" transmits "information" from one friend or associate to another, keeping everyone "informed". In society, one immediately thinks of the hateful rumors of young men about the women they have "laid", or the catty gossip of young women about each other, or about the boys. More damaging still is the gossip of old spinsters, who transmit smutty ideas about the love-lives of young people in the neighborhood, keeping a sharp eye on children, not to

1. *Orgone Energy Bulletin*, IV(3):162-170, July 1952

protect or help them, but rather to crush down their naturalness and sexuality. Such gossip plays an important role in every armored society, to keep people down, preventing them from breaking out and away from the existing *status quo*.

Even the social pioneer or the honest politician is prone to be attacked with sexual innuendo and slander, the most effective kind within our sex-starved world, which undermines any positive benefit to their work. Such gossipy tendencies can actually become organized, and connect with police and the courts, to become a truly powerful force to repress life, nature, and youth. Witness the "neighborhood spy" system of the communist states, or the various "religious policemen" predominating throughout the Muslim nations. These systems give legal power to the neighborhood snoop, who then reports on anybody doing anything "suspicious". This includes snooping on the sexual lives of young people, which is effectively criminalized.

Another difficult aspect of this problem is the occasional reliance upon gossip information within certain orgonomic circles, where information on one worker is passed along to others, without serious consideration about the truth or falsity of the information. There can be no excuse for this. Given that orgonomy deals with hot, burning issues of the day, clarity of fact is most important. Gossip tends to circulate and to be denigrating, mixing just enough truth to catch the interest of the eager listener with just enough poison to shock. Occasionally, therapy patients may act as a pipeline for transmission of misinformation from one orgonomic worker to another. The danger of unresolved negative transferences, which contaminates such "information" with additional poison, is self-evident. Or, questions which are raised after reading something published by one worker will be answered, not by directly asking them, but rather by negative speculating and jumping to conclusions. Without a high degree of caution, and a lot of self-criticism and fact-checking, such misinformation can provoke one group of workers to act towards another group like the FDA behaved towards Reich. This is inexcusable, and constitutes part of the "license ideology in our midst", which Reich warned against. To paraphrase Reich: *Why does plague gossip enjoy such wide circulation, with so many hungry listeners, while the truth is shunned and must come limping behind on crutches, panting with its tongue out?!*

Kollwitz

This question must increasingly be asked regarding the assertions and accusations of one "Reichian" group against another; this is just as important a problem, regarding emotional plague assaults against orgonomy, as attacks by groups such as CSICOP. It seems that, whenever anyone undertaking orgonomic work takes a new step, tries something different, or makes an open speculation which Reich did not previously undertake himself, there is a stir of "serious concern", or even knee-jerk opposition among other followers of Reich. A joke is now circulating which captures the essence of the difficulty here: *Where you have one orgonomist at work, alone, you have a social pioneer; when there are two orgonomists, you have a new Association; with three, you soon have a split.*

This joke is offered with some sympathy, as work in orgonomy is difficult and demanding, without the usual professional rewards. One is indeed lucky just to be left alone to do one's work, without harassment. Neither should my words be taken to mean that criticism should not be freely given. But criticism based upon gossip, rumor, or unsubstantiated allegations cannot be taken seriously, and is more illuminating about the motives of the critic than anything else. A worker undertaking new steps or directions in orgonomy must be allowed an unharassed opportunity to explore new territory or approaches; as Reich put it, *a researcher has the right to be wrong without being hung by the neck for it.*

If the new step proves unhelpful or invalid, they have the right to back up and return to more established lines of work, without censure or condemnation. Or, if they can establish a new approach or finding, and provide evidence for it, they should be congratulated for extending the boundaries of knowledge. On several occasions, the Director of the OBR Lab was forced to strongly confront damaging malicious gossip about our work, and the work of others. These confrontations are never pleasant, and unfortunately often cut off formerly productive lines of communication — but gossip is not a proper method for learning anything about anybody. Mostly, we know who is saying what about us, as the information eventually gets to our ears, like chicken-feather stories. Anyone with a significant question about work undertaken here can obtain a direct and friendly answer by simply writing or calling. Nothing in our work is hidden, and we welcome inquiries and constructive criticism.

Reich's Independence and Strength of Character

Someone once criticized Reich regarding his making strong demands upon his co-workers. "Reich", they said, "its easy for you to talk about being strong and facing up to the plague in one's workplace or community. You publish books and have an organization that supports you, and you are very independent. Its easy for you to speak out!" Reich replied, simply "How do you think that I got into this position? Not by making compromises on important matters!" The message here is the path an individual takes towards personal freedom, or which a social group takes towards collective freedom, is paved with a lot of sweat and sacrifice. Freedom is only maintained in such a manner. It is lost, individually and collectively, through the gradual, progressive abandonment of personal responsibility. While often a difficult task, freedom is preserved through maintenance of personal honesty and integrity, and by avoiding alliances with the emotional plague, no matter how powerful or persuasive the superficial reasons. Life-positive work requires emotional-core contactfulness between individual workers, just as love requires core contact between lovers. Basic human decency and honesty is our best,

and most potent weapon against plague behavior, and for dealing with all forms of human problems.

"Beyond Reich"

A series of six articles on Reich appeared in the *Athens Free Press*, starting on 27 February 1990. Details about Reich's cancer research, the orgone energy, accumulator, cloudbuster, and other aspects of orgonomy, were provided to the reporters by members of the Hellenic Orgonomic Association (HOA). However, when the article series was published, no mention of the HOA was given. Instead, the series presented the "Center for Wilhelm Reich Studies and Psychotherapy" (CWRSP) as the only Reich group in Greece. A letter to the newspaper (published 26 July 1990) by the HOA reminded the editor that much of the material for the article series was provided by them, and pointed out that the CWRSP had never accepted the tenets of orgone therapy, bion research, orgone energy, accumulator or cloudbuster. A reply letter from the CWRSP was subsequently published, with the headline "Why the Reichians Argue", in which the Center's director confessed: *"Reich's thought was the basis of our psychotherapy, but there have been studies that go beyond his studies, such as: Lowen, Johnson, Navarro, Brown, Rispoli, Boadella, Liss. Their studies go beyond Reich's..."* and also *"We believe it is charlatan to promise that if someone puts someone in a box built by an amateur he can cure himself of sickness, even cancer."* When confronted, these people who use the name of Reich in their organizational title, show their lack of knowledge about and actual contempt for the man and his work. Any worker following in Reich's footsteps who claims to go "beyond Reich" has quite a task to perform, in the manner of providing evidence for their claims. Generally, the words "beyond Reich" are used by those who have clearly failed to fulfill the claim, who instead have only grasped a small part of Reich's work, and who speak or write such words with obvious contempt.

Neo-Reichian "Religions"?

From both the USA and Europe, examples are discovered of "Reichian" therapists who preach a new "Reichian moralism" of abstinence prior to marriage, compulsive marriage, anti-abortion, and female subordination. Christian Reichians, complete with photo images of an Aryan Jesus on their office walls, or Jesus bleeding on the cross, are appearing here and there, trained by other neo-Reichians. Also, "Reichians" who advocate the circumcision of baby boys, as part of the "civilizing-socializing" process. These are new twists, indeed. Do we need to even say the following? Apparently so. Any individual who pushes religious fundamentalism in a "Reichian" garb has already lost touch with the essence of Reich's work, and is certainly not a spokesperson for Reich. So far, these individuals have not made any public acclamation of their views, and so beyond this short note, nothing more will be said.

"Orgone Energy" in Webster's Dictionary

Squeezed in between *orgiastic* and *orgy*, one can find the words *orgone box* and *orgone energy*, with definitions not too divergent from the nasty and inaccurate words of Mildred Brady or Martin Gardner: "orgone box, a cabinetlike device constructed of layers of wood and other materials as tin, claimed by its inventor, Wilhelm Reich, to restore orgone energy to persons sitting in it, *thereby aiding in the cure of impotence, cancer, the common cold, etc.*" Now, we observe that Webster's does not yet have an entry for *emotional plague...*

"Summerhill at 70"
A Personal Perspective
by Matthew Appleton *

Introduction

The Channel 4 documentary "Summerhill at 70" was broadcast on British television in March 1992, stirring up a great deal of controversy in the media. The ripples of this controversy were felt as far away as America, where the *Wall Street Journal* ran a derogatory editorial entitled "The Ruins of Education's Past". It is now some six months later at the writing of this article, and the ripples, despite their dramatic intensity at the time, have largely died down. However, in their wake, and as a direct result of the film, we have been visited by the H.M.I. (government school inspectors) and the local Social Services, both of whom have carried out intensive inspections of the school.

On a more personal level, many of us here have been left with a bad taste in our mouths; that particularly unpleasant taste we experience when we feel that our integrity has been abused. As someone featured prominently throughout the film, I feel this very keenly myself. My intention here, however, is not to vent personal venom, which is why I have waited so long to put pen to paper, but to put on record an account of events leading up to the film, the making of the film, and the subsequent effect it has had on the Summerhill community. I want to do this partly because I feel we owe it to all the people who have shown an interest in the school over the years, and supported us in our work here; and also because there are lessons to be learned from this experience that might be of value to others involved in such work.

It is impossible to give a complete overview, especially when so intimately involved, so I have not attempted to give anything other than a personal account. In doing so, I have tried to be as accurate and honest as possible. I am not so much concerned with accusations or justifications, but they cannot be completely avoided, nor are they necessarily inappropriate, either. But an indignant rant would be of little interest to anyone. I hope that this article will go some way to setting the record straight as to the context in which the film was made and answer some of the questions that have arisen in the minds of those who are concerned with the well-being of Summerhill and it's principles.

Background: The School

Filming began in the summer term of 1991 although the bulk of the film came from the autumn term. The summer before this, the group of older children who had been most active in running the community left, leaving us with a very young school, which can happen every now and again. This inevitably means that our self-government is rather weak for awhile as the younger children grapple with the new respon-

* Matthew Appleton is a houseparent at the Summerhill School, Leiston, Suffolk, England. Summerhill was founded by the pioneering educator, A.S. Neill who advocated the self-regulation of children in schooling. See: "The Ecology of Childhood: A View from Summerhill School" by Appleton in *Pulse of the Planet #3*, Summer 1991, pp. 57-61.

sibilities that are thrust upon them; a slow, but powerful process as experience begins to teach them the difference between freedom and license. At such a time, the adults in the community tend to take a stronger stand in the meetings, emphasizing the concerns of the younger and weaker children, and of the community as a whole. It is this mixture of reasoning (usually, and ideally, from the older children) and the possibility to experience through experiment, that leads the insecure or anti-social newcomer towards a more community-minded sense of self.

Sporadically, throughout the history of the school, the community has voted to throw out all the laws. This is with the exception of the safety laws, which are not in the hands of the meeting. Usually, after a short burst of chaos, the laws are quickly reinstated, and life soon settles down again. But when this happened in the summer term of 1991, it was five weeks before the bedtime laws were returned, and not until the beginning of the next term that the main body of laws were reinstated. During this time, however, although a little more chaotic than usual, the community was far from floundering. The children had voted to keep the meetings, even though the laws were dropped, and people could still be charged and fined for interfering with others. There were various attempts at silence hours so that those who wanted to sleep could do so, and every week, as the need arose, one or two laws would be returned. The first ones appeared only days after the laws were dropped, and these concerned the use of wheels inside (bikes and skateboards, etc.), who could use the disco equipment, and the laws governing smoking (i.e. you cannot smoke unless you ask to be an exception). So, although during this time there were actually very few laws in writing, common sense still prevailed on the whole. The most that the community suffered was a general sense of aimlessness and lethargy — essentially a lack of community spirit — as everyone was keeping different hours, and when the bedtime laws came back in the last week of term, a great cheer went up in the meeting.

The following autumn term saw fourteen new kids arriving which, in a community of approximately sixty five children, is a large number. These new kids were mostly 'House kids', the 'gangster age' (11, 12, 13 year olds). They are so named because, although most new kids tend to go through some sort of 'anti-social' stage (a stage in which they vent pent-up feelings incurred in previous schools, or at home where they have been allowed little or no voice of their own) it tends to be at its strongest at about this age. (We do not generally take new children after this age.) This influx of new kids was of particular concern, as there were still, as yet, very few older kids who had fully emerged from this stage, and the lack of laws would mean that what boundaries they did find themselves pushing against would be far wider, and of greater consequence, than is usual at Summerhill. On top of this, there would also be the film crew with their cameras and lights, which, however unintentionally, could only excite the situation further.

With these concerns in mind, one of the staff brought a whole list of laws, which had not been returned in the previous term, to the first meeting of the new term. Each of these was discussed separately and the majority were voted in by the community. The novelty of no laws had, by and large, worn off. Also, new to the school this term was a new teacher for Class 2, the class which caters mainly for the 'gangster age' kids. He was an ex-lawyer from America and we had been somewhat dubious about his suitability to the post. He was middle aged, disillusioned with his work in law, and used to a higher standard of living than would be possible at Summerhill. Also, he would be bringing with him his three children, aged 11, 14, and 17. However, he had experience teaching and was very enthusiastic. Concerned that he was a bit too idealistic for the everyday rigors of life at Summerhill, we initially tried to put him off; but he was persistent in his request to be given a chance. So, eventually, he was invited over with his children to spend a few days at the school. This occurred in the spring of 1991. We did our best to convey the reality of Summerhill to him, stressing the more difficult aspects of adult life here. However, along with his enthusiasm he impressed us with his commitment to the ideas of the school and an air of down-to-earth maturity, which allayed our fears that he might have his head in the clouds.

It is always difficult to know how people, adults and children alike, will respond to Summerhill once they are actually in the community. Sometimes the most unsuitable sounding candidates blossom and flourish, whilst others, who might be expected to take to community life like a fish to water, turn overnight into lone sharks or grounded jellyfish. Most, after a short period of floundering or thrashing about, begin to find their feet, but I think its true to say that life at Summerhill often touches great emotional depths in people, and it is not always possible to judge from surface impressions how they will react to the real thing. Every newcomer to Summerhill is therefore, to some degree, a gamble.

In the case of our new Class 2 teacher, things quickly turned sour. Instead of interacting with the other adults, he rarely ventured out of his room nor took any part in staff meetings unless pushed to do so. His contribution then would be minimal, almost resentful. On the occasions that he did socialize with other staff members, he was quick to criticize the manner in which the school ran, and was derogatory about staff members who were not present. His particular grudge was with the manner in which certain adults took an active part in the school's self-government. He did not believe that adults should speak in the meetings at all. Instead of tackling the issue openly in the staff room, or in the weekly General Meeting, he made unpleasant jibes about individuals whilst they were not there to defend themselves. Nor was his opinion arrived at through the unfolding of understanding that comes from experience and openness. It was a rigid, ideological stance that he arrived with, and was not prepared to question in the slightest.

His influence, although not a powerful one, was an unpleasant one, and in various ways had an effect throughout the community. This was mainly felt in the attitudes of his three children. Often they could be heard repeating, parrot fashion, sentiments that he had expressed on earlier occasions to members of staff, or bad-mouthing certain members of staff, targeting and criticizing them exactly as the father did. His children began to voice many of these opinions in the meetings, but having no basis in actual experience, they were incoherent and intangible, and as such, were not taken seriously by the other children, with the exception of only one or two malcon-

tents. Indeed, the opinionated and sneering nature in which they expressed themselves did little to endear them to the rest of the community.

This was perhaps the most disturbing aspect of his influence, for although it lacked credibility in the community, it did prevent his own children from settling down and living their own lives at Summerhill. They were already caught up in an unpleasant and disturbing custody case between him and his wife. Added to this, they were caught between their own experience of Summerhill and their father's opinions. This conflict was most apparent in his eleven year old son to whom I was houseparent. Almost every evening, either I or someone else had to deal with some sort of aggressive confrontation between this boy and one of the other kids. Nor was this the sort of mild skirmish I am used to at Summerhill; there was a very definite violent edge to his behavior. One evening, after such an incident, he became wildly hysterical, screaming at me that I favored other children (more of which I will say later), that the staff ran Summerhill and were fascists, that it was nothing like Neill's books, that the meetings were useless, and the other children he shared a room with were 'sick'. I and a couple of the older kids tried to reason with him, but it was impossible. It was as though he had been brainwashed; his thoughts were soaring around totally beyond his own experience, flying out of reach every time he tried to get a grasp on them. Later, I went to talk with his father, expressing my concern that this boy could never settle down at Summerhill if he was constantly being told such things as the meetings are useless and the other kids were sick. Confirming that he had expressed these opinions to his son, he concluded that it was his right as a father to do so, and that it was no concern of mine.

The overriding and most traumatic event of this term, however, was the death of Akira, a twelve year old Japanese boy who had been with us since he was six. At the beginning of term, he did not return with the other Japanese kids, and we were told that he had a bad asthma attack a few days earlier. A couple of weeks into term we were informed that he had died. It is difficult to understand the depth of grief into which the community was thrown unless you have lived here. We are more like an extended family than a school, and the relationships forged here are very real and very deep. Akira was a particularly popular kid, with friends throughout the school. He had touched almost all of our lives in some way. A special meeting was called and Zoe [the headmistress of Summerhill and daughter of Neill] informed the school of his death. I remember that day as the most painful day of my life, and I am sure that there are many others who will remember it as such. It was as if a bomb had hit the school. There was none of the laughter, the games, the running around that had been minutes before; only silence and tears.

Shuffling their way through this emotional debris, the new kids must have wondered what hit them. All around, there was grief that excluded them. Months later, one of them cried as he told me how guilty he had felt being surrounded by all this sadness and yet not sharing in it. I had been Akira's houseparent for several years and had become extremely close to him. During that time, I had seen him through several very bad asthma attacks, and although I had always known they were potentially fatal, somehow I had never really considered that he might actually die. After his death, I went completely to pieces, and was given a couple of weeks leave. When I returned, I felt desolate and found it hard to be enthusiastic in my work. What had been a joy before, now became an effort. But I plodded on, doing my best, yet unable to really put my heart into it.

That term, Akira had been due to move up to the 'Shack', the next age group, but for the past few years he had been a 'House kid'. Most of his closest friends were therefore amongst the 'House kids', and it was with these children that the new kids were most intimately in contact. As the houseparent for the 'House kids', I was also the adult they were most likely to have the greatest contact with. Given these circumstances, it was very difficult for the new kids to integrate. They inevitably felt excluded by the sense of shock and grief that united me and the other House kids. This was further aggravated by the Class 2 teacher spreading it around amongst the new kids via his own children, that I was exercising favoritism.

Background: The Filmmakers

I do not remember when I first heard mention of the film, but it sounded like an exciting project. We often have film crews visiting Summerhill, and they usually stay only a few days, doing a couple of interviews, filming a meeting and some shots of kids running around and playing. The end result is usually innocuous, but rarely inspiring. The idea of an in-depth study of Summerhill was very appealing. Personally, I have felt that it is an important element of the school to show the world what kids are capable of, given the chance; that they are able to run their own communities, direct their own lives without constant adult interference, play until their heart's content, and then learn without being bribed and pushed into doing so. An in-depth study could show this at work, while also honestly exploring the difficulties that many children have moving from a system in which there is little freedom or responsibility, to one in which they are regarded as citizens of equal merit. The dynamics of this process would, if charted with sensitivity, be a powerful statement about childhood.

The aim of the filmmakers, it seemed, was to make such a film and to do so, they wanted to live in the community for three or four months, having complete freedom to film whatever and wherever they wanted. The only restrictions would be verbal ones, i.e. if anyone did not want them to film, they would respect that request and turn the cameras off. We were not blind to the possibility that the filmmakers could make a negative film. As I have said earlier, no one knows how anyone is going to react when they actually come to Summerhill. We have had bad experiences even with visitors who stayed a few weeks and were unable to tolerate the liveliness of the children without becoming anxious or resentful. However, these filmmakers seemed very credible. A married couple in their mid-thirties, Peter Gretzels and Harriet Gordon Gretzels, had both studied anthropology before becoming filmmakers. Americans, they had read *Summerhill* as students in the sixties, and it had been an inspiration to them ever since. Having made several documentaries in South America, their great ambition was to make a documentary about Summerhill. They envisaged a powerful tribute to the school's principles that would put Summerhill back in the limelight of the educational debate where, they said, they believed it belonged while also putting them on the map as filmmakers.

So it was that they were welcomed into the community, along with their two daughters, one aged four and the other only six months old. They struck me as sincere, lively people when I first met them. They gushed with good intentions and were very convincing. As soon as any question arose as to how they would portray the school, they urged "we're on your side", "we believe in Summerhill". They seemed genuinely supportive and became upset at any hint that this might be called into question. Over the weeks, they struck up friendships with both staff and kids, and it was in this spirit of friendship that we let them into our lives to make their film.

I did not personally have a great deal to do with them. When they began filming in the last few weeks of the summer term, I was tired from the long weeks of no bedtimes or laws, which had put alot of stress on me as a houseparent living in the heart of it all. Then, in the first weeks of the autumn term, I was preoccupied with getting the new kids settled in, and then the trauma of Akira's death caused everything else to fade into the background. Yet, I was also aware that they were focusing their camera on me a great deal.

They also seemed to be focusing very much on the new kids, particularly upon the two youngest children of the Class 2 teacher and another American boy who came to us full of frustration and rage after a series of traumatic experiences in schools in the States. (The extent to which they focused on these three children is reflected in the assumption of many newspapers that the majority of children are American. In fact, at the time of the filming, there were only three American kids in the whole school!) Apart from these particular children, they seemed to be mainly following around the 'gangster-age' kids, and turning on the camera every time there was a commotion or a confrontation. They did not seem to take any interest in the wider life of the community and everyday events of which that wider life is comprised.

This began to disturb me. On the one hand, I felt that it was important this element of the school should be portrayed. As houseparent for this age group, I am deeply concerned with the details and dramas of which their lives are composed. On the other hand, it worried me that the film crew were seemingly targeting the most aggressive of these kids at their most confrontational, without giving adequate attention to the wider social structure that contained and dealt with these difficulties. It worried me even more when I learned that they intended to use little, if any, interview material or voice overs to set the context, but would rely almost exclusively on the events they filmed to speak for themselves. I was afraid that without proper background, the school could come off as a very aggressive and uncaring place. I expressed my concerns to them.

As always, they seemed pained that their good intentions, or judgement, should be questioned. They assured me that they would structure the film in such a way as to explain what was happening and to put events in their rightful context. I made suggestions to them, such as filming the bedtimes when things generally begin to calm down, and these 'gangsters' who are running around all day letting off steam begin to filter into my room to make hot chocolate and have bedtime stories read to them before settling down for the night. It seemed to me that this aspect of these children's lives was every bit as important as their more boisterous activities, and that the contrast between these two elements gave a fuller and more vivid picture of their nature, and of the school as a whole. They made several appointments with me to be there for the bedtimes, but did not keep them. (In fact, they did eventually venture up, but by then it was a couple of days to the end of the term and the kids were predictably hyped-up, which was aggravated even more by the camera and lights.)

As the term progressed, I grew more and more worried. Rather than settling in, the film crew seemed to become increasingly tense, frantic and chaotic. Although some of this was obviously due to the pressures of their work, it was also obvious they were finding the liveliness and pace of life at Summerhill hard to follow — which they began to acknowledge themselves. It also upset them that their five year old daughter started to drop some of her politeness and become something of a 'gangster' in her ways. They began expressing increasingly negative attitudes towards the school, stating, for example, to my girlfriend who was working for them as a baby-sitter, that they thought the staff encouraged aggressive and anti-social behavior in the new kids. Yet, at the same time, whenever questioned about the slant their film might take, they insisted that they supported Summerhill and their film would be very positive.

The Film

The film was all I feared it might be, and all that the filmmakers had insisted it would not be. It had a frantic, chaotic quality to it; one scene after another depicting tension and conflict with little remission. Minimal information was provided to set the scenes in context, and it was difficult to make sense of what was actually happening unless you had been there at the time. Even then, it was not always easy as they would splice two meetings into one, giving the impression they were one and the same. The train of events became lost in the editing in such a way that it seemed as if all anyone ever did at Summerhill was shout at each other. There was no sense of how things developed, or the underlying dynamics; just disjointed scenes full of angry outbursts and confrontations.

During the time they were filming, they had attended and filmed several staff meetings stating that they felt it important that viewers knew that the adults were aware of, and in constant touch with what was happening in the community. Without this perspective, they said, it might seem as if the kids were running amok with no one caring about what they did. In fact, this is just what it did seem like to many people, and no scenes from the staff meetings were used to suggest otherwise. Even more important than the staff meetings, the film failed to convey the way in which the self-government regulates everyday life at the school, or the high degree of genuine care and spontaneous affection that exists amongst the majority of kids and staff. Although there were many shots of the meetings, there was little sense of anything getting resolved. The older kids were hardly featured at all, and even though there were few older kids there at the time taking a role in the self-government, they were certainly around and quietly getting on with their own activities. A third of the school were Japanese, yet hardly a Japanese face appeared. What of these kids?

Another questionable aspect of the film is why certain scenes were used and what message were they meant to convey. For example, there weren't any shots of the autumn end-of-term party with the sense of community and warmth it embodied. Nor did they show the children hugging and kissing each other and staff as they prepared to set off for the holidays. The end-of-term good-byes are always a moving scene, and I remember the film crew filming this. Instead, they only showed the bleak aftermath of the party — a wrecked lounge covered in end-of-term debris (which, incidentally, a group of staff and older children cleaned up the next day), and empty bedrooms strewn with litter and mattress's askew. It painted a very desolate picture, rather than the very warm and affectionate one it could have painted. Why was this view of the school considered of interest, and the other one edited out?

The main criticisms arising from the film centered around a handful of issues, such as the use of 'bad language', particularly by Zoe, the seeming lack of lessons, the apparent level of aggression, a massage class in which I instruct students on how to perform a back massage, and a theatrical wedding in which, dressed up like a vicar, I 'marry' two of the kids. The single issue that caused the greatest outrage was the killing of a rabbit with a machete by a fifteen year old boy. With a little more information, viewers might not have jumped so quickly to the conclusions that they did. For example, it was not made clear that the 'wedding' was a spoof, a bit of theater instigated by a couple of the kids. Many people thought it was a serious ritual, overseen by the staff, that all kids went through when they became 'paired-up'. Nor was it made clear that the rabbit which was killed by Zoe's son was suffering from myxomatosis [a highly infectious, fatal disease of rabbits].

Looking back at the film some six months later, I am still left with many ambiguities and unanswered questions. In my own mind, I have time and again questioned the motives of the filmmakers. Although I have drawn my own conclusions, they still remain sketchy and incomplete. Of one thing I am certain: it was not simply a matter of wanting to make a sensational film, even though this might have been one element of it. There were other factors, too, of a more nebulous and unconscious nature. Beyond this, though, there is only speculation. Whatever the motives, the film stands as a flawed testimony to documentary filmmaking. It is surely the duty of any serious documentary maker to set the context in which a film

WILD: Boys and girls are allowed to bathe in the buff

Photo and caption that appeared in British newspaper.

is made and to inform the public of essential facts. To quote psychiatrist M. Scott Peck from his book *The Road Less Traveled*:

"...because it may seem less reprehensible, the withholding of essential information is the most common form of lying, and because it may be the more difficult to detect and confront, it is often even more pernicious..."

The Aftermath

If the picture that the film painted was bleak, the picture that the newspapers painted was even blacker. For several weeks the newspapers were full of headlines such as "TV LAD HACKS HEAD OFF RABBIT", "SEX AND VIOLENCE ARE OK AT LORD OF THE FLIES SCHOOL", "PUPIL'S TOPLESS MASSAGES TO BE SHOWN ON TELEVISION", and "HOME MOVIE FROM HELL". The sensationalism of the tabloids was to be expected, but what I found most distressing was the manner in which many of the more 'intelligent' papers used their reviews as soap boxes to air their own prejudices rather than questioning the bias of the film. Then there were the inaccuracies, the misquotes, and the quotes taken out of context.

For awhile it felt like we were under siege. Almost every day there was another article full of inaccurate assumptions and quotes turned inside out. We all felt a deep sense of hurt, anger and grief. As Zoe said at the time, "this is what it must feel like to have been raped". The papers treated us more like fictional characters they could play around with to suit their own plots, rather than as real live human beings with feelings, friends, and a community we cared about. We found ourselves avoiding going into town. There were unpleasant phone calls and letters, and on several occasions, kids were threatened downtown by local youths. Yet, at the same time, many friends rallied around. We received alot of phone calls and letters of support; some from ex-Summerhillians, some from people who had visited the school, some from parents past and present, and some from people who had just read between the lines of the film and glimpsed the essential humanity which is the bedrock of life at Summerhill.

With the knowledge that the film was likely to be sold abroad, the school approached Channel 4 to ask if some changes could be made. These included changing the title from "Summerhill at 70" to something such as "New Kids at Summerhill". It was felt that "Summerhill at 70" implied an overview of the state of the community in it's seventieth year, whereas, in fact, it concentrated on just a small minority within the school. There was also a request for more information to be added so people could understand the context in which events occurred before drawing their conclusions. It was also asked that the 'rabbit scene' be withdrawn, partly because in Britain it had proved to be such a sensational scene, it overshadowed the rest of the film; and, also, because of the distress it had already caused the boy concerned who had been assured by the filmmakers that it would not be included before he gave them permission to film it. Each one of these requests was refused.

The attitude of Channel 4 was that they considered the film to be a fair portrayal of Summerhill, and that if we did not like the finished product, it was our own fault for having given the camera such a free rein. The underlying tone was one of 'well, you should have known we were going to make a film like this', implying that responsibility lay solely with us for being so naive as to have trusted them. They also hinted that they could have made things even worse for us if they had wanted to do so.

For sometime after the film was broadcast, the film crew continued to keep in contact with the school, although never returning. It seemed important to them to try and justify the film to us, and they reacted angrily when we defended ourselves in the media which inevitably involved some criticism of the film. They would darkly hint that if we wanted a battle, they could and would dig up even more dirt on us. Even then, they continued to insist that they supported us and reacted with hurt that we no longer considered them as friends. As far as they were concerned, they had made a radical film about childhood; a controversial, but positive portrayal of Summerhill.

The following term we were subject to an intensive inspection by both the H.M.I. (government school inspectors) and the local Social Services. Although we had been due for a Social Services inspection anyway, they told us it had been brought forward because of the number of complaints they had received following the film. Similar pressure had been brought to bear on the H.M.I., who had conducted a thorough inspection only two years earlier. As a result, they made various recommendations such as more systematic record keeping, new floor covering in some of the bedrooms and corridors, more wash basins and toilets (as always), but specifying this time separate ones for boys and girls, and for adults and kids, new sick rooms (again, separate ones for boys and girls), and the replacement of a couple of roller towels we have with some other form of hand drying...in case one of the kids accidentally hung themself!!! Just how far we will be required to fulfill these recommendations is yet to be ascertained, but at best they will cost us a lot of money, and at worst, they pose an unpleasant threat to our independence and principles. Yet, none of these recommendations is in any way related to the issues arising from the film.

This last year has been a rough ride. The double trauma of first losing Akira and then the film, have shaken the community to it's roots. There is still pain, but there has been much healing, which I know will continue. The film showed that we are able to shout and swear at each other, but what it did not show, and we have known all along, is that we are also able to support and care deeply for each other. It is ironic that the kids who were most prominent in the film were actually with us for that term only. The Class 2 teacher left at the end of the term, disappearing on the continent with his three children when it looked like he was in danger of losing his custody case. The other American boy returned to the States after his father was transferred back there; and his mother writes, "all the staff in his suburban school said that they have seen tremendous growth in my son. He is more focused on his work, more adept in his reading."

In a couple of days the new term starts. I look forward to it optimistically. We lost only one kid as a result of the film, which was sad because it was the first time he had ever enjoyed being at school (ironically, he was bullied at all his other schools). We have a good number of new kids arriving, the majority of whom, for the first time in a few years, are English. (As somebody once said, "The only bad publicity, is no publicity.") Our young community has grown over the past couple of terms, and the older kids have begun to feel their strength and take the reins of self-government. It will be good to see them all again. They always come back much bigger after the long summer holiday. ∎

The Beauty of Children:
Through a Child's Eyes

The artwork on these pages is by Karen Carrino (1953 - 1972), who died in an automobile accident five days after her nineteenth birthday. The drawings reflect not simply Karen's innate talent, but her intense interest in, and love of children. Barely more than a child herself, between the ages of thirteen and nineteen she produced over 300 sketches and paintings as well as several sculptures of children. Before she died, she was looking into opportunities for working in a "free school" system whose principles were based on those espoused by A.S. Neill of Summerhill.

During her lifetime, Karen's work had begun to receive considerable attention. Her pictures capture the special aliveness of children, the very core of their unique characters. Shortly after her death, though, the body of work was sold by her father, who did not keep records of its whereabouts.

For the past 2 years, Karen's sister Deborah, also an artist, has conducted a search for Karen's artwork and has located 260 of the 360 pieces she estimates were sold. The search is not to reclaim the work, but to photograph and catalog it for a book Deborah is writing about her late sister. In December of 1991, Karen's work was given a one-woman show at Drew University in New Jersey. The show was a focus of a front page story in the New Jersey section of the *New York Times*. Several other newspapers and television news programs have covered the story of Karen's work and Deborah's search for it, and collectors from as far as Florida and Michigan have come forward with works to be added to her catalog. For more information and prints, contact Deborah Carrino at 96 Mount Bethel Road, Warren, NJ 07059.

Boy Holding Pencil   pencil on paper, 1968

Fair Haired Friends   pencil on paper, 1972

Seated Boy   scratchboard, 1970

Crying Baby
pencil on paper, 1972

Two Boys Wrestling
pencil on paper, 1972

Michael Sleeping
pencil on paper, 1970

Beauty of Children

Deadly Deceit: Low-Level Radiation, High Level Cover-up
By Jay M. Gould and Benjamin A. Goldman, with Kate Millpointer

Four Walls Eight Windows, Second Edition, NY, 1991, 266 pages, $10.95, Softbound
Reviewed by Robert Leverant, M.A., M.F.C.C.

Out of the libraries come the killers.
Mothers standing despondently waiting,
Hugging their children and searching the sky,
Looking for the latest inventions of professors.
Engineers sit hunched over their drawings:
One figure wrong, and the enemy's cities remain
undestroyed.

Bertolt Brecht, "1940"

On August 10, 1945, a few days after the U.S. dropped the atomic bomb on the unwarned citizens of Hiroshima and Nagasaki, Wilhelm Reich issued a plea and warning to the world community about the dangers to all life and the earth from nuclear energy.(1) Reich was a mature man, a lover of life and guardian of the living, who described himself in his short essay as a professor of biophysics and medicine. He had spent 20 years studying atomic energy in its natural state which he called *orgone energy*, and the destructive effect of unnatural or nuclear energy on this natural energy.(2) Thus, Reich spoke with authority:

"Based on my knowledge of atomic energy, I agree with those who maintain that a safe, industrial deployment of this unspeakable invention is impossible."(3)

In the 37 years since Reich's warning, there have been numerous books and articles published in both professional and lay literature, including films,(4) about the dangers of nuclear energy and also the cover-ups of its effects on those in both Third and First World cultures who have been exposed to both high and low-level nuclear radiation. There have also been studies and exposures of cover-ups of other environmental hazards from nuclear pursuits such as increased earthquake activity resulting from underground

nuclear testing.(5) Nonetheless, the addiction to the promise of a cheap, safe, clean energy resulting from nuclear fission continues to this very day and brings in its shadow the promise of global holocaust.

It is this shadow which Jay M. Gould and Benjamin A. Goldman, two professional statisticians, track with great precision and sound logic in *Deadly Deceit*. By doing so they place themselves in the tradition of the 1950's antinuclear proponents — Linus Pauling, Andrei Sakharov, and Rachel Carson — and the later investigators — John Gofman, Arthur Tamplin, Alice Stewart, Thomas Manusco, Karl Morgan, Carl Johnson, and Ernest Sternglass. It is important to note that these authors, like their predecessors, are now being attacked in official government circles, their work marginalized in scholarly publications and its value distorted in the news media.(6)

Gould and Goldman's invaluable contribution to this evergrowingly ominous body of knowledge is their use of the statistical sciences. As a result, *Deadly Deceit* makes apparent the facts that low levels of nuclear radiation are not harmless and that the pursuit of nuclear power is the pursuit of global genocide. By using actual mortality figures and a different methodology than the nuclear industry, Gould and Goldman are able to estimate the actual number of deaths due to the actual after-the-fact dose response to low-level radiation. Their epidemiological study is unprecedented and quite damaging to the case of the nuclear industry, which bases its "safe" dosages upon data generated by computer models and not actual facts. Official "safe doses" of low-level radiation are also inaccurate because the field equipment used to measure dosages often cannot measure low-dosages. Often fallout data is not gathered in areas where radiation exposures are potentially damaging, but are gathered in other areas where the fallout is within permissible ranges. Sometimes, potentially damaging figures are altered or remain classified. As a result, the official "safe dosage" of exposures to low-level radiation are officially lowered every so often. These are some of the cover-ups documented in this book.

In the three years after the Three Mile Island, Pennsylvania nuclear power plant accident in 1979 — through the ingestion of fission products carried by the wind and deposited in rainfall which then entered the food chain through food crops and drinking water — the U.S. experienced about 50,000 to 100,000 more deaths than was expected. This was

1. "On Using the Atomic Bomb", *Orgonomic Functionalism*, Wilhelm Reich Infant Trust Fund, Vol. 2 / Fall 1990.
2. This research culminated in January of 1951 with the Oranur experiment in which Reich and several coworkers were exposed to low-level radiation effects. They suffered some of the now familiar symptoms of such exposure: dizziness, loss of consciousness, loss of balance, fatigue, headaches, nausea, sensations of pressure, conjunctivitis, liver symptoms, heart problems, etc. In general exposure aggravated long standing health problems, particularly the weak link in one's physical makeup. Some of the symptoms were more aggravated several months later; for instance nine months later Reich, who had a heart condition, suffered a severe heart attack.
3. "On Using the Atomic Bomb", *Orgonomic Functionalism*, Wilhelm Reich Infant Trust Fund, Vol.2/Fall 1990, pp. 46.
4. Of particular relevance to *Deadly Deceit* are: John W. Gofman, MD., Ph.D. *Radiation-Induced Cancer from Low-Dose Exposure: An Independent Analysis*, San Francisco, 1990 and the 1970's documentary film "Paul Jacobs and the Nuclear Gang".
5. Whiteford, Gary T.: "Earthquakes and Nuclear Testing: Dangerous Patterns and Trends" *Pulse of the Planet*, Vol. 1 No. 2, 1989·
6. See Goldman, Benjamin A.: "The Stress and Strain of the Atomic Age." *In These Times*, May 20-26, 1992.

comparable to the one other equally dramatic rise in mortality in U.S. history (7) which followed the 1971 accident at the Savannah River, South Carolina nuclear power plant. There, mortality rates peaked similarly (Figure 1). This peak, as the authors show, was most significant in states within 500 miles of the plant, especially South Carolina. Within South Carolina, the greatest mortality occurred in counties surrounding the nuclear plant. The studies of the effects of the Savannah River accident were more detailed because considerably more data was collected from the Savannah River Accident than after Three Mile Island. The lack of interest and the paucity of money spent to gather hard data following Three Mile Island, and the lack of access to this data are linked by the authors to the official cover-up about the perils of low level radiation. In 1986, within a few months after the Chernobyl nuclear accident, more than 40,000 people in the U.S. died than what would have been normally expected. There has been little interest within the nuclear industry in collecting data and doing health studies on this most recent accident. During the 1950s and 1960s, mortality rates in the U.S. did not improve, as expected; in fact there were 9 million deaths, largely among the very young and the very old, in excess of the expected trend of increased longevity. This period coincided with above-ground atmospheric nuclear bomb testing (Figure 2).

By analyzing public U.S. mortality data from official death certificates and projecting the revealed trends into the present and future, the authors thus solve a great epidemiological mystery — why mortality statistics in the U.S. (and elsewhere, though the authors concentrate largely on the U.S.) have inexplicably stopped getting better after decades of improvement dating back to the discovery of antisepsis early in the 19th century. The authors' methodology, in conjunction with actual mortality figures, reveal that a wide variety of diseases can and do occur after exposure to low-level radiation. These include immune deficiency diseases like AIDS, Chronic Fatigue, Epstein Barr, various forms of Herpes, Hodgkins (in children, too) as well as allergies, anemia, loss of appetite, birth defects in humans and other species, bronchitis, various forms of cancer, cataracts, dizziness, endocrine maladies, headaches, heart and kidney and liver diseases, metabolic changes, stomach pains, thyroid problems, vision loss, and slow weight gain for children and low birth weight for infants.

The authors show that those who die from low-level nuclear radiation are largely the very young and the very old. Today, six years after Chernobyl, we are witnessing an unparalleled increase in diseases of the immune system among adolescents and middle age persons. Thus, when the next nuclear accident (which is highly probable within ten years) strikes the already fragile immune systems of these large numbers of people as well as the very young and the very old, the increase in mortality will be staggering.

In an afterword to the second edition, Gould and his colleague Ernest Sternglass report their findings on the health effects on the general public from fallout episodes and releases from Swiss nuclear power plants and the emissions from the Trojan reactor located just 35 miles northwest of Portland, Oregon. Employing the same methodology detailed in the main text, the authors come up with similar mortality increases due to the effects of increased low-level

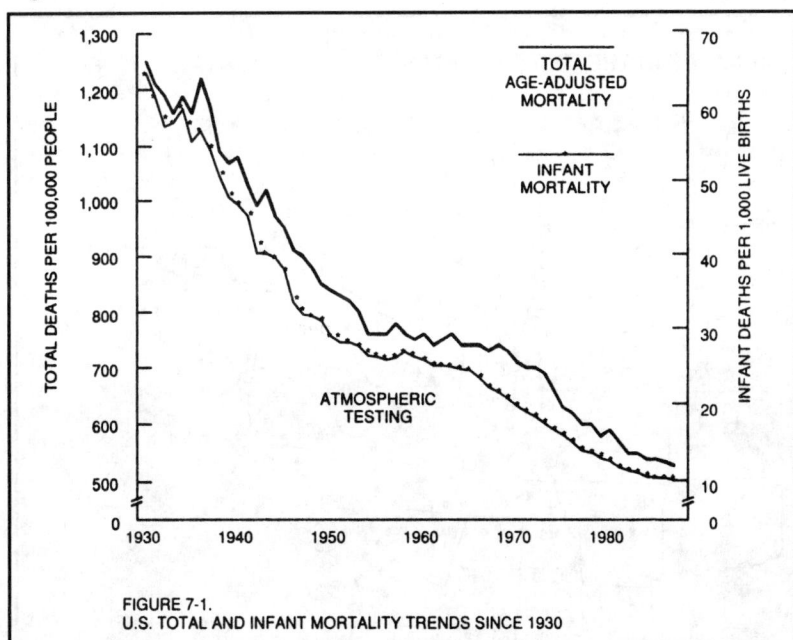

FIGURE 5-2. AGE-ADJUSTED U.S. MORTALITY, 1970 - 1982

Figure 1.

FIGURE 7-1.
U.S. TOTAL AND INFANT MORTALITY TRENDS SINCE 1930

Figure 2.

7. Not including the genocide of the black slaves and native peoples. These populations were considered so marginal by the dominant culture that their existence, hence their deaths, were not included in official statistical surveys of the time. See Howard Zinn: *A People's History of the United States*, New York, 1979. It could be said that the citizens of the U.S. today, like the native peoples earlier, are now being given (by the nuclear agents of the U.S. government) nuclear-contaminated blankets with which to warm themselves.

radiation on the populace. Not surprisingly, antinuclear groups commissioned these studies which were later disparaged by government agencies and their staff scientists.

Readability is one of the great strengths of this book. The non-jargon language, easy access to the authors' logic and the abundant charts and graphs make this whodunit interesting to read. However, this is not an idle armchair mystery. In *Deadly Deceit*, the authors assist the reader in uncovering the actual mass serial killings done by global nuclear madpersons. They show the reader how the killers cover their tracks. There is no crime and no victims since everything is legal; the killers write, enforce, and interpret the laws. By simply not using actual data, as the authors do, the nuclear industry, including establishment scientists and government officials, can deny the truth of what is happening to us all at an increasing and *cumulative* rate.

My criticism of the book is that, due to what I suppose is a lack of available and reliable statistical information, the authors place singular blame with regards to mortality figures, on the effects of nuclear radiation. Yet, in actuality, this is only one environmental insult to the organism; there are many other environmental stressors also damaging to the immune and other biological systems. These include electromagnetic fields, mass vaccinations, overuse of antibiotics and pharmaceutical drugs, the pervasive use of pesticides, the demineralization of the soil, the loss of topsoil, the destruction of the ozone layer, the contamination of the groundwaters from toxic chemicals, the contamination and devitalization of the air, man-made famines, the desertification of the Earth; and, of course, the many violent crimes against others resulting from the emotional plague, such as increased domestic violence and international conflicts. Thus, the particular crime and cover-up of low-level radiation is only one of many against humanity, and all species of life forms, including the planet itself.(8) What is the basis for the perpetration and cover-up of these crimes of which low-level radiation is perhaps the most seamless when seen from the victim's point of view? Gould and Goldman give no concrete answer but suggest (between the lines) greed, ignorance and lust for power. In *On Using the Atomic Bomb*, Reich gives us a clue to the answer by casting light on the big cover-up — namely that the biopaths have not only concealed the facts of the dangers of nuclear energy but have "obstinately and systematically attempted to conceal" the discovery of "natural atomic energy (orgone). This is the big cover-up which lies at the root of what appears as the sheer lunacy described in this book.

The nuclear killers who are murdering us all are simply out of contact with the life force, the orgone.(9) Their wanton killing of life is an expression of this fact. Reich's own death and the disinformation campaign against his work is part of the cover-up about the existence of orgone energy. As documented in *Deadly Deceit*, when the very existence of this energy is denied, all life is murdered. ∎

---

8.   These are acts of "normal" men often highly valued by society. "Normal men have killed perhaps 100,000,000 of their fellow normal men in the last fifty years." See Laing, R.D.: *The Politics of Experience*, New York, 1967.
9.   For an in-depth, cross-cultural analysis of an aboriginal culture which affirms the life force, see: Robert Lawlor: *Voices of the First Day*, Rochester, Vermont, 1991.

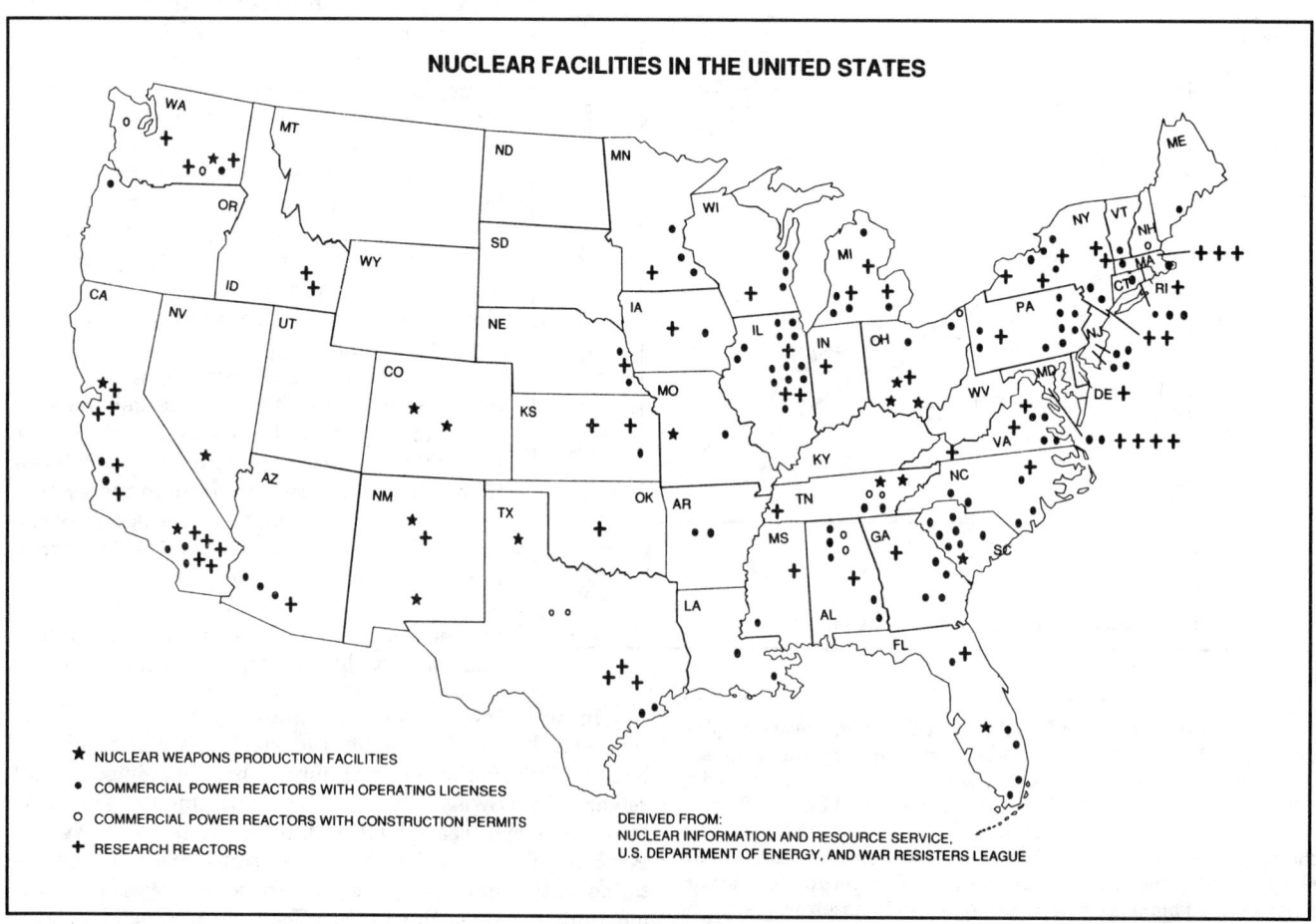

NUCLEAR FACILITIES IN THE UNITED STATES

★ NUCLEAR WEAPONS PRODUCTION FACILITIES

• COMMERCIAL POWER REACTORS WITH OPERATING LICENSES

○ COMMERCIAL POWER REACTORS WITH CONSTRUCTION PERMITS

✛ RESEARCH REACTORS

DERIVED FROM:
NUCLEAR INFORMATION AND RESOURCE SERVICE,
U.S. DEPARTMENT OF ENERGY, AND WAR RESISTERS LEAGUE

The Petkau Effect:
Nuclear Radiation, People and Trees
by Ralph Graeub
Introduction by Dr. Ernest J. Sternglass
Four Walls Eight Windows Press, NY, 1992.
Reviewed by Theirrie Cook, B.A.

This book provides evidence, mostly from European scientists, that low-level nuclear radiation has a much more powerful biological effect than is accepted by traditional physics and biology. The findings are probably not known to many American scientists, because this book constitutes one of the first English-language disclosures of the evidence. This research has not been greeted well in either Europe or the USA, because its findings suggest the need for a quick shut-down of nearly all nuclear energy facilities. For individuals who have studied Reich's work on the *oranur effect* (1) which showed a powerful reaction of the life-energy of people, trees, and the Earth itself to low-level nuclear radiation, this book constitutes an indirect and independent confirmation.

The Petkau Effect is named after Abram Petkau, an associate professor in the department of radiology of the University of Manitoba, who accidentally discovered the very damaging effects of chronic, low-level doses of radiation. In 1972, while a scientist at the Canadian Atomic Energy Commission's Whiteshell Nuclear Research establishment in Manitoba, Petkau conducted experiments on phospholid membranes which, though artificial, are similar to cell membranes in living cells. He irradiated the artificial cell membranes while underwater and found that the membranes would tear with a much lower total radiation dose, over an extended period of time, than if this total dose were given in a short, intensive radiation burst, as from a medical x-ray machine. In other words, the more drawn out the radiation, the lower the *total* dose required to break the membrane.

Most investigations into the biological effects of nuclear irradiation are focused on the cell DNA, which is known to be directly damaged by impacting radiation. From this, the cell nucleus became the primary focus for the major concern of "genetic damage". However, Petkau discovered that a very different, indirect damaging mechanism caused by nuclear irradiation operates on the cell membranes. A cell membrane not only holds a cell together, it also has many important functions in the biological processes which are necessary for health. In the cell fluid, which contains oxygen, the irradiation caused the formation of an unstable form of oxygen, or *free radical*. A chain reaction occurs which successively oxidizes and dissolves the cell membrane causing the cell to leak and die. It is *how* the unstable oxygen is created which is believed to cause the problem: the fewer free radicals in the cell fluid, the greater their ability to damage. Free radicals can deactivate each other to form ordinary oxygen. The more free radicals in the fluid, the more chance they have to neutralize each other before damaging the cell wall. High doses of radiation create large numbers of free radicals which then recombine and become ineffective; sustained low doses of radiation create fewer free radicals, which are then more capable of disrupting the cell membrane. The cells that appear most vulnerable to this form of attack are those connected to immune functions. Due to the Petkau Effect, small, extended radiation doses such as those following atomic testing fallout or exposure to the emissions of nuclear power plants are 100 to 1000 times more dangerous than those experienced by atom bomb survivors in Japan.

The Petkau Effect has been confirmed by numerous other studies conducted in the past twelve years. The effects of low-level radiation on humans have been observed frequently in the past, but were considered inexplicable and therefore were dismissed. Some examples:

— Workers at the Hanford, Washington plutonium facility had an extremely high rate of cancer in 1977 in spite of only minimal, low-level radiation exposures. Attempts to reduce the maximum dose for workers were rejected.

— Navy shipyard workers in Portsmouth, New Hampshire who repaired nuclear submarines had a leukemia rate 5.6 times higher than non-exposed workers, according to a 1978 study.

— Internal studies by the Department of Energy in 1984 on workers in twelve different nuclear facilities found 50% higher leukemia rates and higher rates for lung, lymph, and brain cancers.

Prior to the discovery of the Petkau effect, "questionable" statistics, such as the above, were routinely dismissed as the radiation doses from fallout and emissions from nuclear plants were considered far too low to have any effects upon humans. However, with the discovery of the Petkau effect, these studies now become plausible.

The author, Ralph Graeub, also chronicles the effects of iodine 131, strontium 90 and other isotopes on such factors as intelligence, fetal development, bone marrow and immune systems development. He continually stresses that the subtle effects on the hormonal and immune systems by the indirect chemical action of radioactivity on the human body contribute to premature childbirth, infant mortality, infectious diseases and cancer. Abundant citations to published studies are provided.

In addition to the alarming findings above on the indirect effects of low-level radioactivity, in 1981 the most important high-level radiation protection data for humans was found to be wrong. The Tentative Dose Estimate, developed in 1965, was based upon the radiation doses received by the Japanese A-bomb victims. However, in recalculating the radiation fields of the two bombs dropped over Hiroshima and Nagasaki, the neutron radiation was found to have been overestimated by a factor of 6 to 10, whereas the gamma radiation had been slightly underestimated. This finding shook the entire basis of the radiation protection standards — the currently estimated cancer risk has been shown to be too low, even for short bursts of high-dose radiation. The 1982 report by the United Nations Scientific Committee on the Effects of Atomic Radiation estimates that the risk of cancer is actually twice as great as previously believed, and that all dose limits should be reduced by half — but then nuclear power plants could not operate economically.

The danger is not only to humans and animals. Graeub presents enormously important, but little known evidence, that nuclear plant releases are also contributing to the death

---

1. Reich, W.: "The Blackening Rocks: Melanor", *Orgone Energy Bulletin*, V(1-2):28-59, 1953; Reich, W.: *The Oranur Experiment, First Report (1947-1951)*, Wilhelm Reich Foundation, Maine, 1951; partly reprinted in Reich, W.: *Selected Writings*, Farrar, Straus & Giroux, New York, 1960.

of the forests. "Forest death", as it is now called, has reached epidemic proportions, not only in Europe, but also in North America. Classic forest death has been observed since the dawn of the industrial revolution and was usually centered around coal-fired power plants, metal processing facilities, heating plants, waste incinerators and ceramics factories.

In the 1970s, a new kind of forest decline was observed, first in the central European mountains, and it has gradually spread. A Special Report by the Environmental Council of the West German Federal Ministry of the Interior, published in 1983, states:

> *"The new areas of declining forest are not comparable, or only partially comparable to the known central European areas of smog damage, such as the Ruhr Valley, etc. Moreover, the type and extent of forest decline observed can no longer be explained on the basis of traditional forestry experience."*

This new forest death, instead of affecting only evergreens, or just one species of tree, affects a broad spectrum of all trees, even including fruit trees. The danger emerging is that the basic process of the life cycle of plants, photosynthesis, is being threatened. Plants often show a greater sensitivity to their environment because of their intensive ventilation of air which provides them with carbon from atmospheric carbon dioxide. The effects of air poisoning are therefore noticed much earlier in plants than in animals or humans.

Dr. F.H. Schweingruber of the Swiss Federal Institute for Forestry Experiments in Birmensdorf concluded that the "decisive" physiological damage resulting in current forest death must have begun during the 1950s. This decline was evident in a reduction of density and width of tree rings and in reduced growth, which occurred across the entire Northern hemisphere. The closer the growth rings are spaced, the less growth of the tree. The trees examined in his study show extreme retardation of growth since the 1950s and virtually no growth since the 1970s. Comparable phenomena in historical and prehistoric spruce trunks do not exist, according to Dr. Schweingruber. The Swiss Federal Office on Environmental Protection notes: "This [discovery] is without parallel in the history of forests."

Other symptoms of forest death are "a general thinning of the crown, discoloration of the needles of spruce and firs, weak foliage on individual branches, premature fall coloring in beach trees and twig and leaf deformations." Organisms can call upon great reserves for reproduction if their environmental conditions deteriorate dramatically. Alarmingly, trees showing symptoms of forest death have been uncommonly fruitful in recent years. Sickly apple, pear, and cherry trees are yielding rich harvests. In Switzerland, Operation Noah's Ark is collecting seeds from valuable stands of dying trees in order to make a biodiverse reforestation possible.

Something in the 1950s and 1960s caused this global decline in the forests of the northern hemisphere. First the cause was thought to be SO_2, then acid rain, then ozone, and now, "stress" is suggested as a cause, or perhaps a combination of all these factors. However, the northern hemispheric belt not only contains the world's major industries, it also contains the most nuclear power plants — 300 of them — and almost all nuclear processing centers, which are the world's most important radioactive polluters. In addition, this zone was also the site of the majority of nuclear weapons tests —

especially the above-ground tests of the 1950s.

In 1982, the carbon 14 content of tree leaves was still 25% higher than the natural level prior to the atomic age; the carbon 14 content of human blood and hair has increased in direct proportion with the carbon 14 content of the troposphere. In the vicinity of various nuclear power plants, significantly increased carbon 14 concentrations were found in leaves and bark. An American study even recommends that no agriculture be carried out in the vicinity of nuclear power plants. In contrast to classic pollutants, carbon 14 can't be washed out of the air by rain or snow. The normal production rate of carbon 14 in the atmosphere is dependent on cosmic radiation linked to sunspot activity. However, the unparalleled increase of carbon 14 in the atmosphere, along with other fission products like tritium and krypton 85 due to nuclear bomb testing and power plant emissions, parallels the unprecedented global retardation of tree growth and forest death.

In the early 1980s, Prof. Gunther Reichelt of Germany found spots of forest death near nuclear power plants and uranium mines in Germany and France which could not be explained by air pollution (See Figure below). Reichelt believes the damage is caused by a "synergistic" effect with radioactive emissions. The actual mechanism for the causal link between the radioactive emissions and the forest damage is not stated decisively, however, and it is here that Wilhelm Reich's observations on the effects of the Oranur Experiment can lead to more positive connections.

Emerging from all this new knowledge is the growing awareness of the truly deadly effects of so-called "low-level" radiation on all living systems. To fully understand the causes of these effects — the underlying energetic principles — scientists will have to look beyond the theories of mechanistic physics and biochemistry which have brought us to this impending ecological disaster. ∎

Forest decline around the uranium mines at Wittichen in the Black Forest

Denying The Holocaust:

The Growing Assault on Truth & Memory
by Deborah Lipstadt

Free Press, NY, 1993

Reviewed by James DeMeo, Ph.D.

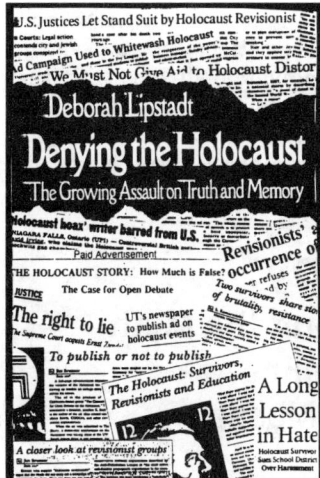

The orthodox scholarly world has a major problem with its narrow-minded attitudes towards unorthodox ideas, and rightfully can be accused of, too often, throwing out the baby with the bathwater. (That is, of discarding valuable research findings along with the worthless materials.) But this does not mean *bathwater* does not exist. For those interested in unorthodox research findings, outside the mainstream, discretion and strict fact-checking are absolutely necessary requirements. There are publications which over the years have made a constructive reputation for themselves by presenting unorthodox ideas to the general public. Some do a better job than others in sorting through the morass of claims and counter-claims. But of late there is a tendency for more substantive and documented unorthodox materials to be passed over in favor of materials which appeal to wide spread prejudice and mysticism and have only the superficial appearance of "scholarship." Particularly, there has been a growing credence afforded to the fringe neofascist groups which claim through blatant lies and distortions that the WWII Nazi death camps and Holocaust are "fabrications of a conspiracy".

A few publications which properly honor eyewitness testimony and photographs as primary evidence for nearly every kind of controversial subject, such as UFOs or the Kennedy assassination, appear willing, suspiciously willing in fact, to embrace Holocaust-denial materials without criticism, as "alternative history": Mountains of eyewitness observations, testimony, confessions, photographs, mass graves, documentary materials, and the sites of the death camps themselves, are all dismissed as part of a "Jewish conspiracy", which itself is completely undocumented.(1) Deborah Lipstadt's book is a powerful antidote against this kind of fascist-apologist propaganda. Lipstadt predominantly focuses upon the backgrounds and methods employed by the deniers. She demonstrates clearly and unambiguously the blatant twisting of truth and fabricating of materials undertaken by these individuals in their publications. These are Big Dangerous Lies. The kind that, when swallowed whole, destroy entire nations. Her analysis sheds considerable light by clearly demonstrating their patterns and methodology. Lipstadt's chapters cover the history and methods of the Holocaust deniers, from their roots in earlier "historical revisionism" of the early 1900s, through the period of Hitler apologism following WWII. Analytical chapters cover the activities, statements and publications of various deniers: Austin J. App, Arthur Butz, Mark Weber and the "Institute for Historical Review", the "Committee for Open Debate on the Holocaust", with revealing information on other notables in the movement, such as David Irving.

For example, Lipstadt cites the case of prison-execution "engineer" Fred Leuchter and his "Report" on the Nazi gas chambers. Leuchter traveled to Germany at the invitation of a neofascist group, to evaluate the concentration camp gas chambers. After visiting Auschwitz/Birkenau and a collecting $35,000 fee for his "services", Leuchter publicly proclaimed that true gas chambers did not exist at the Nazi death camps. His statements and Report were paraded in public as "proof" that mass murder did not take place in the camps. Leuchter was later exposed for misrepresenting his credentials (he had no degree in engineering; only a B.A. in history) and it came out that opponents of the death penalty in the USA had previously cited his gas chamber designs as incompetent, needlessly prolonging death agony. He was charged with fraud, and plead guilty in 1991. However, the "Leuchter Report" is still widely cited as fact within revisionist circles, its publication having been arranged by Hitler-admirer David Irving, who also wrote a glowing "foreword".

The Holocaust deniers agenda is to whitewash the Hitler years, to blame the Allies and "their Jewish advisors" for provocating the Japanese attack on Pearl Harbor and Hitler's invasion of Poland and France, to justify the death-camp murdering of millions of men, women and children, or alternatively, when it suits them, to deny the very *existence* of the death camps. If the Holocaust can be denied, or even seriously challenged, then Nazism itself can be publicly rehabilitated. The methods of the deniers reveal a tricky and deceitful quality second only to the perpetrators of the crimes being whitewashed. It is Emotional Plague writ in large letters, and it makes the poison-pen distorters of Reich's work appear as meek amateurs by comparison.

The Holocaust denial materials are often quite slick, couched in scholarly dress, mixing kernels of truth with whopping lies, cleverly misquoting or quoting out-of-context bona-fide scholars of the Nazi era and Holocaust — all with the aim to portray the victims of atrocity as aggressive conspirators. The David Dukes and Daniel Irvings of the USA and Western Europe don't wear black uniforms or jack boots, nor do they pound the podium in an open rage as did their greatly-admired Herr Hitler. (Although this is the mode of dress and behavior of their openly anti-Semitic cousins in Eastern Europe, in organizations such as Pamyat.) Certainly, it is not they who are out in the streets, throwing bricks and firebombs, beating up and murdering the *auslander*, or ethnically-cleansing the neighborhood. Such tasks are left to the semi-educated, hate-filled street gangs, who read the Holocaust-denial materials, and give it credence, animus, and muscle. Rather, the modern authors of denial material dress in business suits and are very neatly groomed; they produce slick publications, like the *Journal of Historical Review*, and richly-footnoted hardbound tomes, giving the facade of "scholarly objectivity". They present themselves as "controversial scholars", who merely wish to present "an alternative view of history".

Lipstadt explodes these "rational" images of the deniers, ripping away their mask; using their own words, writings and personal histories, she provides necessary background information on the Holocaust denial movement, and the key personalities behind it — they are fully on record with abundant

---

1. A list of resource materials documenting the extermination program of the Nazis is listed at the end of this article.

and quite vicious anti-Semitic statements, often acting as cheer-leaders for hate crimes, and have given prior support to, or were leading members of hate groups such as the KKK, White Aryan Nation and other neofascist organizations. Such groups have, in recent years, developed a growing international network with newsletters, computer bulletin boards, and cooperative financial arrangements. Their materials are translated into many languages and distributed around the world, from Brazil to Japan, as ammunition for neofascism and the whitewashing of WWII Axis crimes. These hate groups are also linked up with traditionally anti-Jewish, fundamentalist-Islamic organizations, such as Hammas and Hezbollah, who have murdered friend and foe alike for years, without restraint, and who likewise circulate translated copies of Holocaust denial materials. There is a clear and obvious death toll associated with the growth of radical hate groups, easily confirmed by surveying news reports during any given week. And there is, indeed, a very real organized secret conspiratorial movement requiring exposure to the light of day: *the neofascist, Nazi-apologist, anti-Semitic, Holocaust-denial conspiracy.*

One might ask why any of this should be in question. Why waste time to refute such obvious racist propaganda. The answer is, the denial movement has been successful in gaining the public podium, in legitimizing and portraying itself as but another one of the dozens of "suppressed findings". It is a message which strikes paydirt among racist groups, political extremists, uncritical conspiracy buffs, and others with an axe to grind against the establishment. But, why no skepticism towards the Holocaust deniers, or fact-checking of their materials? Why the welcome mat for hate groups who *a-priori* deny any legitimacy to eyewitness reports or extensive documentation about the death camps? Eyewitness reports are essential materials for historians, scientists, and the legal system, but

they are completely dismissed by the deniers and their ultra-conservative and extreme-liberal supporters. The problem is *not* the absence of evidence for the Holocaust. That evidence always existed, and is unquestionable. The problem is the willingness of ordinary people to *disbelieve the awful truth*, and to instead willingly swallow this sugar-coated version of history, a poison pill which labels the victims of Nazi atrocity the aggressors, and which contemptuously throws mud in the face of every witness and survivor. The hate literature of the Holocaust deniers should not be confused with honest scholarly work. It isn't. It is deceitful emotional plague venom, from start to finish. For the individual flirting with the Holocaust denial "literature", or its parent, the "Jewish conspiracy", Lipstadt's book is essential antivenom — highly recommended for those who live in snake country. ∎

Against Therapy:
Emotional Tyranny and the Myth of Psychological Healing,
by Jeffrey Moussaieff Masson
Atheneum, NY 1988
Reviewed by James DeMeo, Ph.D.

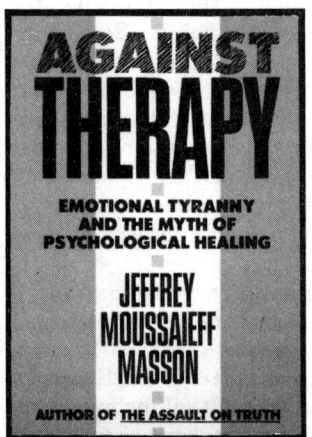

Jeffrey Masson made the headlines in recent years regarding his work as former Projects Director of the Sigmund Freud Archives and his psychoanalytic heresy, with various lawsuits resulting therefrom. As is well-known today, Masson exposed to daylight certain letters between Freud and Fleiss, which demonstrated (to those who required additional convincing) that Freud's descriptions of childhood sexual abuse as "fantasy" or "wish" were developed with calculated measure, to preserve his social situation and approvals from the *Status Quo* of polite, compulsively-tidy Viennese and Germanic society. At the time Freud was tidying-up his psychoanalytic theory, to diminish any significant mention of affect from widespread and real-world childhood trauma (especially sexual trauma), Wilhelm Reich was emphasizing and fighting against this same social pathology. Out in the streets, Reich and his associates distributed banned contraceptives and literature on birth-control, and arranged for necessary abortions; his group likewise promoted laws liberalizing divorce, for the protection of women and children, and for decriminalizing homosexuality and prostitution. Reich attempted to reform society through changes in laws, and by counseling working-class people, en-masse, on principles of sexual hygiene. Today, we know Freud received public honors and awards for his cowardliness, while Reich – expelled from the International Psychoanalytic Association and under threat of death from the enraged Nazis whom he exposed in *Mass Psychology of Fascism* (1933) – had to run for his life.

Masson also came to discover this truth about the Great Compromise of psychoanalysis while working in the Freud

---

Additional Reading on the Holocaust

- *Hitler's Apologists: Anti-Semitic Propaganda of Holocaust "Revisionism"*, Anti-Defamation League, NY, 1993.
- Yehuda Bauer & Nathan Rotenstreich: *The Holocaust as Historical Experience*, Holmes & Meyer, NY 1981.
- Lucy Dawidowicz: *The War Against the Jews, 1933-1945*, Holt, Rinehart & Winston, NY 1975.
- Martin Gilbert: *The Holocaust*, Hill & Wang, NY 1985.
- Israel Gutman, Ed.: *Encyclopedia of the Holocaust, Volumes 1-4*, Macmillan, NY 1990.
- Raul Hilberg: *The Destruction of the European Jews, Revised Ed. Vols. 1-3*, Holmes & Meier, NY 1985.
- Nora Levin: *The Holocaust: The Destruction of European Jewry, 1933-1945*, T. Y. Crowell, NY 1973.
- Robert J. Lifton: *The Nazi Doctors: Medical Killings and the Psychology of Genocide*, Basic Books, NY 1986.
- Jean-Claude Pressac: *Auschwitz: Technique and Operation of the Gas Chambers*, NY 1989.
- Gerald Reitlinger: *The Final Solution: The Attempt to Exterminate the Jews of Europe, 1939-1945*, Second Revised Ed., T. Yoseloff, S. Brunswick (NJ) 1968.
- David Wyman: *The Abandonment of the Jews*, Pantheon, NY 1984.
- Leni Yahil: *The Holocaust: The Fate of European Jewry*, Oxford U. Press, NY 1990.

Archives. Better late than never. The reader will excuse this reviewer if he does not too loudly celebrate "Masson's discovery". However, Masson deserves much credit and respect for the excellent documentation he has gathered regarding the plight of "mentally ill" persons at the hands of rather calous and unhelpful "mental health" professionals. *Against Therapy* is clearly the most significant book written by Masson, far more important socially than *Assault on Truth*, which only added additional fuel to an already highly-heaped bonfire roasting Freud. In *Against Therapy*, Masson broadened his scope, to include a wider variety of mental health professionals and theorems than merely the psychoanalysts. In this hot book, one finds heartbreaking stories about individuals interred in the early asylums of Europe; of individuals who were clearly far more healthy emotionally than the families or lawyers who forcibly incarcarated them, or the doctors who "treated" them. And the examples given are just as real for today's treatment of patients in mental hospitals, as for the asylum wards of 50 or even 100 years ago.

To begin, Masson provides a rather straightforward and demystifying review of a major case history in the development of psychoanalysis: that of Freud's patient, Dora. Freud refused to believe her story regarding an attempted seduction by an older man; claiming poor Dora had imagined it all! He completely mystified the event, refusing to believe that a proper Viennese gentleman would attempt such a seduction, and his mystification became a cornerstone of psychoanalytic theory. (Today, the pendulum has swung in the opposite direction as uncritical, and often unscupulous therapists encourage their adult female patients to view "recovered" memories of past sexual abuse as *always* having taken place, or to insist that such incidents occured even when the patient has no such memories and there is no corroborating evidence; i.e. the female patient is sexually afraid of men and withdrawn, therefore, they conclude, she *must* have been assaulted as a child.)

Masson also provides exposés of Ferenczi's secret diary, and Jung's tenure as a National Socialist (Nazi). This latter chapter on Jung is powerful ammunition against anyone playing apologist for Jung on the Nazi matter. Jung knew precisely with whom he was associating, and he wrote favorably about the Nazis, even after they started down the road of murderous conduct. Jung became president of the Nazi-controlled "International Medical Society for Psychotherapy", and editor of its journal *Zentralblatt fur Psychotherapie und ihre Grenzgebiete*. The first issue of this journal carried a statement by Heinrich Goring (cousin of the more notorious Nazi Prime Minister Hermann Goring): "It is expected of all members of the Society who write articles that they will have read through with great scientific care the path-breaking book by Adolf Hitler, *Mein Kampf,* and will recognize it as essential [to their work]."(p.95-96) Jung willfully and opportunistically ascended to this position of influence and power.

In later years, through many articles and private letters exposed by Masson, Jung would continue to expound in a most disgusting manner upon the "diminished", even "poisonous" psychology of Jews as compared to Aryans. Jung remained as president of the Nazi "Society", and editor of its *Zentralblatt* at least into 1938, well into the period of political murders, mass political rallies, severe anti-semetic repressions, and "street actions." Only after the war, in 1945, did Jung reverse his position, attempting to distance himself from the disaster of Nazism, but without so much as a simple apology to anyone, or admission as to his own antisemitic words and deeds. The

revelations are enough to make one vomit, particularly when one considers the vast numbers of people who today are swayed by the mystical psychology of Jung. (Even Jung's widely discussed ideas on "synchronicity" and "collective unconscious" which have titillated so many in the New Age movement, were stolen and mystified from Paul Kammerer's prior vitalistic ideas on *seriality : Das Gesetz Der Serie* of 1919). Importantly, Masson shows the connections between Jung's spiritualistic psychotherapy to his Nazi sympathies—indeed, most Nazis were steeped in the same mystical esoteric and spiritualist ideologies which today are circulating in Western nations in sanitized, newly-cleaned packages. In the background of Masson's chapter on Jung, I kept hearing echoes of Reich's prior warnings and observations from *Mass Psychology*, about how *mysticism leads, step-by-step, to fascism.*

Other chapters in *Against Therapy* expose John Rosen's "Direct Psychoanalysis" (a form of rationalized sadistic patient-beating), the rationalized sexual seduction of patients by various psychotherapists, and the general absence of social public health benefits from the widespread and popular "benevolent" psychotherapies of Rogers, Erickson, and others. Thankfully, the name of Wilhelm Reich does not appear once in this book, as a target of criticism or otherwise, but it is clear Masson's revelations touch upon issues discussed by Reich in other contexts many decades earlier.

The book is a damning indictment of how worthless and parasitic are nearly all the major professional approaches to mental health, and how they in fact sustain and create more social damage and personal misery than they heal or resolve. The book was nearly impossible to locate, rumor having it that all existing copies were purchased and burnt by various psychotherapists to keep the book out of the hands of their patients. Aside from the failure to discuss Reich's similar observations years earlier, my only other small criticism of Masson's book is the lack of discussion regarding the over-use and reliance upon behavior-modifying drugs by modern psychiatrists, and the resurgence of electro-shock therapy. Both of these produce "results" (and often severe side-effects), but like psychoanalysis, allow physician, patient, and family to engage in collective denial about the real-world effects of repression and trauma.

Masson concludes the book by advocating community self-help groups, a very rational suggestion in light of the social disasters confronting us all, and the absence of significant beneficial help from the vast majority of "professionals". *Against Therapy* is must reading, also, for every orgonomist and patient in orgonomic therapy, as a reasonable and necessary caution against Reich's therapeutic approach being reduced to simply a branch of traditional psychiatry, and as a reminder that the primary task of orgonomy is *not* the therapy of patients, but rather, *the prevention of armoring.* ∎

Sigmund Freud

The Montauk Project:

Experiments in Time

by Preston B. Nichols, with Peter Moon
Sky Books, New York, 1992
Reviewed by James DeMeo, Ph.D.

The Montauk Project (hereafter TMP) puts forth the argument that the US Government, through its military and research institutions, engaged in secret work on the subject of electromagnetic invisibility, the so-called "Philadelphia Experiment", which later branched out to include secret weather-control, mind-control and time-travel experiments. Into the web of this argument, the authors assert that Wilhelm Reich played an important role. Chapter 7 of the book, titled "Wilhelm Reich and the Phoenix Project", identifies Reich's discovery of orgone energy, DOR, and other details suggesting the author has studied Reich in some manner. The author asserts Reich's atmospheric work was followed by US government officials, who, with Reich's cooperation, used his discoveries to develop the radiosonde, a device sent up in weather balloons for measuring upper atmospheric temperature, humidity and pressure. However, *TMP* presents the radiosonde as a "secret Reichian weather control device," developed in collusion with the US government. A separate one-page Appendix, titled "Wilhelm Reich", presents a few additional confused and error-filled paragraphs. The author knows enough about Reich's work to use his terms, such as *orgone* and *DOR buster*, which suggests the fabrications are not accidental. The author cleverly accuses disbelievers and critics of his fantasy tale of engaging in "disinformation", which may be a Freudian slip for the motivation to include Reich in the book. For example: "Despite what disinformation you may hear, the government already knew what Reich could do and considered him a brilliant man. They asked for his prototypes and he was happy to oblige them..." (p.43) Later (p.45), the author asserts that the Reichian weather-control aspects of the radiosonde are cleverly disguised in its electronics. "Because of these precautions, the secret was maintained for over 40 years." The book is filled with such suspicious confusions from start to finish.

To summarize my feelings about this book: it is mediocre science fiction. The "Philadelphia Experiment", for example, is the least-documented of any of the supposed "secret government research" projects. I recall reading about this "experiment" more than 30 years ago, as a teenager, in science fiction paperbacks and comic books. The entire fabric of the story is woven from assertions by a few individuals who claim to have inside knowledge — knowledge which "came" to them after regaining previously-blocked "memories". In an introductory passage, the author admits the book is but "an exercise in consciousness", and states the story is founded upon "soft facts" and "grey facts", in contrast to "hard facts...backed up by documentation". And so by the author's own admission, *TMP* fails to document any of its central premises regarding the purported strange experiments, or the supposed role of Reich (or Tesla) in any of it.

Having seen and weathered far more studied attempts to undermine Reich's solid research, I can't get too worked up about this book. No scholar will take the book seriously because, in addition to lacking documentation, the author admits to disorientation, flights of fantasy, breaks with reality, and open involvement with "psycho-active electronics".

My major annoyance is that a growing number of laypeople who know nothing about Reich are taking the book seriously. It is becoming a hot item on the strangeness circuit. Already I have received a dozen calls asking if the book is true. Several mail-order book catalogs devoted to unorthodox subjects also carry it, alongside other titles on bona-fide subjects, lending an aura of legitimacy to it. And recently, the author Nichols has lectured to eager audiences at various "free energy" and "New Age" groups. The Rim Institute Center in Arizona also scheduled a workshop on "Time Travel and the Alien Presence", with the following description in their catalog:

> "The Montauk Project has been called one of America's greatest modern mysteries. The story began with the pioneering work of Wilhelm Reich and Nikola Tesla, took form in government-sponsored weather control experiments in the early 1940s, and crystallized in the ill-fated 'Philadelphia Experiment' on invisibility during World War II...The incredible story includes: joint human/alien research, abductions and brainwashing, advanced age-regression techniques, psychics linked into Tesla technology, missing Nazi gold, explorers lost forever in alternate worlds... Nichols...regained the blanked memories of his role as chief technician for the Project only after years of struggle."

And so the amazing story of "Wilhelm Reich's secret government research" spreads. The authors of *TMP* will likely find a warmer welcome on the public speaking circuit than anyone who has only researched Reich's findings on fascism, sexuality, the bions, orgone accumulator, cloudbuster, or other "less-spectacular" subjects. In fact, to satisfy the growing public interest in this fairy tale, a second book *Montauk Revisited* was recently released, along with a video *Montauk Project Tour*. It is a strange social phenomenon, indeed. For those who have been emotionally touched and helped by Reich's discoveries, who have worked hard to keep orgonomy clean of mystical distortions, dilutions, fabrications and hostile attacks, the book presents quite a challenge. The public appears thirsty, not for the difficult truths and facts developed in Reich's painstaking research, but instead, for whatever meagre scraps of fantasy and mystical delusion which can be conjured up, to erode away those same "hard facts". Reich is more "acceptable" as the archetypal mad scientist, or as part of a "secret government experiment", moving back and forth into other dimensions. Perhaps this is to be expected, from a popular culture addicted to violence, mysticism and horror films. It makes one wish Reich actually did develop a method for time travel, as there are a few people we'd like to teleport back to the stone age! ■

*"Psycho-active electronics assist
in retrieval of suppressed memory traces."*

July 1992 - October 1993 (Updated from *Pulse* #3, Summer 1991)

Appearing in *Orgonomic Functionalism* Volume 3, Spring 1991:
(Wilhelm Reich Museum, PO Box 687, Rangeley, ME 04970)
- The Developmental History of Orgonomic Functionalism, Part 3, by Wilhelm Reich, M.D.
- Orgonotic Pulsation, The Differentiation of Orgone Energy from Electromagnetism, Presented in Talks with an Electrophysicist, Part 1, by Wilhelm Reich, M.D.
- The Evasiveness of *Homo Normalis*, by Wilhelm Reich, M.D.

Appearing in *Orgonomic Functionalism*, Volume 4, Summer 1992:
- The Developmental History of Orgonomic Functionalism, Part 4, by Wilhelm Reich, M.D.
- Orgonotic Pulsation, The Differentiation of Orgone Energy from Electromagnetism, Presented in Talks with an Electrophysicist, Part 2, by Wilhelm Reich, M.D.
- Orgone Functions in Weather Formation, by Wilhelm Reich, M.D.
- The Attitude of Mechanistic Natural Science to the Life Problem, by Wilhelm Reich, M.D.

Appearing in the *Journal of Orgonomy*, 25(1), May 1991:
(Orgonomic Publications, PO Box 490, Princeton, NJ 08542)
- Orgonomic Hygrometry, by Charles Konia, M.D.
- CORE Progress Report #24: The California Drought of 1990-1991, by Richard Blasband, M.D.
- Aspects of Grief and Mourning: A Case of Chronic Pain, by Barbara Koopman, M.D., Ph.D.
- Two Patients with Obsessive-Compulsive Symptoms, by Howard Chavis, M.D.
- A Phallic Narcissist, by William Frederick, M.D.
- Use of Character Analysis in a Case of Adolescent Misery, by Jack Sands, M.D.
- Orgone Therapy (Part XI: The Application of Functional Thinking in Medical Practice), by Charles Konia, M.D.
- In Seminar with Dr. Elsworth Baker
- Self-Regulation (Part I: Its Roots in Reich and Neill), by Jacqueline A. Carleton, Ph.D.
- Self-Government at Summerhill, by Matthew Appleton
- Work Energy and the Character of Organizations (Part V), by Martin D. Goldberg, M.S.
- Adolescent Sex-Repression, by James DeMeo, Ph.D.
- Wilhelm Reich and UFOs (Part II: Examining Evidence and Allegations), by Peter Robbins, B.F.A.

Appearing in the *Journal of Orgonomy*, 25(2), November 1991:
- The Function of the Orgasm: An Orgonometric Review, by Jacob Meyerowitz, B. Arch.
- CORE Progress Report #25: Two Year Research Summary -- The American West, Greece, and Germany, by James DeMeo, Ph.D.
- Bionous Breakdown in Degenerative Disease, by Alan Cantwell, Jr., M.D.
- Research Note: The Reich Blood Test with Autofluorescence, by Carlos Frigola, M.D. & Pilar Castro, M.D., Ph.D.
- Somatic Manifestations of Ocular Armor, by Charles Konia, M.D.
- A Three-Year-Old Schizophrenic, by Virginia W. Lyon, Ph.D.
- Orgone Therapy (Part XII: The Application of Functional Thinking in Medical Practice), by Charles Konia, M.D.
- Functional Diagnostics, by Charles Konia, M.D.
- Self-Regulation (Part II), by Jacqueline Carleton, Ph.D.
- Marriage and Family, by James DeMeo, Ph.D.
- A Basic Problem in Work, by Martin D. Goldberg, M.S.

Appearing in the *Journal of Orgonomy*, 26(1), Spring/Summer 1992
- Reminiscences of Reich After Four Decades, by Bernard Grad, Ph.D.
- The Source of Time and Length, by Jacob Meyerowitz, B. Arch.
- Orgonomic Weather Control: An Overview, by Richard Blasband, M.D.
- CORE Progress Report #26: California Drought of 1990-1991, Part II. With a Special Note on Underground Nuclear Testing and the Oakland Wildfires, by James DeMeo, Ph.D.
- CORE Progress Report #27: East Coast Reservoir Recovery: Fall 1991, by John Schleining, M.S.
- CORE Progress Report #28: Cloud Signatures in Pacific Coast Operations, by Richard Blasband, M.D.
- Addendum: Bringing Rain to the Pacific Northwest, by Stephen Nagy, M.D.
- The Function of Independence, by Robert Harman, M.D.
- A Diagnostic Dilemma, by Robin R. Karpf, M.D.
- Clinical Brief: The Function of Diagnosis, by John Blake, M.D.
- Orgone Therapy (Part XIII: The Application of Functional Thinking in Medical Practice), by Charles Konia, M.D.

- Bioenergetic Aspects of Consciousness in the Newborn, by Barbara Koopman, M.D., Ph.D.
- Cultism in Orgonomy, by Charles Konia, M.D.
- Contraceptive Herbs in Native Societies, by James DeMeo, Ph.D.

Appearing in the *Journal of Orgonomy*, 26(2), Fall/Winter 1992:
- The American College of Orgonomy's 25th Anniversary, by John M. Bell, M.A.
- The Accumulator Effect on Leukemia Mice, by Bernard Brad, Ph.D.
- The Effect of Stress on Bion Formation, by Steven R. Dunlap
- Hygrometric Function of the Orac in Drought Conditions, by Charles Konia, M.D.
- CORE Report #29: Summer Drought Relief in Southern Oregon, by John Schleining, M.S.
- First CORE Network Conference, August 1992, by Stephen Nagy, M.D.
- CORE Report #30: The Desert Greening Project in Israel, by James DeMeo, Ph.D.
- CORE Report #31: Breaking the West Coast Drought, by Richard Blasband, M.D.
- A Difficult Diagnostic Problem, by Robert Harman, M.D.
- Clinical Brief: Orgonomic Treatment of Anxiety Symptoms, by Dale G. Rosin, D.O.
- Schizophrenia and Epilepsy are Functional Variants, by Charles Konia, M.D.
- Perception and Consciousness, by Robert Harman, M.D.

Appearing in the *Annals of the Institute for Orgonomic Science*, 8(1), September 1991:
(Institute for Orgonomic Science, PO Box 304, Gwynedd Valley, PA 19437)
- Measurements of the Atmospheric Orgone Energy, by Manfred Fuckert, M.D.
- Combined Orgone Therapy and Classical Homeopathy, by Dorothea Fuckert, M.D.
- Human Armoring: An Introduction to Psychiatric Orgone Therapy, Chapter 8, by Morton Herskowitz, D.O.
- David and Saul (1 Samuel 9-20): Expansion and Contraction in a Biblical Narrative, by Kathleen Mosher

Appearing in *Pulse of the Planet*, #3, Summer 1991:
(Orgone Biophysical Research Laboratory, PO Box 1395, El Cerrito, CA 94530)
- The Origins and Diffusion of Patrism in Saharasia, c.4000 BCE: Evidence for a Worldwide, Climate-Linked
  Geographical Pattern in Human Behavior, by James DeMeo, Ph.D.
- Body Pleasure and the Origins of Violence, by James Prescott, Ph.D.
- Three Mile Island: The Language of Science Versus the People's Reality, by Mitzuru Katagiri
- Orgone Accumulator Therapy of Severely Diseased People, by Heiko Lassek, M.D.
- Orgonotic Devices in the Treatment of Infectious Conditions, by Myron D. Brenner, M.D.
- Personal Observations with the Orgone Accumulator, by James DeMeo, Ph.D.
- The Ecology of Childhood, by Matthew Appleton
- Interview with James DeMeo, by Matthew Ryan
- OROP Arizona 1989: A Cloudbusting Experiment to Bring Rains in the Desert Southwest,
  by James DeMeo, Ph.D.
- Thank You For This Honor, by Eva Reich, M.D.
- The Voice of Wilhelm Reich, Conference at Orgonon, by James Strick, M.S.
- An Additional Perspective, by Myron Sharaf, Ph.D.

Appearing in Other Publications:
- James DeMeo, "In Search of the Goddess", (Letter), *East West*, April 1991, p.6; "A Desert Greening Experiment
  in the Desert Southwest", *Annual Meeting Abstracts*, Association of American Geographers, Washington,
  DC, 1991, p.46; "Climatic Causation and Pre-Columbian Contacts in Global Patterns of Human Behav-
  ior", *Abstracts*, Association of American Geographers, San Diego, 1992, p.54-55; "Has the AIDS Tragedy
  been Distorted by Media and Partisan Politics?" Book Review, in *Macrocosm USA*, Ed. by Sandi
  Brockway, Macrocosm Publishers, Cambria, CA, 1992, p.130; "Man-Made Radioactivity: A Cause of
  Droughts? (Interview)", *Explore*, 4(1):64-67, January 1993; "The Petkau Effect", (Letter), *Earth Island
  Journal*, Spring 1993, p.2; "A Global Geographical Pattern in Human Behavior", *Abstracts*, Assn. Pacific
  Coast Geographers, Annual Meeting, University of California at Berkeley, 15-18 Sept. 1993, p.23;
  "Similarities and Differences Between Wilhelm Reich's Orgone Accumulator and Giorgio Piccardi's
  Shielded Enclosures", Abstracts, Int. Symposium on *Relations of Biological and Physico-Chemical
  Processes with Solar Activity and Other Environmental Factors*, Pushchino, Russia, 1993, p.229.
- Ed Gehrman, "Reich", *Anderson Valley Advertiser*, Boonville, CA 10 March 93
- Sergei Kolokoltsev & Vladimir Androsov, "An Accumulator of Subtle Energy", *Aura-Z*, July 1993, p.85-87.
- T. M. Lai & D. Eberl, "Effect of an Energy Accumulator on Phosphorus Availability", *Abstracts, 80th Annual
  Meeting*, American Society of Agronomy, Anaheim, CA 1988, p.240.
- Carl Little, "WR: Functions of the Artist", *Art In America*, 76(3):142-145, March 1988.
- W. Edward Mann & Edward Hoffman, *Yoga Journal*, September/October 1992, p.30-36.
- Jim Martin, "Wilhelm Reich in Hell", *Steamshovel Press*, 6:24-27; "Wilhelm Reich in Vienna", *Steamshovel
  Press*, 7:25-30; "Quigley, Clinton, Straight & Reich", *Steamshovel Press*, 8:40-45, 1993.
- Nina Silver, "The Cosmic Pulse: Where Sex and Spirit Meet", *Gnosis Magazine*, Fall 1990, p.20-25.

SCIENCE NOTES

Bions from the Bottom of the Sea!

Discover magazine recently featured the work of Mike Adams, a researcher who has been cultivating bacteria originating *"from hot springs at the bottom of the ocean — spectacular smoking, sulfur-rich caldrons where pressurized water shoots from volcanic vents at temperatures as high as 700 degrees."*

These deep sea ocean thermal vents were discovered only within the last several decades, and were a big surprise to modern science, with their foot-long clams and other thriving plant and animal communities. These deep sea food chains are founded upon the "bacteria" which come from the volcanic vents — the difficulty here is explaining how organic cellular forms can withstand such high temperatures and pressures, usually sufficient to disrupt biochemistry and rupture fragile cell walls. Life should not exist, much less thrive, under such conditions, and yet it does. Smith has shown that his "microbes" (bions?) actually *crave* high temperatures, multiplying only at temperatures around 220°F, above the boiling point of water!

The probable answer to the puzzlement is that, in the deep sea ocean vents, the organisms are not simply "growing", but rather are being *produced* by a bionous disintegration process deep within the Earth, possibly where magma is cooling from red-hot into cooler (but still super-heated) conditions.

Bions, as discovered and demonstrated by Wilhelm Reich, are tiny vesicular forms, bridging the worlds of the living and non-living. They are about the same size as bacteria, but derive from the break-down and disintegration of both organic or inorganic substances. Reich demonstrated that bions could be produced from substances as diverse as coal, iron filings, clay, Earth, or sand, by firstly heating them to incandescence, and then quickly immersing them into sterile nutrient solutions. The bions could progressively alter shape and form, and could be cultured to yield a variety of microbe forms. It is refreshing to see confirmation of similar natural processes. (*Discover*, May 1993, p.87-91)

Bions from Space!

Polycyclic aromatic hydrocarbons constitute a key family of organic molecules necessary for life, and they recently have been found in interplanetary dusts — or rather, from dusts falling in the Earth's atmosphere, as captured by filtering apparatus on high altitude research aircraft. The isotopic composition of these dusts suggest an extraterrestrial origins, wherein lies the mystery.

Either interplanetary dusts contain organic molecules, or both the dusts and organic molecules were created by meteorites burning up in the Earth's atmosphere — in this latter case, Reich's experiments suggest an origins of the molecules similar to the origins of bions from incandescent sand or iron. (*Science News*, Vol.143, 1993, p.204)

Gold-Plated Bions!

John Watterson of the Denver USGS has theorized that placer gold is not the product of weathering and erosion of gold deposits from an undiscovered "mother lode" on the mountainside. Using an electron microscope, Watterson observed that placer gold is composed of a fine lacy structure, with tiny tubes of .00004" connected to tiny spheres of .0002" diameter.

He speculates that soil bacteria, through a process unknown, have somehow plated themselves with gold as they grew in the flowing waters of mountain streams. The difficulty with his theory is the scarce nature of gold ions in nature, even in streams which are considered to be rich with gold.

Nevertheless, the vesicular structure of natural placer gold deposits is real, suggesting the gold may be the bionous break-down product of some other parent material, possibly in conjunction with biological transmutation processes. Hmmmm, has anyone ever tried making bions from *lead*? (*Earth*, March 1993, p.12)

Beautiful Bions

L'Oreal cosmetics laboratories of France has announced the discovery of the "niosome", a special phospholipid vesicle now being researched for cosmetic and industrial applications. Like mud-packs for bion energizing, or the "beauty masks" of mud used by women for centuries, it appears that a major corporation will soon make use of the bion principle.

Thomas Edison's Bionic Spirit

"Let us consider our body. I believe it consists of myriads and myriads of indefinitely small entities put together, each of them being itself a living unit, and all these units create groups — or swarms, as I like to call them — and those indefinitely small units are living eternally. When we 'die', those swarms of units literally move like a swarm of bees to somewhere else, and continue to function in another form and another surrounding." (T. Edison, *The Diary and Sundry Observations*)

Bionic DNA?

Researchers at Kyoto University have been able to photograph individual DNA "specks" as they move and spin through gels and solutions. First, the researchers label the DNA with fluorescent materials, and then observe and film the specs as they move:

"...like shooting stars: their leading ends shine brighter than their trailing tails...the squiggle that swims across the screen is more than 5,000 times its original size... the DNA specs are difficult to follow...the apparatus must be properly grounded so that motors, lamps and other fixtures do not create spurious background signals..."
(*Science News*, 3 Aug. 91)

"Brownian Motion" Due to Orgonotic Pulsations?

Robert Brown firstly described the subtle pulsating movements of tiny pollen grains within the field of a microscope in 1827. He argued the effect was due to *vital forces*, which put the particles into motion.

Years later, in 1905 (after Brown's death), Albert Einstein wrote a paper claiming the motion was "nothing more" than the result of larger molecules in solution, colliding against the particles within the fluids being observed.

Now, new controversy on the issue. Daniel Deutsch of Pasadena claimed that Brown's particles were either too big or too heavy to be adequately buffeted about by such "big molecules" rather like the impossibility of a battleship being rapidly pushed around by collisions with thousands of basketballs from all directions, every second. The scale of the interactions do not explain the phenomenon adequately.

Other scientists have rallied to the defense of Brown, but one wonders if Brown would have liked Einstein's explanation or not. The controversy appears to open the door to other explanations of "Brownian Movement", and I do recall Wilhelm Reich arguing along lines similar to Brown... (*Science News*, 15 Aug. 92, and *The Economist*, 3 Oct. 92)

Cosmic Theory of Everything, Proven!

"Big Fleas have little fleas
upon their backs to bite-em.
And little fleas have lesser ones,
And so ad infinitum".

(J.B.S. Haldane, 1967)

Chaotic Calendars

In the 1950s, the radical psycho-historian Immanuel Velikovsky asserted that dating techniques routinely used by archaeologists which rely upon radiocarbon and other radioisotope decay-rate differentials were unreliable. He was pilloried for his assertion, and for the radical hypothesis he developed in the books *Worlds in Collision* and *Earth in Upheaval*, that the Earth had been shaped by massive cometary collisions within ancient historic times.

While Velikovsky's new chronology was never widely accepted, his influence did shape the modern psyche about the possibilities of such cosmic collisions. All modern theories regarding Cretaceous catastrophes, or dinosaur extinction by cometary collisions, owe an unacknowledged intellectual debt to Velikovsky.

Lesser known in the USA is the fact that many entire scientific disciplines in some areas of the world do not accept radioisotope dating techniques. For example, among East European and Central Asian historians, radiocarbon techniques are not relied upon, given the wide variety in dates often obtained from the same sample by different laboratories. Control experiments testing the validity of radiometric dating techniques verify this concern. A single sample of organic material, such as a specific layer of wood from a single tree-ring layer, when submitted to the same laboratory as different samples, is often given widely different dates, off by as much as 500 to 3000 years.

In fact, by 1969, specialists in the radiocarbon dating field met at the Upsala Conference, to highlight and address these problems. To date, the problems have never been resolved or corrected, but only *evaded* by mainstream scientists with special theoretical biases to protect. Other conferences were convened every so often, but the controversy remained submerged in the USA.

Recently, however, the radiocarbon problem surfaced again, this time in the public press, with respect to controversies surrounding the Dead Sea Scrolls. The latest radiocarbon study of the Scrolls, suppressed for several years by academics with a bias towards an ancient identity, suggests they date no earlier than 1000 AD to 1500 AD — and that, in turn, brought forth other amazing public revelations, such as the existence of Chinese symbols, Western letters and numbers, Masoretic vowels and other symbols of the medieval period, including Hebrew script mentioning Jesus.

For Scrolls supposedly interred in jars and caves between 300 BC and AD 50, these kinds of evidences are (or were) an unresolved enigma! The Scroll's content suggests they were written in more recent times, and not in such ancient periods as was previously believed from the early radiocarbon tests.
("Dead Sea Hoax", *This World, SF Chronicle*, 28 March 1993. Also see: Mook, W. & Waterbolk, H., eds.: *14C and Archaeology*, PACT, Proceedings of the 1st International Symposium, 1983; various articles in *Pensee*, Student Academic Freedom Forum, Portland, OR, Spring-Summer 1973.)

Magnets Will Give Your Car Gas

"Tests conducted recently by the British Internal Combustion Engine Research Institute, an independent engine test facility based in Slough, have confirmed that applying a magnetic field to fuel immediately before burning it in an internal combustion engine does improve combustion efficiency."

So stated a recent article in *New Scientist* (20 July, 1992) confirming what various maverick scientists in Europe and the USA have been saying for years. Various magnetic devices for increasing fuel efficiency have been on the market, selling for prices between $10 to $150. The cheaper magnets work just as well as the more expensive variety. Better efficiency results from the use of only south-pole magnetism, which appears to promote a more gaseous dispersal of fuel. (Economical fuel magnets are available from *Natural Energy Works*, PO Box 864, El Cerrito, CA 94530.)

Earthquake-Weather Connections

Jerome Namias of the Scripps Institute of Oceanography, verified connections between certain weather conditions and earthquakes — what folklore has often called "earthquake weather".

In California, warm high-pressure conditions are identified as prevailing during a significant number of major earthquakes, including the major one on 17 Oct. 1989. In orgonomic terminology, we observe this weather as *dorish* in nature, associated with an expansion of the nearby desert atmosphere towards the open ocean.
(*Toronto Globe & Mail*, 7 Nov. 89)

Electrical Currents Streaming Through Earth

Geologists researching the question of geomagnetism discovered, some years ago, that natural variations in the Earth's magnetic field were associated with shifts of electrical potential from one part of the Earth's crust to another. Termed "natural electrical currents", these are *rivers* of weak electrical current moving deep in the crust.

Recently, one exceptionally large current was discovered 19 miles beneath Australia, looping some 3,750 miles from Broome in the northwest, southward through South Australia, and then north through Queensland and into the Gulf of Carpentaria. The next largest such current is in North America, moving from Wyoming through Canada and out towards Greenland. The currents are not very powerful, however, having very low amperages. (*Detroit Times*, 9 April 91)

Stars Streaming Through Space

Astronomers may deny the existence of a cosmic energy in space, but they certainly describe the flowing movements of stars and galaxies as if they are caught up and being moved by gigantic streaming forces. The theory of a "Great Attractor" is based upon observations of the clumping and streaming of galactic matter through the cosmos. The Milky Way galaxy, our own, is said to be streaming along at 375 kilometers per second towards this same invisible and unproven "Great Attractor".

The astronomers cannot physically *see* anything in that particular region, such as a large mass which would explain the strong gravitational forces. Since they assume space itself is empty of any form of cosmic energy which might be swirling everything towards that spot, they came up the additional hypothesis of an equally invisible and unproven "dark matter" to explain the attractive energy of the " Great Attractor." (*Science News*, 12 December 92)

Rocks Streaming through Space

Researchers say they have found compelling evidence that meteorites sometimes fall to Earth in clusters, as if carried together on streams. A team led by Michael E. Lipschutz of Purdue University and Robert T. Dodd of the State University of New York at Stony Brook searched through meticulous records kept at the British Natural History Museum.

They found that 17 meteorites which fell to Earth between 1855 and 1895 formed an intriguing pattern — a broad line in the Northern Hemisphere which extends for several thousand kilometers. "These meteorites seemed to just line up," Lipshutz says. "We knew from the data that this was probably not a random event." A group of 13 of the "streaming" meteorites were found to be chemically similar, in contrast to a control group of 45 other meteorites not part of the streaming pattern.

The clustering and streaming patterns of the meteorites have the astronomers baffled, as they cannot explain how such phenomena could come about. "The conventional wisdom about how we think things get here [to Earth] from asteroids just isn't understood." This phenomenon does appear to be explained by the existence of cosmic energy streams which, as described by Reich, carry materials with them as they move through space. (*Science News*, 1 Aug.92)

Rivers of Atmospheric Vapor

"Huge rivers of vapor, some carrying as much water as the Amazon, have been discovered in the lower atmosphere".

The rivers of atmospheric moisture have lengths many times their widths, and they persist over many days. These "rivers" are a new phenomenon for classical scientists, but have been taken for granted by those familiar with Wilhelm Reich's prior research on atmospheric orgone energy streams. The orgone energy streams are water-attracting. They give rise to the long streams of moisture in the atmosphere, and are routinely tapped for successful cloudbusting operations. (*Geophysical Research Letters*, 24 Dec.92, p.2401-2404)

Do Planets & Comets Luminate?

Anomalous brightening and dim-ming of planetary atmospheres have been observed for years, changes in luminosity that cannot be explained on any known physical basis. The effect appears to be the result of interplanetary lumination, a product of planetary alignment conditions, similar to the manner in which microscopical bions luminate when they approach.

A similar phenomenon was observed in February 1991, when Halley's Comet flew by the Sun. After passage and on its way out into the dark cosmos, it was triggered into a brief luminating brilliance. This increasing glow from the comet may have been the product of lumination also, as shortly beforehand, the Sun threw out a flare. The distances were too great for any simple mechanical shining of light to be responsible, but it is very possible that the flare excited the energy field of the comet, resulting in a brief glowing good-bye. (*Science News*, 12 Oct.91)

Clouds from Mountains

While a moist air mass may trigger the formation of *orographic clouds* at the crest or peak of a mountain range, there often are reports of clouds literally streaming off the top of a mountain under essentially clear and dry atmospheric conditions. Meteorologists often dismiss these observations, but some are so persistent and unusual that even the most mechanistic meteorologist will take note. The Bennett Island plumes in the East Siberian Sea are one such mystery spot, first recognized in 1983. Visits to the Islands in recent years have failed to solve the mystery of the plumes, which originate at the Island's mountain tops, and stream downwind for hundreds of kilometers.

In *Pulse of the Planet #2*, we provided photos of similar unusual non-orographic clear-sky clouds streaming directly from mountains near to Sedona, Arizona. Long considered a sacred spot, we postulated that orgone energy was literally surging from deep within the Earth out to the surface, discharging through the mountain tops where clouds spontaneously formed.

In recent months, similar observations have been made by Californians regarding Mt. Diablo — this has prompted alarm from time to time, as Mt. Diablo is a dormant volcano. But geological investigations have not shown any seismic activity. (*Science News*, 27 June 92; *Pulse of the Planet* #2, 1989, p.91)

Strange High Altitude Winds

Classical theory on atmospheric movements attribute movements within the atmosphere to solar thermal surface heat, which creates mechanical movement of air, similar to water boiling in a pot. Based upon this idea, there should not be much wind in areas far removed from solar heating, such as in the mesosphere, which is higher up than most known Earthly winds. Consequently, the discovery of high velocity, high altitude winds was greeted with a bit of shock, as they were not predicted by classical meteorology. The newly discovered winds blow from west to east, and can reach speeds of up to 200 miles per hour. While these may sound similar to the lower-altitude jet streams, they occur at perhaps three times the altitude, around 160,000 feet elevation, near to the edge of space where the air is exceedingly rarified. The existence of such winds is anticipated on the basis of Reich's orgone theory, which asserts that streams of cosmic orgone energy are moving down from space, towards the surface of the Earth, dragging the atmosphere along with them as they move in a west-to-east direction. (*SF Chronicle*, 13 Dec.91)

Jupiter's Spots, Neptune's Winds

The planet Neptune receives only 1/900th of the solar energy received by Earth, and yet its atmosphere has winds reaching speeds of nearly 600 meters per second. Similarly, the planet Jupiter has powerful storms circulating in its atmosphere. One such storm constitutes the Great Red Spot, visible on Earth's telescopes for over 300 years as it circulates through the Jovian atmosphere. There is no known explanation as to how such powerful winds and storms are developed — winds on Earth are described by orthodox meteorology as a by-product of solar radiation and thermal heating, and solar-powered storms on Earth last no more than weeks at a time.

These other planets are simply too far away from the sun for solar radiation to play much of an effect. However, Wilhelm Reich argued that Earth's winds developed from cosmic energy streams which came down to the surface from above, pulling along the atmosphere with the energy streams. The jet streams are said, by orgone theory, to develop in such a manner. The rapid winds of Uranus and storms of Jupiter might also support this idea of Reich; certainly, they are a

blow to the solar-thermal theory of planetary atmospheric movements.
(*Science*, 22 Feb. 91 & 20 April 90)

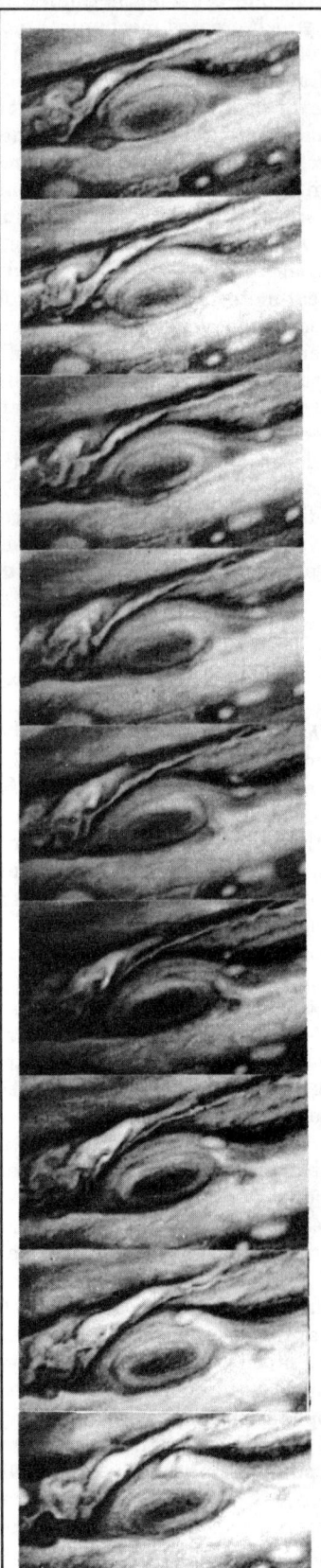

(*Science*, Vol. 248, 20 April 1990, p. 310.)

Left: *Time-lapse sequence of the Great Red Spot of Jupiter at 20 hour intervals showing the counterclockwise flow. Smaller spots approach from the east (right), go once around the GRS, and partially merge with it. Winds around its periphery exceed 100 m/s.*

Below: *Time-lapse sequence of the Great Dark Spot of Neptune. Both the GRS and the GDS have the same size relative to the planets and occupy nearly the same latitudes. They both rotate counterclockwise, but the GDS stretches and contracts as it rotates.*

Jovian Aurora

The giant planet Jupiter was recently observed to have an aurora glow at its poles, prompting immediate speculation on the mechanism. Earth's aurora is attributed to the stimulating influence of ionic winds from the Sun, but Jupiter is five times as far away, and could not be developing an aurora based upon solar wind.

This opens the door to other mechanisms, and cosmic orgone energy may be at work here too, with solar wind only providing some additional excitation. The discovery of an aurora on Jupiter was completely unexpected by the astronomers. "Everything is against common sense, everything is against our predictions" exclaimed Sang Kim of the University of Maryland research team which made the discovery.
(*Science News*, 12 Oct.91)

Calling Dr. Velikovsky!

Researchers located 10 oblong craters in Argentina which suggest a meteorite approximately 150 meters in diameter hop-scotched across the surface of the Earth, forming a 50-kilometer-long line near Rio Cuarto. The largest of the shallow depressions measures roughly 4 km long by 1 km wide. And what's even more interesting, because the craters do not yet show significant signs of erosion, Schultz believes the impact occurred as little as 2,000 years ago, a time when humans inhabited this region and may have witnessed the event.

This discovery, along with the massive meteorite crater discovered on the Yucatan Peninsula by geologist Walter Alvarez give increasing credence to the late Immanuel Velikovsky's theories about events on Earth triggered by catastrophic collisions with meteorites or comets. However, none of these newer researchers ever once mentions Velikovsky in the presentations of their catastrophic theories.

In another related discovery, geologists have identified deposits in Texas which suggest they were left there by a whopper of a wave:

"Along the Brazos River, there are meter thick beds of coarse-grained sandstones and large chunks of clay that were deposited precisely at the Cretaceous-Tertiary boundary. Only a wave rising 50-100 meters above the ocean surface could have created such a layer of uprooted material... Since there is almost incontrovertible evidence that one or several comets or meteorites crashed into Earth at the same geologic time as the wave hit Texas, the researchers say it is likely an extraterrestrial body created the tsunami deposit."

In an even more startling confirmation of Velikovsky's general thesis, a number of researchers at the recent Annual Meeting of the American Geophysical Union put forth the issue that much of the Earth's surface has been shaped by collisions with giant meteors and comets. The presentations shocked many conservative geologists at the meeting, but were well supported by evidence from a variety of sources.

Again, Velikovsky was the first to identify certain moraines and other large debris deposits as possibly originating with huge wave action created by meteor impact. And he was thoroughly vilified by people such as Harlo Shapley and Carl Sagan for his observations. Perhaps, as in the case of the Catholic Church finally "pardoning" Galileo, it will take several hundred years for Velikovsky to be forgiven for his challenge to the new religion of Orthodox Science. (*Science News*, 25 Jan.92; and 30 July 88; "Rebel Geologists Say Meteors Carved Earth" *SF Chronicle*, 10 Dec. 92; also see Immanuel Velikovsky, *Worlds in Collision*, Doubleday, NY, 1950, and *Earth in Upheaval*, Doubleday, NY, 1955)

Arrow marks a person standing in one of the smaller oblong craters in Argentina.
(*Science News*, Vol. 141, 25 Jan. 1992, p.55.)

Glowing in the Dark

"*A number of observations in recent years have found large amounts of ionized, glowing hydrogen in different parts of the universe. The ionization requires the presence of a background flux of ultraviolet light*," reported Adrian Melott of the University of Kansas to *Science News*. "*It's something people have been puzzled about. No one can figure where it comes from.*"

However, Wilhelm Reich created a similar phenomena in his laboratory by soaking a special vacuum tube with a high vacuum in a strong orgone accumulator. The "empty space" of the vacuum would start to glow a bluish color which Reich identified as the concentrated, illuminating orgone energy.

Melott hypothesizes that the glow of space is caused by "the decay of neutrinos in the dark matter," and even invents a new particle, the "eta" to account for the glow. Neutrinos, dark matter, and eta particles have never been observed and exist only in the minds of the researchers to explain away phenomena that shouldn't exist in an "empty space." Perhaps this is why many modern theoreticians rely solely upon mathematical formulations to describe reality: there are a lot fewer contradictions.
(*Science News*, Vol. 133, 6 February 1988)

All Shook Up!

Even though the sun is only 93 million miles from Earth and therefore *comparably* accessible to researchers, the more sophisticated the research undertaken, the more questions seem to arise about it's very nature. For instance: As the sun spins on its axis, a point near the equator takes about 25 days to make a round trip, while a point in the polar region requires 33 days. Since solar astronomers have no concept of a streaming energy in space – a force which would spiral down towards the surface of the sun from above, forcing the movements of the sun's surface – they must rely upon other theoretical mechanisms.

One very popular theory, for which there is no observational evidence, is that the sun's core may be rotating as much as three times faster than its surface. This would cause the observed surface behavior of the sun, but nobody can explain how or why the interior core would be rotating so fast. Whatever, the general theory of solar physics is in a state of confusion, based upon the many anomalous behaviors exhibited by the sun.

In addition to the unusual streaming effects, mentioned above, its coronal temperature is hotter than its surface temperature, and solar flares exhibit non-Newtonian characteristics, violating gravitational "laws" The sun also "quivers and shakes" like a bell, expands and contracts with incredible speed, and resonates at specific frequencies, displaying a characteristic acoustic signature. It additionally displays 11 and 22-year cycles of activity, building up large numbers of storms on its surface, which then gradually, over years, dissipate away to yield a clear and calm surface. (*Science News*, Vol. 134, 2 July, 1988)

Hubble Space Telescope Revisited

In a prior issue of the Pulse, the failure of the multi-million dollar Hubble Space Telescope was discussed as possibly being due to problems with the dominant astronomical theory about how light comes to the Earth from outer space, and not due to a speculated "improperly constructed" telescope mirror. In the next months, NASA will undertake another expensive mission to place corrective lenses on the "defective" telescope. But if the malfunction is not caused by the mirror, then the "corrected" telescope will still fail to function as anticipated. If so, this would again confirm that *the problem lies not in the telescope mirror,*

but rather, in the assumption that starlight is of the same intensity outside the Earth's atmosphere and orgone envelope as within it! (Pulse of the Planet #1:48, 1989 and #3:122, 1991)

The Intelligent Neanderthal

The notion that Neanderthals were a brutish, grunting sub-human specie that went around clubbing each other is again challenged, this time by the discovery of a small neck bone in the basicranium of Neanderthal skulls. A new analysis of Neanderthal and modern human skulls, conducted by David W. Frayer of the University of Kansas indicates that Neanderthal speech and language ability was the equivalent of todays humans. In other words, Neanderthals of 130,000 to 35,000 years ago could conduct conversations — not just grunts. If you combine this information with the *lack* of archaeological evidence for violence appearing among Neanderthals, the picture emerges of a peaceful, social, and now possibly articulate people. (*Science News*, Vol. 141, 11 April 1992)

Pre-Columbian Diffusion

One of the earliest transitions to a politically stratified society in the Americas took place not among crop growers, but among villagers who hunted, fished, and gathered wild plants along Mexico's southwestern coast about 3,500 years ago. The findings indicate that many New World coastal societies developed without relying on agricultural techniques, which anthropologists often consider essential to the growth of highly stratified civilizations.

This research inadvertently supports the possibilities of pre-Columbian contact because the stratified societies were found to exist in predominantly *coastal* areas where contact with sea-going traders or conquerors is most likely. In contrast to the standard anthropological view which stresses the generation of agricultural surplus and irrigation technology as leading influences on the development of hierarchical societies, pre-Columbian contact theorists (particularly the Saharasian research of James DeMeo) attribute the development of stratified and hierarchical coastal societies in the New World to migrations of conquering, sea-going, patrist peoples from Asia, the Middle East and Africa. (*Science News*, Vol. 141, 8 February 1992; also see "The Origins and Diffusion of Patrism", by J. DeMeo, *Pulse of the Planet* #3, 1991.)

NUCLEAR NOTES

Exposable Workers

Untrained, temporary workers hired at French nuclear facilities to save the costs of more skilled and trained employees, were exposed to radiation that "left them horribly burned and mutilated". The workers were not educated to the dangers of their work, which involved repair of mechanical equipment located in high radiation environments. Their supervisors were charged with civil offenses which, at most, would lead to a year in prison and a few thousand dollars in penalties. One worker was left with second and third degree burns over 2/3's of his body following only 30 minutes of exposure. His hair fell out, parts of his ears and fingers required amputation, and skin grafts were required on his arms, legs and chest.
(*SF Chronicle*, 23 April 1993, p.A21)

American Nuclear Guinea Pigs

A new book *American Ground Zero: The Secret Nuclear War*, by Carole Gallagher (MIT Press, 1993) details the callous use of American citizens and military personnel for biological experiments during nuclear bomb tests. It is filled with first-hand accounts of the atmospheric nuclear bomb testing program, which took place in Nevada in the 1950s and 1960s. Said Reason Warehiem, a former military man with lung cancer who witnessed a bomb detonation,

"...nobody out there knew what they were doing. It was one big goof-up, supposed to be a 23-kiloton bomb, twice the size of Hiroshima. It was 51 [kilotons]! When it went off, you felt you were in a vapor, like a vacuum, everything still as death — and then this real bright light, so bright I had my hands over my closed eyes and I could see all these bones just like you were looking at an X-ray. The fireball was right straight up over our heads. We had to be in the stem of it. We were only 300 yards from ground zero. The sand had melted into a glaze, like a brown glass. Then we got a sunburn, and the guys all started throwing up in the truck going back. Sick as dogs, all of them."

Citizen LaVerl Snyder lived near Ruth, Nevada, and witnessed the tests at the time when she was carrying her unborn child:

"I remember seeing lots of clouds. Different clouds. I broke out in a rash, my whole body, burns and blisters. I was sick, nauseous all the time. My toenails fell off and some of my fingernails fell off and I lost a lot of hair. It almost killed me."

Doctors in Salt Lake City diagnosed heat exhaustion, sunstroke and neurosis. Her baby was born with cancer, for which radiation treatment was given, causing more problems. The daughter today has congestive heart failure and pulmonary hypertension, with a right lung that no longer functions. None of the nuclear physicists, politicians or generals have yet been charged or brought to trial. (cf. "Tales from Ground Zero", *This World*, 11 April 93, p.11.)

Radiation Hazards Revised

Dr. Alice Stewart has studied the health records of 35,000 workers at the Hanford nuclear weapons facility in Washington State, for the period 1944 to 1986. Her findings demonstrate low level radiation carries an even greater risk than previously acknowledged by nuclear advocates. Small doses of atomic radiation are four to eight times more likely to cause cancers than previously suspected. Also, older people are more vulnerable to radiation-induced cancer than previously believed. And finally, radiation delivered in low doses over time is far more damaging than intensive radiation delivered in a single dose.
(*SF Chronicle*, 8 Dec.92)

Chernobyl

So great were the calculated deaths from nuclear bomb testing, that Andrei Sakharov, the "father" of the Soviet H-bomb, eventually concluded that the nuclear bomb was primarily a biological weapon. He conservatively calculated that, for each 50-megatons of nuclear explosion that took place in the atmosphere, between 500,000 and 1 million people would perish, worldwide. He was punished for his public revelations, and banished to Siberia.

Now comes the book by Vladimir Chernousenko, *Chernobyl: Insight From the Inside* (Springer-Verlag, Berlin/New York), which validates Sakharov's prior predictions of disaster, and exposes the many official lies and cover-ups which took place. Chernousenko claims that between 7,000 to 10,000 volunteer workers were killed in the immediate control and clean-up of the area around Chernobyl, and that a full 80% of the reactor core materials were released into the atmosphere, not just the 3% which was "officially" announced. Chernousenko asserts that in some large regions, such as Belarus, nearly every child suffers from some kind of mild to serious immune deficiency disease. Radioactive food products were also knowingly exported from the contaminated areas to all parts of the former Soviet Union, resulting in a sickening of the entire Soviet society.

The findings of Chernousenko are in agreement with those previously published in the USA by Dr. Jay Gould and Dr. Ernest Sternglass, who also have been treated with silence and "official" denial. Chernousenko, a Ukranian physicist previously ordered to "liquidate the consequences" of the Chernobyl accident, and who therefore had a front-row seat to the entire appalling situation, is today himself dying of radiation poisoning, along with thousands of others who were engaged in the emergency cleanup. Following publication of his book, he was fired from his post at the Ukranian Academy of Science. (See the book review article on *Deadly Deceit* in this issue of *Pulse*, and also "Chernobyl, The Hidden Tragedy" by J. Gould, *The Nation*, 15 March 1993, p. 331-333)

Winds from Chernobyl: shaded regions have contamination levels of 1-5 curie of radiation per square kilometer. (*Science*, 31 May 1991, p. 1245.)

Nukes into Windmills

U.S. Windpower of Livermore, California has been drafted by Ukraine to supply 5,000 windmills that will replace 1/6 the power generated at Chernobyl and hopefully speed up the closure of that facility. The company created a barter deal with the ex-Soviet republic and will be paid in spare windmill parts made in former Soviet military factories. These parts will be used to repair and maintain thousands of windmills in the U.S. and Europe.
(*SF Chronicle*, 19 Feb. 1993)

Chelyabinsk

Chernobyl is not the only Soviet nuclear disaster. Chelyabinsk is worse. Formerly a secret nuclear complex where atomic bomb materials were fabricated, Chelyabinsk is today considered one of the most polluted spots on Earth. Officials callously allowed nuclear waste to be poured into the air and water throughout the cold war period, without any warnings to workers or local residents. Massive quantities of radioactive sludge and wastewater were simply dumped. The accumulated radiological doses are so great that in some parts, such as Karachay Lake dump, you can absorb a lethal radiation dose in just a one hour walk along the shoreline. The Lake has leaked its contents into groundwaters.

Many nuclear disasters have occurred at the site. In 1957, liquid atomic wastes exploded, contaminating a huge area with 20 million Curies of radiation; over a quarter million people were exposed, and all the pine trees in a 20 square kilometer area died within 18 months. That incident was covered-up by both KGB and CIA operatives, who wished to protect the growing nuclear programs of both nations. Even though the soil and water was contaminated afterward, no attempt was made to move people off the land, or to warn them.

In 1967, drought caused the evaporation of moist surface deposits of radioactive wastes at Karachay Lake, after which winds carried away the highly radioactive dusts across the region. In that one accident alone, some 25,000 square kilometers were contaminated with 5 million Curies, an amount roughly equal to the Hiroshima bomb; 436,000 people were living in the area at the time. Radiologically-induced birth defects, cancers and immune dysfunctions are now abundant.
("From Here to Chelyabinsk", *Mother Jones*, Jan/Feb 92, p.51-72)

Ocean Dumping of Radioactive Waste

The Russian Federation recently admitted how the former USSR repeatedly broke international rules and dumped highly radioactive wastes in the Atlantic and Pacific Oceans. The amounts were *twice* the combined reported totals of the 12 other nuclear nations, some *2,500,000 Curies*. Other nations had dumped a total of 1,238,465 Curies during the same time period. A single Curie is equal to the total radiation given off by one gram of radium, and this is roughly equal to *37 billion disintegrations per second*. For comparative purposes, normal background radiation yields around 20-50 disintegrations per second on a Geiger counter, while an old-style radium-glow watch face might yield around 500 disintegrations per second.
(*SF Chronicle*, 27 April 1993)

Radioactive Bullets

Uranium is the heaviest of the naturally-occurring elements. In its pure metallic form, it is very dense and harder than steel. In recent years, military engineers have use it to make armor plating for tanks, and also for armor-piercing anti-tank weapons. Mostly, the radioactive armaments are made from depleted uranium, a by-product from the making of nuclear bombs or reactor fuel. Such radioactive armaments were widely used in the Gulf War, against Iraqi tanks and armored positions, and the battlefields are today littered with this new form of "radioactive waste". American soldiers were also exposed to the rad waste, by touching, breathing, or ingesting the materials.
(*SF Examiner*, 31 Jan.93)

Atomic Bikini

In 1954, when the first hydrogen bomb was tested at Bikini Atoll, it produced an explosion more than twice as large as predicted. The force was 1000 times that of the Hiroshima bomb, and "spewed radiation over inhabited islands and so frightened everyone involved that it marked the beginning of the end of atmospheric testing." The blast created a crater a mile wide and 200 feet deep. For more details on the Bikini tests, see the article by Katagiri in this issue of *Pulse*. ("The Fallout From Bikini", *Destination Discovery*, April 1993, p.16-23.)

Atomic Sardines!

The Soviet submarine *Komsomolets* sank in the North Atlantic off Norway in 1989, killing 42 crew members. Now, according to Russian scientists issuing a public warning, it is learned that there were two nuclear-bomb tipped torpedoes on board which will soon begin to corrode and leak their plutonium warheads. The water is more than a mile deep at the spot where it sank, but currents would carry the toxic plutonium into major fishing grounds of the North Sea.
(*SF Chronicle*, 21 May 93)

Рис. 32. Дезактивация жилых помещений
FIG. 32. DEACTIVATION OF LIVING QUARTERS

The above illustration is from a Soviet handbook published in 1987: *Dolzen Znat' i Umet' Kazhdyi (What Everyone Should Know.)*

Deforestation, USA

Shocked and disgusted by what they saw, employees of the U.S. Forest Service have formed an organization to inform the public about the mis-management and degradation of our wild lands by the agency that was chartered to protect and preserve them. The Association of Forest Service Employees for Environmental Ethics details how the U.S. Forest Service colludes with lumber companies to actually set quotas, known as "timber targets" which specify how much timber *must* be cut in each national forest each year. If a Regional Forester decides that the quota is environmentally unsound and fails to cut the required amount, that person will be faced with reprimands and firing, as happened to the head foresters in Idaho and Montana.

To make matters even worse, the Forest Service actually operated these timber sales *at a loss* to the taxpayers of more than $350 million last year! That's how much it cost for taxpayers to build new roads into formerly roadless areas, maintain existing roads, and mark and sell trees to private timber companies. This figure does not include the losses incurred by selling the trees far below market value as well as other practices such as leasing U.S. grazing lands to private cattlemen far below its real value. (*AFSEEE*, PO Box 11615, Eugene, OR 97440)

Deforestation, Canada

The area of Earth with one of the highest rates of tree-cutting and deforestation is Vancouver Island, British Columbia. Under the greedy promotions of Canadian, US, and Japanese businessmen, there is an apparent attempt to "get as much down as possible" before the word gets out and the forests are protected legally.

Recent articles in the S*F Chronicle* (July-Aug. 1993) gave graphic photographic testimony to the clear-cut, slash and destroy techniques, devastating entire mountains and ranges. The articles triggered a subsequent series of denials and allegations, but several facts emerged: Certain western Canadian regions are threatened with deforestation, little tree-planting is in progress, and rates of cutting far outpacing rates

of regrowth. As usual, little thought is being given to the future of the forests, or the future generations of forest lovers and forest users. The issue is presently before the Canadian courts, with land-developers and logging companies on one side, and environmentalists and Native American groups on the other.

Deforestation, Central America

The Maya Biosphere Reserve in Guatemala, a unique 4 million acre reserve of rainforest containing 225 species of migratory birds, is being progressively deforested and burned by peasant farmers and lumbermen, fueled by corrupt politicians. Open roads constructed by government funds allow easy access to developers. Little attention is given to the needs of native peoples of the area, and lack of suitable family planning efforts have led to high populations of poverty. It is a no-win situation, as the peasants have few jobs or support in the urban areas, and see the forest as a place to live and grow food, albeit in a meagre fashion. (*SF Chronicle*, 4 July 93)

Deforestation, Panama

"If I go to Panama City and stand in front of a pharmacy and, because I need medicine [but have no money], pick up a rock and break the window, you put me in jail. For me the forest is my pharmacy. If I have sores on my legs, I go to the forest and get the medicine I need... without having to destroy everything, as your people do." Panamanian Kuna Indian. (*Greenpeace*, May/June 1991).

Desertification, South America

Brazil's northeastern province of Sertao is undergoing progressive conversion into harsh desert, replete with sand dunes and cactus. The area is climatologically identified as a semi-arid environment, and for the last four years has received only spotty rains. Poor planning and social/political corruption have left little food reserves, and an estimated 10 million are suffering from hunger. Malnutrition similar to that identified in Africa is currently affecting around 15% of the population. In April of 1993, food riots and looting of food stores and warehouses took place. Reservoirs are at record low levels in many areas, and over 90% of the northeastern

corn, rice, and bean crop has failed. Hot, dry air associated with the Pacific Ocean El Nino are partly blamed for the situation.

Deforestation & Floods, India

The Cherrapunji region of India once received over 400 inches of rain each year, before the massive forests of the area were cut down. Khasi hill people living there had described the rains in terms like nowhere else on the planet. The word *hynniew-miat* means: "rain lasting 9 solid days and nights", while *khadsaw-miat* means the same thing, but for 14 days and nights, instead of only 9.

Over the last 30 years, the forests were cut, as population in the Khasi villages swelled from 5,000 to nearly 70,000 people. Now, according to local residents *"at most we'll get a three-day rain, but not a hynniew-miat, and certainly not a khadsaw-miat."* And what rain does fall drains away quickly downslope, to cause floods in Bangladesh. Much of the region's soil has also washed away to Bangladesh, where siltation has aggravated the flooding problem. Interestingly, the local people rarely get sick from the rain, having developed an immunity to the colds, sniffles and sneezes which afflict drylanders. *"This beneficial side effect was overlooked by the British settlers who first chose Charrapunji as their Assam capital in 1832, but then retreated under the barrage of raindrops the size of large-caliber bullets."* (*SF Examiner*, 11 July 93)

Deforestation, New Guinea

Over the last 16 years, the Japanese lumber company of Honshu Paper clearcut more than 170,000 acres of tropical rainforest in New Guinea. The local Gogol-Naru peoples who inhabited the forest were promised better roads and social services. None of the promised benefits were delivered, and logging has destroyed the subsistence base of the area. The forests are gone, soils are compacted and eroded, and streams and rivers are polluted and silted up. The locals have blockaded roads to stop further logging and to demand the payment of promised benefits, but with most of the forest gone, the firm appears unwilling to negotiate. Honshu Paper likewise has not paid any taxes over the years to the government of New Guinea, due to legal loopholes. The company converts forests into woodchips, which are then used for packaging material and cardboard. (*Greenpeace*, May/June 1991).

The Gogol-Naru people protesting Japanese logging giant Gonshu Paper.

Deforestation, Malaysia

The fastest rate of tree-cutting in the world is occurring in the rainforests of Sarawak, Malaysia. *"Despite international condemnation, the rate of cutting has increased in the past year, and now approaches 3,000 acres daily (up from 2,200 acres daily.) Since June, 450 people from different indigenous tribes, including the Penan, have set up blockades of logging roads to stop the logging"* (*Worldwatch*, Dec.91, p.6)

Signs of Devitalization

Sorry to sound so pessimistic, but:
- Per capita food consumption will decline as populations grow around the world.
- A "doomsday" population, when the exponential population curve soars towards "infinity", will be reached sometime around the year 2025.
- Neither farms, livestock ranches, or fisheries will be able to keep pace in food production with the soaring world population.
- World per capita grain output climbed 50% from 1950 to 1984, but has fallen 8% since then.
- Meat production likewise rose 78% from 1950 to 1990, but fell 1% thereafter.
- Ocean fisheries also peaked out at 100 million tons in 1989, declining by 7% since.
- 91 million people are added to the Earth's population each year.
- The refugee population of the world climbed to 18 million in 1982.
(*Vital Signs*, Worldwatch Institute, 1993)

Atmospheric DOR Kills

Researchers are finally beginning to analyze atmospheric haze, what Reich called DOR for Deadly Orgone Radiation which he believed was a stagnant, toxic form of orgone energy. By correlating daily weather, air pollutants and mortality in five U.S. cities, a federal scientist has discovered that non-accidental death rates tend to rise and fall in near lockstep with daily levels of atmospheric haze — but not with other pollutants such as sulfur dioxide, a gaseous pollutant, which showed no effect on mortality rates. The correlation held up for even very low haze levels. Moreover, the magnitude of the haze effect on mortality proved nearly identical in each U.S. city.

What is this atmospheric haze? In England, it is called "British smoke" and is also causally linked with mortality in London where it is measured every day. The EPA measures only what they consider to be respirable particles — with a diameter of 10 microns or less — and not all particles suspended in the air. But what these particles actually are, besides "soot and sulfates" is not made clear in the report. There is a tacit, unproven assumption at work in all such studies on atmospheric haze, that such haze is composed primarily of particulates. Another way the researchers gauged the amount of haze is by the *visibility index* often compiled at airports. It is interesting to note that the correlation between atmospheric haze and mortality held up even when the levels of measurable particulate matter was very low.

The new findings also suggest that haze is more toxic than smog ozone. But exactly how this might contribute to mortality remains unknown. "I have no idea what the mechanism is," reported Dr. David Bates, a chest physician and air pollution epidemiologist, "nor has anyone else." The above findings confirm the observations made on the effects of DOR energy by Wilhelm Reich and other orgonomists over the past 30+ years. More research is required to clarify the relationships between "atmospheric haze", particulates, and the *energetic* qualities of the air.
(*Science News*, Vol. 139, 6 April 1991)

About that Arctic Haze...

Pollution levels in the Arctic can often reach levels observed in large cities. This is because prevailing wind patterns transport the air from the large cities and industrial areas of the USA and European-Russian region northeast, towards the Arctic in a spiraling manner. Particulates in Arctic haze sometimes contain sulphur compounds comparable to that observed in large coal-fired power plants. (*Bull. Am Met. Soc.*, Nov.91, p.1712-1713)

Record Low Ozone Levels

Stratospheric ozone levels reached record low levels, between 9% to 20% below average, in the arctic region during this last winter. It is the second year in a row with such record low levels. The low levels of stratospheric ozone were matched with record high levels of chlorine monoxide, an ozone-destroying chemical. (*Science News*, 20 March 93)

Record High Ultraviolet Radiation

The connection between decreased stratospheric ozone and increased surface UV radiation is finally, and unfortunately, receiving empirical support. Measurements in Argentina during 1990 and 1992 indicated levels of UV radiation at the ground level some 45% higher than anticipated. The researchers feel the increases were related to the movement of ozone-depleted pools of air moving from the Antarctic towards the equator, passing over their measuring station. They have not yet determined what biological damage is developing from this significant change.
(*Science News*, 3 July 93)

Electromagnetic Hazards

"A new study of 585 pregnant women employed in banking and clerical positions in Finland is the first to find an increased risk of miscarriages for women who work at VDTs that emit strong magnetic fields. The women were employed for at least three months during the first trimester of pregnancy — and 191 of the group (33%) had miscarriages. The study concludes that pregnant women who work with VDTs with strong magnetic fields are 3.5 times more likely to have miscarriages than those working with VDTs with low magnetic fields. The research, reported at an international scientific conference last September in Berlin, also asserted that women exposed to medium levels of extremely low frequency magnetic fields had nearly twice as many miscarriages as those exposed to lower fields. The Finns were the first to do the obvious: They measured the magnetic fields of 23 different computer models, the women's exposure and the outcome. Dr. Marija-Liisa Lindbohm, primary researcher on the Finnish study, concludes that 'pregnant women should not work at VDT terminals with high magnetic fields'. She points out that newer computers have lower — and safer — levels of electromagnetic radiation."
(From the *Pegasus Computer Network*, as reported in *Nexus*, Feb./Mar. 93, p.7)

Low-Level EM Fields & Childhood Leukemia

A 5-year study by the University of Southern California has linked childhood leukemia to electric power lines, television sets, electric clocks and video games. The study of 232 cases of childhood leukemia in Los Angeles County built upon earlier studies, though not all uncertainties were eliminated. The risks were particularly associated with two types of appliances: television sets and electric hair dryers.
(*Am. J. Epidemiology*, Nov. 1991)

Missing Bioelectromagnetic Mechanism

Research presented at a joint Bioelectromagnetic Society/ Biochemical Society symposium (25 July 1991, Salt Lake City) focused upon a common perplexing problem: classical theory is not sufficient to explain the magnitudes of observed biological effects from exposures to low-level, extremely low frequency electromagnetic fields (ELF). Here are some pertinent observations on the problem from Dr. Beverly Rubik, Director of the Center for Frontier Sciences at Temple University:

"The basic objection of the physics community [to the existence of bio-effects] has been that these fields are below the random, collisional thermal energy of tissues at body temperature. ... One of the obstacles to an objective analysis of the possibility of ELF effects at low field strengths has been the absence of a mechanism of interaction that is generally believable, withstands careful scientific scrutiny, and suggests experiments to verify its predictions."

Another problem with such effects has been the almost animal-like nature of low-level electromagnetic field phenomena. A powerful emitting transformer may be on a power pole right outside your home, but it will be the home three houses away which shows the highest field strength. Likewise, slight differences in electrical grounding, or changes in the weather, can result in ELF fields either to appear or to disappear. The acronym "ELF" appears to have a dual meaning. Consider this quote from *Science News* (28 Sept.91):

"Life is tough for researchers investigating the health effects of electromagnetic fields. Power companies berate them for scaring the public, and the public berates them for not being able to say for sure whether a high-current electrical wire running across the backyard might induce leukemia. Even their experiments play tricks on them. Changes induced by electromagnetic fields are fickle phenomena — here one day, gone the next. And colleagues provide little solace. Anyone advancing an explanation for how these fields might affect biological systems can expect a grilling from every other researcher stalking such effects, plus the scorn of a raft of outside critics."

The Editor of *Pulse*, once again, wishes to suggest the *oranur effect*, observed and described by Wilhelm Reich

in the 1950s, very likely constitutes this "missing mechanism".

Police Ban Radar Guns

Connecticut police recently banned the use of hand-held speed-detector radar guns following complaints by officers that their cancers were caused by the guns. Testicular and lymphatic cancers are among the stated effects. Police radar guns utilize microwave frequencies long associated with problems of cellular degeneration.(SF Chronicle, 17 Oct. 91)

Brain Tumors from Cellular Telephones

Hand-held cellular telephones—the kind which have a small antenna behind the user's head, and which can be used away from home—are being linked with increases in brain cancer. The numbers are small, but the reports surface at the same time the giant telecommunications companies are gearing up towards a completely wire-free communications system. Microwave radio frequencies are used by the telephones for long distance communication, but such frequencies have for a long time been associated with health-related problems. People living near cellular telephone relay towers have complained about health problems consequent to the installation of such facilities, but neither the telephone firms or the government have paid much attention to the complaints, other than to ridicule or dismiss them outright.

Sperm Go On Strike

A Danish study has detected major declines in sperm counts, of up to 25%, over the last 50 years. The reductions are postulated as the result of widespread environmental pollution. The hypothesis of an environmental causation is supported by correlated dramatic increases in male genito-urinary abnormalities and testicular cancer.
(*SF Chronicle*, 11 Sept.92)

Birds and Frogs in Decline

All around the world, biologists are observing gradual or even dramatic decreases in the populations of amphibians and birds, sometimes with entire species vanishing. The problem is partly due to environmental toxins, but also to loss of natural habitat. There are simply too many people swarming over the globe, destroying natural ecosystems, and taking up living space once occupied by nonhuman species. (*SF Chronicle*, 20 Apr.92)

New World Order Toxic Alphabet Soup: EEC/GATT/NAFTA

The desire of citizens to develop decentralized economies, and to increase democratic controls over issues that affect their daily lives, are powerfully threatened by EEC, GATT and NAFTA. The new EEC/GATT/NAFTA bureaucracies will have the authority to overrule local environmental quality, consumer protection and labor laws, and undermine local democratic control of social institutions and economic life with layers of unelected bureaucrats who rule by decree. Nations which rule their peoples with a heavy hand thereby become the "least common denominators" for dictatorial bureaucrats, who will use the treaties to undermine the higher standards of the democracies.

For example, Mexico, a one-party police state rife with corruption at both the local and highest political levels, will be given power to veto or by-pass American laws on consumer, worker, and environmental protection by bureaucratic fiat. Already, the Canadians, who have a stronger sense of social responsibility than their American cousins, have suffered from "free trade" treaties with the USA: high-wage Canadian jobs have shifted to low-wage factories in rural America; medical costs in Canada have been forced upwards artificially by bureaucrats, to "harmonize" them with the more expensive American system. American laws requiring the labeling of food products subjected to nuclear irradiation, and the banishment of foods containing unsafe levels of pesticides, are already under attack by Central and South American food growers (often subsidiaries of major US corporations).

Unlike in Europe, nobody is asking American or Canadian citizens what they think about the New World Order bureaucracy. If they did, these "treaties", which benefit nobody but the rich and powerful, would be soundly defeated. Another example follows:

"Britain's booming health food industry is under threat from European Commission plans to classify all but the smallest doses of vitamins and minerals as drugs, rather than food products. The Commission also plans to move against sales of herbal teas, royal jelly and slimming aids. The move, which could see the removal of most brand name vitamins from the shelves of health food stores and chemists, will seriously threaten the livelihoods of thousands of people in the 200-million-pound-per-year health food industry. 'Harmonisation' would require the UK to fall into line with other European countries, where vitamins and minerals are classified as pharmaceutical products if they contain as little as 1.5 times the recommended daily intake." (*Sunday Telegraph*, 9 August 1992)

Note: similar bills are now being pushed through Congress; see the article on the FDA in this issue of the *Pulse*.

America: Top Arms Merchant for the World

While America's basic manufacturing infrastructure has been decimated in recent decades, one industry is going strong—the making and selling of weapons of death and destruction. Not only is the USA the world's number one exporter of arms, according to the Stockholm International Peace Research Institute, fully 45% of all the major combat systems sold around the world in 1992 were American made. In 1991, some $900 billion was spent worldwide on military hardware.

We're Still Number One!

For two years in a row, the United States of America has held the world record for having the highest percentage of its population in jails or prisons. Our nation incarcerates 455 individuals per 100,000 population, well above the second ranking nation of South Africa, which incarcerates 311 per 100,000. The population of incarcerated Americans has tripled since 1973, and increased by 6.6% since 1991 to a 1992 total of 1.1 million individuals. The number of black inmates is roughly at 500,000 or 3,370 per 100,000 blacks; this number is roughly five times the incarceration rate of blacks in South Africa, which has only 680 per 100,000 in prison. The cost of this soaring "police solution" to social problems is $20 billion per year, and growing. The fastest growing employment sector of the US economy is *prison guards and private security firms*. The USA currently has *more private security guards than public police forces*. These grim statistics suggest the continued, even accelerated reliance upon policemen to "solve" social problems.

(*The Sentencing Project*, 918 F St. NW, #501, Washington, DC 20004; also Robert B. Reich, *CNN interview*, 2 June 92)

World's Richest Man

The Sultan of Brunei, with a fleet of 165 Rolls Royce automobiles, is worth an estimated $37 Billion.

Research Funding

"Renewable energy received only 5% of the Energy Department's budget over the past 15 years, far less than nuclear power or fossil fuels. 70% of all pollution control equipment used in the US is manufactured overseas. Meanwhile, military research gets 60% of all federal research and development funding."
(Rep. G. Miller, *Congressional Newsletter*)

Skyrocketing Executive Pay

Time-Warner chairman Steve Ross received a $78 million pay package for 1990, the same year the company laid off 600 employees whose total earnings amounted to around 1/3 of Ross' pay. ITT chairman Rand Araskog doubled his pay to $11 million in one year, at the same time the company's stock performed poorly. CEOs' salaries at major US corporations can range as high as 85 times that of the average factory worker, contrasted to Japan, where executive salaries are only 17 times as high as the average worker. This bloated-salary philosophy appears fully disconnected from the performance of the executives, and rather reflects a "Royal Family" ideology, that "them in power deserves more".

Unfortunately, this ideology is likewise afflicting public service. Presidents Bush and Clinton have both expressed justification for giving bloated salaries to politicians "in order to attract qualified people". What is wrong with this belief is the assumption that the vast numbers of hard-working Americans who never received more than $30,000 or $50,000 yearly salary are somehow incompetent to hold such executive jobs. The reverse, however, is more likely true — that the current crop of CEOs, with the overbloated paychecks, perks, stock options, etc., are among the *least* competent individuals one could pick to run such large firms. In large measure, they simply do not know what they are doing, and are selected not for their knowledge or working capacities, but rather, for their family connections, whom they know, their country club memberships, powerful affiliations, and class loyalties. It is reminiscent of the Kings of France or the Emperors of China, who were so surrounded with luxury, including special foods, concubines, and pampered care, that they had no grasp of the real world, no understanding of the forces which shaped their nations or sustained their unnatural lifestyles.

"Health Care" or Sickness Industry?

The total combined private-public cost of health care in America traditionally held around 5% of the gross national product, up until around 1960. After 1960, it skyrocketed. By 1991, "health care" consumed a total of $837 billion, or 13% of the gross national product. The total cost in 1992 was 14% of the GNP, or $3,200 per person. By contrast, the Japanese spent only $600 per person on health care in 1992. Not only do Japanese live longer and have better health than Americans, they also have no Food and Drug Administration lording over their health care. Increases in health care costs continue to outstrip inflation; by the year 2000, Americans will spend over 17% of the GNP on "health", more than a trillion dollars. Cancer afflicted only 1 person in 4 in 1970. Today, it is 1 in 3, heading towards 1 in 2. Just what are we getting for all this expense?

POSITIVE SIGNS

Unorthodox Viewpoints Are Legal

The US Supreme Court recently ruled that scientific evidence may be presented to a court of law even if that evidence has not been published in a "mainstream" scientific journal. Two lower courts had previously ruled that research data and interpretations must be previously published and peer-reviewed before they can be used to decide legal claims. The Supreme Court, thankfully, did not agree. Justice Blackmun wrote that if judges were allowed to label scientific evidence "invalid" simply because of its unpublished or non-mainstream status, it might "sanction a stifling and repressive scientific orthodoxy".

Fully Informed Jury Association

A new organization has formed to put the legal system back into the hands of ordinary citizens. It is the Fully Informed Jury Association (FIJA), whose simple message is causing a revolution in the legal system whereever it has been spread. Simply put, FIJA is mounting an educational effort to reinform Americans about their Constitutional right and obligation, if they are called for jury duty, to vote on matters of *both fact and law*. When legislators, prosecutors and judges want to railroad a citizen, using bad law, the only hope is an independent jury. When a judge informs a jury to "ignore this" or "ignore that", to "ignore their own feelings about whether a law is bad or good, and just vote on the question of guilt or innocence", they are at that moment abrogating the very purpose of juries as established by the founders of our constitutional Republic. In short, informed juries are the last bulwark against tyranny.

Jurors have a right and responsibility to rule on matters of both fact and law, and for much of America's history, bad law passed by legislative bodies was nullified by juries who refused to convict people for violations. Jury nullification of despotic laws was, and remains, the major reason for having juries in the first place. We need to be reminded of these facts of history, that our personal sense of justice is legally valid, and does indeed count for a lot when we serve on a jury. (*Fully Informed Jury Association*, PO Box 59, Helmville, MT 59843. 406/793-5550)

Health Reforms

*The National Institutes of Health have established an Office of Unconventional Medical Practices, with a mandate to study unorthodox methods of healing. The preliminary budget is quite small, but assuming it can maintain its independence from the AMA, FDA and corporate medical interests, it might help to lift the current oppressive climate against unorthodox medical research.

*The states of Alaska and Washington have passed laws forbidding local medical peer review committees from harassing physicians or revoking their licenses for using alternative or natural healing methods. Maryland may become the third state to enact such a law. (*Townsend Letter for Doctors*, May 92)

*The new Surgeon-General has finally embraced breast-feeding, advising mothers to breast-feed their children for the first two years of life.

*Approximately 7 out of 10 German physicians employ alternative or natural healing methods, and many insurance companies pay for such treatments. The German Science Ministry launched a research program on alternative treatment for cancer some years ago, and within the last several years, German medical schools have included major new courses in their curricula on natural healing methods. We fully expect to see the day when Reich's orgone accumulator therapy will be taught in German medical schools to all new physicians. Hopefully, when this day arrives, the American medical profession will have reversed its present trend towards repression of such methods.

Renewable Energy

*Record efficiency was recorded for a two-layer solar cell which demonstrated a 31 percent sunlight-to-electricity conversion efficiency. (*Science News*, 20 Aug.88)

*The world's wind power generating capacity doubled to 2,652 megawatts between 1986 and 1992. Wind generators in California now supply enough power to meet the needs of San Francisco and Washington, DC combined. (*SF Chronicle*, 18 July 93)

*US Windpower of California recently concluded a contract with the new Republic of Ukraine to supply 5,000 wind-electric generators to the region of Crimea. The Ukranians hope the power will allow a complete shut-down of the Chernobyl nuclear complex. The company presently operates over 4,200 wind-electric generators in California. (*SF Chronicle*, 19 Feb.93)

Is the Atmosphere Getting Cleaner?

Recent reports in science journals suggest the Northern Hemisphere atmosphere might be improving in quality. A slight reduction of particulate haze in the Arctic has been reported. Atmospheric transparency has slowly increased since 1982, according to records gathered at NOAA laboratories in Barrow, Alaska. Similarly, the acidity of precipitation over the continental USA has decreased between the years 1980 and 1991, with the measured pH of rains increasing. The beneficial changes are attributed to air pollution controls and a switch from coal to cleaner-burning natural gas in the USA, Europe and Russia since 1980. (*Science News*, 10 July 93; *Bull. Am. Met. Soc.*, July 93, p.1401)

SEX - ECONOMIC NOTES

Somalia: What the News Doesn't Say

One aspect which the journalists have not mentioned with respect to the recent UN military missions to Somalia is the widespread sexual mutilation of women. Over 90% of young girls in Somalia are subjected to severe mutilations of their genitals at the hands of the older women. Often called "female circumcision", the practices actually are far more butchering than the term implies. The entire external female genitalia (labia majora, labia minora, clitoris) are sliced or scraped away, with the inner walls of the exterior vagina being excoriated to a bloody mess so they will fuse together during healing, aided by the girl then being stitched up with thread or thorns, to "insure her virginity". An uncircumcised woman is viewed as something unclean and dirty, akin to a prostitute, and is at risk for mob actions against her.

Much of the population of Somalia is additionally addicted to the narcotic *qat*, a leaf which is chewed, with physiological affects similar to cocaine and hashish combined — paranoia and psychosis are products of the drug, and this can often be seen in the faces of the average man on the street. Widespread religious fundamentalism certainly contributes to this paranoia, particularly with its identification both of the female and of sexuality (and Westerners in general) as "devilish" influences. Additionally, the USA and Soviets had been pumping massive armaments into the region for more than a decade, fueling various massacres and tribal wars, helping to create the current situation. Far more women and children have been dying than men, given the tendency of qat-chewing thugs and gunslingers to dominate the food supply and political situation.
(*Women's International Network News,* 187 Grant St., Lexington, MA 02173)

Drought Blamed on Women

ZINDER, NIGER: Hundreds of people attacked bars and bordellos used by women accused of causing a drought, the official Niger Press Agency said yesterday. Police imposed a curfew after the mob injured three people, the Agency said. The mob was urged on by "marabouts", self-claimed Moslem holy men. (*Sunday Star Ledger,* NJ, 19 July 92)

Official Government Rapists

A new book by Kanan Makiya, an Iraqi reformer, gathers evidence that the regime of Saddam Hussein had employed on its payroll a special group of policemen whose sole responsibility was to go out, kidnap women who were "making trouble" for authorities, bring them back to special prisons and subject them to repeated sessions of rape. The rapes were officially sanctioned and approved by the higher-up authorities, with the goal to destroy the will of dissenting women. Many ordinary, non-political women who happened to be at the wrong place at the wrong time were imprisoned and raped. Makiya provides the names of some of these "bureaucrats", with chilling precision. Example:

"Mr. Aziz Salih Ahmad, civil servant, paid a salary to rape Iraqi women... When the prisons of the mukhabarat [secret police] and the army were stormed during the March 1991 uprising inside Iraq, which followed the end of the Gulf War, scores of women with children born to them in prison were released. Every major prison seems to have had its own specially equipped rape room (replete in one case with soft-porn pictures stuck on the wall opposite the surface being used)."

These reports come from native-born Iraqis and are in complete agreement with what we already know about Saddam Hussein, a man who used poison gas against villagers along the Iraqi-Iranian border, and who previously set up death camps in Kurdish territories for the systematic butchering of entire village populations. One might consider these facts as justification for Operation Desert Storm, and there is a certain truth to the idea that those who helped create Saddam Hussein should take the responsibility to bring him down — but the poison gassing of civilians, the massacres of the Kurds, and other atrocities of Saddam Hussein were public knowledge for years, even before and during the time when Washington politicians were funding him illegally (with multibillion dollar diversions of Department of Agriculture taxpayer dollars, secretly

Kollwitz

channeled through banks in Atlanta and Italy). The USA also illegally shipped nuclear materials to Iraq, with full knowledge and blessing of the State Department. Both the Bush and Clinton Justice Departments have been actively covering it all up.

Makri also provides evidence of intensive police investigations and aggressive preoccupations with female sexuality in other Arab nations, part of the widespread "honor system" where even the slightest hint of sexual display or "misconduct" (such as failure to wear a veil, or walking outside your house with an unrelated man) is taken as an Offense Against The State. Special "Religious Police" today roam the streets of Saudi Arabia, Iran, Jordan, and other Arab nations, snooping about for women to round up and imprison.
("Rape in Service of the State: Power and Patriarchy in Iraq", *The Nation,* 10 May 1993, p.627-630; *Cruelty and Silence: War, Tyranny, Uprising and the Arab World,* W.W. Norton & Company, 1993; also, under pseudonym of Samir al-Khalil, *Republic of Fear,* Pantheon)

Iranian Discipline

When the Ayatollah Khomeini died in 1989, it was anticipated that Islamic Puritanism might wane, and for a few years, the government did "lighten up" a small bit. The dreaded "komitehs", neighborhood social spy organizations who kept "law-n'order" throughout Iran, were subordinated and renamed the "Disciplinary Forces". Recently, however, the "Disciplinary Forces" were mobilized to crack down on "growing social vices". Women wearing makeup, or who might have a lock of hair showing outside of their veils, have been arrested in new police sweeps against "immorality". Their fate is uncertain and unknown. (*SF Chronicle* 5 Aug.92, *SF Examiner*, 26 July 92)

Military Rapists-Turned-Pornographers

Reports from the former Yugoslavia, now torn by civil war, indicate that rapes of Muslim women by Serbian troops are taking place *enmasse*. Additionally it is reported they are making videotapes of the rapes, which are often gang-rapes or rape-mutilation murders. Some of the videos have been broadcast on Serbian television, and made their way into the international pornography market. (*MS Magazine*, July/August 1993)

Public Hugging and Kissing!

During the last 10 years, India has seen a surge of music videos depicting young lovers dancing together, holding hands, hugging and even kissing! Such open displays of romance were formerly completely taboo among the puritanical Hindu and Moslem populations; however, at least among the Hindu youth, a sexual revolution of sorts is starting to occur. Likewise in Japan, where formality and the holding back of public display of emotion has long been the enforced norm. In the last several years, however, one can see young couples holding hands, lying together on blankets and smooching in public parks. As recently as the mid-1980s, this would not have been seen.

No More Public Hugging & Kissing!

Following the machine-gunning of students and reformers in the Tiananmen Massacre, Chinese officials have targeted another serious threat to their totalitarian regime: public hugging and kissing by students at Beijing University. Calling it "an offense against decency", over 100 students had been cited by policemen for "displaying affection", and repeat offenders may risk fines and school demerits. These efforts come as Chinese leadership is discovering what every sex-economist knows — that the docility of character and unquestioning obedience to authority required for maintenance of a fascist state is underlain by a social background of severe sex-repression. (*SF Chronicle*, 18 Oct.91 & 26 May 92)

Anti-Sex Reformers

The conservative president of Nicaragua, Violeta Chamorro, ordered the replacement of school textbooks which gave explicit education on human sexual reproduction. Explicit textbooks have been replaced with ones promoting monogamy, the Ten Commandments, and condemning premarital sex, in harmony with the wishes of the Catholic Church. Nicaraguan women currently have around five children each, and 25% of them become pregnant prior to age 20. An opposition politician charged: *"What the government is doing is crazy. They have put a group of fundamentalist Christians in charge of the Education Ministry."* (*Seattle Times*, 21 March 91)

Philippines Family Planning: Destroyed!

Everything is not always as it appears to be. Ferdinand Marcos was a iron-fisted dictator who murdered his political enemies and used his power to accumulate a gargantuan personal fortune. But he also assisted family planning efforts in the Philippines. Some 10,000 clinics existed at the time a popular uprising ousted him. The family planning programs of Marcos were one reason Muslim groups in the south islands were revolting. When liberal Aquino took the reins of power, she repaid a political debt to the Catholic Church, and purposefully destroyed the Filipino family planning program. Only 200 clinics were remaining at the time she was replaced by Ramos, a former General who supported Aquino against Marcos.

Ramos is in favor of family planning, and has built the number of clinics back up to 2000. The population growth rate in the Philippines is 2.6%, the total population doubling every 27 years, but the annual growth rate of food production is only 1%, with a limit on available new lands for development. New jobs, schools, housing and other facilities cannot be developed rapidly enough to meet the needs of the growing population, and so there is a relatively permanent underclass living in poverty and squalor, worsened by the Aquino "pro-life" policies, which also were anti-abortion.

The Filipino Catholic clergy railed against the brothels around Subic Bay, condemning the US soldiers for "turning our women into whores" — and with significant justification. But by opposing family planning, the Catholic Church guaranteed the perpetuation of poverty in the Philippines, plus a steady stream of unwanted, throw-away children, who

as teenagers would readily sell their bodies to anyone for basic food and shelter. The Principle of Population, discovered by Malthus over 100 years ago, appears as basic as gravity. One cannot preach it away, or pray it out of existence. The only proven way around the Principle is family planning. A similar situation exists in overpopulated, impoverished Haiti, where the liberal Catholic priest Aristide is against family planning, while the military dictators at least tolerated its existence. (CNN Special Report, Sept. 93)

Throw-Away Children

Several years ago, Pope John Paul II visited Brazil, and railed against contraception and divorce at a time when the Brazilian Parliament was voting on a liberalized divorce law. At that time, record numbers of Brazilian women were being murdered by angry husbands for the "crime of disaffectionado" (falling out of love) — the Brazilian Constitution guarantees a man the "right of dignity", and such murders for this reason were *legally permitted*. The Pope continues to step into the bedrooms of ordinary people, railing against abortion, contraception, and divorce despite the fact that Brazil's largest cities are already swamped with people, with so many homeless children who must live in sewers and engage in petty larceny in order to get food. Brazil's homeless children are now being routinely murdered by police and businessmen, like stray dogs. During his last trip to Brazil, the Pope called contraception "a crime worse than murder". But, by opposing birth control programs, the Pope has directly contributed to not only increased poverty, crime and murder, but also to more abortions. Abortion rates in Catholic Latin American nations are among the highest in the world.

Anti-Abortionists Promote Abortion

"Abortions are more common in countries that ban or restrict the procedure than in those where it is widely permitted."

The above conclusion comes from a report by International Planned Parenthood, and is no surprise to anyone who has studied the issue of contraception, family planning, and the problem of unplanned, unwanted pregnancy. Aggressive anti-abortion laws are successfully promoted in nations where generally antisexual attitudes predominate, and this includes attitudes against contraception. Anti-abortionists are rarely, if ever, supporters of contraception. They are, instead, promoters of antisexual propaganda, such as "abstinence" or other unreliable methods of birth control, such as the rhythm method.

"In western Europe, where abortion is legal except in Ireland, there are about 14 abortions per 1000 women, the study said. In Latin America, where abortion is restricted, the rate is between 30 and 60 per 1000 women... Abortion rates are lowest in countries that not only permit the procedure, but offer family planning and sex education services. Among 22 countries that allow abortion, the rate increases as availability of family services declines... the Netherlands, which has widespread sex education, had the fewest abortions — 5.6 for every 1,000 women in 1984. The United States ranked 13th with 27.4 abortions for every 1000 women... the Soviet Union ranked last, with 181 abortions for every 1000 women..." (SF Chronicle, 29 May 93)

Abortion Clinic Attacks

The National Abortion Federation reports that since 1977, abortion providers have been hit by 36 bombings, 76 attacks by arsonists, 53 cases of attempted bombing or arson, 277 bomb threats, 119 death threats, 84 assaults, 55 stalking cases, 28 burglaries, 452 cases of vandalism and 2 kidnappings. Then, of course, there was the gunshot murder of Dr. David Gunn by a devout, bible-quoting Christian fundamentalist. (In These Times, 5 April 93, p.11)

Soaring Chinese Divorce

When communists took over China after WWII, initial efforts to reform the traditional Chinese treatment of women and girls was met with extreme public resistance. For instance, early divorce reform frequently resulted in the murder of a wife by her angry relatives when they learned of her application for a divorce. The early reforms were rescinded quickly by the moralist Mao Tse Dung, who instituted a regime of repression in all spheres of life. More recently, however, the Chinese divorce rate has been "soaring" ever since a new liberalized marriage law was introduced. The increase is attributed not only to the new law, but also to economic liberalization. Divorce is increasing, especially among women working outside of the home. (SF Chronicle, 21 Oct.92)

Taoistic Sexual Alchemy versus Sex-Economic Freedom

A lot of people confuse the sexual rituals of Taoism with Reich's sex-economic findings, partly due to the misrepresenting of Taoism by its advocates. Here's a quote from a recent article advocating Taoism, "Harnessing Sexual Energy", which is clearly different from Reich's findings:

"After a night of excess love-making, I have a dull headache the next day. I also feel like my brain is in a fog, and I often have a nagging low back pain. Many men I have spoken to confirm these observations. This is nothing new to the ancient Chinese Taoists... If we're not making babies and sex is more enjoyable without orgasm, why are we throwing our lives away through orgasm? ...The baby-making way involves getting all charged up then discharging all the stored energy through orgasm. This leaves people discharged most of the time and can leave them with the impression that all of life is dull except during sexual intercourse. The monastic way involves pretending that the opposite sex does not exist. ... It is a healthy life-style but unacceptable to most Americans. A Taoist way involves building up energy through sexual stimulation but not releasing it through orgasm... The Taoists teach women to regulate their menstrual flow and men to conserve their seed."
(China Healthways Newsletter, July 93, p.4)

What is not mentioned in these modern-day articles about Taoism is the fact that, in China at the time when it was developed, female sexual slavery was rampant, and men following the "Taoist way" routinely bought numerous slave women (captured from conquered territories or purchased as children out of poverty) for orgasm-avoiding Taoistic rape sessions. The most "desirable" women were those who went completely limp, both unpassionate and unresisting. And the early Chinese sex manuals did not just advocate "pretending the partner does not exist", but rather called the female "the enemy", and described intercourse in military terms. Slave girls were raped in large numbers, but with ejaculation held back (coitus obstructus, coitus reservatus), on the assumption that a man would accumulate a large amount of female Yin essence from the slave girls. After doing so over a period of time, he would then sleep with his legal wife and ejaculate — the accumulated "yin essence" would thereby help guarantee the production of strong and healthy sons. A wife who did not produce a son was considered a failure, and her marriage and position in life would be threatened. The entire Chinese system was developed at a time of rampant female infanticide, female sexual slavery, and the ritual murder of widows. This system of sexual abuse was not formulated upon love, but rather designed to fit the fantasies and sadistic urges of dominating warrior-caste males. Anyone advocating Taoistic sexual alchemy today must hide the facts of its history, as those facts would also be "unacceptable to most Americans".
(cf. R.H. Van Gulik, Sexual Life in Ancient China, E.J. Brill, Leiden, 1961)

America's Children in Poverty

"Almost half of all new American families are handicapped from the start because they are founded on single, young or poorly educated mothers who will have a tough time raising healthy, productive children... Fewer young people are graduating from high school in four years. Only 69% of all teenagers and 42% of Latino teenagers graduated on time... Teen pregnancy rose... 26% among whites, higher among blacks. 45% of all new births in 1990 were founded on families where the mother was under 20 years old, had not graduated from high school, or was unmarried."
(SF Chronicle, 29 March 93).

America's Suicidal, Violent Children

When we deny our adolescents the right to a full and natural sexual life, a stable home life, and rewarding education, the price they and all of society pay is high. As reported by the U.S. Centers for Disease Control in the federal health agency's Morbidity and Mortality Weekly Report, one in every 12 high school students (8%) has attempted suicide and one in four says he or she had carried a weapon at least once in the past month. Up to 19% of all high school students have planned to take their own lives with twice as many female students attempting suicide as males. Across the board, males were about four times more likely than females to carry a weapon. These reports come with others indicating that gunshot wounds are a leading cause of death among inner city teenage males; the problem is particularly acute within the black communities, where school dropout rates, unemployment, and impulsive violence are at high levels. (*SF Chronicle*, 16 Oct.92)

America's Runaway Children

More than 1/3 of all children living on the streets had been in foster care or in a group home within the previous year. The children report reasons for running away which are more severe than in years past, such as physical or sexual abuse by parents (66%), severe alcoholism at home (33%), severe drug abuse at home (25%), trouble with the justice system (25%), or a personal drug or alcohol abuse problem (25%). Nationally about 1 million youths run away each year. Half eventually return, while the other half go to relatives, friends, foster care, or group homes. About 200,000 youths form a street population in US major cities; they are so distant from social services they are not even counted in the ranks of the homeless. (*SF Chronicle*, 2 Jan.92)

Sexual Harassment in the Kindergarten

"*As the bus pulled into Sacramento traffic, an 11-year-old boy named Charles gave in to his friends' taunts. He walked to a girl seated in back, yanked one side of her halter top down, and ran back down the aisle. The malicious prank quickly brought consequences: Charles, whose real name remains confidential, was charged last year with attempted rape. He was thrown into juvenile hall. He was kept there for several weeks — until a judge was so startled by the course of the case that he stopped proceedings and referred the boy for counseling. The case is dramatic, but child therapists and legal experts say they are seeing similar cases with unnerving frequency. Incidents of sexual abuse by children are on the rise, they say, but the legal system is poorly equipped to deal with them. Children who exhibit typical sexual curiosity can become victims of overzealous investigators and social service agencies, while others who are profoundly troubled may not be taken seriously.*" (*SF Chronicle*, 21 Sept.93)

Many individual states have passed legislation to deal with childhood sexual expression in a heavy-handed manner, and children are now being jailed in the USA for offenses no worse than the example cited above. New federal "gender-equity" legislation is also in the works, sponsored by Senators Kennedy, Harkin, Simon, Moseley-Braun, Mikulski and others, which would make sexual expression by toddlers a criminal offense. It is all being done under the banner of new "health care" ideology, where healthy heterosexual expression of young children is lumped into the same "sexual harassment" category as rape or adult-child incest. The new Liberal Puritanism identifies healthy heterosexuality as a sickness, to be dealt with by policemen, while compulsive celibacy and homosexuality are given greater legal sanction and protection, its advocates receiving federal funds to develop anti-heterosexuality "educational programs" for distribution to schools. Consider this quote by Sen. Edward Kennedy:

"*You have first-, second- and third-grade harassers. You have kindergarten harassers. We're reaching out and identifying them at the earliest grades, disciplining these individuals. As with every aspect of heath care, early intervention can have a big impact.*" (*SF Chronicle*, 23 Sept. 93)

Sexual Feeling During Breastfeeding is Natural

The child's suckling of the breast can be an exciting experience for both child and mother, and nothing about this is immoral or dirty, except in the minds of the breast-denied and sex-repressed. Many midwifery and breast-feeding support groups acknowledge the naturalness of breast-feeding emotions. There is a slow but growing public appreciation of the value of breast-feeding, partly reinforced by the stupidities of various moralists, in and out of government, who have attempted to banish infants back to the bottle.

Consider the case of Denise Perrigo and her two-year-old daughter. While calling a local New York community volunteer center, trying to get the telephone number of the La Leche League, she mentioned to the telephone operator her questions about sexual feelings during breastfeeding. The operator secretly referred her name and number to a nearby Rape Crisis Center, which immediately dispatched policemen and social workers. Perrigo was still on the telephone when the officers arrived at the door to arrest her for "child sexual abuse".

The child was taken away by social workers, and a policeman on the scene remarked "*Having a two-year old suck on her breast would be like me having a little boy suck on my penis*".

Perrigo was jailed overnight. She was charged with "sexual abuse and neglect" and forbidden to be with her own child for nearly a year. Social service workers fought attempts by Perrigo's parents to obtain temporary custody of the child because, "*they would not acknowledge that abuse had taken place*". Perrigo's case eventually came to the attention of *Mothering* magazine, and later the *New York Post* ran a story, which brought her case to the attention of the public. According to various letters and articles which were triggered in the wake of the Perrigo case, she is not alone.

Social service workers have routinely harassed mothers engaging in extended breastfeeding (cross-culturally, the biological norm for spontaneous weaning of children is between two to four years of age). The charge is "sexual abuse". Similarly, parents opting for home birth are often harassed and charged with "child neglect". Such is the nature of our "social services" now too-often in the hands of emotional plague anti-sex moralists. (*The Birth Gazette*, Spring 92, p.11-12)

Don't Monkey with Alcohol

In a laboratory experiment, monkeys separated from their mothers for the equivalent of two years were found to drink alcohol excessively when exposed to it. While the predominant emphasis in science is to find genetic causes for social ills like alcoholism, studies such as this support the earlier work of Harry and Margaret Harlow and James Prescott on the devastating effects of maternal separation on young monkeys. As more and more human mothers return to work after a brief six-week "maternity leave," these monkey experiments may portend an even more troubled future ahead for our children. (*Science News*, 17 July 91 & 16 Nov.91)

Kill Your Television

By the age of 18, the average American child will have watched 22,000 hours of television, compared to only 11,000 hours of classroom time. These hours will have included 200,000 acts of violence, including 25,000 murders. (Nat. Coalition on Television Violence, 1992)

HEALTH & BIOLOGY NOTES

Epidemic of War Deaths

"Although medical research often addresses the causes of homicide, suicide and other 'private' human-caused deaths, it rarely addresses the more 'public' deaths of war. But the scale of such deaths in the 20th century is comparable to the scale of deaths in prior centuries due to epidemic diseases... Since 1700, wars have claimed more than 100 million lives worldwide, and more than 90 percent of these deaths occurred in the 20th century... The ratio of civilians to combatants in the death toll has also increased steadily: Historically, about 50 percent of war-related deaths were civilian — but by the 1970s, civilians accounted for 73 percent of war deaths, and in the 1980s so far, the figure has risen to 85 percent..." (*Sci. News*, 20 Aug. 88)

Americans Should Go Primitive

Researchers from many different fields presented findings at a recent meeting of the American Association for the Advancement of Science, suggesting we would be better off without all the trappings of civilization: colicky babies simply need to be picked up and held, breast fed on demand, and to sleep with their mothers. Breast cancer rates would decline if women breast fed, and if first childbearing (lovemaking??) were not delayed so long into life. Eating food grown organically, straight from the garden, leads to longer life and fewer diseases. (*SF Chronicle*, 16 Feb. 93)

Breastmilk: The Best Vaccine!

A protein, mucin, found in human breast milk destroys one of the major viruses that causes diarrhea, which is a world-wide killer of one million infants and children each year. Breastfeeding has also been found to reduce the incidence of ear and respiratory infection, pneumonia, meningitis, crohns, colitis, diabetes, childhood cancers, constipation, allergies, urinary tract infections, tooth decay, and obesity. It also increases intelligence and reduces the incidence of breast cancer for the mothers. (*The Compleat Mother*, PO Box 209, Minot, ND 58702, Spring 1993)

However, researchers at the Stanford School of Medicine have also found that microwaving breastmilk to reheat it diminishes the milk's infection-fighting properties. The breastmilk used in the experiments had been frozen, then microwave heated and innoculated with *E. coli* bacteria. The heated milk grew bacteria 18 times faster than the milk which had not been heated. The researchers state that heating alone does not fully explain the increased bacterial growth. They are, of course, unaware of Experiment XX conducted by Wilhelm Reich, in which a frozen strained solution made from boiled earth developed microscopical bionous forms upon thawing. Perhaps heating simply advances a pleomorphous process of bions to bacteria? Storing breast milk in freezers and heating it in microwave ovens is now a matter of course in many intensive care nurseries.

(*Microwave News*, May/June 1992)

Midwives Still Under Attack

The legality of midwifery varies from state to state, and the situation is in flux. There is organized lobbying by midwives and their supporters to make legal what is already going on "underground" in rural areas. Due to numerous and very justified lawsuits against incompetent obstetrical bungling, many MDs are withdrawing completely from the childbirth business. In other areas, doctor groups, teamed up with policemen and prosecutors, have raided midwifery clinics, and even the homes of midwives, in attempts to crush the growing home-birth and midwifery movements. In California alone, at least four different midwives are fighting legal battles initiated against them by the colluding doctor-prosecutor arrangements. The Gentle Birth Center of Los Angeles, which provided perinatal care and home births, was recently raided and shut down — five practitioners were charged with felonies. This included Linda Bennett, who was involved in the notorious Santa Cruz midwifery arrests over 20 years ago. Having failed to stop the pro-midwife movement through rational argument, or by demonstrating that midwifery or home birth is unsafe (it is very safe, much safer, in fact, than birth in hospitals), the doctors have once again resorted to police-state tactics. Midwifery in the USA is a bona-fide social movement which will, if allowed to flower productively, lower medical costs and make for safer births and healthier babies.

Midwives, particularly lay midwifes (empirically trained), have *in general* displayed more concern for the emotional aspects of birth than the average MD. Statistically, the ob/gyn specialist still is the *least safe* practitioner for any birthing mother to be with. Even hospital-trained nurse-midwives have a worse track record than the lay midwives — though exceptions to the statistical rule abound; there are many gentle and caring MDs, and some rather rough and aggressive midwives. The basic fact to be remembered is: Pregnancy and childbirth are *not sickness* — however, the more they are treated as sickness, with drugs and interventionist techniques, the more pathology develops. The great majority of birth pathology observed in hospitals is a by-product of the hospital environment, a consequence of misapplication of various insane and unscientific procedures and medications, and the product of incompetent meddling with the natural birth process. While the growth in popularity of home-like *birthing rooms* within hospital settings can mitigate against these factors, birthing rooms *per-se* are only a step in the right direction — more important are the *attitudes* of the attending nurses and physicians towards childbirth, and their knowledge (or lack thereof) regarding the necessity of the birthing mother to be left in peace and quiet, and sheltered from various "do-gooder" attempts to "make" the birth process proceed more quickly than the physiology of the baby and mother would have it. These factors, more than anything else, determine the general emotional tone of the delivery, and whether or not potentially dangerous or interfering medications and procedures are used.

Emotional armor of the mother at birth is also *not* a fully-adequate explanation for the pathology of American births, given the numerous controlled studies of balanced population groups, contrasting the outcomes of midwives delivering at homes against doctors delivering in hospitals. Most ob/gyns are simply *not trained* in the basics of a natural and uneventful vaginal birth. As a group, they just *don't know* what a natural birth is like. Most have never even seen a natural birth, as occurs only in a quiet, unhurried and relaxed home-like environment.

Too often, mothers are blindly subjected to routine procedures which have no demonstrable benefits, but which are demonstrated to correlate with increased mortality and morbidity for both mother and infant: intravenous infusions, labor-inducing drugs and procedures (such as artificially breaking the amniotic waters, etc.), forcing the laboring mother into unnatural positions, application of dangerous and scientifically-unjustifiable electronic devices to her belly or to the unborn infant's scalp (fetal heart monitor), the use of unnecessary and dangerous pain-killing drugs, episiotomies, and/or forceps. At worst, a laboring mother in a modern American hospital is treated like a guinea pig in a laboratory, in an environment of loudness, bright lights, porcelain, stainless steel, and hospital smells. The outcome in such cases is generally predictable.

The most immediate consequence of such physician ignorance about natural birth is the dramatic increase in surgical births: Caesarean sections are now around 25% of all US births, and still growing. Add to this the various sadisms vented upon the infant immediately after the birth — separation from the mother, isolation, stinging eyedrops, circumcision, failure to breast-feed, and so forth. Many hospital-trained nurse-midwifes are likewise not well-trained for natural delivery; some often rely upon labor-inducing methods, drugs and even episiotomies; this writer has seen hospital nurse-midwives subjecting newborn infants to the same cruelties once associated mainly with the MD. Some nurse-midwives are even advocating that *circumcisions* be performed by them, to increase the "profitability" of their profession. The medical establishment in total, still chooses to submit women and babies to routine and compulsory medical treatments which have no scientifically demonstrated benefits, and generally do far more harm than good.

(*The CALM Connection*, PO Box 922, Davis, CA 95617; *The Compleat Mother*, Box 209, Minot, SD 58702; also: Jessica Mitford, *The American Way of Birth*, Dutton, NY, 1992)

Vitamins Vindicated:

Here is a short selection of reports published over the last few years which verify what "health food nuts" have said for years:

Vitamin E For Vascular Health

Vitamin E, in moderate to large doses, will protect the user against heart troubles. The protective effects range from 37% to 46% reductions in heart disease among groups ingesting vitamin E of 100 IU or more per day for a period of two years. Significantly greater health benefits were observed when vitamin E was ingested in higher doses, with one study indicating a ten-fold reduction in heart disease among those taking 400 IU per day for more than 10 years. (*Health Federation News*, March 1993, p.7)

Vitamin A For Skin Health

Retin-A, a synthetic form of vitamin A, was recently announced in two medical studies to have an anti-cancer influence upon the skin, thus verifying claims from health food advocates made decades ago. (*SF Chronicle*, 18 May 93, p.A-1)

Vitamins & Mineral Supplements Reduce Cancer Risk

"*Daily doses of beta carotene, vitamin E and selenium reduced the incidence of cancer deaths by 13% in a study conducted in rural China. The five year study, involving 29,584 people in an area where cancer rates are among the highest in the world, showed that some vitamins and minerals can be of benefit against cancer, according to the National Cancer Institute researchers. The study is the first randomized trial to show a significant reduction in cancer in a population supplemented with vitamins and minerals.*" (*SF Chronicle*, 13 Sept. 93)

The above report appeared at the same time the FDA is attempting to reduce minimum standards for nutrition in American foods, and unleashing an all-out war against high-dose vitamins for human use to prevent or combat disease (see the article on "The Anti-Constitutional Activities and Abuse of Police Power by the U.S. Food and Drug Administration and other Federal Agencies" in this issue of *Pulse*).

Vitamins For Plant Health

An entomologist at the University of Wisconsin at Madison, Dale N. Norris, has found that plants suffering from a range of environmental stresses respond extremely well to treatments of Vitamin C and E. Norris observed that special "sentinel proteins" in plants were being damaged by oxidation; so, he tried using nature's premier antioxidants — vitamins C and E — to halt this cell deterioration, and it worked! Not only do the treated plants have better growth, but they are disease and pest resistant and can even fight off the effects of mechanical injury (such as bruising) and drought.

"We've been able to apply them (C and E) in every conceivable way," from drenching the soil or painting a band around a tree trunk to spraying foliage or immersing a few leaves in a dilute bath, Norris says. "We've even treated seeds prior to germination and gotten good results on the eventual plants." The vitamin seems to stimulate the plant to react systemically: treating a single leaflet can elicit an effect throughout the plant. What's even more interesting, the vitamins are applied in extremely dilute solutions — at mere parts-per-million concentrations — which appear to work best. Such dilutions are similar to homeopathic preparations. (*Science News*, Vol.141, 8 February 1992)

Food Irradiation Alert

Following the deaths of several Americans from food poisoning after eating contaminated meat and bad mayonnaise at several fast-food restaurants, one would think there would be a crackdown by health and food inspectors at the nation's meat packing and food processing houses. For years, consumer organizations and reporters have publicized direct evidence showing the nations packing houses and food processing plants were riddled with unsanitary practices, while food inspectors were often governed by bribes or personal threats. The food inspection programs were drastically reduced by the Reagan and Bush Administrations, who took more actions to silence conscientious inspectors than it did to curb unhealthy violations of existing laws. Under Bush, the industry producing the nation's rapidly-putrefying poultry supply was given the green light to use food irradiation as a method to "deal with" contaminating fecal bacteria, instead of healthier and cleaner methods for growing and slaughtering chickens. .

The Clinton Administration had promised to clean up this mess with reforms. But no, there will not be any increased surveillance or monitoring of the food industry. Instead, the new Secretary of Agriculture used the widely-publicized deaths of several Americans (including children) by food poisoning to announce an expensive new federal program devoted to the nuclear irradiation of beef. This announcement comes upon the heels of a report that the nation's only food irradiation facility, operated by Vindicator Corporation, suffered a $940,000 financial loss during its first 9 months of operation. The major reason was consumer protests, and the unwillingness of major supermarkets and chain stores to purchase irradiated food products.

"Irradiation is claimed to kill 99.99% of salmonella; this looks very efficient. But when you consider that, for example, an unirradiated food contains one million organisms, irradiation reduces this to 100 (the food is not sterilized). These 100 salmonella, once in the GI tract, divide about every 20 minutes and therefore reach one million in 6 hours. You thus delay onset of symptoms by 6 hours by food irradiation. You do not decrease the incidence or severity of illness. The only thing accomplished is that you are now dealing with a population of salmonella which is by definition radiation resistant, and no one knows how these organisms differ from the wild type. It will also be harder to trace the source of contaminated food because of the greater time interval. Nothing net is thus gained. The same is true for trichinosis. Hence, non-irradiated as well as irradiated food must be cooked properly to avoid these two diseases. Irradiation does nothing to botulism. For this zero benefit, the consumer pays for the cost of irradiation and with an increased risk of leukemia and lymphoma from the free radicals formed during radiation..."

The USDA has additionally increased the opportunity for Americans to consume dangerous and unhealthy food by giving the green light for "Frankenstein Food"; this is patented, genetically engineered foodstuffs, the long-term safety of which has never been demonstrated, and which, due to higher prices and the need for specialized chemicals and technology, cannot be grown by ordinary local farmers. (*Safe Food News*, Winter 93, RR.1, Box 30, Old Schoolhouse Common, Marshfield, VT 05658; *Coalition to Stop Food Irradiation*, PO Box 3294, S. Pasadena, CA 91031; *Food & Water*, 225 Lafayette St., #612, New York, NY 10012).

Modern Medical-Genetic Quackery

Genetics Does Not Equal Heredity

The big push in medical genetics is to identify various "genes" for diseases, with the often unstated assumption that, if a disorder expresses itself within a given family lineage (e.g., grandparent to parent to child) then it must be due to "bad genes" of one sort or another. So thoroughly has the biochemical theory of DNA and genes taken over as the assumed mechanism for the observed phenomenon of heredity, that few scientists or laypeople today seem aware that DNA chemistry and genetics are only *theories* which attempt to explain the phenomenon of heredity (the inheritance of characteristics). Certainly, Mendel's work on the genetics of bean plants was a breakthrough in understanding the transmission of many basic traits from parent to offspring, and so was the discovery of DNA itself — but, the theory of biochemical DNA and genetics has limitations to its predictive power. Textbooks on genetics abound with "exceptions to the rule" of the basic theory, which are in turn explained by jumps in reason and logic that defy gravity, and common sense. This would not be so bad, were the alternative theories for heredity given a fair and equal hearing in the marketplace of ideas — the ideas of Sheldrake on morphogenetic fields, for example; Reich's orgone energy may also play a fundamental role in heredity, as it does in health and disease. But these ideas are heresy, and modern genetics has become a religion, offered up without proof as the "cause" of a myriad of socially-difficult character traits and illnesses.

Identical Twins Reared Apart

Advocates of genetic determinism of character traits and behavior often point to identical twins reared apart for support of their argument, given the fact that, so often, identical twins reared apart behave so strangely similar. But while such behavior may be a proof that different environments could not create such identical behaviors, this does not automatically mean that cellular genes and DNA chemistry are the answer to the riddle of similar behavior. Consider the following:

"The study of identical twins separated shortly after birth and reared apart are the only human studies where the genetic component is constant while environmental components are variable. As expected, physical characteristics such as height, weight, and menstrual symptoms are found to be greatly alike among such twins. However, there were surprises. In many cases, these twins laughed alike, described symptoms in the same way, smoked similar numbers of cigarettes, chose similar creative pursuits, and sometimes even married the same number of times. In addition, there was an inexplicable trail of similar names sometimes associated with such twins. For example, there were two adopted infants both named Jim by their adopted parents. When they were reunited at age 39 they found that their lives were marked by a trail of similar names. Both had dogs named Toy. Both married and divorced women named Linda and had second marriages with women named Betty. They named their sons James Allan and James Alan, respectively. Another pair of long separated twins, Briget and Dorothy, named their sons Richard Andrew and Andrew Richard, respectively, and their daughters Catherine Louise and Karen Louise. In the case of Berta and Herta, the twins had the same nickname of 'Pussy' yet the nicknames were in different languages since the twins lived on different continents and had not met since the age of four. Are all these 'genetic' factors? Another surprise was that identical twins with the <u>least contact</u> appear most frequently to be the <u>most alike</u>. Generally, the more separated the twins, the more similar they appear to be on personality tests. Twins with no contact were more frequently alike than those with ample opportunity to 'identify' with each other." (W. Gough, "The Mysterious Link", *Foundation for Mind-Being Research Newsletter*, 442 Knoll Dr., Los Altos, CA 94024, Jan. 1992)

To the above, the Editor of *Pulse* can add a personal anecdote: As a young man I knew two brothers, identical twins of age 16 who lived together. Their personalities were not very similar, and over the years I knew them, they drifted apart, living apart as well. One day, for no apparent reason, one of the brothers became catatonic, withdrawing into a fetal position, sitting inside a dark closet, unable to speak; we gently tried to communicate with him for hours without success. After around 24 hours, he regained lucidity and spoke with us, unable to remember anything, except an extreme immobilizing sense of loss and despair. About a day after this, it was discovered that his identical twin brother had been murdered, shot in the head, and left to die in a swamp. The time of the one brother's death was the precise time of the identical twin's catatonia!

This example, like the strange naming behavior of identical twins, also cannot be explained on the basis of either "genes" or "environment". Rather it is stark testimony to a powerful *energetic* connection between such identical twins, something which is more akin to extra-sensory perception, and requiring of a mechanism which binds and connects the individuals together, no matter how far apart they physically move. This mechanism would appear to be the orgone energy fields of the two identical twins, working in coordination with the connecting orgone energy field of the Earth, in which both are immersed. Assuming this is a correct hypothesis, then we are forced, by the nature of the phenomena, to the conclusion that the orgone must have the capacity to transmit quite specific and detailed information, in a manner similar to Rupert Sheldrake's *morphogenetic field* theory.

Inheritance of Acquired Characteristics

A research paper of this same title recently appeared in the mainstream publication *Annual Review of Genetics* (1991), with a shorter essay in *Scientific American* (March 1993, p.150), by Professor Otto E. Landman, of Georgetown University. Landman reminds the biological profession, with dozens of explicit citations from published journals, that there is plenty of experimental and observational evidence to support the inheritance of acquired characteristics: this is the capacity of an organism to pass on to its offspring basic physical characteristics acquired by the parent during its lifetime — such as the strong hands of a violinist or pianist or the strong legs of a race horse being passed on to offspring. Landman points out, correctly, that most biologists reject the idea without examination, simply because the evidence was never presented to them in their university textbooks.

From the Editor's perspective, the inheritance of acquired characteristics leads in the direction of vital force, or the orgone energy, because it requires some mechanism beyond DNA or genetics as a mechanism for inheritance, implying that somatic processes and basic protoplasm can be affected by life experience. For those who are never taught the important differences between biochemistry and biology, or between genetics and heredity, these issues probably appear confusing at best, or downright heretical at worst. As Reich continually pointed out, *one must make a sharp differentiation between facts, and theories about facts.* The observed phenomena of biology and heredity are the facts, while biochemistry and genetics (specifically, the role of DNA) are only *bodies of theory* which attempt to explain those facts. Evidence for the inheritance of acquired characteristics cannot easily be explained by DNA-genetics, and opens the door for other hereditary mechanisms, such as those which involve emotion, bioelectricity, electromagnetism, life energy, and so forth.

Bad Science + Social Policy = *Disaster!*

When a society undertakes to implement socially a factually inaccurate or patently wrong scientific theory, social disaster awaits. Genetic theory formed the basis of the Nazi race theories earlier this century. As expressed politically through National Socialism, gene theory provided the facade of a "scientific rationale" for the urge to kill the outsider, the "auslander", those who were different in appearance, ethnicity, or those with infirmities or crippling diseases. Genetic theory formed the intellectual frosting on the cake of National Socialism, which sprang from the sexual frustrations, buried passions, longings for paternal authority, and sadistic urges of the masses. As revealed in Wilhelm Reich's milestone work, *The Mass Psychology of Fascism*, Nazi Germany constantly identified Jews, Gypsies and other foreign elements as sexually and genetically contaminated figures, which society needed to purge in order to remain sexually and racially pure.

Like Original Sin, the modern theory of genetics is a ripe and moldable ideology by which "scientists" can identify the "real causes" of social ills and health complaints in a manner which does not require much social criticism, analysis or change to the status quo. Consequently, we are not surprised to see modern genetic theory being unscientifically incorporated into new modern theories, which likewise attempt to explain major social and health problems in a manner which leaves their essential cores untouched, such as the new genetic theories of homosexuality or cancer.

In other parts of this issue of *Pulse*, we have detailed the unscientific theories of the HIV theory of AIDS, which has led to thousands of iatrogenic (physician-caused) deaths, and to a culture-wide increase in hysterical sex-repression. Likewise, the unscientific theories of childbirth hazards, and the "dangerousness" of the vagina, widely held by obstetricians, has led to numerous iatrogenic problems and deaths in the newborn. Physicians, particularly surgeon-ob-gyn specialists, are mostly responsible for this epidemic, but we can also cite the epidemic of unnecessary hysterectomy surgeries (around 700,000 per year in the USA), and unnecessary male genital mutilations (infant circumcisions). There is a lot of unnecessary and scientifically unjustified cutting-up and slicing-up. We should therefore not be too surprised to see genetic theory creeping into the world view of this same group of "health" providers.

Heil Genome!

The marriage of genetic theory to surgery is a very real example of "official" medical quackery in its most virulent form. It must be stated up front that the hypothesis of the genetic causation of cancer, like the viral hypothesis of cancer, always was and remains *an hypothesis*. There is no real proof for the role of the so-called "oncogene" in the formation of cancer. In fact, honest researchers into the oncogene idea will admit that, if every cell had a dormant gene for cancer, with the trillions of cells in our bodies, we would all be dying of cancer at a very early age. And while there is an increase in cancer within recent decades, this also suggests the failure of any genetic mechanism — why should the genes suddenly become more "active" than in past decades? Rather, the hypothesis of oncogenes is championed by those physicians who, via political power and brute police force, have crushed down the competing ideas that cancer has roots in either emotional/sexual factors, or in exposures to toxic substances in foods, air and water. ■

Modern Horrific Medicine

The following reports may utterly shock and offend many people. Others may feel the editors are unfairly portraying the medical industry and what it perceives to be "heroic" medicine. Our outrage about these discredited practices stems in part from the increasing suppression of alternatives to the surgically-mutilating, radiation-burning and chemotherapeutic-poisoning of sick, and increasing numbers of not-so-sick, people. To understand the scope of this repression, see the article on the "Anti-Constitutional Activities and Abuse of Police Power by the U.S. Food & Drug Administration" in this issue of <u>Pulse</u>.

Eskimo Medical Experiments

"Alaskan Eskimos and Indians were fed radioactive drugs in a 1950s Cold War medical experiment to learn whether American soldiers could better survive in the Arctic... Doctors hired by the Air Force gave pills containing small amounts of radioactive iodine to 102 Alaskan Eskimos and Indians, measuring the drugs' effect on their thyroid glands." (SF Chronicle, 4 May 93, p.A-16.) "More than 100 mostly Eskimo women in Canada's remote Northwest Territory charged that the all-male surgical team at the area's lone hospital refused them anesthesia during abortions. One woman said her doctor told her, 'This really hurt, didn't it? Let that be a lesson before you get yourself in this situation again'." (Health, Jan/Feb 1993, p.57)

Infant Medical Experiments

Articles from the late 1980s in *The New England Journal of Medicine, Washington Post,* and *New York Times* revealed the ghastly fact that, for some lengthy period, surgeons have been undertaking deep-cutting organ surgery upon infants *without providing them any anesthetic whatsoever!!* Like the laboratory rats and rabbits upon which they practiced during medical school dissection classes, the hospital doctors simply strapped the infants down and started cutting away, blind and deaf to whatever signs of distress (screaming?? struggling??) were being exhibited. This horrific revelation was not volunteered by the doctors themselves, who apparently were somewhat upset to have the facts go public, but rather by the pro-midwifery magazine *Birth*.

After being exposed in print, the doctors began undertaking damage control. An emotionless, admit-no-wrong resolution was subsequently issued by the American Academy of Pediatrics: "...there now exists a theoretical consensus among anesthesiologists, surgeons, and neonatologists that infants do feel considerable pain..." According to *Birth*, "What remains to be accomplished is full implementation of these ideas [to give anesthetic to infants] in hospital settings not yet internalizing the new techniques and ethics." This is really an understatement, however, given the fact that several physician organizations, such as the American Academy of Anesthesiologists, initially hesitated to support the resolution, relying upon scientifically discredited "Doctor's Tales" about the "risks of anesthesia to infants" and the "insufficiently myelinated nerves of infants...incapable of transmitting pain" — both these unproven assumptions were refuted by reformers in the AAP. However, the reluctance of many doctors to consider the facts about infant feelings would suggest that parents need to be on guard, ready to protect their infants against zealous "baby-can't-feel-pain" doctors. These facts demonstrate blatant physician sadism towards infants, similar to prevailing cultural attitudes towards infant genital mutilations (also generally performed without anesthesia),

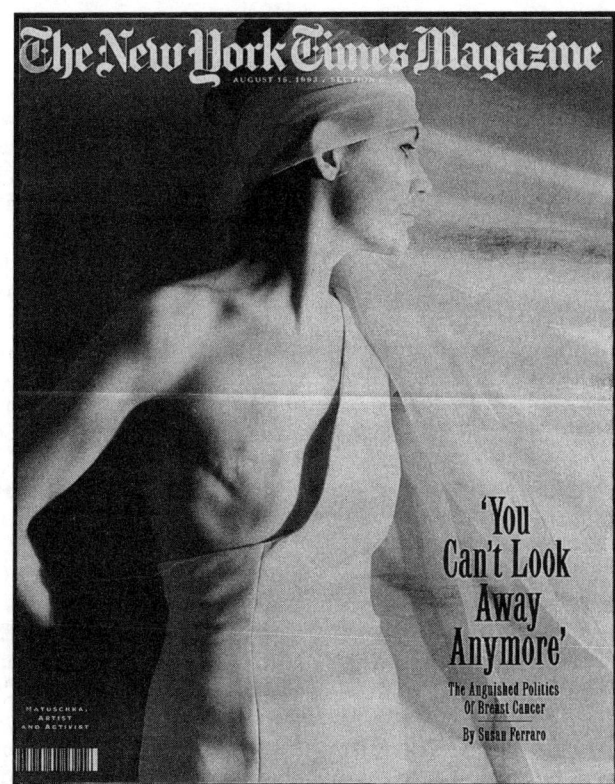

Breast amputation as a fashion statement on the cover of the New York Times Sunday Magazine, 15 August 1993.

but of a more intensive variety. Just ask yourself how many years have passed since the discovery of anesthesia! (Birth, 15:36-41, March 1988)

"Preventative" Mastectomy

The sadistic butchery of cancer surgeons is most clearly revealed in those specialized groups who mutilate and disfigure healthy young women, often teenage girls, who do not have a trace of cancer in their bodies — only the "theoretical" traces of unobservable "cancer genes", or textural changes in breast tissue. I speak here of the growing practice of "preventative mastectomy", in which the surgeon firstly identifies an increased tendency for breast cancer in a given family line, and secondly, based upon an unwavering faith in his genetic calculations, diagnoses those women, often young girls, as being "at high risk for breast cancer". With the woman or young girl so diagnosed and properly frightened, the surgeon doctor then "counsels" her to have a double mastectomy "to prevent the cancer before it develops and kills you".

No attempt is made to persuade the "high risk" family to avoid habits known to correlate with increased cancer risks, such as smoking, heavy drinking, or exposure to pesticides. No attempt is made to evaluate the risks of exposure to carcinogens in the home, food, or workplace. No attempt is made to counsel the woman or her family away from the sex-negating "traditional" lifestyles which are also correlated to breast cancer (as discovered by Wilhelm Reich and detailed in *The Cancer Biopathy*), or if she has babies, to breastfeed them (a factor which is correlated with reduced breast cancer risk). The primary attitude of such surgical specialists is, with the presentation of any kind of complaint (breast pain, textural changes, occasional benign lumps) to simply *cut off the offending body parts* before they "cause trouble". And, of course, no attempt is made to employ non-toxic forms of treatment, such as vitamin therapy, orgone accumulator therapy, or various detoxification techniques.

This editor first heard of "preventative mastectomy" more than 20 years ago, when it was heralded by medical journals as an "advanced breakthrough" in the treatment of cancer. Then, it was isolated to a few doctors in training hospitals in New York City. Today, it is nationwide Big Business, with *thousands* of women visiting surgeons across the nation, to be evaluated by quack genetic calculations. In one major hospital alone, Memorial Sloan-Kettering, over 150 "preventative mastectomies" are performed each year, some 20% of the total number of breast surgeries performed. Girls so evaluated as "high risk" are apparently persuaded — by the entire medico-magical "health care" system, and by their typical sex-anxious families — into having their sexual organs amputated. *No confirmed traces of cancer need be present.*

Lest you think your editor is making a sick joke here, or exaggerating, I point to a recent National Public Radio "Talk of the Nation, Science Friday" broadcast (21 August 1992) wherein two surgeons, one male and one female, spoke for nearly two hours about the new "breakthrough" procedure of "preventative mastectomy". I was totally shocked. The doctors boasted of having "saved" several thousand young girls from the *potential* ravages of cancer. The doctors also claimed to be part of a larger group of "preventative" surgeons across the USA. Therefore, it appears that virtually thousands of these operations must be performed each year. And worse, about a half-dozen young women called in to the radio program, most of whom already had the mutilation performed, profusely thanking the doctors for "saving" them!!

Upon listening to this program, I was struck by how similar is our American medicine to the most sadistic, bloody, and superstitious tribe you could name. Ritual female genital mutilations are occurring here, in our most modern hospitals, and all with the emotional collusion and agreement by the women upon whom it is perpetrated. Indeed, the women who had just undergone the mutilation appeared to be its biggest advocates, just as many women now demand caesarean births and hysterectomies so they won't have to be "bothered" with natural functioning and sexual feeling.

The Mammogram

The mammogram is being pushed as a diagnostic tool by which "scientific" decisions about mutilating breast surgery can be made. Such assertions of a scientific basis to mammography are untrue, however. Mammograms can give both false-negative and false-positive indications, both of which can pose a danger to the health of the woman if her doctor is overly-reliant upon mammography technology. For example, even if a woman does not have palpable lumps in her breast, the mammogram might still show a shaded area on the resulting x-ray image, prompting concern by her doctor. Depending upon the character structure of the physician, and whether or not the woman has medical insurance (and not for any scientifically discernable reason), the doctor may or may not rely upon a biopsy for confirmation of cancer. Ambiguous cellular changes, in association with a family history of cancer, might prompt the surgeon to advise "preventative" mastectomy. Or, if the mammogram is negative, and does not show any breast tissue shading on the x-ray image, additional mammograms might be ordered up periodically. As the mammogram exposes the breast to cancer-causing x-rays, a sufficient number might eventually provoke a general energetic contraction within the breast, leading to breast pain,

textural and cellular changes, or even to the appearance of breast lumps. This, in turn, satisfies the urges of the doctor to "find something", and reinforces the fears and discomforts of the patient about their sexual organs.

Through such "broadened diagnostic criteria", a larger and larger number of women could be surgically mutilated, even when no clear trace of cancer would exist. Considering that not all breast lumps constitute breast cancer, that some American doctors are too eager to cut a woman without much more reason than a lump, and, as discussed above, some breast cancer surgeons will advise to amputate breasts without a trace of cancer, a major question is raised: *Can it be that the "epidemic" increase of breast cancer in American women is partly or even largely fueled by hateful misapplication and misinterpretation of mammogram technology, from unscientifically broadened diagnostic criteria, and from "preventative" mutilations?* Many hospitals appear to not even keep separate records of the percentage of "preventative" mastectomies performed. These concerns would also explain the claim of supposed "increased survival" for breast cancer treatments — the doctors appear now to be giving their horrific treatments to larger numbers of healthier women, who do not have cancer, and who therefore can more readily survive the side-effects of conventional radical treatments. Note: The use of another "breakthrough" technology, *the fetal heart monitor*, has been causally linked to an *increase* in caesarean deliveries: the apparatus itself interferes with the normal pace of birth, frightening obstetricians into ordering up unnecessary caesareans.

"Preventative" Colon Surgery

As if the madness outlined above were not sufficient, we recently obtained evidence that similar "preventative" surgery is being advised for members of families in which colon cancer has predominated. "Preventative" colon removal surgery, including colostomy, is being performed in the USA on unknown numbers of people who *do not have a trace of bowel or colon cancer!*

Radical Heart Surgery

Remember Barney Clark, the first man to receive an artificial heart? He lived 112 days. According to his widow, "America needed a hero, and Barney filled that role"... but at what a price! A few days after his death, the doctors who operated on Barney held a news conference, in which they discussed the problems encountered. Barney was simply too far gone, said the doctors. If the artificial heart program was to continue, they would need to try it out on people who were *not so sick*. Consequently, they introduced to the reporters a younger man, who walked into the room and sat down for questioning. The man had a problem for which the surgeons prescribed that his heart be replaced. They spoke of the great benefits this man was performing for the social good. The young man was emotionally preparing himself for his heroic act, and was observed by television cameras to take a long pensive walk on the beach the night before he would ascend into the "operating theater", where his heart would be cut out and replaced with a new marvel of modern technology.

It was amazing to observe how this man could be so sick that he needed an artificial heart, yet he could easily take a walk down the beach! Somehow, that young man had been brainwashed, by doctors, family and friends, to the point that he was going to just walk into the operating room, lie down, and like the sacrificial victims of the Aztec priests, have his beating heart cut out, and held up to the television cameras for all the world to see!! How absolutely striking are the parallels of our modern hospitals to the sacrificial Aztec pyramids. One wonders why the surgeons did not just find a *completely healthy person* to experiment on, perhaps someone with a "genetic predisposition" to heart disease!

Note: There are numerous alternatives to surgery for heart disease, such as chelation therapy, vitamins A, C, and E, organic, whole foods diet, and an emotionally satisfying life.

Horrific Transplant Experiments on Children

A three year old child in Great Britain was paraded before television cameras in late August 1993, after which both parents and doctors discussed how they were going to cut out her pancreas, liver, stomach, kidneys, and small and large intestines, and replace them all at once with donated organs. The child walked into the room on her own power. None of the reporters asked if alternative treatments had been attempted, or how the doctors felt about undertaking radical experiments similar to those of the Nazi death camp doctors, on small children. Other recent experiments on children have included heart transplants using human and baboon hearts, and also the use of children testing positive for HIV antibody as guinea pigs for experimental toxic AIDS drugs.

Kollwitz

Priest-Surgeons and the Altar of Medical Sacrifice

The growth of these kinds of mutilating procedures in our modern "health care" system, the joining of the procedures to quack genetic theories, and the growth of political police power by the existing medical establishment, with the unashamed suppression of dissent in the sciences by police attack and bald censorship, is all taking place simultaneously with a general sexualization of social ills and anxieties (the "AIDS crisis"). It is a dangerous trend which history suggests, if unchecked, will spiral towards social consequences far more disastrous for America than the hospital holocaust already occurring at the hands of Big Medicine.

In ages past, priests would subject women and men to mutilating torture and burning at the stake, all done in order to "save" their souls from the devil, who was always portrayed as a sexual beast — and in fact, given the prevailing sexual repressions and hysterical neuroses, many young girls often willingly and quickly confessed to having "intercourse with the devil", and were burned. (Probably, many quickly con-

fessed rather than suffer torture, knowing that in the end, they would be burned no matter what they said.)

"Preventative" medicine has now taken a similar sadistic turn. No longer the domain of epidemiologists, public health researchers, social pioneers and reformers, nor environmentalists or home economists — instead "preventative medicine" is a new and highly lucrative enterprise for surgeons, who willingly and enthusiastically "protect us" from diseases we do not have, with their scalpels. Stripped of their "scientific" cloth, what we see here are simply sadistic assaults upon the sexual organs of young people by sex-hating and life-hating high-caste priest-surgeons. It is functionally the same thing as what happened when the Church was given absolute power over the lives of people. What both hospital doctor and church priest are really against, and what the "silent majority" in society are likewise uncomfortable about, is the *uncut* breast, the *intact* penis, and the *intact* uterus — in short, *the sexually whole individual*. We are no different from the genital mutilating cultures of North Africa, except perhaps that we are more self-deceiving than they, who openly proclaim the deeper reason for cutting up private parts: to *extinguish sexual feeling*.

Hope: American Alternatives Increasing

According to a recent study in the *New England Journal of Medicine* (Eisenberg, et al, 328:246-52, 1993) about a third of all American adults use unconventional medical treatments, such as chiropractic, therapeutic massage, relaxation techniques, special diets and megavitamins. The percentage is growing. Perhaps this is the result of average people voting with their feet and pocketbooks, against the above forms of modern horrific medicine. ■

Orgone Accumulator Experiences

Dear Editor,

I recently made a small orgone blanket. I had been having trouble with an osteomyelitis infection in my leg (a complication which followed a compound fracture of the bone). Doctors had said I could expect this problem to go on indefinitely, and further surgery had been planned after mega-antibiotic treatment had failed. I decided to try one of Reich's inventions — the orgone blanket that brings in orgone (life) energy and rebalances the system. A couple of weeks ago I made one, layering wool fabric with steel wool, and began wrapping it around my leg at night. After the very first session the wound in my leg closed and stopped running for the first time in nineteen months! It stayed closed for the next five days before a slight swelling occurred, emitting a small bone chip. Since then, the wound has stayed closed and appears to be healing. It itches like mad, however, and every few days emits a pin-head amount of clear serum: a vast improvement over the situation before. I have had a few inquiries about it ... and will take the blanket today to show my pharmacist, and I will try to figure out a non-threatening way to tell my doctor about it. I find it so amazing that these technologies are around and are suppressed, feared, and generally unknown. Thank you Dr. Reich!

Oscar Mann, Nairobi, Kenya

Dear Editor,

I have devised an extremely simple orgone wrapping for one hand and one foot. I am hemiplegic on the right side since September of 1988 when I sustained a moderate CVA [stroke] and had to be hospitalized for six months. I was totally aphasic and incontinent. To document the improvement in my aphasia, I have been reading my poetry in public at coffee houses since 1990.

I first got the idea of making an orgone wrap when I plunged my paralyzed hand into an orgone can [accumulator] and experienced a warming sensation. I went to a fabric store and purchased a bit of grey felt and velcro fastener. From a hardware store, I bought a plastic bag of rough steel wool; not too rough. I cut a piece of felt 2 inches wide for the hand; the length was enough to wrap around the hand (excluding the fingers), then spiral around the wrist and part of the forearm to the radial protuberance. I had two pieces of velcro sewn onto the felt at the distal end, and two pieces sewn at the proximal end. Then I lined the inside of the wrapping with strands of steel wool (be careful: it has to be on the *inside*, not the outside, otherwise it won't work). The steel wool will stick to the felt and has to be replaced after several week's usage due to brown rust marks appearing on the hand. I then applied the device by wrapping it around my hand distally to proximally.

The effect was immediate: a very agreeable, slight warming sensation. I routinely wore this device while sleeping. After the first application, I didn't bother to unfasten the distal end, but slipped the loop over my four fingers and then wrapped it around my hand and wrist until the two pieces of velcro at the proximal end came together.

The effects on the motor system were subtle. Normally, I can't make a fist with my right hand. Wearing the device did not at all enable me to make a fist, but I noticed that the forefinger which normally stuck out when I tried to make a fist, now lined up with the other fingers. This was true whether or not I was wearing the device.

In contrast, the following subtle effect happened only when wearing the device. What I am talking about is the swinging of the arms while walking which is said to be a function of the extra-pyramidal motor system. I have a defect on the right side due to my stroke. Wearing the device in the daytime while walking restored the ability of my right arm to swing. This defect had been particularly bothersome since it called attention to my limp right arm by other pedestrians.

The device for the foot is made in the same way as the device for the hand, except that 3 inch rather than 2 inch strips of felt are cut, and also the total length is greater. A loop which slips over the foot is made and secured with velcro. The felt is wrapped around the foot once, bypassing the heel; and then it is wrapped around the ankle twice and fastened proximally with velcro. Notice that multiple layering of felt with steel wool is possible by this method, achieving a multiplication of the orgone energy effects. This is also true of the hand device.

Since I didn't sustain quite as heavy a motor loss in my foot compared to my hand, I didn't expect an effect, and I didn't get any. I don't require a cane to get around, although I have a noticeable limp and I am not as fast as other pedestrians. The orgone wrap for the foot did nothing for my gait. However, it did cut down on the paresthesia in my foot at night; this is a pins-and-needles sensation resulting from damage to the sensory apparatus and is more bothersome than painful. I am wearing these devices every night and will switch from night time to day time usage for the hand device. My thanks to Faye Clipson who sewed on the velcro.

Teddy Weiler, Ph.D., California

Dear Editor,

Following are some of the related relief and cures resulting from the usage of orgone blankets, accumulators, and usage of the glass tubes [orgone wand: a pyrex test tube filled with steel wool and charged up in an accumulator] as related to me, and also my own results.

One lady broke a bone in her shoulder, diagnosed as such by a doctor. She went to the doctor on a Monday. She proceeded home and started using the tubes [orgone wands] that had been charged up inside the accumulator. She did this conscientiously twice a day, everyday, and on Friday of the same week she went back to the doctor. He was amazed at the healing of the bone and wanted to know what she had done to make it heal so fast. He said she would not have to come back unless she had problems.

A young lady stopped by our house and said her migraine was really bad. I proceeded to get some of the tubes from the accumulator and told her to hold them on her head for a short time. She did this for approximately six minutes. She had to go home to meet her daughter, so she left. The next day my wife asked her how the headache was after using the tubes. She said, "I went home changed my clothes and went out for dinner." Normally, she said she would have gone home, got sick, and would have gone to bed, and that would have been it.

One lady who is in her upper sixties had a leg hurting so bad she said she was about to cry. I took her an orgone blanket and she put it on her leg for 30 minutes. She proceeded to go out and start the lawn mower and mowed the lawn and said the leg didn't hurt.

A lady with sugar diabetes had a toenail removed. The doctor said she would probably have problems with it healing because of her diabetes. She went home and used the tubes for 10 days, twice a day. She then went back to the same doctor. He was amazed at the healed toe and said he had never seen a toe heal that fast. He wanted to know what she had done. He also said she didn't have to come back unless complications arose, and they didn't.

My daughter-in-law broke a bone in her ankle, diagnosed by a doctor with x-rays. She was put on crutches to start with and this did not help the pain and swelling. Next, the doctors put her foot in a cast for quite a spell. This also did not solve the problem. Approximately one year passed with these doctor-recommended remedies. The doctors in the end said the ankle with the break would always be bigger than her other ankle. As she was doing acrobatic swimming, the pain and swelling worsened. I proceeded to send her a small accumulator and she started using the tubes. In about two weeks I asked her how her ankle was progressing and she informed me the pain was gone and the swelling left. Her broken ankle was down to normal in size.

There have been many more wonderful happenings with the energy accumulator systems. Soreness in necks eliminated, sore throats, arthritis in hands, arms and legs alleviated. One person said if they didn't have the accumulator they wouldn't be walking today as their arthritis would be so bad it would have them in bed.

Also, the blood pressure of people in the sixties plus are more like a young person after using the orgone accumulator.

My wife has had some good results using the blankets and tubes. My wife had cataracts removed and in doing this they gave her intravenation in her hand. When they took the needles out of her hand, it turned black and blue like dead blood. She used the tubes and in a few days it was all cleared up. She also burnt her arm while reaching in the oven and touching the side. She proceeded to use the tubes and in less than two days the pain left and a scab formed.

My daughter has used the tubes on her allergies and sinus and in doing this, it has made her breathing a lot better. Her feet hurt, and in using the tubes and blankets the pain and swelling has left.

My own personal help has come from sitting in the accumulator plus using the blankets and tubes. My legs and feet were hurting, arthritis in elbows and finger joints hurting, neck muscles hurting — these pains have all disappeared and with constant usage, the pain stays dormant.

In conclusion, I would like to say this: There are great results to be gained by having these energy systems and the cost is minor when you look at what you save in avoiding diseases. 　　　　　　　　　　Kenneth Dirkes, Montana

The Editor welcomes our readers to write in about their personal experiences with the orgone accumulator, or about other matters discussed in the pages of the *Pulse*.

Classical Biology Rediscovers the Bion

Dear Editor,

I read an article in *Der Spiegel* (26 July 93) which referred to recent publications in *Medical World News* and *Science* magazines, and almost got a heart attack when realizing they were giving an exact description of bionous disintegration. But they failed to mention Reich. If you compare Reich's report with what they have found out now, it is 90% the same. The only difference is that Reich did it 55 years ago (!), and they now present it as a brand new spectacular result of their own sophisticated high-tech research.

They call the phenomenon of bionous disintegration "apoptosis". The article says that during the process of dying, human cells "wildly twitch and convulse", then they form "small vesicular structures at the periphery", after which one can observe "vesicular *pulsating* (sic!) protuberances at the cell membrane"; then the entire cell body disintegrates and the fragments are digested by macrophages. They also state that cancer is due to dysfunctions occurring during this physiological disintegration process.

However, the qualitative difference of the writing styles is most striking. While Reich describes bionous movement in a way that makes you think of energetic attraction and sexuality, *Der Spiegel* article notoriously chooses associations of militarism and death, thus reflecting the whole dilemma of mechanistic science. They speak about the "death program against tumors", "suicidal self-elimination of human cells", "the killer program of cell death", the "cell harakiri", and so on, and therefore the only consequence of "their" discovery is that they are now searching for the "commando center which controls the cell suicide". And they indicate they may have already found it in the "genetic sequence p53", which can be pharmacologically manipulated by the "bcl-2 gene". Horrifying! 　　　　　　Stefan Muschenich, Marburg, Germany

Dear Dr. Muschenich,

Reich's scientific priority on the bions, and other issues, is constantly being ignored by the academic world today. It must be pointed out that the failure to cite, as well as the appropriation of the work of other scientists still constitutes a serious breach of scientific ethics. It may, in some cases, constitute *fraud*, where the researcher clearly knows about Reich's work, fails to cite him, and presents Reich's observations (re-worded) as his own. It is a growing problem in the academic world, and is not limited to the pirating of only Reich's work.

The worst example I ever identified, with respect to the stealing of Reich's ideas on the bions, and twisted rationalization of the failure to cite his priority, is found in the book *Complementarity in Biology: Quantization of Molecular Motion*, by J.P. Isaacs and J.C. Lamb (John Hopkins Press, Baltimore, 1969). In this book, the authors postulate the existence of sub-cellular units which build up to compose the cells, and they blatantly call these units "bions". Furthermore, the "bion" of Isaacs & Lamb interacts with its environment energetically, through "bionic radiation". They do cite the "mitogenetic radiation" of O. Rahn, who in 1936 published a Monograph on *Protoplasma* (Monographia Vol.9, Verlag von Gebruder Borntraeger, Berlin) — this citation should be investigated by German-speakers for its relationship to Reich's discovery of orgone radiation from SAPA bions, which took place around the same time. This question aside, the authors of *Complementarity* attribute none of "their" findings to Reich's empirically derived, observed and published descriptions, but rather, to the "...broad application of quantum reasoning to molecules, which reflects the phenomenological conditions of many crucial living processes." (p.4) Their language is, also, as dead and emotionally horrifying as the examples you give from *Der Spiegel*. Consider the following passages:

"The assumption is justified of supra-mechanical stability of stationary states in atomistic or discrete living units, which we refer to as 'bions' (sic). Bions are not equivalent to cells. An organized cell is not a bion, but is composed of bions. Bions are a more fundamental living unit than cells... A new classification of biological organisms is developed from a consideration of basic biological units or bions."(p.4)

Now, one would wonder how they could get away with using a term so clearly connected with Reich, and so explicitly defined by him. Indeed, Chapter 5 of *Complementarity* is titled "The Bion: Basic Atomistic Living Unit", while Chapter 6 is "Applications of the Bionic Concept", etc. The dismissal of Wilhelm Reich is accomplished in a single footnote, the only place in the book where Reich's name is even mentioned:

"After the completion of this book, we learned that Wilhelm Reich had employed the term 'bion' to name 'fundamental living units' (Cancer Biopathy, Rangeley, Maine: Wilhelm Reich Institute. 1948). In our work, the theoretical basis for the existence of the bion, and the operational meaning of the term are quite different from that used by Reich, however."(p.86f)

The authors dissemble further, by stating "...another word such as viton, vion, bio-atom, biological atom, small living particle, or the like could be substituted to designate this fundamental living unit" — but the fact remains they did not use another such word, and did stick with a definition and terminology directly derived from, or so close in agreement with Reich that it makes the disclaimer appear suspicious. Also, one wonders why they did not, having learning about Reich's specific discoveries prior to their publication, dedicate a chapter to him in their book — that would have been the most ethical procedure, and would have provided important empirical support for their own quantum-mechanical reasonings. The probable reason they did not is because Reich is so hated a figure among the mechanistic biologists that to have included his name as more than a footnote would have condemned the book to unpublished status — John Hopkins Press would not have touched the book with a 10 meter pole.

We have seen this kind of piracy with respect to Reich's other discoveries, such as his work linking the psyche and soma (today blandly subsumed under an emotionless, de-sexualized "mind/body" terminology, *sans* Reich). Unfortunately, I predict we will see more of this unethical stealing of Reich's research findings. It is therefore the responsibility of those scientists who have followed Reich, who have replicated his findings in various ways, to start writing clarifying letters to the various scientists and publication editors, reminding them of the facts of Reich's priority. The pages of *Pulse* are also open to our readers to expose any such breaches of scientific ethics. For more discussion on the bions, see the "Science Notes" section of this and other back issues of the *Pulse*.

J.D.

Atmospheric Deterioration

Dear Editor,

Are there any articles in *Pulse* which deal with the relatively recent incidence of the white "fog" or "mist" which always surrounds the sun now, even on cloudless, sunny days? I suspect there is a problem with the orgone (life) energy. The sky is also a paler blue than it used to be.

Margie Fyfe, New Jersey

Dear Ms. Fyfe,

Each issue of *Pulse* discuss the deterioration of the atmospheric life energy. This problem is specifically the focus of our work at the *Orgone Biophysical Research Laboratory*, and a central topic of the *Pulse of the Planet*. Wilhelm Reich was the first to give detailed descriptions of this problem, which appears to be caused by a literally dying-off of the atmospheric life energy — the life energy (orgone) itself has a deep bluish color, and the Earth is surrounded by an orgone energy envelope. One can see this blue color as an energy field which surrounds the planet. However, where the forests and plant cover of the Earth have been stripped away, and as deserts spread across the planet, this bluish energy glow is lost and reduced, leaving only a dull-blue-grey, or milky color in the atmosphere.

We know, for example, that healthy, vibrant forests and mountain ranges will glow with a soft bluish coloration. This is most apparent to the eye when seen from a distance, though on occasion it is starkly apparent even at a relatively close distance. We now have good color photos of this blue-glowing environmental phenomenon, from various highland areas of the world. A related phenomenon is the fact that, when good strong storms pass over an area, such as following a hurricane, the atmosphere itself will glow with a profoundly deep and rich blue color. Likewise, snowfall from a vigorous storm will have a bluish color and a very high moisture content, reminding one of bluish glacial ice, which also is derived from highland areas with intensive storms and snow accumulations. In short, this pale white mist or fog you describe appears to be a product of atmospheric deterioration and loss in quantity of orgone (life) energy charge at the Earth's surface.

J.D.

Dear Editor,

I have been in Eritrea [formerly a northern province of Ethiopia, now an independent state]... the drought situation in Asmara and the whole of Eritrea is far beyond any imagination. Coming with the airplane from Italy to Eritrea, I noticed how the major part of the territory is desert-like: locally the sky appears as horizontally split, with the upper layer bright blue, and the lower one lacking brightness and full of haze. The actual rainfall rate has dropped from the usual 450 mm per year some 20-25 years ago to the 250 mm per year of the last 4-5 years, and a minimum of 210-215 mm between 1990-1992. The natural underground reservoirs of water in the highlands has completely dried up. The government is trying its best to preserve water by digging pools everywhere in the territory and inviting the population to preserve the vegetation. One gets the impression of a deep block of orgonotic pulsation in the local atmosphere, which is strictly connected to the dorized conditions of the Sahara and Arabian Deserts. In the highland city of Asmara (2,400 meters elevation) the sky is blue and highly orgone charged; [but] you can see the forming of clouds without the subsequent discharge in rain. Another curious phenomenon happened in Asmara (Eritrea) and Addis Abbaba (Ethiopia)... the sun was blurred by a large circular "diaphragm" surrounded by a blue halo, and sometimes a rainbow halo. All observers noted...that the sky was bright, that it was possible to look at the sun without blinking and sometimes light clouds were passing by. ...Local meteorologists registered it without any explanation. Foreign TV reports referred to it as a "globular cloud".

Aurello Albini, Asmara, Eritrea.

Dear Mr. Albini,

The phenomenon you observe is generally explained by classical meteorology as the product of light refraction at high levels, due to obscuring clouds of ice crystals from condensing moisture. However, Reich observed the phenomenon of a related "ring around the moon" as a product of contraction of the energy field of the Earth. In moister regions, this lunar ring is correlated to rains, and folklore in North America and Europe often stated the moon ring was a sign of rain. In the moist areas of the Midwest where I formerly lived, moon rings were a fairly reliable predictor of rains. However, in semi-arid regions, such as in southern or central California, we cannot make such direct associations. Moon rings appear quite often, generally in association with moister air moving inland at high altitudes from the Pacific Ocean, but the moisture simply rides up and over the low-lying dor-layer, and so rains are not predictable from this observation alone. Perhaps in Eritrea and Ethiopia, both arid or semi-arid in climate, a similar situation exists. The layered quality you describe, with an "upper layer bright blue, and lower one lacking brightness and full of haze", sounds similar to our experience in the deserts of the American Southwest, though we do receive more rains than you do, at the edge of the Sahara or Arabian deserts. The lower layer of haze and diminished brightness is the typical dor phenomenon described by Reich, and is the major factor at work preventing the development of cloud growth and rains... If I interpret your observations correctly, there must be a lot of moisture and healthy energy just above this stagnant haze layer. Historically, the progressive reduction of rains in your area is connected to a similar progressive drying-out and desertification along the entire southern margin of the Sahara. Rains on the Ethiopian highlands have progressively diminished since hundreds of years ago, and the Nile River itself has been reduced to a trickle from time to time. Khartoum, the capital city of Sudan (northwest of Eritrea) was surrounded by knee-deep grasses, with grazing elephant, giraffe and zebra only 100 years ago. Today, it is surrounded by barren rock and drifting sand dunes — the nearest grasses being perhaps 100 miles or more to the south. It is a serious problem indeed, one which is affecting not just Africa, but the entire Earth.　　　　　　　　　　　　　　J.D.

Sun rings photographed in Eritrea.

TRAVELER'S REPORT:
A Journey to Southern California
by Chris Nelson

Marlene and I have lived in Fort Collins, Colorado for fifteen happy years now. Though we enjoy the well known Colorado environmental amenities, we have lately begun to think of relocating closer to family members in the southern California area. We decided to do some exploring and it was with this in mind that we set off by car in early October of 1990, bound for Los Angeles.

As an ardent orgonomy buff and faithful reader of both the *Journal of Orgonomy* and *Pulse of the Planet*, I resolved to make notes and keep a record of the atmospheric energy conditions we encountered during our trip and our subjective reactions to these conditions. As a way of quantifying energy conditions, I chose the Baker DOR Index.(1)

I work outdoors in my job which lets me observe the sky daily. I can report that the northern Colorado atmosphere has enjoyed unusually fine health all this past spring and summer (1990). DOR index readings have been consistently in the

Baker DOR Index

Movement

Still; leaves drooping; no breeze; animals quiet	2
Occasional breeze	1
Consistent breeze; animals active, any occasional but vigorous wind	0

Humidity (subjective)

Oppressive and sweltering	2
Heavy, humid	1
Comfortable	0

General Subjective

Irritable; fuzzy, weak; lethargic; thirsty; out of contact; fingers swollen	2
Slow or restless; uncomfortable	1
Comfortable; vigorous; well being	0

Sky (color)

No blue; white haze; full milkiness; very thin, diffuse white; glare	2
Solid overcast (color not visible); steel gray; some milkiness; purple; pepper in sky; brown haze;; milky blue	1
Soft, clear blue	0

Sky (clouds)

Thin overcast; milky clouds; white haze; no discreet clouds; no significant structure	2
Any discreet but fuzzy clouds; differentiated overcast; thin wispy (but discreet) clouds	1
Any completely discrete, sharp clouds	0

1. First developed by Courtney Baker, M.D. The index is calculated as the sum of the observed values.

sparkling to good range with regular pulses of rain. Appearances by our famous high altitude *brown cloud*, have been at a minimum. Subjectively, the feeling has been one of ease and contentment.

Our first full day of driving saw us heading west across Utah on I-70 and then south on I-15. We both felt strong and relaxed as we marveled at the clear air vistas of surrounding mountains. Distant features had good color. The DOR index was zero. Even after six straight hours behind the wheel, I felt little fatigue. Then we began to notice a change. We were crossing into Nevada and the temperature was on the rise. The sun began to glare and gave a burning heat. After some time, we topped a rise and spread below us was Las Vegas in all its hazy brown glory. We recoiled in surprise at the sight of a deep, dense brown haze layer stretching all across the horizon. On the left, it was actually a thick white haze and it completely obscured terrain features behind it. Mountains on the opposite side of the valley were almost invisible, hazy silhouettes. The expression was of sickness and impending doom. In the space of an hour and a half, the DOR index had rocketed from zero to eight. We had thought that we would stop in Las Vegas for food, but after seeing the pollution and experiencing a traffic jam on the freeway through town, we were just glad to get out quick.

We continued on across the desert toward Riverside, California. By now, my nasal passages had thoroughly dried and become raw. Marlene's were plugged. Our water container was in constant use, but strong thirst was persistent. The heat was oppressive right up until sundown. We passed Riverside after dark and headed down into the L.A. basin. The traffic was incredible; ten lanes at 75 miles per hour; thousands of cars spewing tons and tons of carbon dioxide into the night sky. How does our poor atmosphere survive this onslaught? We arrived at Marlene's daughter's house in Torrance at around 9 PM, exhausted, but glad to be there.

The next day was spent relaxing in the immediate Torrance area. The milky sky featured one or two wispy cloud areas and a distinct brown haze all around the horizon. Our sinuses were still dry and we were both experiencing mild headaches and a sense of lethargy, but we felt reasonably good and had fun at Marlene's seven-year-old granddaughter's soccer game. The DOR index was fair at from four to five.

The following morning we set off on our planned exploration of the region. Our first destination was to be San Luis Obispo which we had heard from several sources was a great place to live. It is about four hours north of L.A. in the mid-coast area of the state. The day was much the same as the previous one in Torrance. However, conditions rapidly worsened at Oxnard and Santa Barbara. We were treated to a couple of Las Vegas-like long views which were distressing to say the least. The now familiar brown or white haze layer in every direction, coupled with more thousands of cars at high speed, propelled our stress levels ever upward. I noticed that pollution was evident all around the horizon, even out to sea, and yet, if you looked straight up, the sky was a nice clear blue. This seems to aid one in denying the seriousness of the situation because it gives the impression that the pollution is "over there", not here. Subjectively, I was becoming irritable in addition to the dryness and mild headache. The DOR index was now at least six.

We arrived in the San Luis Obispo area around noon and our first stop was Pismo Beach. The visual evidence of pollution and DOR was significantly diminished here. Still, distant coastal features were hazy and devoid of color; and out to sea, there was a whitish layer with tinges of violet at its edges. Sitting on the beach, Marlene felt relaxed and content to read her box. I definitely felt the energy of the sea, and wanted to get out there and play in the shore break. Though I felt energized and expansive, I was aware that the sun was still glaring and my throat and nose were dry and raw. The DOR index was at three.

In our travel literature, we had a 1986 brochure about San Luis Obispo. It described the climate as having sunny, warm summers and rainy winters. Upon inquiring at the Chamber of Commerce, we found that 1986 was the year it stopped raining in winter. San Luis is about to enter its fifth year of drought. "Water Crisis" signs are on every restaurant table and in public rest rooms. The situation is critical.*

Subjectively, we both felt much better in San Luis. I was rating DOR at two on the index and I felt comfortable and safe which was a marked contrast to the way I felt in L.A. I even found a couple of very early issues of the *Journal of Orgonomy* in a used book store which made me feel good. The town seemed to have many of the requirements on our list. We liked it. We stayed overnight and spent the next morning exploring the area further. By the time we left for L.A., I had decided in my own mind that though it had several good points, the lack of rain bothered me. My business is grounds maintenance and no rain means no business. Also, I love rain very much, and the prospect of even less rain than in Colorado did not sit well.

As we plunged headlong into nerve rattling traffic and heavy DOR, I felt a return of previous physical and psychological sensations. I began to worry that Marlene and I would come to conflict about moving, although she had said nothing to make me think so. I then realized that I was actually beginning to lose contact with her. I felt isolated and anxious.

Over the next two days, my subjective sensations remained about the same or got worse. We found much the same conditions in San Diego as we experienced in L.A. It occurred to me that my reactions to high DOR could be cumulative and that a large part of what I was feeling might be more the result of a week-long exposure than the result of the present reading on the DOR scale. At any rate, these were all unusual feelings. I was now completely withdrawn from Marlene, afraid even to ask her what she thought of this or that area we had looked at for fear that she would say she liked it and wanted to move there. I had a couple of sudden temper outbursts and was also experiencing feelings of worthlessness and fear of the future.

Our last day in L.A. was a Friday and Marlene's daughter, Sue, had the day off from work. She and Marlene wanted to go to Tijuana to shop. I had never been to Mexico at all so I decided to come along. Sue drove, so my stress level was lower. On the way down, I asked Sue to tell us the things she liked and disliked about southern California after having lived there for five years now. Sue has her M.S. in Sociology from the University of Colorado and is on the staff at a college in L.A. She said that when she first moved there, she hated the freeways and the traffic, but now she is used to it. She dislikes the fact that one must wait in lines and plan further ahead

about going out to eat or to the movies because of the high population density. She knows that the pollution looks bad, but she does not know how it is affecting her, if at all. She does like the economic and career opportunities she has found and feels good that she has been able to better her quality of life since moving to L.A. She said that she is a "doing" person and experiences boredom unless she is on the move. To her, L.A. is an exciting place.

Tijuana, I found, was simply unbelievable. I was not prepared for what I saw there. We were in the heart of the business district. The buildings were old and almost totally neglected. I had the impression that just enough upkeep was done in this city to keep the buildings standing and no more. Thousands of people jammed the sidewalk. Incredibly old and battered buses roared and smoked up and down the streets. Mexican men stood on corners loudly offering to call a cab for us. Hawkers beckoned from storefronts. Street peddlers approached us every other minute with necklaces draped over one arm. "Which one you like? Almost free." Despite the choking heat, all the men were dressed in long sleeved shirts and long pants.

All this was hard to take, but it was the little children that moved me the most. There were dozens of them on every street, each with a small box of candy or trinket to sell. Every minute or so, one would be in front of me, holding up his or her small merchandise for me to see; six or seven years old, saying nothing. Their eyes had a lifeless, gone-away look; their faces dirty and expressionless. I thought that perhaps if I bought something, I might get one to smile, but there was no reaction, no contact, whether I bought or not. There was a little girl sitting on the sidewalk with a battered accordion and a little basket for tips. She was supposed to be playing, but instead she was crying. There was no one there to comfort her. Hundreds of people walked by and kept on going, me among them. I felt a big sadness moving in me. I wanted to cry but I choked it off. Marlene and Sue would definitely become alarmed if I started bawling right there on the street. It would have put a damper on their festive shopping spree. So, I swept it under the rug.

Later, we went to a beach just south of Tijuana. The Pemex oil refinery was at the north end, right on the beach. It belched a plume of black smoke that darkened the sky. It stunk. There was garbage in the sand.

On the way back to L.A., north of San Diego, we saw a strange sign with figures in black silhouette. Instead of a man walking or whatever, the silhouette was of a family: the father, mother, and a small child. They were huddled together and running. The mother's hair was flying and she was pulling the child along by the hand behind her. It was very striking. What did it mean? Later on we saw a sign that said, "Watch for people crossing highway." What people? This was a ten lane freeway jam packed with cars 24 hours a day and they were all going 75 miles an hour. There was a chain link divider fence topped with barbed wire. Who would try to cross such a thing? Well, of course we realized that it must be illegal Mexican immigrants, desperate to escape conditions in Mexico even worse than Tijuana and having to brave the San Diego freeway to do it.

The next day saw us saying good-bye to our loved ones and heading back out for Colorado. Beyond Las Vegas the DOR index again dropped to zero and we started feeling much better. We could again see color in distant mountains. I found myself asking Marlene what she liked about the various places

---

* Editor's Note: Winter rains were restored throughout all of California in the winter of 1993. See the CORE Report in this issue.

we had seen and was no longer afraid of her answers. Returning to a healthy atmosphere and the concurrent wondrous improvement in physical well being and psychological outlook was confirmation that, what I had been feeling for the last week was, in fact, due to the stagnant energy conditions of southern California and not to some sudden personal fault or weakness in my character.

The human organism is so adaptable. All of what I have commented on here is really a chronicle of conditions that humans have adapted to. Pollution and over-crowding in L.A., the soul murdering poverty of Mexico, the years of drought in California, and ten lanes of traffic at high speed everywhere we went. Just what would it take for a relatively healthy organism from a low DOR environment to "get used" to all of this? I wondered. Getting used to it means ingesting enough of it, for long enough, until a stage of DOR exposure is attained where the organism is deadened to its effects. It reminds me of an addiction. One of the symptoms of the addict's disease is that it disguises its symptoms as something else. I think denial is at work in long term DOR exposure as well as in addiction.

In Colorado I have my home, my mountains, my plains and my sky. I can see them all clearly and colorfully almost every day. I can see the clouds breathe and the orgone streaming. I can feel the changing expressions of the vast galactic ocean of life energy both in the atmosphere and in my own body. I do not want to become dead to these effects.

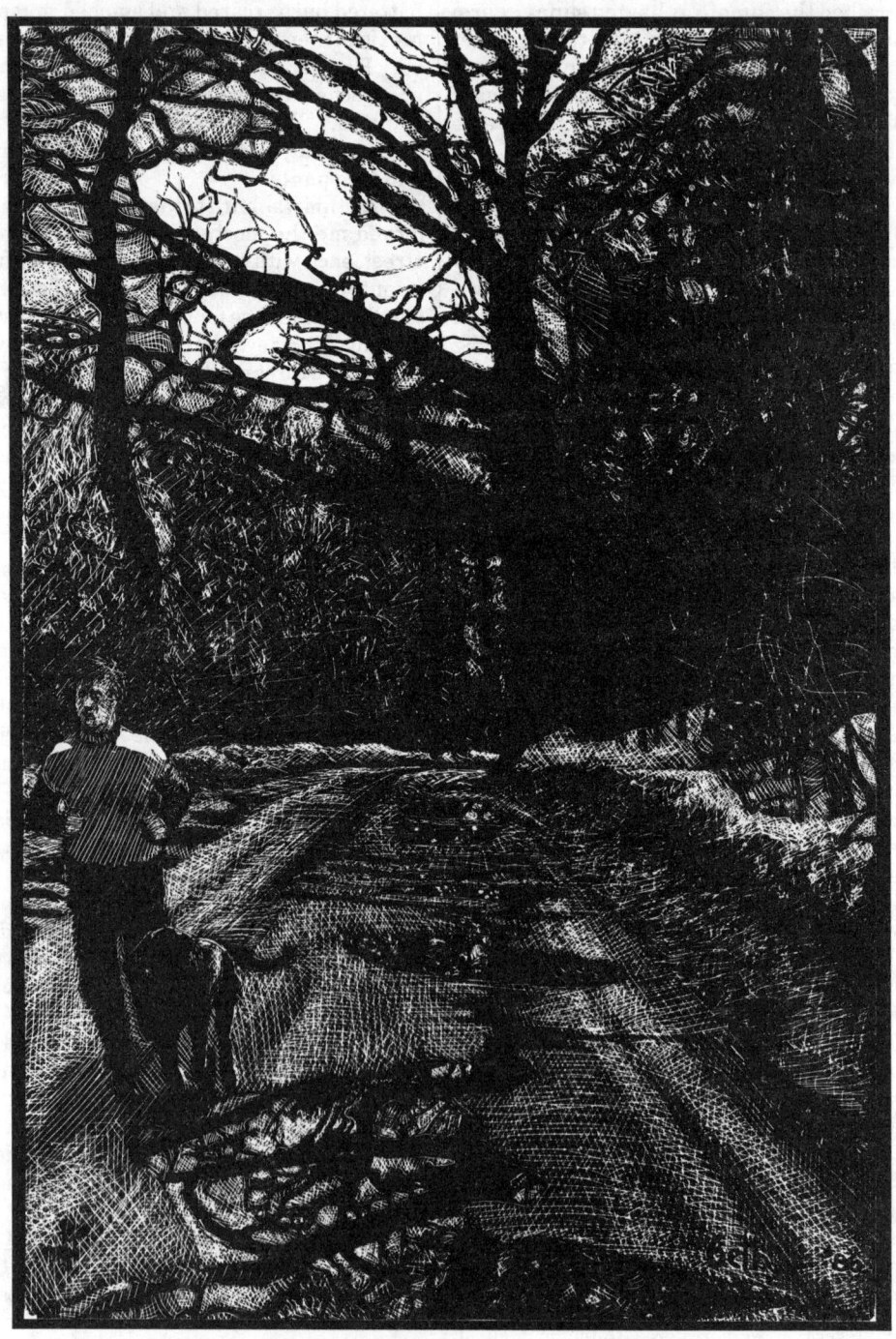

Winter Running by Beth Cook, Scratchboard

Orgone Biophysical Research Lab, PO Box 1395, El Cerrito, CA 94530, Telephone 510/ 526-5978.
- Publishes *Pulse of the Planet*, and other *Special Reports*. Occasional public educational seminars, lectures and workshops on Wilhelm Reich and orgonomy. Active program of orgonomic atmospheric & environmental research.

Natural Energy Works, PO Box 864, El Cerrito, CA 94530, Telephone 510/ 526-5978.
- Mail-order sales of books, products, and research instruments related to the topic of the orgone (life) energy, and to electromagnetic and nuclear energy pollution issues. Send $2 for Catalog.

Institute for Orgonomic Science, PO Box 304, Gwynedd Valley, PA 19437. Tel. 215/ 732-1200.
- Publishes *Annals of the Institute for Orgonomic Sciences*. Active program of orgonomic biological and physical research. Training for orgone therapists.

The Wilhelm Reich Museum, PO Box 687, Rangeley, ME 04970, Telephone 207/ 864-3443.
- Preserves Wilhelm Reich's home and laboratory (called Orgonon). Publishes *Orgonomic Functionalism* and a *Newsletter* for members. Sales of books by Reich, including xerox editions of various out-of-print books and journals. Occasional public seminars and workshops.

The American College of Orgonomy, PO Box 490, Princeton, NJ 08542, Telephone 908/ 821-1144.
- Publishes the *Journal of Orgonomy*. Occasional public symposia, seminars and workshops. Training for orgone therapists.

Center for Functional Research, 2175 Mar East, Tiburon, CA 94920, Fax: 415/ 435-2815.
- Active program of orgonomic and related consciousness research; occasional public symposia.

Individual Contacts, Orgone Therapists, and/or Study Groups on Reich & Orgonomy:
- A separate list is available from the Orgone Biophysical Research Laboratory, PO Box 1395, El Cerrito, CA 94530. Include a stamped, self-addressed envelope.

Foreign Research Journals on Orgonomy:
Bioenergy, 3-27-5 Kodatsuno, Kanazawa, 920 Japan.
Emotion, Karlsbergallee 25-E, D-1000 Berlin 22, Germany.
Energia, Caracter y Sociedad, Publicationes Orgon, C/. Serpis, 36-34^a, Valencia 46022 Spain.
Greek Journal of Orgonomy, Hellenic Orgonomic Association, T.O. 10837, Thessaloniki, 30136 Greece.
Lebensenergie, Memelstr.3, 6930 Eberbach, Germany.
Revista de Ciencias Orgonomicas, Fundacion Wilhelm Reich, c/Paris, 147 3° 2^a 08036 Barcelona, Spain
Sciences Orgonomiques, "La Rose des Sables", Alle due Chene Vert, Parc Liserb, 06000 Nice, France.

Of Related Interest:
Summerhill School, Leiston, Suffolk, IP16 4HY United Kingdom. Telephone 44/ 0728/ 830-540.
- Democratically operated school founded by A.S. Neill, educator and pioneer on self-regulation for children, and the non-coercive educational environment.
- Publishes *Friends of the Summerhill Trust* Journal, 280 Lordship Lane, London SE22 8LY U.K.

Group for the Scientific Reappraisal of the HIV/AIDS Hypothesis, 2040 Polk St., #321, San Francisco, CA 94104, Fax: 415/ 775-1984. Scientific group opposing the HIV hypothesis of AIDS.

H.E.A.L.: Health Education AIDS Liaison, PO Box 1103, Old Chelsea Station, New York, NY 10113, Telephone 800/ 410-4325. Clearinghouse for information opposing the HIV hypothesis of AIDS.

Cancer Control Society, 2043 N. Berendo St., Los Angeles, CA 90027, Tel. 213/ 663-7801.
- Information on alternative, non-toxic and natural therapies for degenerative disease.